THE GREAT MOVIE SERIALS
Their Sound and Fury

Other Books by Jim Harmon

THE GREAT RADIO COMEDIANS
THE GREAT RADIO HEROES

THE
GREAT
MOVIE
SERIALS

Their Sound and Fury

Jim Harmon
and
Donald F. Glut

DOUBLEDAY & COMPANY, INC., GARDEN CITY, NEW YORK
1972

Library of Congress Catalog Card Number 70–171269
Copyright © 1972 by Jim Harmon and Donald Glut
All Rights Reserved
Printed in the United States of America

Dedication

This book is especially dedicated to our friends,
Kirk Alyn
and
Spencer G. Bennet,
and to Buster Crabbe, Roy Barcroft, Adrian Booth, John English and William Witney, Howard and Theodore Lydecker, George Plympton, Jean Rogers, Dave Sharpe, Dale Van Sickel, Linda Stirling and Tom Steele without all of whom the sound serial could not have existed as we knew and loved it; and finally to
Alan G. Barbour
to whose research and private publications the authors are outrageously indebted.

Preface

It is certainly an honor to have this excellent book on serial films dedicated to me and to be given such extensive coverage in the sections on Superman, Blackhawk, and my other "chillers."

Jim Harmon and Don Glut are completely dedicated "buffs" and their tireless enthusiasm for their avocation has resulted in this thoroughly researched volume which might easily be called *An Encyclopedia of the Serial Era*.

As one who actively participated in the making of the last of these exciting "cliffhangers," I can testify to the accuracy of the author's information. Don and Jim were just youngsters when the films they discuss so authoritatively were first shown, so they are to be doubly congratulated for catching the spirit of the serial years while faithfully recording the minutest details.

This book, like Harmon's other books and articles on various aspects of show business, will arouse the reader's nostalgic memories. Fond recollections of long-past Saturday afternoons at the movies will flit through his head. He will again experience the same excited anticipation for next week's solution to this week's terrible dilemma.

I wholeheartedly recommend this book to buffs, collectors, and all those who retain pleasant memories of serial motion pictures.

It is also a privilege to have this opportunity to salute each of you who recalls favorably my small contributions to that thrilling era.

KIRK ALYN
Hollywood, California

Acknowledgments

The authors wish to thank the following people who lived through the wonderful era of the cliffhangers, either as creators or audience members and who have shared their memories with us:

Forrest J Ackerman (editor, *Famous Monsters of Filmland* magazine), Dave Amaral, Richard Alexander (the last surviving classic villain of the "B" Western), Richard Alexander (animator extraordinary, Superman serials), Kirk Alyn ("Last of the Serial Kings," so invulnerable he eats curry at nine in the morning), The Kirk Alyn Fan Club (Box 1362, Hollywood, California 90028), Dick Andersen, the late Bart Andrews (stuntman), the late Roy Barcroft (best of the bad men), Alan G. Barbour (editor, *Screen Facts, Serial Quarterly, The Serial* limited edition publications, Box 154, Kew Gardens, New York 11415), Spencer G. Bennet, Larry Byrd, Ed Connors, John Cooper, (*Hero Hobby* magazine), Alan Copeland, the late Kenne Duncan, Buster Crabbe, Ray Craig, Skip Craig, William K. Everson, Gene Fernete, Jack Gold, M. C. Goodwin, Alex Gordon, Richard Gulla, John Hagner (*Falling for Stars* magazine), Jim Harmon's Radio Heroes Society (serial-related radio characters, P.O. Box 38612, Hollywood, California 90038), Ron Haydock (writer, actor, star of Batman parody film, *Rat Pfink*), George Henderson (publisher, *Captain George's Whizzbang* and *Comic World,* 594 Markham St. Toronto 5, Canada), Judd Holdren, Eric Hoffman (owner of one of the world's largest information libraries on serials and other popular culture media), Larry Ivie (*Monsters and Heroes* magazine), Al Kracalik, Kalton C. Lahue (author, *Continued Next Week* and *Bound and Gagged*), Woody Langley, Dan Leavitt, the late Howard Lydecker, Ferris Mack of Doubleday, Robert Malcomson (*Those Enduring Matinee Idols* magazine), Ken Maynard, Chuck McCleary, Rick Mitchell, Lloyd Nesbitt, Olive Stokes (Mrs. Tom) Mix, Kris Neville, Bill Obbagy (President, American Bela Lugosi Fan Club), James Pierce (movie and radio Tarzan), Bob Price, Kane Richmond, Robert M. Rosen, Gene Roth, Mike Royer (associated with Russ Manning in illustrating the *Tarzan* newspaper comic strip), Sam Sherman, Jim Schoenberger (President, The Cliffhangers Club), Tom Steele, International Tom Steele Fan Club, (P. O. Box 4334, North Hollywood, California 91607), Glenn Strange (who followed Boris Karloff in the role of the Frankenstein Monster, but who was also one of the most dependable villains in Westerns and serials), Bill Warren, and Jim Warren (Warren Publications, *Spacemen, Screen Thrills Illustrated, On the Scene presents Superheroes, Wildest Westerns, etc.*).

J.H. and D.F.G.

Contents

List of Illustrations

A Note to the Reader

Movie serials were the best action films of any kind ever made.

The scenes of action in many major motion pictures, especially ones in recent years, do not approach the professional skill and excitement of movie serials, especially those of Republic Studios, and especially during the very brief Golden Age of 1939 to 1942. The A pictures had more spectacle, yes. Serials could not afford massive armies pitted against one another. But the spectacles of major films borrowed on the skills of serialmakers. The classic example may be the fact that the burning of Atlanta and other spectacles in *Gone with the Wind* were actually directed by second unit chief, B. Reeves Eason, who directed Tom Mix's only talking serial, *The Miracle Rider.*

Boris Karloff received his early training in silent and talking serials. Jennifer Jones and Carole Lombard got early exposure in serials. Due to the tight *caste* system of Hollywood, the stars of the serials were, for the greater part, locked into the B market, but Buster Crabbe, Kirk Alyn, and Ralph Byrd could easily have carried major productions, and came off well when they did appear in them.

The greatest shortcoming of serials was a lack of such story values as characterization and credibility. In areas that other B films always scrimped on, such as special effects and musical scores, serials did very well.

With a new generation of film enthusiasts who have only a minor interest in plot (they have seen every conceivable plot on television since they were born), there is a new interest in serials as well-made films and only secondarily, we believe as "camp"—something so old and corny it is funny. Some serials are not funny at all. They are good films.

Strangely enough, many writers on the history of films seem literally unaware that there were serials made in the sound era, or completely dismiss the talkies. The silent era has been well documented, especially in the books of Kalton C. Lahue. We are offering the first essentially original text history on primarily the *sound era* serials, with coverage of the silents only where it is pertinent to the grasp of the over-all subject. Publishing delays of several years prevent this from being the first book of *any* type on sound serials.

Silent serials differed from the later talkies in two major ways (beside the lack of a soundtrack, of course): they were made for adults as well as children, and their plots were much more complicated. The first factor influenced the second. Early talking serials such as *King of the Kongo* retained the complex plotting of the silents. By the forties and *Perils of Nyoka,* the plots were basic but serviceable. By the late forties and *The Purple Monster Strikes,* the plots had become absolutely mindless, far underestimating the intelligence of even young children. Only the action remained. There was always the *action.*

In this work, we have discussed many films, both serials and related short subjects and full-length features. We have tried scrupulously to refer always to serials as either serials or chapterplays. Feature films that are complete in one showing of over an hour are referred to as features. Television series and television episodes are properly identified.

The source materials for serials—often comic strips, or more rarely radio programs or books—have been discussed because they are pertinent to screen adaptation, and because, we feel, that those interested in these serials will be interested in the parent source as well.

While this is primarily intended as a book of nostalgic entertainment, we believe it can also serve as a reference work. To help the reader avoid extensive cross-checking, certain facts have been repeated. You will read that John Hart not only played Jack Armstrong on the serial screen, but did only one season as the Lone Ranger on television more than once.

As a collaborative team, it is Donald F. Glut who has the greater personal interest in serials and information on them, and Jim Harmon who has had a wider background in general writing. However, we hope that neither Glut nor Harmon will be subjected to immediate mob action if somewhere in this mass of names, dates, and facts there may prove to be an error. Rather than treating us to your outrage, please correct our ignorance so we may use the new information for any future editions.

Meanwhile, we have done our best.

> Jim Harmon
> Donald F. Glut
> Hollywood, 1972

THE GREAT MOVIE SERIALS
Their Sound and Fury

1

The Girls
"Who Is That Girl in the Buzz Saw?"

THE PERILS OF PEARL

The headliners of the early silent serials were primarily pretty young women, who engaged in breathtaking perils and a seemingly endless list of situations designed explicitly for their slow, drawn-out elimination.

In the early part of the twentieth century, when women had not yet attained the freedoms they enjoy today, the motion picture serial primarily featured girls in the leading roles doing business at once risky and risqué. A woman who would be out of place puffing on a cigarette in the opening decades of this century would, on the other hand, reap no scorn for plunging off the side of a cliff in a careening touring car. Nor would she be whispered about behind her back for pumping her railway handcar into the cowcatcher of an onrushing locomotive, or hanging with tiring fingers from the top of a high building and slipping . . . slipping . . . slipping . . .

And as did the male serial stars of later years, these heroines managed to thwart the masculine baddies despite every obstacle, triumphing over the mysterious doings of their masterminding archenemies in the last episode. In many instances, the situations endured by these seen but not heard chapterplay queens were *more* spectacular than those encountered by the men. And certainly, they were more original, since during that era of movie-making the perils were still new and fresh to the screen. It was only in later years that the cliffhangers presented an endless catalogue of car crashes, warehouse explosions, and falls from cliffs, the solutions to which were always predictable.

These serial queens, although naïve in trusting their unknown enemies, were brave and rugged. Despite the apparent glamour, they underwent their trials and overcame them. Perhaps these silent serial queens were living proof, as reported by men of science and medicine, that females are actually better suited for strain and hardship than men. We might, then, re-evaluate our definition of the "weaker" sex.

The very first movie serial ever made starred a girl as the one to fall under the evil gaze of the villain and become the victim of his devious machinations. It was *What Happened to Mary?*, made in 1913 by the Edison Company. A slightly overweight Mary Fuller starred in this virgin serial. She portrayed an innocent young girl (as were all serial queens) with a sizable inheritance. Naturally, the money was coveted by the villain who devised a number of ways to dispose of Mary and gain the inheritance for himself. (This was a standard plot in silent chapterplays.)[1]

Serials of this period differed considerably from the later chapterplays, primarily in their endings. While the standard serial episode ended with a cliffhanger—a climactic scene in which the hero or heroine is apparently killed or slated for imminent death, the name coming from the standard scene of the star hanging by slipping fingers from the edge of a cliff—those of the early silent chapterplays were relatively complete stories, connected by a central though sometimes hard to discover plot. Mary would then find herself in some dangerous situation concocted to get her life and money, would somehow be rescued, and then, after the suspense had been relieved, the end titles would flash on and the chapter would fade out. Apparently, Thomas Edison and other serial producers either felt that audi-

[1] Featured in the cast was Charles Ogle, who played the Monster in Edison's version of *Frankenstein* made in 1910.

ences would not have a sustained interest in the story or characters to make them come back a week later to find out how Mary and her kind would somehow regain consciousness and chew through their bonds before the log upon which she lay fed the whirring buzz saw, or else they just never thought of the cliffhanger ending.

Some of the things that happened to Mary included her pursuit by the bad guys to a window, from which she escaped on a makeshift rope of joined bedsheets. If that weren't enough, Mary continued fleeing to safety to the very doors of the Salvation Army. Such a heroine should know it was not always the smartest thing to be overly courageous, but found nothing wrong with waiting behind a screen for a crook to rob an office safe, then to engage him in a brief struggle, and hold him at gunpoint until the police arrived.

What Happened to Mary? was a success, due to its uniqueness, however far it was from any semblance of art. But just as Edison's production of Edwin S. Porter's *The Great Train Robbery* brought the "story" to film-making, so did this episodic curiosity give birth to a type of entertainment that would flourish for forty-three years, and leave countless fans clamoring for more even today (there was more: a sequel, *Who Will Marry Mary?* in 1913).

It was the following year, however, that the serial motion picture was really established. In 1914, the chapterplay which, although differing substantially from most of the serials ever made (especially those of the talkie era), *The Perils of Pauline* was produced. What is most remarkable is the fact that, although the production is more like the serials abandoned soon afterward and is extremely primitive in all respects, *The Perils of Pauline* remains today as the one serial the average man knows by name. Say the word "serials" to most anyone walking down the street and (aside from the enduring folk humor about

Post Toasties) you will most frequently hear something to the effect of, "Oh, you mean like *The Perils of Pauline?*"

The star of this eclectic serial was a pretty, wide-eyed young woman, who covered her natural red hair with a blond wig on the screen. She was an actress who looked good in both formal gown and dirty dungarees . . . Pearl White, who is now regarded by film historians as *the* Serial Queen. Just as the *Perils of Pauline* has become the most famous movie serial of all time, so does Pearl White remain in memory as the most famous star of cliffhangers.

In the first chapter, "Through Air and Fire" (although chapter numbers and titles were given only after the serial's reissue), Pauline was left a fortune to rival that of her predecessor Mary by her late guardian. Pearl, pure and honest, trusted everyone including the not-to-be-trusted Koerner (played by eye-shifting Paul Panzer). Koerner then attempted to steal the inheritance through a series of extravagant schemes—the perils. His first try at doing away with Pauline was to send her adrift in a sky-climbing balloon which took her high over the Hudson River to the Jersey Palisades. The girl was saved from death by her ever-faithful, though chaste, boyfriend, Harry Marvin (played with sincerity by Crane Wilbur), who was always nearby when the perils arose. Rescued from the danger of Air, she had yet to experience the Fire to justify the chapter title. Pauline was kidnapped, then trapped in a burning building. She was left for dead until heroic Harry arrived just in the nick of time and saved her. Again, the chapter closed *after* the resolution of the perils instead of ending with the apparent death of Pauline.

Pauline's perils, although centered around the villain-wants-inheritance theme again, seemed a set of unrelated stories with equally dissimilar locations and casts of supporting villains. In the second installment, "Goddess of the Far West," Pauline went to Montana to forget the perils of the balloon and the

flames, but found anything but relaxation. She was again kidnapped by Koerner's thugs and spirited off to an Indian reservation. In this second chapter we were given reason to speculate
as to the schooling, or lack of it, the people responsible for the
serial's title cards had before getting jobs in the film industry.
Misspelling a word is one thing, but creating a new word with
an hilarious new meaning is another. Thus, imperiled Pauline
was not described in the titles as being in danger of her "immortal soul" . . . but of her "immoral soul." The oversight
failed to attract the attention of director Louis Gasnier, whose
efforts in this serial were exciting and remain nostalgic—but
certainly not artistic or entirely adequate.[2]

Assisting Gasnier with the directing of some of the Pearl
White serials was a young man named Spencer Gordon Bennet,
who would one day be known as the most prolific action director
in the motion picture industry.

In "Goddess" the Indians, attempting to dispose of the "immoral" Pauline who now wore the traditional attire of a squaw,
were carrying on like savages. They were dressed in full war
costume and hooting from their place at the top of a canyon.
Then they rolled a huge boulder down the canyon wall to
splatter Pauline, who was helplessly waiting below. Luckily,
Harry Marvin was nearby, and, with a rope, yanked the dis-
traught Pauline away from the crushing chunk of rock.

Koerner's vast legions of cutthroats to keep Pauline in peril
ranged from the more subtle gangsters to the more spectacular
savage and warring (1914) Indians and related types. Pauline,
always believing in the "benevolent" Koerner, was subsequently

---

[2] William K. Everson, in "The Silent Serial," published by Allen G.
Barbour in *Screen Facts*, first issue, 1963, stated: "PERILS was sloppily
constructed and badly directed by one of the worst directors the movies
have ever known, Louis Gasnier. (Not surprisingly, though, he kept working steadily, and was busy turning out mediocrities for Paramount well
into the thirties, at a time when such former giants as D. W. Griffith and
Herbert Brenon were pointedly ignored by Hollywood.)"

almost killed in an airplane, the wing having been cut by her
unknown enemy; nearly blown up as her ship was destroyed by
a maniacal pirate; nearly drowned in a sinking submarine; and
nearly poisoned by the fatal bite of a viper, placed in a basket
of flowers by a gypsy woman. (Gypsies in silent films were in-
variably cast as thieving, conniving, kidnapping villains, as were
Mexicans and other low-pressure minority groups.)

In another episode, "The Floating Coffin" (a favorite chapter
title of the later sound serials), Pauline and Harry took a boat
ride across the lake and encountered engine trouble. Of all
places for the boat to stall—and coincidence was one of the
things serials were made of—Pauline and her beau found themselves in the United States Navy's firing range, right on target.
The Navy opened their guns, riddling the small boat with
bullets. This time all seemed lost, as Harry, who usually
rescued Pauline from her predicaments, was also in the *same*
predicament! But Pauline was a quick-thinking girl, and had
thought quick enough to bring her faithful dog along for a boat
ride. Writing fast, Pauline tied a note to the dog's collar and told
the canine to swim to safety with the message that saved their
lives.

It was only in the last chapter, not surprisingly, that Pauline
discovered the true evil nature of Koerner, and with the help of
Harry Marvin defeated him, leaving the two virtuous characters
free to marry. Harry had been as pure as Pauline through all
her dangers, and now his honor would be rewarded with a home
life in the most conventional of suburbs (he must have asked
himself if it was worth it).

The Perils of Pauline had come to an end. But Pearl White
continued to star in the type of film she had become identified
with—the chapterplay, all of them being shot in Ithaca, New
York, and Fort Lee, New Jersey.

In 1915, she made a similarly titled serial, *The Exploits of
Elaine,* a better chapterplay than *The Perils of Pauline.* It

featured an unknown or mystery villain called the Clutching Hand, the prototype of all the Scorpions and Crimson Ghosts and Captain Mephistos of the future. The next year, Pearl battled another titled villain in *The Iron Claw*.[3] This chapterplay boasted all the trappings of the mysterious Orient—dagger-throwing Chinese assassins, secret passageways, staring eyes, and other yellow perils. Both the Clutching Hand and Iron Claw were played by the menacing actor Sheldon Lewis, whose villainous silent movie roles included a version of *Dr. Jekyll and Mr. Hyde* in 1920.

Most serials of the talkie era—even some Westerns—incorporated some element of science fiction into their themes. In this sense, *The Exploits of Elaine* was prophetic, bringing into the plot a weird ultrascientific device whose beam was fatal, in the ninth chapter, appropriately named "The Death Ray." Episodes with titles such as "The Frozen Safe," "The Poisoned Room," "The Vampire," "The Blood Crystals," and "The Devil Worshippers" give an idea of only some of the terrors and perils faced by Elaine. The tenth episode actually saw Elaine killed—literally. This was a condition which most serials threatened, but which never became actualized. Elaine's friend, Craig Kennedy the scientific detective, must have been reading Mary

[3] These villains proved durable. In 1936 Stage and Screen made a sound serial called *The Clutching Hand* starring the ever-popular cliffhanger star Jack Mulhall as Craig Kennedy, assigned to stop the villain of the title. The Clutching Hand was attempting to secure for his own greedy ends the secret for a new process for manufacturing gold. Detective Kennedy was to get the secret for the good of the U.S.A., never stopping to consider that his own heroics might *destroy* that same company and his own salary by upsetting the national—and world—economy. Luckily, the formula turned out to be a phony.

The Iron Claw was remade by Columbia in 1941 as a fifteen-episode production starring hero Charles Quigley and heroine Joyce Bryant. The Iron Claw, a diabolical villain out to steal a hidden trove of, again, gold, not only wore the glove-like device which gave him his name, but also facial bandages, dark glasses, and a pulled-down hat that made him look more like the Invisible Man of Universal Features.

Wollstonecraft Shelley's *Frankenstein*. The chapter was called
"The Life Current." And Kennedy used his own invention to
restore Elaine to life so that she could endure the perils of four
more installments.

Pearl White continued making serials until 1923. During
those years she encountered a vicious ape man in *Plunder*
(1923), and various henchmen and traps in chapterplays like
The Black Secret (1919) and *Pearl of the Army* (1916). In the
latter serial, she fought a black-masked criminal, The Silent
Menace, in hand-to-hand combat. After the struggle, the
stronger male pushed Pearl out of the window, ending another
of her perilous chapters.

Despite the long list of Pearl White serials, it is with *The Perils
of Pauline* that her memory truly remains.[4]

With the success of Pearl White in silent serials, many other
actresses with a yen for action and thrills began starring in cliffhangers and falling victim to their own 1920s perils. Helen
Holmes preferred serials that involved railroad settings. In one
of these, also starring Helen Gibson, *The Hazards of Helen*
(1915), a title designed to capitalize off *The Perils of Pauline*
with a total lack of subtlety, Helen saved a freight train by

[4] As some of Pearl White's serials were later remade in sound, so was
her classic that first presented her to theatre audiences. A later talking
version of *The Perils of Pauline* starred Evalyn Knapp as the girl of
perils, which included attacking jungle cats and bombing airplanes, plus
the evil workings of a sinister Oriental villain. The cast of this twelve-
chapter epic included Pat O'Malley, William Desmond, Robert Allen,
James Durkin, and the Satanic-looking John Davidson. It was written by
Ella O'Neill and directed by Ray Taylor. The production was rated "Excellent serial" by *Motion Picture Herald*. A highly fictionalized biography
of Pearl White, starring Betty Hutton, titled appropriately *The Perils of
Pauline,* was made in color by Paramount in 1947. And in 1967, in the
color Universal feature *The Perils of Pauline,* Pamela Austin starred as
Pauline with Pat Boone her loyal and wholesome beau. This latter film
tried in vain to recapture the flavor of the original and to capitalize on
the then-flourishing "camp" craze.

shooting at a semiphore from a locked room. In another installment, she found herself tied in classic fashion to the railroad
tracks as the train came ominously nearer. The serial had an
unbelievable list of one hundred nineteen chapters! Ruth
Roland, whose serials exploited the grandeur of the great outdoors, became entangled with more spectacular perils. She was
once rescued from the top of a freight train by her boyfriend
who swooped down in his biplane and dropped her a rope
ladder. Another time, Ruth was on the roof of a freight car that
had broken free of the train and was speeding along the tracks
to a sheer drop-off.

All seemed lost until her boyfriend, true to form, swung
down with a rope—à la Tarzan—and saved her from the plunging doom, leaving the train car to fall off into space. Yet in another cliffhanger, Ruth Roland slid across two mountains on a
rope hung over a wire, which joined one peak to the other.
Then the wire . . . snapped! Ethlyne Clair found herself carried
away by one of the screens first werewolves, The Wolf Devil, in
the serial *Queen of the Northwoods* (in 1929) directed by
Spencer G. Bennet and Thomas L. Storey. This might not
have been a werewolf in the standard movie tradition. But it
did comply with some species of werewolf in legend and super-
stition wherein a man masquerades and acts like a canine. This
villain dressed as a wolf, complete with an all-concealing wolf's
headpiece to disguise his real identity, and mysteriously commanded a pack of snarling wolves. After the Wolf-Devil disposed of Ethlyne's boyfriend, he chased her to the top of the
stairs, into a room, approaching like a bloodthirsty beast. The
window being her only way to freedom, the girl climbed outside
where she hung over an even worse type of death. Below was
the villain's yelping, salivating pack of hungry wolves.

None of the girls could keep the wolf from the door forever.
By the 1930s and the advent of sound, men had taken over doing the heroics in cliffhangers.

QUEENS OF THE JUNGLE

Republic Pictures made the first sound serial to star a cliff-hanger queen. It was *Jungle Girl* in 1941. The studio had decided to try something new—new to talkies that is, since serials had tended to cast male leads in the chapterplays of the 1930s. Republic had plans to return to the old proven formula of placing a pretty heroine amidst the terrors created by some scheming mastermind, this time in a jungle locale. But now the archfiend would attempt more than merely pilfering the hapless girl's inheritance. And in at least one example, that arch-enemy would be another girl.

The serial queen had returned with the added quality of sound. Before we could only see the heroine face apparent doom and watch her pretty countenance contort with a silent scream. Now there was the added realism of actually hearing her shrieks as she neared the jagged flesh-hungry teeth of the revolving buzz saw.

The first Republic serial to star a girl in the lead was set in the familiar jungles of Africa. It was very loosely based on a 1932 novel, *Jungle Girl,* written by the creator of Tarzan, Edgar Rice Burroughs. Republic retained the title of the book for their serial, then went about in their usual manner and changed things according to their own discretion. The hero of the novel, American physician Gordon Kin who battled a nutritional deficiency existing in a lost jungle civilization, was ignored. Instead, Jack Stanton (played by Tom Neal), a typically heroic white hunter, was substituted for the serial role. The Jungle Girl herself was given the name of Nyoka—a name which would eventually become famous through a second serial and a long series of comic book adaptations, totally ignoring the Burroughs origin.

Nyoka, the Jungle Girl, was portrayed in the serial by one of the sexiest-looking actresses ever to battle evil on the chapter-play screen, young and dark-haired Frances Gifford. Frances was completely enticing in her tailored leopard-trimmed jungle minidress and boots. It is not surprising that many fathers, who would otherwise have preferred staying home to listen to Joe DiMaggio going to bat on the radio or to putter around the garden, personally took their children to the theatre for fifteen consecutive Saturdays to see each installment of *Jungle Girl.*

Nyoka "Meredith," as Tarzan of the Apes, was raised in the wilds of Africa. Her father was a physician who was forced into self-exile because of the actions of his criminal and identical twin brother, Bradley (both portrayed by Trevor Bardette). He then joined forces with a jungle medicine man named Shamba (Frank Lackteen) and an American crook, Slick Latimer (played by Gerald Mohr, who bore an uncanny resemblance to real-life public enemy, John Dillinger). Together, they stopped at nothing to get at an invaluable diamond supply. But Nyoka, with the help of Jack Stanton and his humorous sidekick Curly Rogers (Eddie Acuff), managed to thwart the trio of villains, but not before barely escaping from hazards like plunging into a seemingly bottomless chasm, killed by poison darts, incinerated in a jungle fire, and crushed by a smiling gorilla (played unconvincingly by Emil Van Horn).

Jungle Girl was an exciting serial, directed by the greatest team of action directors, William Witney and John English. The chapterplay's forte lay in the stunting Dave Sharpe did for Frances Gifford. If he had been too embarrassed to dress as Nyoka and swing through the trees, the Jungle Girl would have been less impressive on the screen. For the footage of Sharpe doing his acrobatics from vine to vine and limb to limb were better, more spectacular, than those performed in the higher-budgeted Tarzan features made by Metro-Goldwyn-Mayer.

The serial was well received by audiences, but died prematurely with no chance of future theatrical or television revivals

due to copyright complications.[5] But Republic looked toward
that future when the studio decided to film a sequel to *Jungle
Girl*. Since it was Republic that created the name Nyoka, they
were within their rights to do another serial using that name,
but not basing the character on the Burroughs novel. In this
way, they would have all rights to the serial, and not have to pay
royalties to Burroughs. The second chapterplay was the 1942
Perils of Nyoka, a title which recalled the silent days of cliffhanging. Directed solely by William Witney, this fifteen-episode
serial lavished in increased production values, making *Perils
of Nyoka* far superior to *Jungle Girl,* and possibly the best
jungle serial ever made.

Nyoka had a new serial, a new last name ("Gordon") and a
new actress to portray her on the screen. Kay Aldridge was
striking, full breasted, yet somehow boyish, slightly out of character every time she called "Fahther!" She wore the more civilized garb of a female big game hunter. Apparently, the Jungle
Girl no longer made her own clothing, but purchased it down
at the local African trading post.

Also, the Jungle Girl was given a new boyfriend and defender, Dr. Larry Grayson, portrayed by Clayton Moore years
before he donned the black mask as television's Lone Ranger.
Larry and his superior, Professor Campbell (Forbes Murray),
had acquired an ancient papyrus which told how to locate the
lost Tablets of Hippocrates. There is only one person who can
translate the inscriptions on the papyrus—the queen of the jungle, now going under the new name of Nyoka Gordon.

[5] The contracts made between Republic Pictures and the various
sources from which they made many of their serials often resulted in
legalities stating that certain productions could not be shown after a particular date. Therefore, the Republic serials like *The Lone Ranger*
(1938), *The Lone Ranger Rides Again* (1939), *Drums of Fu Manchu*
(1940), *Adventures of Red Ryder, King of the Royal Mounted* (1940),
King of the Mounties (1942), *Captain America,* and *Haunted Harbor*
(1944) have been unfortunately withdrawn.

INT. PROFESSOR CAMPBELL'S STUDY—DAY

> NYOKA *holds the ancient papyrus, reading aloud and translating from same. Gathered around her are* DR. LARRY GRAYSON, PROFESSOR CAMPBELL *and* TORRINI, *supposedly an ally of hers.*

PROFESSOR: What does it say, Nyoka?

LARRY: Can you translate it?

NYOKA: Yes. (*beat; reads aloud then*) The first section tells of the Golden Tablets of Hippocrates on which are inscribed medical secrets—including the cure for a dread disease.

PROFESSOR: Undoubtedly that refers to Cancer.

NYOKA (*reading aloud*): When Egypt was conquered by the Romans these tablets together with a vast store of treasure were removed and hidden away.

TORRINI: Does it say where?

NYOKA: Not exactly. But it tells a way to find out. We must go to the Lair of the Eagles and after penetrating to its far end we will come to the Tunnel of the Bubbling Death.

PROFESSOR: Tunnel of the Bubbling Death! Weird sort of name, isn't it?

NYOKA: Passing through the tunnel we will then reach the Ancient Valley of the Tauregs.

TORRINI: Tauregs?

PROFESSOR: Originally they were cave dwellers.

NYOKA: Within the Taureg Caves there is an inscription which points the way to the Golden Tablets of Hippocrates.

LARRY: And the priceless medical knowledge to aid humanity.

TORRINI: Of a certainty, Doctor. But many dangers lie ahead of us.

Within a very short while their expedition into the Arabian desert was underway, with Nyoka all the while searching for her missing father, Professor Gordon (portrayed by elderly and lean Robert Strange).

When news of the Campbell expedition reached the area, another female, the wicked Vultura (played by luscious

Lorna Gray, later known as Adrian Booth) and her band of converting-by-the-sword Arabs, stole the papyrus. Together, Nyoka and Larry made their way into Vultura's temple. But Vultura had an ace up her robes—a furious, yet comical gorilla named Satan (again, Emil Van Horn), who attacked them, pulling the pillars that supported the temple, tearing down the building on Nyoka and Larry, and ending Chapter One, "Desert Intrigue."

Only their quick reflexes—and a broken wall providing an exit—permitted Nyoka and Larry to escape the falling debris which could have made the shortest serial on record.

Perils of Nyoka continued through a total of fifteen weeks, presenting more than the standard jungle fare. There were frequent slashing sword battles between Larry and the savage Arabs. And many of the cliffhangers were placed in elaborate and imaginative settings, with powerfully directed furious action, extremely effective lighting, and quick cutting to liven the pace. In Chapter Three, "Devil's Crucible," Nyoka plunged down toward a bubbling, steaming pool of molten lava, luckily falling to a stone ledge at the beginning of the next episode. Chapter Four, "Ascending Doom," took Nyoka and Professor Campbell on a moving floor, rising toward a ceiling of stalagtite-like spikes, until Larry rescued them the following week. In the sixth installment, "Human Sacrifice," Nyoka learned the whereabouts of her lost father—or fahther. But her knowledge had come too late. For she had been captured, bound, and was being lowered by a crude apparatus into a fiery pit. And the chieftain carrying on with the execution was her father, suffering from the amnesical loss of memory so frequent in popular entertainment of the 1940s. Again, it was Larry who saved Nyoka, by roping her Lone Ranger fashion and pulling her to safety. Among the other perils undergone by Nyoka, the Jungle Girl, was a plunge off a cliff in a chariot, being burned at the stake like a witch, and tied beneath a descending, swinging bladed pendulum, a contrivance that would have gladdened the heart of Edgar Allan Poe.

Supporting Vultura in her schemes were the Arab killer Cassib (Charles Middleton, "Ming" himself) and a youthful, dark-haired Torrini (played by Tristram Coffin, whose name was misspelled in the album cast as "Tristam"). Torrini appeared to be an ally of Nyoka and Larry until later revealing his true allegiance to the exotic ruler. In the tenth chapter, "Treacherous Trail," Torrini had tried kidnapping Nyoka and Larry. When his station wagon plunged off the side of a cliff and exploded, it seemed evident that all three had met a violent death. But Nyoka and the young doctor managed to escape from the car before the catastrophe occurred.

In the final episode, "Satan's Fury," Vultura had escaped to her temple with the discovered and stolen Tablets of Hippocrates. But Nyoka and Larry were after her and broke into the wicked lovely's lair. The wrestling match between the two girls, their naked legs entwined, had something for everyone. Satan the gorilla went berserk and hurled a spear during the fight at the Jungle Queen. But the weapon whizzed by its intended victim and thudded with fatal impact into the shapely body of Vultura. Larry blazed away time after time with his gun at the ape, but finally the monster was stopped only by a dagger thrust from Nyoka. Outside, the rest of the expedition finished Vultura's Arab hordes. The shock of all these events restored Gordon's mind. The wonder is it didn't cost his daughter hers.

Perils of Nyoka has outlived *Jungle Girl,* since it was not based on the Burroughs' book. It was rereleased years later as *Nyoka and the Tigermen.* And a feature version, *Nyoka and the Lost Secrets of Hippocrates,* can be seen on television. The latter title was one of a package of twenty-six Republic serials re-edited to one hundred minute full length movies sold to television in 1966.

Kay Aldridge, after her role as Nyoka, continued her serial

career with Republic, making two more chapterplays, *Daredevils of the West* in 1943 and *Haunted Harbor* the next year. While the locales for these two productions were nowhere near Africa, they did present Kay with an equally dangerous set of perils. *Daredevils of the West* was a twelve-episode adventure, starring Allan Lane (later "Rocky" Lane) and featured Eddie Acuff, who had appeared in *Jungle Girl,* again as a sidekick. The serial, involving a war between competing stagecoach lines, presented the usual Western cliffhangers, several of which involved death by fire. *Haunted Harbor* (rereleased as *Pirate's Harbor*), based on the story by Dayle Douglas, and starring Kane Richmond, was the story of hidden treasure, a giant mechanical sea monster that rose from the water with steaming breath, and a hero wrongly accused of murder. In various episodes of this one, Kay was nearly speared to death, trapped in a burning truck, and squashed as an automobile tumbled down a hillside to fall on top of the vehicle containing her and Richmond. As her male counterpart Tarzan had learned, the "Jungle Girl" discovered civilization could be a jungle itself.

Republic Pictures attempted a revival of the jungle queen during the last years of serial-making. Attractive Phyllis Coates, just out of her role of Lois Lane on the *Superman* television series, starred with "Clay" Moore in *Jungle Drums of Africa* (1953), an uninteresting arrangement of stock footage and clichés involving uranium in the jungle.

It was not, however, until 1955, in the second to last serial ever made by Republic, titled *Panther Girl of the Kongo,* that Phyllis shed her city clothes and donned scanty jungle garb. The resemblance to Frances Gifford's Nyoka was more than coincidental. She wore the same costume, giving more than suspicions that audiences were in for plenty of stock footage from *Jungle Girl.* The Panther Girl suddenly emerged wearing leopard-trimmed attire.

But serials had greatly declined by the 1950s in all respects.

The elaborate and thrilling chapter endings, as seen in *Perils of Nyoka,* had been reduced to the standard falling tree, the groping and shoddy gorilla, and the plunge from the always present cliffside. To boost the dying entertainment form, Phyllis as jungle girl Jean Evans (even the names had lost their exotic sound) was given a threat to tangle with that was totally unlike the usual Republic hazard. This menace was an enormous crab, appearing in the first chapter, "The Claw Monster," enlarged through the scientific madness of the sinister Dr. Morgan (Arthur Space). Dr. Morgan used such monsters, plus a band of animal-suited hirelings, to frighten the superstitious jungle people away from his diamond mines. But despite this added injection and excuse for special effects photography (Phyllis Coates running before a process screen showing close-ups of the arthropods), *Panther Girl of the Kongo* could not save the Republic serial from extinction. The first and last female serial star from that studio wore the same jungle garb. But the clothes and every setting and situation they appeared in, in 1955, was secondhand and worn out.

REPUBLIC'S REIGNING QUEEN

The Tiger Woman, filling her spotted outfit with curves, and her boyfriend, handsome Allen Saunders, his expression and his shoulders carved from the same block of wood, were trapped inside a house used as a bombing target by the merciless crook, Morgan. The hoodlum was circling the small building in his monoplane, dropping grenades, each exploding with more telling accuracy. In another drop, the building would be hit, and the Tiger Woman and Allen blown to bits.

Allen Saunders considered the situation in a flash as he grabbed up a machine gun. He could not allow the Tiger Woman, so beautiful in her brief jungle outfit of slightly inappropriate "leopard" skin, yet so efficient when it came to fighting evildoers, to perish in the impending holocaust.

He took careful aim with the tommy gun as Morgan's plane swooped in for the kill. Then Allen let out a burst of hot bullets, spraying the dive-bombing craft. Morgan slumped forward, struck fatally. But there was still enough life in the villain for one last effort to destroy the Tiger Woman and her boyfriend. With grim determination, Morgan guided his wavering hands to the control stick of his plane, then aimed his explosive-laden ship kamakaze style toward the target house. A moment later, there was a tremendous impact of plane and house, both exploding into a cloudy barrage of flying, burning debris.

The chapter was the eleventh, and suitably entitled "The House of Horror." But it was not, of course, the final chapter of this serial, Republic's 1944 outdoors adventure, *The Tiger Woman.*

In the next episode we saw the Tiger Woman and Allen flee the building scant moments before the airplane collided into its walls.

The Tiger Woman, a twelve-episode production directed by Spencer Bennet and Wallace Grissell, was Republic's major attempt to create another Pearl White. The studio wanted to mold its own action female who would star primarily in their own chapterplays and program features. The ideal selection, who would wear the leopard garb in *The Tiger Woman,* was a statuesque, young actress with a firm jaw and sensual lips, named Linda Stirling. Added to these qualifications which were required in this role of another female Tarzan was her athletic abilities.

In a sense, Linda Stirling's success was partially due to the late star of silent cliffhangers, Ruth Roland. Ben Bard, Ruth Roland's widower, had opened an acting school using the money left by his wife. It was at this school that Linda learned much about acting.

Linda followed her dramatic schooling with various modeling

assignments. Luckily, one of the magazine advertisements featuring Linda Stirling fell before the gazes of the "right" people at Republic Pictures. They immediately contacted her agent, who passed on the news that her big break might be on the horizon.

It was, but Linda was still not sure of what awaited her. For, instead of a screen test, she was given a test, more or less one that might be given a rodeo contestant, to see just how athletic she really was. Linda was put astride a horse and asked to show what she could do—including leaps over fences, fast dismounts, and lightning gallops. She did them all, but none of her stunts were recorded on film.

Linda, tired and still confused, was told the next day that she had the part. It was the lead role in the first of many serials for that studio, *The Tiger Woman*. Republic Pictures had a new girl star.

Some part of the reason for a return to the serial queen must have been a knowledge of the sexual appeal of the dominant woman to many males. Miss Stirling slapped, kicked, flipped, spun, and whiplashed countless men in her serials. She was in turn struck and bound with ropes and chains. The erotic element may have been subliminal, but it was present. Linda Stirling combined two elements, one or both of which were absent in earlier sound era serial heroines. She had both "sex appeal" and "class." The first made her attractive and the second made her "acceptable."

Linda Stirling's first serial involved the rivalry between two oil companies for deposits located in the South American jungle. The head of the villainous company was Walton (played by perennial Western bad guy, LeRoy Mason), who would stop at nothing to get the deposits for himself. In his employ was the hoodlum Morgan (Mexican actor George J. Lewis) and a band of hired thugs capable of any type of crime.

Allen Saunders (played by Allan Lane, in his first serial since *Daredevils of the West,* with the second Nyoka, Kay Aldridge) was working for the opposing and good oil company, and went to the jungle for help. At first, the natives prepared to drop the gringo into a pit of flaming oil, but he was pulled back to safety by the Tiger Woman, a strangely civilized white goddess ruling the tribe of primitives. The Tiger Woman agreed to fight alongside Allen, and together with another oilman, José (played by Duncan Renaldo who would become famous as television's Cisco Kid), they fought the greedy villains.

139. EXTERIOR JUNGLE TRAIL: MEDIUM:

A point where the limb of a tree overhangs the trail just a little higher than the rider's head. MORGAN *spurs through, dragging the girl's horse behind him and as she comes under the limb, the* TIGER WOMAN *reaches up and seizes it. The horse goes out from under her and the saddle, leaving her hanging from the limb the saddle dangling from her ankles.*

139 A & B. COVER CUTS FOR ABOVE ACTION

140. EXT. *Jungle Trail:* MED.

SHOOTING BACK *along the trail as* MORGAN *rides to f.g. still leading the riderless horse.* THE TIGER WOMAN *lets go of the limb and drops to the ground.* MORGAN *turns and sees this and starts to check his horse. But just then* JOSÉ, *on* BOLTON's *horse, appears galloping in from the background firing as he comes.* MORGAN *changes his mind and continues ahead and out* PAST CAMERA, *dropping the reins of the riderless horse.*

141. EXT. JUNGLE TRAIL: MED.

THE TIGER WOMAN *lies on the ground, her hands still bound and her feet lashed to the stirrups.* JOSÉ *skids his horse to a stop, drops from the saddle and runs to her.*

142. EXT. JUNGLE TRAIL—MED. CLOSE.

On JOSÉ *and the* TIGER WOMAN *as he starts to cut her loose. She speaks quickly and breathlessly.*

TIGER WOMAN: Quick, José. There has been a terrible mistake. One of my warriors sent a message to the Temple that Allen Saunders had lied—
She breaks off with a gasp as the distant rumble of the ceremonial drums is heard. Then:
TIGER WOMAN: The Death Drums! They will kill your friend—Hurry! Hurry!
He slashes her free and she runs to his horse, makes a flying leap to the saddle and rides hard. JOSÉ *gazes after her.*

142. A & B. TO COVER ABOVE ACTION AND DIALOGUE

143. INT. TEMPLE: FULL
All the natives are now in their ceremonial poses, the hole in the floor has been opened and ALLEN *hangs above it. His feet are just below the floor level and smoke seeps up around them. The drummers are pounding out their death chant, the* PRIEST *stands stiffly in his position beside the rope and the dancing girl, the sword in her hands, poses for a moment, and then starts her routine.*

The Tiger Woman saved Saunders from *this* peril, with José's aid, but before the trio finally brought up a gusher to the righteous oil company, and defeated the scheming Walton, and learned that the Tiger Woman was an heiress, they encountered such dastardly perils as an elevator car plunging down in free-fall, a boat which crashed with explosive impact into a ferry boat (the captain of which was the thin actor, Tom London, who seemed to turn up in virtually every serial and Western feature, including silents) and being caught in the crumbling debris of a collapsing jungle temple à la Nyoka Gordon.

The Tiger Woman was a slick Republic serial, with the fast action scenes that were a mixture of Western, jungle, and detective elements, and perfect special effects that became a trademark of the studio. Linda Stirling made a thoroughly captivating Tiger Woman, starring opposite Allan Lane. The serial's only major fault, however, lay in the scripting, where an endless set of predictable situations were substituted for a developing plot. (Unfortunately, that was the case with too many serials.) There was nothing surprising when Allen Saunders held two crooks at gunpoint while the Tiger Woman watched; then one of the hirelings would kick or toss a box or other object into Allen's hand so that he dropped his weapon and a fight immediately started, usually with the jungle woman bumping her head so that she'd be unconscious when the building or whatever blew up. Still, *The Tiger Woman* was a popular serial, released years later under the titled *Perils of the Darkest Jungle*. Most important, the chapterplay established an immediate fan following for Linda Stirling. Republic had made her a star, and cast her that same year in another episodic film, *Zorro's Black Whip*.

The fact that Miss Stirling was cast in the *title* role of *Zorro's Black Whip* made some of us wonder if the famed black-clad avenger had gone to Sweden for one type of operation or another. But Republic, with its knack for changing the identities of already established characters, resorted to less drastic measures of turning the courageous Zorro into a woman. (The rationale was that her brother was the original phantom rider and when he was killed in the first chapter, "The Masked Avenger," Linda replaced him.) The title was a misleading one, since the name "Zorro" did not appear in the film at all. The character was called "the Black Whip." Under this name, Linda lashed her way through the villains, led by the elderly Hammond (Francis McDonald) who was leading his own reign of terror in order to acquire land. Linda Stirling played the role of Barbara Meredith (perhaps a distant relation to Nyoka Meredith), alias the Black Whip, who was aided by her boyfriend, cowboy Vic Gordon (played by the usually villainous George J. Lewis, who had tried blowing Linda up in *The Tiger Woman*). He occasionally dressed up himself in the embroidered black clothes and all-concealing face mask of the Whip in order to save the girl's secret identity. This was a case of a man impersonating a female who was, in turn, masquerading as a man. What still remains a mystery to viewers of *Zorro's Black Whip* is that those crooks could wrestle around the barn so many times with the avenger without *somehow* discovering the true sex of the "masked man."[6]

The Whip, after going through a secret panel behind a painting of the original Black Whip, rode out of her secret cave, the entrance of which was hidden behind a waterfall. She might have better not left. She narrowly missed death in the form of an avalanche, a plunging stagecoach, and even a pitchfork slammed toward her supine body. Luckily, in the latter cliffhanger, it was a saddle and not Linda's shapely form that met those four sharp prongs of metal.

Zorro's Black Whip was Republic's first and last attempt to create a female Zorro,[7] but it was only the beginning for Linda. The studio directly followed their pseudo-Zorro serial with *Manhunt of Mystery Island,* in 1945. In this one, Linda played Claire Forrest, the daughter of a scientist (Forrest Taylor) who had invented the Radiatomic Power Transmitter, a device capable of sending electrical power through the air by radio waves. Claire, with the help of her criminologist friend Lance Reardon (played by Richard Bailey in his only serial), proceeded to Mystery Island in the Pacific. The island was owned by a quartet of men, all sharing a common ancestor, the tyrannical governor of two centuries past, the flamboyantly costumed swashbuckler, Captain Mephisto (Roy Barcroft). Mysteriously, Captain

[6] As it was, Linda Stirling's costume and man-abusing actions were remarkably similar to those of women in certain forms of underground erotica. The point is made as a minor but valid one, and hopefully will not spur either the P.T.A. or the Serial Fans of America into action.

[7] In 1946, Republic produced *Daughter of Don Q,* starring glamorous Adrian Booth (known as Lorna Gray when she played Vultura in *Perils of Nyoka*). Although Don Q was the son of Zorro (a version of this was made as a silent feature starring Douglas Fairbanks, Sr.), there was no attempt at making Miss Booth a costumed avenger in this serial. In fact, the chapterplay was a detective thriller set in modern times.

Mephisto—the original, as portrayed in a life-size painting—had somehow returned to life. It was in the clutches of the pirate-clad Captain Mephisto that Claire's father had fallen, forced to work some scientific wonders for the villain. Actually, Captain Mephisto did not return from the grave. Instead, one of the four owners of Mystery Island had invented a remarkable Transformation Machine—a chair set in a room of electrical apparatus which transformed any man into the exact likeness of the Captain. In order to gain the entire island for himself, one of the quartet had used the guise of Mephisto to cover up his crimes.

The scenes in which Captain Mephisto changed into the shadowed personage of whomever it was that wanted the other three out of the way—and the reverse scenes—became monotonous when used at least once per chapter. Stretched over a length of fifteen episodes, the overuse of those particular shots exceeded the boring to approach the unbearable. But the direction of three capable men—Spencer Bennet, Wallace A. Grissell, and ex-stuntman Yakima Canutt—made up for it in action.

Linda barely made it alive through *Manhunt of Mystery Island*. Captain Mephisto tried drowning her in the entrapment of a net; she was splashed out the side of a mountain in a raging tunnel flood; and Mephisto guided her robot-controlled plane to almost a sure crack-up in the mountains. But she survived them all, and it was with a breath of relief that Lance finally defeated and exposed the man who *was* Captain Mephisto.

That same year, Linda Stirling again tangled with Roy Barcroft, who exchanged his pirate clothes for a shining uniform of a Martian invader in *The Purple Monster Strikes*.

In 1946, she was again at the mercy of a heartless archfiend, this time a robed and hooded menace wearing the grinning face of the Grim Reaper. The serial was *The Crimson Ghost*, in which Linda played Diana Farnsworth opposite hero Charles Quigley as criminologist Duncan Richards. The Crimson Ghost was after another remarkable invention called the Cyclotrode.

The device could short-circuit all electric current within the radius of its vibrating rays. The Ghost's chief henchman was the cold-hearted and dark gangster, Ashe (played by Clayton Moore, one of the few principals to constantly shift from villain to hero and back again). Ashe employed all the practices of the Underworld in attempting to get the Cyclotrode for his masked boss.

The casting of the part of the Crimson Ghost was most unique —and most devious on Republic's part to fool the audience as to the character's real identity. Wearing the scarlet robes of the Crimson Ghost was the late stuntman-actor, Bud Geary. The voice that came from the stationary skeletal mouth, was that of I. Stanford Jolley, whose name appeared fourth in the cast despite only a brief appearance in the serial as *another* character. To add to the confusion was a scene in which the Crimson Ghost spoke to Jolley over a two-way radio. We heard Jolley's voice dubbed into the skull of the masked villain. But the reply heard over the radio was that of yet another actor, dubbing for Jolley. It was no surprise when, after hapless Linda was almost blasted apart on an exploding bridge and in a crashing airplane, that the Crimson Ghost was unmasked to reveal the face of still another actor.

Linda Stirling's last serial for Republic was *Jesse James Rides Again* in 1947. This starred Clayton Moore, apparently compromising between his hero and villain roles by portraying a "good" badman, an unfortunate victim of circumstances, sorry for his own crimes and trying to clear his name from crimes done by others in the name of Jesse James. Directed by Fred C. Brannon and Thomas Carr, this thirteen-episode adventure was mundane Western entertainment, with the standard and expected cliffhangers. And it featured that most reliable—and most villainous—of chief villains, the portrayer of Captain Mephisto and the Purple Monster, sturdy, growling Roy Barcroft.

Linda Stirling did not make any more serials. But she continued performing in feature length films, and later on television. Republic had tried to give audiences a new Pearl White. They succeeded. Linda gave viewers as much action as had Pearl thirty years before, and with the slicker, more convincing production values of the sound era. Linda Stirling was the only real serial "queen" of the talkies, appearing in many different chapterplays of major interest. Her reign was one of hard riding, accurate shooting, and a thousand thrills, some of them for the big boys as well as the small ones.

2

"We Come From 'Earth,'
Don't You Understand?"

Flash Gordon flashed into theatres when the hero was most needed by his planet. The United States still recalled grimly the great Depression of the 1930s. The economy of the planet Earth was such that the best place to be seemed somewhere else, someplace where the American dollar sign would be a meaningless slashed S and where new thrills would replace old hardships.

Movie serials were about to fire people off to richer worlds, beginning with *Flash Gordon.* On Sunday, January 7, 1934, Alex Raymond, one of the true craftsmen of illustrated storytelling, saw printed in gorgeous color the very first installment of his King Features Syndicate newspaper comic strip which shot our imaginations away from the heartaches of this world and into the hazards and beauty of another.

The strip was titled *Flash Gordon.* The hero was a perfect specimen of blond-haired manhood, a "Yale graduate and world-renowned polo player." Flash Gordon, and a lovely, dark-haired girl named Dale Arden, were passengers in an eastbound transcontinental biplane. Around their craft, the sky was loud and bright with hot colored explosions and debris, as an unknown planet rushed toward the Earth to inevitable collision. A fiery comet severed one of the plane's wings, and Flash bailed out with Dale Arden in his arms. After landing, the two were confronted by a fanatical, bearded man, who addressed them at gunpoint before a weird craft poised for vertical takeoff.

"Now get into the rocket!" said Dr. Hans Zarkov, the great scientist who could be the only man alive capable of saving the world. "I intend to shoot this ship at the comet which threatens the Earth. The ship will deflect the comet from its course and save the Earth. We three shall die, martyrs to science!"

It was impossible to reason with the apparent madman. There was a flare of yellow, orange, green, and blue power. And Dr. Zarkov, with the two captives, Flash Gordon and Dale Arden, streaked toward the onrushing sphere, leaving behind a red and yellow wake of burning fuel.

Flash Gordon's adventures on this new world, the planet Mongo, involved a number of extraordinary characters, most of which were based on actual historical or popular fictional people. Among the residents of this sphere were:

Prince Barin: (later to become King Barin) the most noble of rightful rulers, dethroned when but a youth by Mongo's evil dictator, later to emerge as an extraterrestrial Robin Hood.

King Vultan: The fat and bearded winged ruler of the Hawkmen that were anything but holy as their angelic appearance would suggest, the monarch of the elevated Sky City, and Mongo's embodiment of drumstick-devouring King Henry VIII.

Thun: Prince of the Lion Men, with an impressive mane and tail that would almost hint that M-G-M was inspired by him for the Cowardly Lion of *The Wizard of Oz*.

King Kala: Lord of the submerged race of Shark Men, who pompously swirled his toga about with the dialogue and mannerisms of a hybrid Julius Caesar and Caligula.

Worst of all, Ming the Merciless, the sneering bald-headed Emperor who commanded his subjects to shave their heads; the self-claimed conqueror of the entire universe, with a hanging mustache and a waxed beard and the mandarin-like garb that suggested the worst aspects of Fu Manchu. Ming was so evil that there was no doubt that he could conquer the cosmos with his several rocketships and small band of soldiers.

Finally, Princess Aura, the light-haired daughter of Ming, in love with Flash, and capable of killing him before losing him.

Two years following the advent of Flash and his beautiful and bizarre friends and enemies in the color Sunday newspaper strips, Universal Pictures, realizing the tremendous popularity of the property, decided to film his adventures as a thirteen-episode serial, and boasting a budget of over a million dollars. That figure is small by today's production standards, especially when considering the total length of any serial. But in 1936, when applied to a string of chapters that would usually be produced under the cheapest possible conditions, that million was staggering. Universal, however, was not a studio to waste money. And even with a good budget, Henry MacRae, Universal's most prolific and capable producer of cliffhangers, knew how to cut Mongo's rugged corners.

Mongo was a strange world, as shown by Alex Raymond's drawings. Although its weaponry and gadgetry was vastly superior to that of Earth, in many ways the planet was incredibly primitive. Costumes were throwbacks from Earth's Roman Empire, with swords used more often than the more deadly ray pistols and rifles. Palaces reminded one of ancient China, and the animals lurking about the jagged mountains and valleys of Mongo were enormous, salivating reptiles, of dinosaurian proportions and appearances.

Thus, Universal had but to scour their own props department and stock footage library to ease that budget. The watchtower that gave birth to the Monster in Universal's 1931 *Frankenstein,* plus the machinery and various scenes of electricity in action, suddenly turned up on Mongo. The idol of the "Great God Tao" mysteriously resembled an Egyptian deity from the studio's horror film of 1932, *The Mummy.* Fox's 1930 science-fiction feature, *Just Imagine,* provided some of the rocket ships for this and later Flash Gordon serials, which was curious in that the movie version of Dr. Zarkov's craft resembled that featured in the

Buck Rogers comic strip. Even the shots of Earth seen by Zarkov through his telescope on Mongo were borrowed from a Universal feature of 1936, *The Invisible Ray.*

There was more, and not as contemporary as the talkie era. Good lengths of silent newsreel footage showed the destructive effects of Ming the Merciless's evil on Earth. And a weird Ballet Russe segment from Universal's 1927 *The Midnight Sun,* with numerous half-clad women writhing about a gigantic, moving idol, served to amuse the lecherous Ming who sat at the controls in another room and watched with glee.

The selection of music was also an economical venture. While many serials, primarily those of Republic Pictures, featured action music as exciting and original as that of the big "A" features, no original strains were written for *Flash Gordon.* Instead, scenes that should have been enhanced by action music were lifted from the then recent Universal horror films, including *The Invisible Man* (1933), *Werewolf of London, Bride of Frankenstein* (both 1935), and *The Invisible Ray.* Added also were selections from *Romeo and Juliet* by Tchaikovsky. Strangely, this unlikely set of musical compositions intended to convey terror, melodrama, or romance, worked tremendously over the sword battles and rocket chases in the serial, and have come to be identified, not with their original sources, but with the science-fictional escapades of Flash Gordon.[1]

A further monetary savings came in the use of sets. Most of *Flash Gordon* was shot either on interior sets, or on the back lot of Universal, avoiding the costliness of location shooting. Some of the exterior scenes were filmed, however, in Hollywood's

[1] In the later Flash Gordon serials, further musical scoring came from horror films such as Universal's *Son of Frankenstein* (1939), and from *Les Préludes* by Franz Liszt. *Les Préludes,* also associated with *The Lone Ranger* on the radio, retains an extremely powerful association heard by anyone in the civilized world, recalling the daring and resourceful masked rider of the plains to some, and to others, the fantastic adventures of Flash on the Planet Mongo.

famous bowl-like Bronson Canyon,[2] a section of land in the Griffith Park area with staggering 250-foot high walls of rock and an impressive tunnel with several cave mouths. With such a location, the prehistoric aspects of Mongo were instantly actualized.

Flash Gordon was scripted by Frederick Stephani, who doubled as the serial's director, George Plympton, Basil Dickey and Ella O'Neill, who transcribed a faithful adaptation of the Alex Raymond story appearing in the newspaper and reprinted in three consecutive "Big Little Books" from the Whitman Publishing Company, *Flash Gordon on the Planet Mongo* (1934), *Flash Gordon and the Monsters of Mongo,* and *Flash Gordon and the Tournaments of Mongo* (both 1935). The script followed Raymond's text extremely closely, going off on its own after the ordeal of the Mongo tournaments. Raymond's comic strip was virtually a movie storyboard for whole sequences and the costumes, which Hollywood's Western Costume Company fashioned with the most meticulously accurate detail.

While the special effects and fight scenes[3] in *Flash Gordon*

[2] The origin of Bronson (also known as Brush) Canyon is not as dramatic as the films in which it was used. In 1907, the site was a quarry, its minerals used for construction purposes. The cave was cut through the rocky wall to make the transportation of the minerals easier, where trucks would take their cargoes out of the canyon. In later years, a railroad line enhanced the efficiency of removing the rocks. The quarry remained in use until the early 1930s. Bronson Canyon has served as movie locations since the silent era of films, doubling as remote areas of the world, as any number of alien planets, and primarily as a section of the Old West. To even attempt a comprehensive list of serials, features, and television shows to use the canyon and its cave would be impossible. It is the most used exterior site ever to be featured on the screen, utilized today as much as before.

[3] Eddie Parker doubled heroes Flash Gordon and Buck Rogers at Universal. Parker, a six foot four actor-stuntman who also appeared in serials made by Republic and Columbia, doubled such stars as Boris Karloff, Bela Lugosi, and Lon Chaney, Jr. in Universal's horror features of the 1930s and '40s. He continued his role as an unbilled monster through the 1950s until his death just before the change of the decade. The majority of Parker's serial acting roles consisted of being a hired thug or outlaw.

were crude when compared to the slick formula shots in the Republic chapterplays of the late 1930s and through the '40s, director Stephani interjected something else into his cliffhanger that keeps the serial even today in a niche reserved for only the greatest entries to the genre. The *Flash Gordon* characters had personality, individuality, qualities lacking in most serials, especially those of later years. And they worked within the limits of a *good* script with a real plot. In storytelling, characterization precedes plot in importance. For this reason, various bits of business between Flash and his friends still hold one's fascination while a hundred spectacular stunt fights and car chases are forgotten. But even a director as capable as Stephani could not work without actors able to make such unearthly characters as Ming and Dr. Zarkov believable. The choice of players in *Flash Gordon* was barely short of perfect.

Prince Barin, the powerful man dressed like a Roman centurion, with chest armor emblazoned with a dragon, a helmet, gauntlets, and even a flowing cloak, was played by Richard Alexander,[4] whose portrayals in serials and features usually were of the brutal villain variety. But despite his audience's familiarity with Alexander as a bad guy, he indeed made a physically impressive Barin, although he had trouble delivering some of the archaic dialogue.

John "Tiny" Lipson wore the wings and beard of King Vultan in one of his only film roles, but with tremendous characterization, growling uproariously with a wide open mouth and a shaking belly.

Prince Thun's role was enacted by James Pierce, who had

[4] Richard Alexander actually helped design the costume he wore as Prince Barin in *Flash Gordon*. "I almost completely designed the chestplate and all that out of real heavy leather," he related. "It was painted gold, and had all the pectoral muscles shaped right into the leather. And we could accentuate the wide shoulders and so on. The object of it was to look like metal."

already played Tarzan on both the screen and on the radio. Pierce did not wear the long feline tail that Thun boasted in the comic strip, but was granted the hirsute mane of the chief Lion Man.

"Flash Gordon was a wild science-fiction deal," Pierce reminisced, "that seemed crazy then, but today the same things are real more or less. Buster Crabbe, as you know, was also a Tarzan. It took about two hours each morning to get the Lion Man make-up on. I was selected as Thun because I had played in several serials at Universal and the producer wanted me. Production techniques in those days were crude compared to today's. We doubled many times in helping lug equipment, holding reflectors and playing other parts in disguise. That was before the Guild took care of all of that sort of thing. Also, the labor unions, etc. But one thing that was OK was that we started a picture on salary and stayed on to the end. Today, they bring them in on a day-to-day basis and cut them off as soon as possible. There were few retakes—they would cut and pick up or cover it with a quick close-up and put the fluff in the close-up as it should have been in the first place."

Irish character actor Frank Shannon played Dr. "Alexis" Zarkov as a little older and less dynamic than his counterpart in the funnies, but fans did not seem to mind.

Dale Arden did not lose any youth as did Zarkov in the serial, but actress Jean Rogers, naturally a brunette, was forced to dye her hair blond for the part for two reasons. First, Dale was black-haired in the comic strip. Second, during the 1930s era of films, the dark-locked girl was usually identified with good, the blonde being the temptress. The change in hair color apparently capitalized on the popularity of Jean Harlow. Even more curious, when Jean Rogers re-created the role in the second Flash Gordon serial, she was allowed to keep her natural hair color which did not match up with the flashbacks to the original.

Charles Middleton, the most hissable serial villain of them all and the most believable, was Ming the Merciless, and a more merciless Ming there could never have been. His daughter, Princess Aura, appeared with darker hair in the serial through the enactment of Priscilla Lawson. Neither Ming, nor Aura, or any of the inhabitants of Mongo, were mentioned as having yellow skin as colored by Alex Raymond every Sunday (in later years, they all suddenly became Caucasian in the comics).

Just as *Flash Gordon* co-starred the world's meanest cliffhanger archfiend, it also boasted the most popular chapterplay hero of them all. Clarence Linden Crabbe, whose hair was dyed a striking gold to portray Flash, was muscular Olympics swimming champion, whose first screen appearance was doubling Joel McCrea in RKO's *The Most Dangerous Game* in 1932. Changing his name to Larry "Buster" Crabbe, or simply Larry or Buster, his first major film featured him as the star, Kaspa the Lion Man, no relation to Thun, in Paramount's *King of the Jungle* (1933).[5] Eighteen productions later, he was Flash Gordon, with the distinction of being one of the only actors who literally looked like a comic strip hero and who played the role with total believability. Crabbe was *the* serial hero, showing the zenith in bravery and sheer determination to vanquish evil from Earth or anywhere. Many actors have tried to imitate his screen courage, but none have equaled him.

For the role of Flash Gordon, Crabbe's hair was dyed a shocking blond to match the image in the Alex Raymond strip.

---

[5] *King of the Jungle* was an obvious imitation of Tarzan. In 1933, he played the Ape Man himself in a serial, Principal's *Tarzan the Fearless*. In addition to the Flash Gordon serials, Crabbe also starred in the following chapter adventures: *Red Barry* 1938, Universal; *The Sea Hound* 1947, *Pirates of the High Seas* 1950 and *King of the Congo* 1952, all Columbia. Currently, Buster Crabbe is the director of water sports at a large resort hotel in which he has a large interest. He played Flash Gordon again recently on a radio-type record album, not without revealing the passage of time. Still, there was spark in the old Flash.

According to writer George Plympton, Crabbe was extremely self-conscious of the fact that the golden hair and his powerfully constructed frame made his appearance questionable. He never took his hat off in public, even when there were ladies present. In a lengthy interview published in *Kaleidoscope* magazine, Volume 2 Number 2, 1966, the actor stated:

"I didn't give a damn if they were all ladies—my hat stayed right on, I was so conscious of it. And to have guys whistle at you—that really burned me up."

Chapter One, "The Planet of Peril," re-created the destruction on Earth caused by the approaching alien world. Flash Gordon's father (Richard Tucker) feels relieved that his son has seen fit to "cancel his polo game so that he might be with us during Earth's final hour," which was a noble gesture for even one of the blond hero's stature. After Flash and Dale fled the Earth in Dr. Zarkov's rocket ship and landed on the planet to encounter some gigantic iguana lizards whose very breath is fatal, they spotted a fantastic flying ship not too different from their own. Dipping its nose, the ship blasted the reptilian monstrosities to death and landed. A heavily armored man named Officer Torch (Earl Askam) and two soldiers dressed like human robots and holding bizarre alien rifles confronted and arrested the Earthlings and took them to the throne room of Emperor Ming, tyrant of the planet Mongo. Ming lecherously took a more than friendly liking to Dale and an immediate hatred to Flash, "the blond giant" who attacked the soldiers of Mongo at the slightest frown.

Dale, Ming decided, would be his bride, while Flash would serve as sport in the arena of death. There, before the leering faces of Ming and his subjects, and Princess Aura who loves Flash, the Earthman Gordon was pitted against three-fanged subhuman wrestlers (in the comic strip they were red apes), meeting apparent defeat during the last seconds of the episode.

Flash was rescued by Princess Aura, and both plunged into a

pit overlooking a number of sacred dragon lizards and into
twelve more episodes of adventure. Ming, convinced by Zarkov
in Chapter One not to destroy the Earth but to conquer it in
order to save the human race from immediate doom, put the
scientist to work in the laboratory, giving him everything he
required except his freedom, a situation which was the most
recurring fate of the bearded doctor. Then Ming turned to preparing for his wedding to Dale before the statue of the Great
God Tao. Meanwhile, Flash has found a rocket ship with the
distinctive clothes that would identify him as plainly as Superman's "S" outfit. In an air battle, he downed one of the Gyro-
ships of the Lion Men, weirdly shaped devices reminding one
of birthday cake candle holders. After defeating and refusing
to slay Prince Thun, the two, both enemies of Ming, set out to
defeat the monarch and save Dale from her fate worse than
death. To rescue the girl, Flash and Thun had to first defeat
a flank of Ming's Roman-styled soldiers, then face the "great
beast" that guards the rear cave entrance to the nuptial chamber.
Thun continued to battle the soldiers as Flash enters "The Tunnel of Terror," the lair of the monster, a towering dinosaur-like
creature (played by Glenn Strange), stomping about on two
legs, with a hideous horse-like head and enormous lobster
pincers (the beast was patterned after the comic strip's Gocko,
an eight-legged horror that lived underwater). As the monster
yanked the comparatively tiny Flash Gordon off his feet at the
climax of the second installment, he seemed surely doomed to
be split in two.

Thun defeated his adversaries and rescued Flash by firing
a ray, scratched directly on the film emulsion, destroying the
beast, and the hero rescued the woman he loves.

The original reason for heroism had changed. At first, the
mission of the Earthmen was to save their home world. With
Zarkov's assurance that the two planets would not collide,
Flash's sole motive for remaining on Mongo was to save the

woman he loved and, if possible, to enact his vengeance of Ming whose very glance could violate the pure Dale Arden. Dale's feelings for Flash were no less ardent. When she says "I'd do *anything* for Flash," the grown-ups in the audience undoubtedly grinned.

In the succeeding installments, Flash and his friends encountered such characters as the Shark Men, whose King Kala trapped Flash in a flooded tank with a dreaded Octosac with its grasping tentacles; the Hawkmen, a race of winged men living in a Sky City supported by light beams; Prince Barin, who helped them to fight Ming and who secretly loved Aura; the sacred Tigron, one of many sacred beasts, which was forced to give up the horn it sported from the head in the strip; and a titanic Fire Dragon that guarded the fiery Sacred Palace of the Great God Tao.

After Dr. Zarkov caused a disaster in the Sky City's deadly atom furnace room where Flash, Barin, and Thun toiled as slaves, threatening the destruction of the metropolis, he agreed to save it with a ray he invented while working in Vultan's laboratory with everything he required except his freedom, providing his friends were released. Vultan agreed, swearing by Tao, and Zarkov steadied the city with his "new ray" which he cleverly disguised as a Jacob's-ladder. When Ming, a guest of Vultan, refused to free the Earthlings, the winged monarch sided with them. Ming cackled that Flash must now enter tournament battle to prove his freedom.

> *The first ordeal was sword duel with the mighty Masked Swordsman of Mongo. As* FLASH *in chain-mail clashed blades with his stocky, hooded opponent, the royalty of the planet exchanged comments.*

VULTAN: Who is your champion, Ming?
MING: The finest swordsman in all of Mongo—heh!
VULTAN: He'll have to be the best to win from the Earthman.

MEDIUM SHOT

> *As* FLASH *and his opponent strain against their locked swords,* FLASH *twists the tip of his sword so that it rips off the hood from his head, revealing the face of* BARIN.

DALE: Barin!

FLASH: Barin!

BARIN: I'm sorry, Flash . . . I was forced into this.

FLASH: I might have killed you.

VULTAN: So your champion was Prince Barin. Clever trap, Ming, but the Earthmen won.

MING: Heh! He won the right to fight the mighty Beast of Mongo!

Barin has been "forced" into the fight in a hope to be able to best Flash, but without killing him, so that Barin could have his chosen bride, Aura.

The "Mighty Beast" proved to be the Sacred Orangapoid, a horned, hairy ape with Ray "Crash" Corrigan inside the costume. With the help of a spear thrust from the dedicated if misguided Princess Aura, Flash finished off the monster.

Later, Ming ordered Flash's immediate execution, a measure he should have taken in Chapter One.

But as the Torch's firing squad aimed to shoot, the Earthman backed against a mechanized wall under the suggestion of Zarkov. The doctor flicked switches, there was a peculiar sound of power, and Flash Gordon disappeared, causing sheer panic, ending the chapter. Flash had not disintegrated, but was rendered invisible by Zarkov. Then Flash proceeded to release Vultan who had been jailed by order of Ming. Back in the laboratory, the soldiers of Mongo engaged in a fight against Vultan and the unseen Flash wherein the villains were again thwarted.[6]

[6] Glenn Strange, who wore the make-up and raised boots of Frankenstein's Monster in three Universal features of the 1940s, and who eventually became a regular on television's *Gunsmoke*, as Sam the Bartender, had a non-speaking role in *Flash Gordon*. "In *Flash Gordon*, big old

In the last segment, "Rocketing to Earth," Thun and his shaggy-maned Lion Man invaded Ming's palace. Seeing his forces defeated, Ming took the coward's way out and fled to the Sacred Palace of the Great God Tao from which no man returns, apparently the victim of his own suicide. Flash, Dale, and Zarkov, safe from the threat of Ming and Mongo, left their friends, Aura to become the wife of Prince Barin, and blasted off for Earth. After disposing of a time bomb placed aboard the ship by Ming's evil and obviously maniacal high priest (Theodore Lorch), they found their adventure finished.

But Flash Gordon's adventures were not finished. In 1938 he returned along with the same Dale, Zarkov, Ming, and Barin in an adaptation of the 1936 "Big Little Book" version of the newspaper strip, *Flash Gordon and the Witch Queen of Mongo*. But 1938 was also the year in which Orson Welles terrified the nation with his Halloween Mercury Theatre presentation of Martian invaders, "War of the Worlds." To capitalize on this, the location of Zaura the Witch Queen's domain was switched from Mongo to Mars, where Flash, Dale, Zarkov, and a comic relief newspaper reporter stowaway, "Happy" Hapgood (Donald Kerr), went mysteriously not in the doctor's ship but one that belonged to Ming, to investigate a ray that was sapping the Earth of nitrogen needed for plant life. The title was *Flash Gordon's Trip to Mars*.

On Mars, the Earthlings again discovered Ming whom they believed dead. They also discovered and befriended a race of Clay People, once living, breathing, and otherwise normal men who had been so changed through the witchcraft of Queen Azura (Beatrice Roberts). Mars had advanced from the Roman Empire of Mongo. There was a vast squadron of stratosleds,

---

Tiny, John Lipson, who had the wings in that one, jumped on my foot and broke my little toe. Just crushed it. I was the guy Buster Crabbe tossed around when he was supposed to be invisible. We wore those—they looked like 5-gallon oil cans over our heads."

carrying powerful bombs. A secret rocket subway connected the palace of Azura with the dark abode of the Clay Men. People walked high above the city supported only by glowing "light bridges." And the enormous Nitron Lamp continued extracting nitrogen from the Earth.

Queen Azura, like all female villains, falls in love with Flash. But he was nonetheless committed to defeat her. With the help of Prince Barin, the Earthmen battled the primitive native Forest People, who fought with knives and blow guns, and occasionally managed to slip in a televisor or deathray which they had secured from who-knows-where, put the Nitron Lamp out of commission, and restored the Clay People to their former human selves by destroying the magical Black and White Sapphires of Queen Azura. The jewels that gave her the power to even vanish and teleport herself.

In the fifteenth and last episode, "An Eye for an Eye," Ming, now characterized more like the Devil than Fu, who had shown his true intentions by ordering the death-by-bombing of Azura, escaped to the laboratory where, raving like the madman he was, threatened to turn his destructive wrath on Mars. Tarnak (Wheeler Oakman), once loyal to both Azura and her supposed ally, Ming, realized that his own planet was about to die and forced the Emperor at ray rifle-point to enter the disintegration room. Moments later, Ming the Merciless was totally reduced to a pile of ghastly rubble. And Flash and his Earthling friends returned to Earth again in one of Ming's rockets.

Flash Gordon's Trip to Mars, though only two years later than its predecessor, seems surprisingly modern when viewed today. While *Flash Gordon* remains somewhat primitive in style and production values despite its appeal, the Martian adventure appears as though it could have been filmed recently.

The *Flash Gordon* comic strip was actually not an original concept at all, but King Features' imitation of the rival *Buck*

Rogers—2429 A.D. which began in 1929, written by Phillip Nolan and illustrated by Richard Calkins. Buck's adventures, though the original, in no way compared with Flash's five years later. Though possessing a distinct charm and fascination, the drawings were crude, without the refinements of Raymond. The stories were sometimes ludicrous, with a twenty-fifth century cowboy with chaps, gunbelt, and ten-gallon hat, and people flying through the futuristic skies in biplanes! But *Buck Rogers* did not want for popularity. And in 1939, Universal released its own *Buck Rogers* as a twelve-part chapterplay.

However, despite the title, fans knew that this newest science-fiction opera from Universal was merely a Flash Gordon opus in disguise. It starred "Larry" Crabbe as Buck, who played the part with the same style as Flash. Only his costume and hair color were different. The music was also the same as that heard in Flash's serials; and many of the props, the secret rocket subway, and the whole style all resembled Flash Gordon.

Buck and Buddy (Jackie Moran) crashed in Chapter One, "Tomorrow's World," on an icy mountain in the Arctic in a dirigible containing a new gas called Nirvano. Breathing the gas, the two slept in suspended animation until their discovery in the twenty-fifth century where they learned that the world was dominated by a futuristic gangster named Killer Kane (Anthony Warde) and his legion of henchmen.

In the comic strip, the first daily titled "The Sleeper," Buck was the only one to sleep for five hundred years. In this original version, Buck was a surveyor trapped in a mine cave-in.

Buck and Buddy were taken in Chapter One, "Tomorrow's World," to the Hidden City, where Dr. Huer (C. Montague Shaw) and Wilma Deering (Constance Moore) used science to combat the ruthlessness of Killer Kane (in the comics, Buddy was Wilma's brother, not a time-traveling stranger).

The serial took our heroes from the Earth to Saturn, where we learned that aliens were Oriental but not necessarily evil.

We also learned that Saturnians could be Caucasian stuntmen, like Tom Steele and David Sharpe, who could conveniently battle Buck and Buddy without the use of doubles, and also fill in for the stars.[7]

Buck Rogers, though not haunted by as many monsters as *Flash Gordon,* was not devoid of horrors. There was the Robot Battalion, made up of men whose minds were sapped away by the gadgets on their heads, reducing them to servile human zombies; and the Zuggs; horrible low intelligence humanoids that obeyed their human robot leaders. And there were numerous fantastic devices like trapezoid-shaped rocket ships, invisibility devices, and rocket belts that predicted those used in real life by today's Air Force.

By Chapter Twelve, "War of the Planets," Buck had finally managed to convince the Saturnian Prince Tallen (Philson Ahn) of "The Leader Kane's" evil ways. And the Oriental alien agreed to help defeat the twenty-fifth century mobster. After a thrilling rocket battle in the skies, Killer Kane and his flight force were defeated, Buck was rewarded with the marshalship of the nation's air forces, and with the amorous glance of Wilma.

Despite the production values of *Buck Rogers* it was an imitation of the thing fans preferred, Flash Gordon. And so Universal returned to their original blockbusting property in 1940 with a twelve-segment thriller, *Flash Gordon Conquers the Universe,* again based on the comic and the "Big Little Book," *Flash Gordon and the Ice World of Mongo.*

This last Flash Gordon epic again set on Mongo, is perhaps the most "pretty" serial ever made, with emphasis on costuming

---

[7] Tom Steele, who played several parts in *Buck Rogers,* which was typical of his serial performances, said of his partner David Sharpe: "Dave once told someone he could jump up and touch the ceiling. His friend laughed, because Dave isn't tall. The way he did it was to do a back flip and kick the ceiling with his feet."

and set design. Everything in this chapterplay is elaborate, aesthetically beautiful, right down to the military plumage of the vilest of fiends, Ming, who had mysteriously returned to Mongo whole and entire, without even a blister resulting from his previous disintegration.

Location shooting moved at least partially away from Bronson Canyon, taking the crew to California's Red Rock Canyon, where parts of *Flash Gordon's Trip to Mars* and *Buck Rogers* were shot.

Flash Gordon, Dr. Zarkov, and Ming were again played by Crabbe, Shannon, and Middleton, the latter now more of a wicked general than Satan. But considerable changes were made in the other principals. Carol Hughes became the new Dale Arden; handsome, slender Roland Drew was the new bow-and-arrow-slinging Prince Barin, to correspond with the slimmer version currently appearing in the newspaper feature; Shirley Deane was the "blonde" Mrs. Barin, Princess Aura; and Don Rowan played "Captain" Torch, a character missing from the screen since 1936. Also in the cast were Anne Gwynne as the beautiful traitor Sonja; Donald Curtis as Ronal and Lee Powell as Roka, both loyal to Barin. Ronal, Roka, and Barin are all three dark-haired men with mustaches, difficult to keep mentally separated.

"The Purple Death," Chapter One, had Dr. Zarkov finding his original spaceship that had undergone some variations, completely avoiding that questionable Ming ship of the second serial, and returning to Mongo from which the fatal malady had struck the inhabitants of the Earth. On Mongo, the Dale, Zarkov, and Flash who seemed a bit less energetic than in the first two chapterplays, met the restored Emperor Ming who now claimed to *be* "The Universe." The Earthlings also found the usual giant lizards of Mongo, a giant warrior, a stiff-walking robot army, and that planet's answer to the Clay People, the Rock Men.

The speech patterns of the Rock Men were indeed a curiosity. Their words came out backwards! But Zarkov, brilliant scientist that he was, knew that they were actually speaking the language of the lost tribes of Earth's own Gobi Desert in Mongolia—a place that did at least resemble Mongo in name. Zarkov conversed with these primitives, whose origin seeds apparently were the same as the corresponding Earth tribes, by himself speaking backwards, then translating the sucked-in words to the less brilliant men at his side. Surprisingly, when played backwards, the language of the Rock Men did not reveal any off-color phrases or in-jokes, but exactly what Zarkov translated on the soundtrack.

Much of *Flash Gordon Conquers the Universe* was set in the frozen wastelands of Frigia, using much stock footage from a previous Universal feature of 1930 about snow and mountain climbing, *White Hell of Pitz Palu.* Unfortunately, the serial used excessively long sequences of the characters, and their stock shot counterparts which strangely changed their numbers, rambling about the ice for long minutes where virtually nothing happened. The serial was the most picturesque of the trilogy, but surrendered much compelling charm to its cinematic sophistication.

"Doom of the Dictator," the last episode, sent Ming and his henchmen to a destructive climax as their ship crashed into a tower loaded with explosives. Ming was dead—for the third time. But he had survived greater demises. And had Universal decided to make a fourth Flash Gordon serial, he would doubtlessly have returned from the grave without a scratch, for Zarkov stated that there *was* indeed one possible escape for the fiend. In his terror, however, Ming apparently never thought of it. He never returned.

Flash Gordon had won again, returning Mongo to the rightful rule of Prince Barin. And Zarkov mused that since Ming called himself "The Universe," and Flash Gordon conquered Ming . . . well, he solved the problem implied by the title wherein fans wondered why a hero like Flash would ever want to do a terrible thing like conquer the universe.

Flash Gordon and Buck Rogers have appeared in countless forms, including comic books, bubble gum cards, hard-cover books, paperbacks, and various whatnots. There were also Flash Gordon and Buck Rogers radio programs, and later, television shows. But these visual adaptations for television of the 1950s could only make one pray for a rerun of the original four Universal chapter adventures. The two series, *Buck Rogers* done live, *Flash Gordon* (starring Steve Holland) filmed in Germany, were vastly inferior, even to most space operas of that era of television. They lacked many things, including good scripts and concepts, and adequate production values. But most of all, they lacked Buster Crabbe, who *is* Flash Gordon.

DESTINATION: THE MOON, ATOMA, AND ERGRO

Science fiction was a popular and important ingredient in movie serials. Even the most mundane police chapterplays and Westerns might center upon some weird buzzing and crackling device capable of tremendous destruction or similar extraordinary power. But the number of straight space opera chapterplays due to the costliness of constructing other worldly sets and costumes to outfit entire alien races, are relatively few.

Columbia Pictures attempted to imitate the superadventures of Flash Gordon and Buck Rogers with three rather shoddy, low-budget space cliffhangers—*Brick Bradford* (1947), *Captain Video* (1951), and *The Lost Planet* (1953). The trio were produced by Sam Katzman, the quickie king also known as "Jungle Sam" due to his list of films set amongst the vines and the elephants. Spencer G. Bennet directed each of these serials

as best he could considering the lack of production values and
the uninspired scripts. But it was rather obvious that even
Bennet, who had directed so many better than average action
pictures since the silent days, had realized that serials were on
their way out, their loyal audiences deserting the medium they
loved so well in favor of that new upstart, television. Therefore, although the actors seemed to believe the impossible lines
foisted upon them by the less caring script writers, it was often
difficult for audiences to take them seriously. And so, facing
the problems of the dying serial, Bennet continued directing
them for Columbia without the verve that had characterized
earlier chapterplays bearing his name in the credits, grinding out
the last five, culminating with the final theatrical cliffhanger ever
made in the United States, *Blazing the Overland Trail* (1956).

Brick Bradford, starring Kane Richmond in the title role, was
based on the science fiction newspaper comic strip appearing
through the King Features Syndicate. Three writers produced
the script, George H. Plympton, who also worked on *Captain
Video* and *The Lost Planet;* and Lewis Clay. And it is of considerable interest to see each writer's interpretation of the
Brick Bradford concept.

Chapters One through Six illustrated Plympton's lingering
fondness for the Flash Gordon masterpieces that were born in
his typewriter in 1936 and 1940. The first installment, "Atomic
Defense!", opens with Brick Bradford protecting the Interceptor
Ray anti-guided missile device invented by Dr. Tymak (John
Merton) from a gang of crooks led by Laydron (Charles
Quigley), Dr. Tymak fled into a strange Crystal Door that im-
mediately teleported him to the moon, where he hoped to secure
some lunarium, an element required in his experiments. After
avoiding death by searing rays and less spectacular hazards,
Brick and Professor Salisbury (Pierre Watkin) entered the
Crystal Door, becoming the "Prisoners of the Moon" of
Chapter Three.

The moon sequence of *Brick Bradford* proved that extra-terrestrial life forms had undergone their own depression since the flamboyant days of Flash and Buck. Gone were the elaborate costumes of Ming and his subjects. The inhabitants of the moon were forced to exchange their Roman soldier uniforms in favor of, worst of all, the costuming of married, middle-aged, suburban Earthmen! Yes, these moonmen sported such familiar attire as white T-shirts, Bermuda shorts, and of all things, white tennis shoes. Their capes and helmets did little to enhance the ridiculous image. It would not have been surprising to see these men puttering around a lunar rock garden or watching the ballgame on television on weekends. And the antics of Brick and a group of Earthlings who managed to become stranded on the moon, all unaffected by the lack of atmosphere and decreased gravity as they cavorted under the bright afternoon sky, was difficult to accept, especially at such a late date. Scientists like Brick—and writers like Plympton—should have known better.

Chapters Six through Ten, in which Brick and his young sidekick Sandy Sanderson (Rick Vallin) crash into an eighteenth-century jungle via a device called the Time Top, are perhaps the most interesting. Hoerl's scripting laughed at the whole idea of the story. Where the general rule of serials stressed that the performers believed their dialogue and situations regardless of the incredulity and acted with total conviction, these middle chapters showed Brick and Sandy laughing at themselves, fighting with such devices as exploding cigars! When they were tied to a stake by a tribe of savage natives and Sandy quipped that "This is a hot one" or "I'd like to smoke, do you have a match?" as the flames spread around them, the suspension of disbelief required a bit of straining.

The last five installments by Lewis Clay were neither interesting nor funny. Despite the invisibility device introduced in a previous episode, the remainder of the adventure was a mun-

dane yarn which seemed to offer nothing more than the crooks'
capture of a good guy and Brick's subsequent rescue, repeated
again and again. The fact that Brick Bradford knew the location
of the villains' hideout did not stop them from re-enacting their
kidnapping schemes. Nor did Brick phone the police to raid
their headquarters. A curious attempt at comedy spanning
several chapters in which the heavies' car tires flattened just as
another one was repaired was less laugh-provoking than the
episodes set on the Moon.

Space operas reached their greatest popularity in the television programs of the early 1950s. It seemed as though any
children's show that did not feature cowboys or puppets starred
interstellar heroes, all fighting against their own enemies that
threatened the Earth by either conquest or destruction.

Of the many raygun-slinging heroes that rocketed across the
black and white television screens of Saturday mornings and
weekday dinnertime, the most popular was a combination
soldier and scientist working from a secret mountain headquarters on Earth. He wore what appeared to be a futuristic
army uniform, and occasionally donned a football helmet with
goggles. A teenage sidekick called only the Video Ranger, which
was curious since that was also his rank, accompanied him on
adventures that took him all over the universe. The hero's name
was simply Captain Video.

Captain Video and his Video Rangers began as a five-day-a-
week television serial, live except for the filmed special effects
sequences, presented by the defunct Dumont network. Richard
Coogan and Don Hastings starred in the early days of the show
as Captain Video and the Video Ranger (who apparently was
christened with the title), respectively, in the late 1940s. By
1950, however, Coogan felt his dramatic talents suited for more
roles and left the show, his combat boots to be filled by the most
famous and popular Captain Video of them all, former *Green
Hornet* radio star, Al Hodge. Hodge and Hastings shared inter-

planetary adventures through the mid-1950s, blasting off in their sleek rocketship, the Galaxy, and suppressing such adversaries as Dr. Pauli and Tobor, the indestructible super-robot.

In 1951, during the most successful period of the television series, Columbia released their fifteen episode filmed version, appropriately titled *Captain Video,* starring Judd Holdren, a young actor with a truly heroic visage, and Larry Stewart, the son of the casting director for that production, as a miscast Video Ranger. It was the only time a movie serial was adapted from a television show.

Some attempts were again made to capitalize on Flash Gordon in *Captain Video.* Whole sequences were tinted by Cinecolor to convey the feeling of alien atmospheres. Thus, when the Captain and the Ranger landed on the planet Atoma, they encountered pink hues; everything on Theros was green. A similar "color" technique made the Red Planet look green in *Flash Gordon's Trip to Mars.*

To further remind audiences of the greatness of Flash Gordon's installment adventures, a counterpart of Ming the Merciless emerged in the personage of Vultura (Gene Roth), the tyrannical ruler of the planet Atoma. But where Ming reeked with the class of flowing robes and sinister snickers, Vultura appeared as an overweight character in a cheaply assembled costume of tights, leather cape and helmet. He did, though, look better than he did in his moonman uniform in *Brick Bradford.*

Perhaps the serial's true appeal rested in the conglomeration of weapons, props built by propman Wes Morton. These included the Opticon Scillometer, a Peeping Tom device for looking through walls; the Isotopic Radiation Curtain, which could make even sizable objects disappear; the Radionic Directional Beam and its Radionic Guide, which sent out traceable electrical impulses; the Mu-Ray Camera, that photographed the lingering image of a man after he had vacated a room; the miniature Door Hinge Recorder, ideal for eavesdropping; and the Psychosomatic Weapon, which produced a temporary madness in its victim. Seeing these weapons in operation was not nearly as much fun as hearing stars Holdren and Stewart attempt pronouncing them.

In the first episode, "Journey into Space," we learned that Dr. Tober, no connection with the TV robot (George Eldridge), had made an alliance with Vultura, the Genghis Khan of Atoma. Captain Video and the Ranger left their hidden Earth headquarters and blasted off, via a crudely animated cartoon spacecraft, to the planet where Dr. Tober had already arrived. Vultura, watching the approaching rocketship of Captain Video, guided a remote-control comet to intercept with and explode the craft, ending Chapter One in a splash of violent light.

Captain Video and the Ranger escaped this and various other cliffhanger perils, including being frozen alive, strange flames that turned out to be cold, and a number of smiling Tin Woodsman robots left over from Gene Autry's *Phantom Empire* escapade. At one point, the duo actually escaped death by falling from a speeding rocket and landing safely in a haystack! In the fifteenth installment, "Video vs. Vultura," the crusading Captain, disguised as one of the tyrant's own subjects on Atoma, switched the villain's own ray cannon on him, disintegrating Vultura with his own devious device.

The Captain Video serial with its shoddy sets, unbelievable costumes, phony special effects, unconvincing action, and laughable plotting and dialogue showed that the serial had but a few remaining years before extinction. But the production company behind *Captain Video* was not yet ready to toss in the towel. Two years later, with Judd Holdren and Gene Roth again battling each other on another world, *The Lost Planet,* was discovered in fifteen cosmic episodes.

In *The Lost Planet,* Rex Barrow (Holdren), a reporter, learned of the traitorous activities of an occultist-electronics genius, Dr. Ernst Grood (Michael Fox). Barrow was captured along with pretty Ella Dorn (Vivian Mason) and a photographer ally, Tim Johnson (Ted Thorpe), and transported to the Lost Planet, Ergro, via a spacecraft dubbed a Cosmojet. On Ergro, Dr. Grood and his assistant Reckov (Roth) had forced Ella's brilliant father to help them conquer the universe. Traveling to and fro, between Earth and Ergro, Rex and his friends encountered scientific gadgets to not only rival, but to surpass those used by and against Captain Video and the Ranger. There were the Prysmic Catapult, the Cosmic Cannon, the De-gravitizer, the De-Thermo Ray, the Axial Propeller, the Thermic Disintegrator, and a machine that sounded like something involving Captain America in 1944, the Sonic Vibrator. The total number of the bizarre mechanical creations of *The Lost Planet* was a staggering fifty-two! Enough to fill a year-long serial, one gadget per week. With that many devices to cope with, it was a true miracle that Rex and his accomplices escaped death and Dr. Grood and Reckov were shot by Cosmojet to an eternal trek through the void of space, ergo climaxing "Sentenced to Space."

The Lost Planet was followed by only six more Columbia serials, which would terminate this American form of Saturday afternoon entertainment. Each of these would get progressively worse. Even fighting Rex Barrow and Captain Video, the heralded Master of the Stratosphere, could not save the movie serial, in fact, *certainly* not them!

"WE HAVE BEEN MONITORING YOUR RADIO BROADCASTS FOR YEARS!"

While Universal and Columbia took their heroes to other worlds to battle the menaces of the solar system, Republic preferred keeping the battles generally on the home front, with invaders of Earth usually migrating from their world, Mars.

The original Republic Martian invader chapterplay was the fifteen-episode science-fiction marathon of 1945, *The Purple Monster Strikes*. The Purple Monster was actually not a monster at all; nor was he purple. This villainous character with the rather absurd name was in reality a Caucasian Martian space soldier, the advance guard preparing a vast invasion of Earth, dressed in a blue serge tight-fitting outfit, trimmed with a scaly gold, metallic material and wearing a matching gilded hood. Among the Purple Monster's alien abilities was the power to become a transparent phantom and enter the body of another, controlling his actions, thereby donning the ultimate disguise.

Chapter One, "The Man in the Meteor," began with Dr. Cyrus Layton, an astronomer and inventor of a fantastic jet-plane capable of interplanetary travel, watching through his Griffith Park Observatory telescope the Earthward descent of a weird, purple meteor. Layton, played by James Craven, an actor who became typecast in serials as a traitor, and often a man who betrayed the Earth to invaders from space, drove where his calculations told him the projectile would collide with the ground. The thing from the sky was now clearly visible, and revealed itself as a man-made—or alien-made—container. The casket-like object crashed, exploding with an array of flames.[8] A strangely garbed man, with a case strapped over one shoulder, fled from the projectile seconds before it completely blew up. Layton, staring in wonder, asked the creature his identity.

"My name would mean nothing to you," said the alien. "I've come from the planet you people on Earth call Mars."

"From Mars!" Layton was amazed. "But—you speak English! Our language!"

---

[8] The rocket explosion was shot by special effects experts Howard and Theodore Lydecker in a vast area of rocks that stretched for acres. Running underground was a water line. It was more bad luck than miscalculation that the rocket struck that lone pipe, sending a geyser of water over everything, forcing a retake.

"Yes, I speak all languages. You see, many years ago my people invented and perfected a remarkable instrument, known as the Distance Eliminator. With the help of this device, we have been able to see and hear everything that happens on Earth." He indicated the case.

The strange creature, who later revealed himself as the Purple Monster (Roy Barcroft), admitted knowledge of Layton's identity and his jetplane. Back at Layton's observatory, the Martian gleefully blurted out his plans to pave the way for an invasion, using Layton's ship to transport his people across space. The scientist watched helplessly as the Purple Monster hits him with a bursting capsule of Martian atmosphere, poisonous to Earthlings. Dr. Layton breathed the fatal vapors and fell to the floor. After propping his victim into a chair, the Purple Monster was discovered by legal counsel Craig Foster (Dennis Moore), friend of Layton's daughter Sheila (Linda Stirling). The Martian defeated Craig (who usually fought at least *two* heavies) in a fight, then became intangible and entered Layton's body. The Plan to take over the Earth and enslave its inhabitants for no apparent reason other than the sheer villainy of it was underway.

After Craig and Sheila evaded many of the Martian's traps, the more unearthly including a disintegrating ray, and after the Emperor of Mars (John Davidson) sent a female assistant, Marcia (Mary Moore), to Earth only to fall from a cliff to a plunging doom, the Purple Monster ended his mission with a "Take-Off to Destruction." Fleeing into the giant interplanetary jetplane, the Martian villain zoomed out of the launching tube protruding from the mountainside. The silvery craft angled upward toward the Red Planet. But Craig, still in the cavern workshop from which the ship was fired, grabbed the Martian's own Annihilator, swinging it around on its turret, aiming it out the tunnel. Seconds later, the Purple Monster and the jetplane were a ball of flame.

The Purple Monster was not always called by that misleading name. During production of the chapterplay, the more meaningful title of *The Purple Shadow Strikes* was used. There was no denying that the Martian's ability to become phantom-like made him more a shadow than a monster. For some unexplained reason, hero Craig was known as Larry Foster even in the final shooting script. Both names were crossed out and others penciled in to show the changes.

Roy Barcroft, an actor usually associated with Western movies, made an extraordinarily convincing Purple Monster, although he exercised considerable restraint by meticulously pronouncing all of his "ings" and giving such words as "FAST" the Martian inflexion "fahst." It was Barcroft who devised the elastic bands that pulled back his eyes to give an unearthly effect. Of the role, Barcroft related:

"I didn't live too far from Republic when we did *The Purple Monster Strikes,* about a mile away, and I used to have to dog trot to work and try to keep in condition for that job. When they told me I was going to do the part, they said it's in tights. I said, 'What?' and they said, 'Yes, in tights.' And I said, 'Oh, oh. Well, I better get off a little weight and get trimmed down.' I think I took off thirty pounds in thirty days. Boy, it was rough. I had to hit the road and walk to work. The serial was first called *The Purple Shadow Strikes,* and then it was changed to *The Purple Monster Strikes.* But I called it *The Jerk in Tights from Boyle Heights!*"

The Purple Monster Strikes, what might be termed a typical Republic mid-1940s serial with formula plot, formula stunt fights, and formula cliffhanger resolutions, probably contained more automobile hazards than any other chapterplay of the time. It became predictable hearing Craig Foster save the heroine from an exploding or plunging car by blaring into the two-way radio, "Shelia! Jump!"

The science fiction installment production also established a precedent for future Republic serials of the same type. That is, an alien menace arrives on earth and solicits the criminal services of a gang of crooks who seem to be unconcerned with what their fate will be after the takeover of the world has been accomplished. Fighting them is but a single hero—or in later serials, also a sidekick or secondary hero to help him—who never seems to think of informing the police, the Army, the FBI, or the Boy Scouts, and who is never questioned about littering the highways with dark-suited corpses.

In 1945 it was not the end of the Purple Monster. As with Republic's flying hero Rocket Man, the costumed Man from Mars returned in various personages and identities, the first being in 1951, *Flying Disc Man from Mars*. This sequel to the original Purple Monster epic relied on much stock footage from that and other chapter adventures including *G-Men vs. the Black Dragon* (1943) where villain Harry Lauter mysteriously became Japanese and *Secret Service in Darkest Africa* (1943) wherein the new serial's star Walter Reed conveniently entered a chase of older style automobiles.

Mota (Gregory Gay) with a suspicious "foreign" accent, arrived on Earth to finish the job of conquest started six years earlier by his predecessor. The entire rocket crash sequence from *The Purple Monster Strikes'* initial episode was used right down to identifiable shots of Roy Barcroft. James Craven again played the Earthling in charge of meeting the invader, only to betray the world. Mota, setting aside his slightly altered Purple Monster uniform for a less conspicuous suit of clothing, blitzed various Earth bases and industries with a flying disc ship, complete with an impressive and misleading Japanese Rising Sun emblem, courtesy of stock footage from the wartime *King of the Mounties* (1942). Mota, like the more American Purple Monster, failed in his mission, defeated by Walter Reed, another brave Republic hero.

The Purple Monster outfit and film clips appeared in two

more Republic productions. In *Radar Men from the Moon* (1952), Roy Barcroft again wore the famed gleaming hood as Retik, tyrant of the moon. In the twelfth episode, "Take-Off to Eternity," rather than to "Destruction," the veteran actor put on the complete uniform again in order to match the stock shots of the seven year younger performer on a doomed return flight to Mars. The Purple Monster with the accompanying Roy Barcroft stock shots, and with his voice dubbed in over a radio as another character, appeared in "Atomic Peril," the third segment of *Commando Cody* (1955). The wearer of the blue and gold suit and agent of the menacing Ruler (Gregory Gay) this time was Stanley Waxman.

Earth heroes have journeyed to other worlds by Crystal Door and spaceship. Our own planet has been invaded many times by alien menaces bent on dominating the Earthlings. In all these instances there have been mighty conflicts between good and evil. But after the holocaust of ray zapping and atomic blasting had settled, the audiences huddled in the safety of terrain movie houses admitted one important fact: There was only one alien tyrant capable of conquering the universe, Ming the Merciless. And there was but a single hero able to defeat *him* —Flash Gordon.

3

Science Fiction/Westerns
"Drop That Zap Gun, Hombre."

RADIUM RUSTLERS

Gene Autry's round, smiling face is most closely identified with movies dealing with the "modern" West, complete with automobiles and airplanes, as well as cowboys and rustlers. Moreover, his first starring Western was more than modern—it was futuristic.

Phantom Empire was a serial about a superscientific lost civilization, which happened to be located in caves beneath Gene Autry's cattle ranch. The mixture was a weird one for 1935, and a brash experiment for introducing a new star to the screen. Somehow, both the production and its star had enough appeal to succeed with the public. Incredibly, due to a total lack of experience on Autry's part in acting (which showed every second) and the cheapness of the production, certain critics have said *Phantom Empire* was "twenty-five years ahead of its time."

In 1933, Autry was a popular Country-Western singer on the *WLS Barn Dance,* originating from that Chicago radio station. He wrote Mascot Studios' boss, Nat Levine, pointing out his popularity throughout the Midwest, and asking for a job in the movies.

Out of the thousands of such letters sent to studios, fate decreed that this one would get some action. Levine brought Autry and some of his radio troup with him to Hollywood. He put Gene Autry on salary at $100 a week and his chubby sidekick, Smiley Burnette, at $75 a week.

Radio broadcasting was making the public even more conscious of the speaking—and singing—voices of the actors of the silver screen. The public's curiosity to actually *see* what the stars they listened to looked like had brought out an audience for more than one movie of the early '30s (although their expectations were usually disappointed).

However, the soft-voiced if iron-willed Levine had not fully realized what he was letting himself in for. He found out when the Autry troup got to Hollywood.

Gene Autry had a pleasant, somewhat nasal singing voice, but he delivered lines of dramatic dialogue with all the feeling of the telegraph he had once operated as a railroad employee. Levine had understood that Autry was a "real" cowhand from Texas. That may have been true, but Autry was so long away from the ranch, he could hardly remember the proper way to get the stirrup in the horse's mouth.

Finally, Gene Autry was not tall and rangy, but rather of average height, and he looked lean only in comparison to rotund Smiley Burnette.

Levine must have reasoned that he had survived making other mistakes, and he would survive this. And get his money's worth out of it.

Autry and Burnette were placed in small supporting roles in the Ken Maynard (silent screen veteran and rodeo champion) serial *Mystery Mountain*.

"All I can remember about that one," Ken Maynard recalled to the present writers, "was that I kept tearing masks off people, chapter after chapter, looking for this mysterious 'Rattler' fellow. None of them were the right man—just somebody the real Rattler put the mask on. People began joking me about it when the serial came out. 'You got the wrong man again this week, I see, Ken,' they would say to me."

The Rattler was attempting to stop the construction of a railroad over Mystery Mountain for his own nefarious purposes.

Directors Otto Brower and B. Reeves Eason put Maynard through the usual assortment of dangers from explosions, gun shots, and one incredibly archetypical cliffhanger where a heavy sent Ken over the edge of a cliff with a kick, only to have Ken grab a rope that just happened to be tied to the saddle of his wonder horse, Tarzan, who pulled him to safety.

Tarzan was a mighty useful horse. Smart too. Besides disguising himself in a false nose, mustache, dark glasses and black cape, the Rattler could also assume the appearance of any male member of the cast by use of a rubber mask that could fool anybody. Anybody except Tarzan. Wearing a mask of Doctor Edwards (Hooper Archley), the Rattler purposely exposed himself to Ken Williams (Ken Maynard) and then rescued a prisoner of Ken's being guarded by the faithful Tarzan. Returning, accompanied by heroine Jane Corwin (Verna Hillie), Ken saw the gang member gone and Tarzan hurt.

KEN: Where did he go Tarzan?
JANE: Look, he's bleeding.
KEN: Beat you up, did he? How come you didn't kill him?
JANE: Look! His rump is caught in the rock.
KEN: Oh, that's what happened, huh? Doctor Edwards has got something coming from both of us.
JANE: Doctor Edwards!
KEN: Yes, I got a look at the Rattler's face, Jane. It was Doctor Edwards . . . I'm going to prove that a horse has more sense than most people. Tarzan's gonna pick the Rattler. Funny thing about a horse. He knows his friends and he knows his enemies. Not through sight, as most people may suppose. But through that delicate sense that all animals have. The Rattler beat him up pretty bad . . . Now I believe he'll sense that man when he comes to him . . .

That was a difficult feat even for a wonder horse, for the Rattler was supposedly either construction boss Blayden (Edward

Earle), telegrapher Matthews (Lynton Brent), or a man named
Lake (Edward Hearn), but in a bit of cheating the cloaked
disguise was always worn by Edmund Cobb who did not otherwise appear.

Another double in some scenes was stuntman Cliff Lyons for
star Ken Maynard. As for the horse Tarzan, he had *three*
doubles. Maynard did do much of his own stunt work throughout his career, especially riding scenes. One of the doubles for
Tarzan was a horse so nearly blind, Ken could have ridden him
straight toward the edge of the Grand Canyon for an attempted
leap across it. (Only less awesome gulches were actually
attempted.)

Gene Autry and Smiley Burnette next worked with Maynard
in a feature film, *In Old Santa Fe*. This story of bad guys on a
modern dude ranch might well have proved the prototype for
the modern Westerns Autry would make in later years. As it
was in this one, Autry and Burnette merely plunked a ten-
minute musical right in the middle of the picture, without any
significant other appearance. Ken Maynard himself sang a few
songs in the film, as he had in several earlier features. His voice
was pleasant enough, but somehow he lacked the spark that
Autry had to sell the public on a singing cowboy.

Producer Levine was not happy with Ken Maynard's attitude
on the set of this picture. In bygone years, Maynard had been
his own producer and director and he had his own ideas about
how things should be done.

One of those ideas was that it was his own business when,
where, and what he ate and drank.

After Ken Maynard left Mascot for a series of steadily declining B pictures for the next ten years, Levine placed his
money on Gene Autry's singing and radio popularity.

The move from a merely "modern" Western to one that was
futuristic was only a logical progression. The Rin-Tin-Tin, Jr.
serial for Mascot, *The Wolf Dog,* had combined the Canadian

wilds with a mad scientist and his death ray invention. Publicity releases had it that the idea for Autry's serial, *Phantom Empire* came to scriptwriter Wallace MacDonald while under gas for having a tooth extracted. When he and Gerald Geraghty and Hy Freedman finished writing it, the story did turn out to be "a real gas"—a lot of fun for those willing to suspend their disbelief.

Gene Autry became the first cowboy star to use his own name in the body of the film itself. That was natural, since he was playing the part of radio-singer Gene Autry. (This practice of using their own family names may have proved somewhat embarrassing for some stars in later years when they were given fictional brothers who had just got out of prison, etc.) Smiley Burnette appeared in the film, along with Frankie Darro and Betsy King Ross as the two kids, Frankie and Betsy. The subteen-age girl was a rodeo performer and Darro was a good horseman. They did all their stunt riding themselves, and were as fine at it as they were at acting. The veteran child stars helped carry the totally inexperienced Autry. (It could be noted that in later years, Autry did become a competent professional actor.) The two youngsters were Mascot's answer to Jackie Cooper and Shirley Temple.

The production was "supervised" (that is, produced) by Armand Schaefer who would stay with Autry right through the half-hour TV films that supplied Autry's last acting roles. His business enterprises became too vast for Gene Autry to be very interested in trying to perpetuate a vogue that had passed.

The beginning of that profitable Autry career was *Phantom Empire,* a marked box-office success.

The first chapter opened with Frankie and Betsy discovering a troop of strange, helmeted and caped riders on Gene Autry's Radio Ranch. (*Radio Ranch* served as the title of the featurization released in 1940.) The kids called these apparitions "The Thunder Riders." Fascinated by these figures, they made costumes like theirs for themselves and their friends, and organized a "Thunder Riders Club" whose main function is to listen to Gene Autry's radio broadcasts.

Despite the devotion they inspired, the Thunder Riders were actually menacing invaders from the subterranean civilization of Murania. It is the city of such wonders as rayguns, robots, and television sets, ruled by a Queen who had a strange passion for Autry's chunky body.

When Autry's riderless horse came back after a bout with the mysterious Muranians, the Junior Thunder Riders rode out shouting their motto: "To the rescue!"

Betsy and Frankie found the stunned Autry in a gully, and he rapidly came to himself.

AUTRY: Say, we got a broadcast at two o'clock. If we miss it, we'll lose our contract.

FRANKIE: And that means we'll lose Radio Ranch. We'll have to ride like the dickens.

CUT TO:
QUEEN TIKA *and henchman watching the above scene on a television screen in Murania.*

ARGO: There is the key to our entire situation.

QUEEN: Explain yourself, Argo.

ARGO: If we capture Gene Autry, Radio Ranch would soon become deserted. And the entrance to our underground kingdom would forever remain undiscovered.

QUEEN: We can never allow Murania to become desecrated by the presence of surface people. Our lives are serene. Our minds are superior. Our accomplishments greater. Gene Autry must be captured . . . Get the Captain of the Thunder Riders on the wireless telephone . . . (*To the captain*) Gene Autry approaches Thunder Valley. Capture him!

By a convenient literary license the Queen began referring to her royal guard at this point as the Thunder Riders—the name given them by the top-side youngsters. As the Thunder Riders approached, Gene, Frankie and Betsy attempted to escape by lowering themselves over the edge of a cliff by a rope.

However, the relentless pounding hoofs of the passing mounts rapidly wore the strands of the rope in two, sending the three Radio Ranch hands plunging toward apparent doom.

Fortunately, a convenient tree limb, and shortly, new ropes tossed down by the *Junior* Thunder Riders saved the trio.

The point of each following cliffhanger seemed to become not whether Gene Autry would live or die from the explosion or the plunge from the cliff, but whether or not he would get back to Radio Ranch in time to sing that song, to save his contract, and his ranch. He not only had to contend with the Muranians but with another menacing group of ground-level criminals who also wanted Autry to lose the ranch so they could move in and claim the secret deposits of *radium* on that destiny-touched parcel of land.

Time after time, the disaster barely averted, Autry would dust himself off and race for the broadcast. Meanwhile, Frankie and Betsy were stalling at the microphone.

"Gene is just tuning up his guitar now, folks," one of them promised. Then Gene rushed in and sang "Silver-Haired Daddy of Mine." It wasn't always "Silver-Haired Daddy of Mine," but it was often enough that it seemed as if Gene Autry *always* sang that particular one of his own compositions.

The story moved in and out of the strange city of Murania. When Autry followed the Thunder Riders down their high speed elevator that dropped them 25,000 feet to the lost city itself, he met many dangers from the Oz-like robots armed with torches of fire and the restless natives themselves. One cliffhanger had him zapped by a raygun and falling back against some weird mechanical devices that showered him with electricity.

Finally, Gene was actually *killed* by one of these perils. However, some friendly Muranians brought him back to life with their advanced superscience. (All this may explain why Autry acted like a zombie through much of this picture.)

In other scenes, Frankie and Betsy were captured while trying to help Gene. Smiley and a friend followed, and disguised themselves as robots but were discovered and made prisoners.

A revolt of the friendly Muranians gave Gene Autry and his friends their chance to escape through the weirdly undulating underground city being melted down by the "atom smashing deathray." Finally, as the group made their way out of the cave that held the entrance to the Phantom Empire, the ultimate weapon totally destroyed friend and foe alike among the Muranians. But Gene and all his friends of the surface world were safe. He was free to go on singing "Silver-Haired Daddy of Mine."

The serial offered a lot of fun and innocent charm. It influenced the pattern of later serials that followed it.

Serials about Mounties, most of them inspired by Zane Grey's newspaper strip, *King of the Royal Mounted,* tended to combine elements of superscience with those of the modern West—at least, Northwest. The first of these came in 1940 under the title above, directed by the Witney-English team, and a concerned miraculous substance with at least two amazing diverse properties. "Compound X" could cure infantile paralysis on the one hand, and on the other, it contributed to a magnetic sea mine which could wipe the oceans of the ships of any enemy to the nation controlling the compound. The inventor of the substance, a mine-owner named Merritt, was murdered by enemy agents who wanted control of Compound X for their country. Sergeant King of the Mounties (Allan Lane) was tracking down Garson (Harry Cording), henchman of the master spy, Kettler (Robert Strange), when the traitor trapped him in a swirling inferno of a forest fire. That closed Chapter One, "Man Hunt."

In the following chapters, Sergeant King did his best to aid

Linda Merritt (Lita Conway) and her brother, Mountie Corporal Tom Merritt (Robert Kellard) bring their father's murderer to justice and to see that the supply of Compound X got into the right hands.

The Sergeant's own father, Inspector King (dignified Herbert Rawlinson) was mortally wounded in one encounter with the enemy at a sawmill. With his last measure of strength, the elder King managed to stop the conveyor belt that was carrying his unconscious son toward that classic cliffhanger doom, a roaring buzz saw.

By horse, automobile, motorboat, and airplane, Sergeant King carried on the struggle, barely escaping crashes in all those vehicles, not to mention being boiled in oil and smashed flat by a massive weight in an elaborate trap. In the twelfth and final chapter, King and Tom Merritt were both taken prisoner on Kettler's submarine and locked in the torpedo room. King determined to blow up the torpedoes at the cost of his own life to destroy the enemy. However, anticipating a similar situation in Republic's later *Spy Smasher,* Merritt knocked out King and shot him to safety through a torpedo tube, then carried out King's somber plan at the cost of his life.

If Sergeant King had troubles in his first movie serial adventure, they were nothing compared with those of the sequel *King of the Mounties* (1942). In *Mounties* all three Axis powers seemed to take a personal disliking to King. Perhaps it was due to his constant interference with their plans to destroy the United States.

The Japanese superscientists had invented "bat plane" which soared over American targets at incredible speed and blasted them from the air. Eventually King entered the hideout of the enemy, an active volcano into which the incredible flying craft descended. During a rousing fight within the volcano, King and his opponents accidentally knocked some explosives into the steaming lava. Hurrying into the "bat plane," King maneuvered the ship out of the volcano only seconds before it belched apart in a tremendous eruption.

Republic also made *Dangers of the Canadian Mounties* (1948) starring Jim Bannon and *Canadian Mounties vs Atomic Invaders* (1953) with Bill Henry. These did not *admit* the Zane Grey inspiration but contained many of the same elements (and stock footage). *Dangers* introduced the weird concept of liquid diamonds in a plot centering around the treasure of Genghis Khan which had been mysteriously found in Canada. There was little if any science fiction in *Atomic Invaders* despite the title. A foreign power (presumably Russia) planned to bombard the United States with superpowerful missiles for twelve chapters. When the missiles finally arrived in the last installment "Cavern of Revenge" they proved to be no more than a few prop air torpedoes left over from *King of the Rocket Men*.

These all were Republic serials about modern Mounties. It remained, as usual, for Columbia to make the most absurd serial in this category, as they managed to do in every category. *Perils of the Wilderness* (1956) was the second-to-last motion picture serial ever made (followed only by *Blazing the Overland Trail,* the same year, bearing some of the same distinguishing marks and having one of the same stars as *Perils,* Dennis Moore). Dennis Moore played Laramie, a supposed outlaw but obvious undercover agent, and Richard Emory was Sergeant Gray of the Mounted. Both men were after Bart Randall, self-styled "Gun Emperor of the Northwest" (the perfect saloon-gambler villain of countless Westerns, Kenneth MacDonald). The "Emperor" was stirring up the Indians to raid wagon trains to aid as a diversion from Randall's own smuggling activities.

So far, so good. The plot was familiar but acceptable.

The incredulity began when we found out that Randall was smuggling out uranium in his hydroplane, which he was frightening the ignorant Indians into believing was some kind of magic bird (not the regular Air-Canada evening flight).

Director Spencer Bennet did what he could with what was handed him by producer Sam Katzman and scriptwriter George Plympton. The cliffhangers had the undercover agent (a U. S. Deputy Marshal) and the Mountie dropping on a collapsing bridge into a canyon, going over cliffs, into mine pits, caught in fires and explosions. In Chapter Thirteen, Laramie was saved from a Medicine Man's sacrifice by the brave Little Bear (Rick Vallin). In Chapter Fourteen an R.C.M.P. plane engaged two outlaw planes in a snarling dogfight. Following victory in the air, a raging six-gun battle in Chapter Fifteen brought law and order to the Canadian Northwest of 1956. *Nineteen fifty-six?*

Perils of the Wilderness really may have been no more ridiculous than *Phantom Empire,* but when the Gene Autry serial was made, film-makers were about equally as innocent as their audience. By the mid-'50s, they knew better and their flippant insincerity showed.

In the *mid-'30s,* producers and fans alike could accept the concept of a mysterious aircraft frightening an Indian tribe as quite believable. This was the opening gambit of the Tom Mix serial, *The Miracle Rider,* the most historically important of all the zap-gun Western serials.

THE MIRACLE RIDER

Tom Mix's last film and only talking serial, *The Miracle Rider,* has probably been referred to in more books on the movies than any other serial; simply because it marked the last screen appearance of its landmark star. Most of the descriptions and comments on this production are highly inaccurate.

The typical film historian presents this production as being a disaster, a sad farewell to the screen for a great star. Other reports have it Mix himself worked only in the tight close-ups, and all his long-shots and even most of the medium shots were doubled for him; that Mix was bored with the whole thing and delivered all his dialogue unintelligibly. Finally, it is stated that the film was shoddy, with a confusing, repetitious script. Allowing for divergences of personal opinion, most of these statements can be demonstrated to be untrue.

Within the limitations of a serial budget (but one obviously far higher than most), *The Miracle Rider* was a solidly constructed Western action film, above the average for the B feature films of the era, much less a serial. The production is as interesting and exciting as any of the Universal talking feature films Tom Mix made in 1933, such as the first *Destry Rides Again,* despite its lower cost. The sound track (recorded by Mascot by the Walt Disney organization) is better than that of many *features* of 1935. Mix's dialogue is intelligible and spoken by him with complete conviction. His voice is admittedly not the voice of an actor—it is nasal and strained, due in part to such injuries as a one-time broken nose and having been shot through the throat, in one of his many real-life adventures. The handicap is overcome by his sincerity.

While perhaps not at the peak of his form as demonstrated in such silent features as *Just Tony,* Tom Mix displayed his unequaled skill at riding in *The Miracle Rider,* and clearly performed himself such stunts as horse falls, flying mounts, climbing and swinging from ropes, and rough and tumble fighting. In some scenes, stuntman Cliff Lyons did flying mounts, horse falls, and parts of fight scenes, but he did nothing Tom Mix himself did not do in other parts of the picture. The stunt expert, who has gone on to second unit directing, helped conserve the time and energy of an expensive star. At this time, Mix was perhaps not the fifty-five he admitted to in official studio releases, but as much as sixty-four years of age according to several of his surviving friends. Certainly he appeared no more than of middle-age, and he would continue actively performing in his own circus for another five years, although this was to be his last film.

The present writers lack the psychic insight of some reviewers to know whether Tom Mix was bored with the serial or not, but certainly, what appears on the screen in private showings is a quiet professionalism. Tom Mix had ridden these familiar trails many times before, but nobody knew how to ride them better.

The storyline was complex, and developed far more inventively than most of the serials that followed it. *The Miracle Rider* contained the large cast of characters with interlocking conflicts that carried over from the silent serials of Pearl White and Houdini. But the fantastic science-fiction inventions and most of the cliffhangers belonged to the sound era.

The theme of Texas Rangers and a fantastic airship would be repeated when Mascot evolved to Republic, in *King of the Texas Rangers* from its pioneer appearance in *The Miracle Rider*. Republic would use another great silent Western star in *The Painted Stallion*—this time, Hoot Gibson, making only token appearances in each episode as a wagon train master who sent Crash Corrigan to do all the dangerous work. The "modern West" theme would be repeated in *Zorro Rides Again*.

Certainly Tom Mix's nemesis in *The Miracle Rider*, Charles Middleton, would cause much further havoc for Republic heroes in *Dick Tracy Returns, Daredevils of the Red Circle,* and *Perils of Nyoka* (although remaining most famous as Emperor Ming in Universal's three Flash Gordon serials).

Middleton played the part of Zaroff, owner of a ranch and oil company, who wanted to drive the Ravenhead Indians from their reservation so that he would be free to mine a rare element he had discovered, X-94, which could be refined into a superexplosive, one the nations of the world would have to come to Zaroff for. "Kings and Queens will grovel at my feet," the saturnian-faced Zaroff ranted. "I'll be the most powerful man on Earth!" (He said that in virtually every chapter).

Pitted against Zaroff was Tom Morgan, Chief of the Texas Rangers. The prologue of Chapter One, "The Vanishing Indian" (a forty-five-minute episode, one of the longest in the sound era) showed how such great American heroes as Daniel Boone, Davy Crockett, and Buffalo Bill had defended the Indians from unscrupulous whites, building up to the appearance of "Tom Morgan" who continued that role in the present era. This was before it became traditional for cowboy stars to use their own names, but transparently, Tom Morgan really was Tom Mix, who was accepted as being himself as near a legendary American hero as Buffalo Bill.

Publicity agents had made a field day of Tom Mix's exploits as a soldier of fortune during the Spanish-American War, the Boer Rebellion (he switched to the Boer side after first supporting the British), and Boxer Rebellion, and his later career as a sheriff in Oklahoma, a U. S. Marshal and a real-life Texas Ranger. Despite some embroidery, these stories *are* basically true, supported by documents, photographs, and still living eyewitnesses. Occasionally, some disgruntled senior citizen will come forth yet today and present a case that he knew Tom Mix when he was actually a whiskey salesman from Omaha and he couldn't even ride a Shetland pony. However, these exposés are simply not true. Tom Mix was the genuine article. As stuntman Tom Steele, a movie hero himself of some stature, has said: "Tom Mix was the only celebrity I ever met who seemed as great in person as he did on the screen."

In 1935, despite some years of relative inactivity, Tom Mix remained one of the *four* greatest stars in the history of motion pictures, the others being Charlie Chaplin, Mary Pickford, and Douglas Fairbanks, Sr. On the strength of popularity alone, on how much money earned, Tom Mix was probably *first*. (There was only greater *critical* acclaim for stern-faced William S. Hart who dealt in what some critics still equate with realism, but is rather an overripe sentimentality.) He was certainly the biggest star ever to headline a *serial* up to that time, or since. (In real life he needed quick money to support his floundering circus. He got it: $40,000 for four weeks' work.) His serial nemesis, Charles Middleton, was one of the great prototypical villains of the screen, even though he never was featured in a major production. It was to be a classic confrontation.

Middleton's Zaroff was a character who would go to any lengths to achieve his goal of gaining control over the deposits of fabulous X-94. In order to frighten the Indians off their reservation, he sent a radio-controlled "rocket-glider," the Fire-Bird, over the land to represent one of their angry gods. A mysterious heat-ray from Zaroff's land base set the redskins' tents and wagons on fire from miles away. Zaroff prowled through his laboratory with its bubbling test tubes and flashing television screens, gloating.

Meanwhile, some money destined for the needy Indians was stolen by what apparently was a separate band of crooks. Tom Morgan went after the thieves. A handful of cartridges thrown in a campfire routed the outlaws, sending them to their horses. The saddles of the horses had been tied to a tree by a series of ropes, and half a dozen men went flying through the air. When they landed, Tom had them covered.

A picturesque Indian ceremony followed in which Tom was made an honorary chief with a lavish war bonnet placed on his head. "This is last of many times you help Ravenhead nation. You are he who is spoken of in our old stories. *You are Ho-Tan —THE MIRACLE RIDER!*" The Indians chanted their approval.

Like so many scenes in his films, this paralleled an event in the true life of Tom Mix. The pressbook for the serial quoted Mix on the subject. "The story of *Miracle Rider* casts me as a Texas Ranger who helps the Indians . . . As a matter of fact, I was a Texas Ranger for years . . . and often-times I was able to do little favors for my Indian friends . . . In 1905 . . . I was a ranch foreman in Oklahoma, then known as Osage Indian Territory . . . A big 'smoke council' was called by the Cherokees, Poncas, Otos, Delawares, Kaws and Osages . . . After passing the pipe they explained how they need a white brother to arrange fair distribution of quarantines on their cattle lands . . . I'm part Cherokee on my mother's side and I've tried never to overlook doing a good turn to the Indians . . . figure they got a pretty raw deal . . . So I went to Washington for them." In real life, Tom Mix's Indian name was Chief Wah-tig-nea—meaning "Comes Home Victorious."

After the Indian ceremony in the serial, Zaroff, the rancher and oilman approached Texas Ranger Tom Morgan. "These Indians know a good man when they see him," said Zaroff with a faint sneer. The old chief nodded. "We know all kind of men when we see them."

Certainly Zaroff was a bad man. When the Indians would not yield to the threat of the mysterious Fire-Bird, the oilman arranged to have the Chief murdered by an arrow shot through an open window by a crook, Chapman, disguised as an Indian. The murderer chose a not-unincriminating means of escape—a Zaroff Company oil truck. Tom followed on Tony (or rather Tony Jr. since the original Tony had been retired). He made a transfer to the speeding truck and began a fight with the renegade Indian and the truck driver. More of Zaroff's men on horseback spotted the careening truck, and after their own men had jumped, fired an explosive rifle shell of the superpowerful X-94 into the truck, blowing the truck and everything in it to atoms!

Naturally, Chapter Two, "The Firebird Strikes," revealed that Tom had leaped to safety a scant second before the explosion. Tom returned to the reservation to comfort the murdered chief's daughter, Ruth (definitely a friendly Indian, played with assurance by pretty Joan Gale). Then he questioned both Zaroff and storekeeper Emil Janss (Edward Hearn), both of whom had aroused his suspicions. At the Janss store he caught sight of the murderer, Chapman, in his Indian disguise. Immediately Tom gave chase.

EXT. WESTERN COUNTRYSIDE—DAY
> TOM *pursues* CHAPMAN—*who looks back suddenly and sees* TOM *is riding hard after him. Abruptly then* CHAPMAN *changes his course and rides up a steep embankment.*

FOLLOWING TOM MORGAN

> *He sees* CHAPMAN *changing direction.* TOM *changes his own course and now takes a shortcut.*

EXT. ANOTHER WESTERN COUNTRYSIDE—DAY
> CHAPMAN *rides by. A moment later* TOM *appears, coming from a new direction. He chases* CHAPMAN *again, now considerably closer to him. As he rides he gets out his lariat. He throws out the rope, catches* CHAPMAN *and brings him down to the ground.*

MED. SHOT—TOM MORGAN AND CHAPMAN
> TOM *jumps from* TONY's *saddle and runs to* CHAPMAN. *He grabs the man roughly.*

TOM: Who do you take your orders from? Better tell me that than rot in jail.

CHAPMAN: The boss would surely kill me if I squealed.

TOM: Headed for your hideaway, were you? CHAPMAN *whines.* TOM *gets an idea. He makes* CHAPMAN *mount* TONY *and ties the man's hands securely. Then* TOM *drapes himself over the pommel of the saddle.*

TOM: Now go on. And one false move will be your last!
> TOM *and* CHAPMAN *on* TONY *ride off in the hideout direction.*

SHOTS TO COVER
> TOM *and* CHAPMAN *riding.*

EXT. HIDEOUT CAVE—DAY
> VINING, HATTON *and* SEWELL. *They see* CHAPMAN *riding up with* TOM *an apparent prisoner.*

VINING: Good work, Chapman!
TOM and CHAPMAN ride into the cave. The others follow.

INT. HIDEOUT CAVE—DAY

They halt. Nearby is the glider, "The Fire-Bird," on the launching catapult. VINING, HATTON and SEWELL begin to take charge of their prisoner. But TOM suddenly surprises them by jumping down from the saddle and covering them with his guns.

TOM: Reach for the sky, hombres!
The outlaws put up their hands. TOM disarms them and then sees the glider there.

TOM *(scornfully)*: So that's the Fire-Bird!
CHAPMAN takes advantage of TOM's momentary distraction. Still mounted, he comes charging down on TOM. The others take opportunities and pile onto TOM. A furious melee begins.

SHOTS TO COVER

TOM fights the outlaws. During the battle TOM gets knocked into the cockpit of the glider. But before he falls unconscious he strikes HATTON who reels backwards off balance. HATTON falls onto the catapult lever.

FULL SHOT—THE GLIDER

The flying machine starts up with a great hissing roar. Then with TOM unconscious in the cockpit the glider zooms forward off the catapult and streaks out of the cave.

EXT. CAVE ENTRANCE—DAY

The glider zooms out and into the sky.

INT. CAVE—DAY

The outlaws recover. They see the glider streaking away.

HATTON: Notify Zaroff!
VINING runs to the telephone and makes his connections.

INT. ZAROFF OFFICE—DAY

ZAROFF answers the call and listens for a beat.

ZAROFF: What! Morgan on the glider! *A fiendish smile lights his face. He breaks connection and moves to a table where sit the wireless controls to the glider.*

ZAROFF: Morgan's on his last ride!
He starts operating the controls, evil joy spreading on his face.

EXT. WESTERN SKY—DAY
The glider zooms by—then starts descending rapidly to the ground. Inside, TOM revives and sees where he is.

EXT. WESTERN COUNTRY—DAY
The glider plunges rapidly down from the skies and crashes into a hillside.

Fortunately, with no more a strain to credulity than most serial cliffhangers, but certainly with no less a one, Tom happened to find a parachute in the strange flying missile and bailed out before the Fire-Bird crashed into the Texas plains below.

It was the end of the Fire-Bird, by only Chapter Three. The wrecked remains were shuffled back and forth by the outlaws and the Texas Rangers since they had some value as evidence to prove to the Indians that the Fire-Bird was not supernatural, but even the tattered fuselage was completely destroyed in a flaming wagon wreck that was the cliffhanger for Chapter Four, "A Race with Death."

With the destruction of the Fire-Bird, most of the science-fiction elements went out of the serial. The only one that really remained was that X-94 was presented as being a superpowerful explosive (and motor fuel) and the fact was occasionally demonstrated using it in a manner designed to send Tom Morgan to his doom. A bottle of the deadly stuff was hurled at him at the end of Chapter Eight, "Guerrilla Warfare," only to be shot in mid-air by Tom's infallible aim in Chapter Nine, "The Silver Band." This proved the weakest chapter of the serial, since Tom Mix spent all of it flat on his back, recovering from the temporary blindness caused by the explosion.

The end of the science-fictional elements after the third episode of *The Miracle Rider* may well have been planned by the producers to save money on the cost of special effects. Seemingly, however, the same shots of the Fire-Bird in flight could have been repeated endlessly (certainly such stock footage gimmicks were being constantly repeated in other serials). The object seemed to be to "hook" the movie audience on the serial with the long, forty-five minute opening chapter, replete with Tom Mix stunts and fantastic gadgetry, and even, most unusual with Mascot, *background music*. But only for the *first* episode. Even before the Fire-Bird went, so did any musical swipes from Stravinsky's *Firebird Suite* or some other classic.

While *The Miracle Rider* can be compared to Mascot's earlier *Phantom Empire,* that first Gene Autry starring vehicle certainly remained far more fantastic throughout than Tom Mix's last picture. The fantasy element was the main body of the Autry picture, but superscience only added a few touches to the Mix serial.

After the fateful crash of the Fire-Bird, *The Miracle Rider* became basically the familiar "modern Western" with automobiles and radio co-existing with cowboys on horseback. One great fun scene had Tom chasing a motorcycle on Tony (certainly the only horse in the world who could keep up with a motorcycle). On the motorcycle were those two eternal Western heavies, Charlie King and Tom London. London, even *then* advanced in years (though still acting in the 1960s) clearly leaped from the speeding motorcycle without benefit of stuntman or trick photography. (If he had been killed, he would not have been the first actor to die while filming a Mascot serial at breakneck, money-conserving speed.)

Although on more familiar Western ground, *The Miracle Rider* did not go around in endless circles in the fashion of many serials before and since. One plotline concerned the storekeeper, Janss, who was falsely made to look guilty by Zaroff, but who was hardly innocent in any case. He was not in on the crooked goings-on, but he *wanted* to be. Finally, he became partners with Zaroff. Another sub-plot concerned the schemes of Janss's sneaky clerk, Stelter (played by the movies' most perfect stool-pigeon, Ernie Adams). These plans culminated in a shoot-out with Zaroff in his laboratory from which only one man could emerge alive—Zaroff, of course, since he was the *main* villain, and the serial was not yet over.

Longboat (Bob Kortman), a traitorous Indian who hoped Zaroff would somehow help him become chief also had eyes for the dead chief's daughter, Ruth. But she, of course, worshiped Tom Morgan, the legendary Miracle Rider of her people. (Although in fine shape for a man his age, Tom Mix nevertheless did look old enough to be the girl's father.) Inevitably, Longboat met the fate of all traitors.

So did Emil Janss.

One of Zaroff's own henchmen tried to turn Janss into the Rangers for the reward that had been placed on his head when he had been found out. Another crook, loyal to Zaroff, who still had use for Janss, sported the graying storekeeper away in an empty oil truck, inside the metal tank. As Tom pursued the truck, it went off the road and Janss was killed in the accident.

The minor crooks had been disposed of. There remained only the master villain, Zaroff. While searching for evidence at Zaroff's ranch, Tom was confronted by the villainous oilman and his henchman with leveled guns. We traveled down the long line of leveled weapons, their barrels gaping black wells. Zaroff intoned, "You're dead, Morgan."

It wasn't much of a cliffhanger, since it seemed to go back to the era of the *silent* movie serial, or to suggest the ending of a *radio* serial chapter, such as the then current *Tom Mix and his Ralston Straight Shooters,* based on the career of Tom Mix, but wherein he was always impersonated by such radio actors as Russell Thorson and Curley Bradley.

Chapter Fifteen, "Justice Rides the Plains," opened with Tom still facing Zaroff and his gang. In something of a *tour de force,* Tom went through first one then another of the clichés heroes used to disarm villains. He asked for a final smoke before he died, and started building a cigaret from the makings. Zaroff dashed the tobacco aside impatiently. "Trying to blow tobacco in our eyes," sneered Zaroff. "Old stuff!" Finally, a disturbance caused by Tom's horse, Tony, let the Ranger turn the tables on Zaroff. No sooner than he had grabbed a gun than Zaroff knocked it from his hand, not by turning the tables, but by spinning a swivel chair about to knock the six-shooter from Tom's hand.

Discretion being the better part of valor, Tom quit the battlefield and dashed outside to receive help from a group of the Rangers be captained, including Burnette (played by Wally Wales, also known as Hal Taliaferro, one of the "six Ranger suspects" suspected of being *The Lone Ranger* in that later serial).

Tear gas soon took the fight out of all the crooks left inside. But Zaroff and his chief aide, Carlton, were no longer inside. They were escaping with the secret of the superexplosive X-94, and a way to synthesize it "from common sand."

Tom mounted Tony and cut across country to head off the speeding touring car. The Ranger dismounted, and spread oil on the road, sending the car to a sliding, screeching halt. "How about a lift to Ranger headquarters, boys?" drawled Tom in a way that always produced applause from the audience.

But Zaroff was the craftiest of villains, a man who gloated over being "the most evil man on Earth." He sent the hapless Carlton flying against Tom, and took off again, his wheels fighting for traction, finding it, and speeding away.

Again Tom pursued Zaroff. He leaped from the saddle into the back seat of the car. He struggled briefly with Zaroff, but soon saw that the car was hopelessly out of control, perhaps from the oil on the tires. "Jump!" he warned the renegade oilman and leaped out himself. It was too late for Zaroff. The car went over an embankment and the supply of X-94 it was carrying exploded with devastating results.

Later, at the Ravenhead Reservation, Tom read a letter praising him for "doing more for the Indian than any other man in history" and appointing him to represent the Ravenheads in Washington. The Ravenheads would be wealthy from the mining of X-94 on their lands. The chief's daughter, Ruth, did not seem appropriately happy over these events. Not until Tom invited her to go along with him to Washington as his secretary. "Do you mean it?" Ruth gasped. Tom removed his glove. "Here's your contract."

R. Reeves Eason used his long experience in films from the silent days, in collaboration with Armand Schaefer, to direct a well-made movie serial. The script by John Rathmell from the original story by Barney Sarecky, Wellyn Totman, and Gerald Geraghty was developed nicely. The production, of course, lacked the budget of many of Tom Mix's lavish Westerns for Fox in the 1920s. It was not *possible* for the chapterplay to contain the carefully choreographed fist fights so loved by many serial fans, since this style of film fighting did not come into existence until the very late thirties. For what it was—a Western movie serial of 1935—*The Miracle Rider* was great.

It was not the most fitting screen farewell for a great star, but it was nothing for Tom Mix to be ashamed of. Even the minor efforts of significant artists are of interest.

It might be noted, as an example of a vanished phase of the Western movie, that in all the long, *action-packed* serial, Tom Mix was never represented to take a single human life.

4

*The Boys   "Sir, I'd Advise You
to Duck That Spear!"*

Frank Merriwell was the champion of any and all sports he engaged in at his college. When off the playing field, this Big Man on the Campus was certainly capable of collaring a few puny crooks who might be rifling the Dean's office for the receipts from the charity raffle. He had his enemies—jealous weaklings —and his loyal friends, and his adoring girl friend.

Long before the appearance of 1936 Universal movie serial about him, Frank Merriwell appeared in an 1890s series of weekly magazines—"dime novels"—written by Gilbert Patten under the pen name of Burt L. Standish. The Saturday morning radio series based on Merriwell's exploits carried him in the late 1940s, making him a boy hero for fully a half century.

If Merriwell might seem passé in today's era of allegedly politically and sexually liberated youth, one might observe that the largest-selling comic magazine of 1970 was *Archie,* a somewhat humorous, but still adventurous, version of Merriwell, with a little bit of radio's Henry Aldrich (and the tiniest trace element of Tom Sawyer). Only a few years ago, there was an adventure comic magazine about Merriwell himself.

Merriwell was the rather frank model for radio's Jack Armstrong, who followed his inspiration to the serial screen in 1947. Both had names that were puns, or at least plays on words. Merriwell was always straightforward—*frank*—as well as one who always kept his sense of humor in adversity—*merry*—

and always, of course, in tip-top physical condition—*well*. Jack Armstrong had an arm that was strong—as suggested by a box of Arm & Hammer baking soda seen by his creator, Robert Hardy Andrews—and it has been suggested that he must of had plenty of "jack" to finance his many trips around the globe.

The *Adventures of Frank Merriwell* movie serial differed somewhat from the original novels. Most prominently, it was set in the period of the year it was made, 1936. Even the radio series retained the gaslit, cobblestone streets of the 1890s.

The tone of the original novels was set early in *Frank Merriwell's False Friend,* No. 70 in the series.

> Frank Merriwell . . . had been depended on as the mainstay in the pitching department of the team.
>
> Of course, Bart Hodge would fill his old position behind the bat, and there were one or two promising men who might serve as substitutes in case any accident happened to him . . .
>
> The anxiety and restlessness caused by Frank's unaccountable failure to return spread to the professors, who began to inquire about him day after day.
>
> Merriwell's enemies had been keeping pretty quiet, for they realized that it would not be best to say too much at first, as he was the pride of the college, and slurs against him would not be tolerated.

The photoplay opened with a somewhat similar situation—a baseball game in which the services of Frank Merriwell were urgently needed.

In Chapter One, "College Hero," Merriwell (husky Don Briggs) arrived as his school was being beat 3 to 0. Immediately, the coach sent Frank in to pinch hit for his rival, House Peters (House Peters, Jr.—one of several cast members bearing the suffix "Junior" who used their own names in the film—or at least their fathers' names since the *characters* were not identified with the suffix). Being deprived of his own chance at glory by Frank could have hardly endeared Frank to

Peters—one could even see his side of it. (In later years, both Briggs and Peters became more active in dramatic radio than films. Briggs was perhaps best known on radio as *The Sheriff of Death Valley*.)

With two out and the bases loaded in the ninth, Frank Merriwell hit a home run, winning for his team 4 to 3. Merriwell's college was called in the serial by the fictional title of Fardale, instead of Yale as in the famous novels, perhaps to keep from alienating any Harvard men attending the Saturday afternoon matinee.

Watching Frank's triumph were his girl friend, Elsie Belwood (striking Jean Rogers) and Bruce Browning (John King, one sidekick actually handsomer than the hero). Browning had been a supporting character in the books, but in the serial he took the place of Frank's best friend, Bart Hodge.

Shortly after the game, Merriwell—or "Merry" as he was sometimes called for short—received a telegram from his mother to come immediately. Frank's father had disappeared, and shortly before his disappearance, a "mysterious stranger" was seen rifling the contents of the elder Merriwell's desk. (This "mysterious stranger" became one of the few "mystery men" serial villains to remain unnamed by some colorful title.)

Elsie and Bruce went to the station to see Frank off on the train. The engineer proved a friend of cheery Frank, and the two boys were allowed to climb into the cab of the engine. Some favor! At that moment, a second huge engine came down the tracks, running wild, and crashed into the locomotive bearing Frank and his friends with devastating results!

The escape revealed in Chapter Two, "The Death Plunge," was the familiar shorter plunge for life out of the engine cab a bare instant before the collision. Finally reaching home, Frank was told by his mother of the sinister events. She gave him a ring of mysterious origin which she felt was what was sought by the "mysterious stranger." Hoping that the prowler might return to renew his search for the ring, Frank decided to spend the night in the plundered room along with a faithful old Negro servant, Jeff. Sure enough, the prowler returned and Frank grabbed him, beginning a terrific struggle in the darkened room. Attempting to help Frank, old Jeff only succeeded in knocking out Frank by mistake. (These Uncle Toms were damned clumsy, also deemed too unimportant to be included in the cast credits.)

However, Frank was shortly recovered sufficiently to return to Fardale and help win the track meet for his class, the sophomores against the team of the juniors. Afterward a henchman of the "mysterious stranger" named Judd (Bert Young) managed to steal the vital ring from Frank. Frank and his sidekick, Bruce, followed Judd's car in their own. At breakneck speed, Bruce made a spectacular transfer from one automobile to the other in an attempt to capture Judd (which ultimately proved successful). Unfortunately for Frank, he lost control of his own car and it hurtled off a dock into the chilly depths of the sea.

In Chapter Three, "Death at the Cross Roads," Frank managed to jump clear of the car just in time, once again.

By the third chapter, the pattern of the serial was clearly established. The interesting and varied plot allowed Frank Merriwell to demonstrate his skill in such other sports as boat-rowing and—of course—football. The story took Frank, Bruce, and Elsie to sea where Frank narrowly survived the cliffhangers of an exploding cargo of powder kegs, and in a later episode, an encounter with an octopus while in a diving suit beneath the water (what soft-living, long-haired, trouble-making student of today could cope with an octopus!)

The setting of the serial became the ship's destination, the lumber camp at Point Dixie (although there would be side trips for those vital games at Fardale). As the gang of the "mysterious stranger" persisted in trying to seize the ring and the treasure to which it represented a key, Frank Merriwell found himself hurled into the raging rapids of a river, narrowly missing being crushed beneath an avalanche of tumbling logs; attacked by a wildcat in one episode and by a circus lion in another; and in the next to last episode, caught in a situation similar to that in the Chapter Two cliffhanger: his car plunging off a bridge into raging waters.

Naturally, "Merry" survived all these dangers, rescued his father from the cave where he was being held by a tribe of Indians (in 1936); found the treasure chest of gold; exposed the "mysterious stranger" as a distant relative named Dagget (Bentley Hewlett); and of course managed to win the big football game for Fardale.

This serial has a reputation for being dull among serial devotees. Insufficient action.

However, with the production being unavailable for viewing, the present writer must judge from the pressbook and publicity stills and comment that it appears a well-made chapterplay with a lot of fun and variety. The screenplay by George Plympton, Maurice Geraghty, Ella O'Neill, and Basil Dickey was directed by Cliff Smith.

If nothing else, the serial offered employment to a lot of relatives: Wallace Reid, Jr., Bryant Washburn, Jr., Carlyle Blackwell, Jr., Edward Arnold, Jr., Herschel Mayall, Jr., and in an important role as Elsie's friend, Carla Rogers—Carla Laemmle, obviously a relative of studio head Carl Laemmle. Reportedly she was spectacularly ill-equipped for the acting profession.

"WAVE THE FLAG FOR HUDSON HIGH, BOYS!"

Jack Armstrong was radio's answer to the Frank Merriwell dime novels. The program was perhaps the top afternoon radio serial for children all through the 1930s and '40s. During that time, no motion picture was made of the property, probably because the owner, General Mills, makers of Wheaties, wanted too much money from the studios. Curiously, Jack Armstrong never made it to the screen until the radio series was faltering and on the way out.

From his first appearance on the air in 1933, Jack Armstrong had been a high school boy attending Hudson High with his friends, Billy and Betty Fairfield. The appearance of the Fairfields' relative, Uncle Jim, a flier and explorer, marked the departure of the three young people for distant lands and tropic climes—jungles, deserts, the high seas.

By 1947, this format had paled and Jack had become an agent of a sort of fictionalized FBI—the SBI (Scientific Bureau of Investigation). Uncle Jim had disappeared from the radio series and had been replaced as a father figure by a version of J. Edgar Hoover called Vic Hardy. Eventually the program would become entitled *Armstrong of the S.B.I.*

The 1947 movie serial, *Jack Armstrong, the All-American Boy,* reflected few of the innovations current in the radio series. As produced by Sam Katzman and directed by Wallace Fox, the screenplay by Arthur Hoerl, Lewis Clay, Royal Cole, and Leslie Swabacker, reverted to a large degree to the Armstrong radio format of the '30s, such as presented by the script of Episode No. 893 from the middle-'30s.

ANNOUNCER: The Silver Albatross is on her way up the Congo River. Uncle Jim is at the controls, with Betty beside him. Three thousand feet below, between giant forests, there roars the unnavigable gateway into Darkest Africa—the plunging cataracts known as Stanley Falls . . . Billy is seated beside Jack . . .

BETTY: What are those specks . . . look . . . four, five of them, between that island and the riverbank?

BILLY: Are they logs . . . or crocodiles . . . or what are they?

UNCLE JIM: Those are native canoes.

JACK: Gosh, those native boatmen must be pretty skillful!

In the movie serial's first chapter, "Mystery of the Cosmic Ray," Uncle Jim (distinguished Pierre Watkin, an ideal choice) was still interested in airplanes but had moved ahead to the world of 1947 and was heading an aviation company interested in developing atomic powered motors. His chief scientist was Vic Hardy (Hugh Prosser is a slightly different version of the radio character). Uncle Jim revealed his plans for the atomic motors to his nephew (bumpish Joe Brown) Billy, his niece, Betty (Rosemary La Planche) and their friend and college classmate, Jack Armstrong (played by John Hart, whose color and handsomeness was fine for the role).[1]

Meanwhile, an important customer of the Fairfield Aviation Company, Gregory Pierce (sleek villain John Merton) learned of another company secret. Vic Hardy had discovered that experiments with cosmic radiation were being conducted at some location outside the United States. Promptly, Pierce had his henchmen kidnap Hardy to find out all he knew. The scientist was to be taken to a mysterious location known as Point X.

Jack Armstrong, Billy, and Uncle Jim traced the gang of kidnappers to a waterfront warehouse as the first chapter neared its climax, and engaged them in a desperate hand-to-hand fight. During the melee, a stray pistol shot set one of a pile of gasoline drums afire. The gang members managed to spirit Hardy away, leaving our heroes trapped in an inferno that would shortly become a holocaust as the drums burst with one final explosion!

In Chapter Two, "The Far World," the three men were trying to force open the outer door as the explosion occurred. The door was blown open, and the heroic threesome fell out on top

[1] John Hart played the Lone Ranger on television for one season. Curiously, one of the radio actors who played Jack Armstrong, Michael Rye, also later did the voice of the Lone Ranger for TV animated cartoons. It all proves, perhaps, that the Lone Ranger is really only Jack Armstrong grown up.

of it. (The present writer recalls seeing this escape as a boy and being especially pleased with it. Being an ultra-purest, he did not even approve of events being recapped with the escape inserted before the final moment of the cliffhanger. The solution should only be shown *after* the cliffhanger climax, he felt, even though it is generally regarded as "cheating" only if events that never happened are shown in the climax, i.e., the explosion does not actually occur; the shot is never fired, etc.)

Back at the laboratory, Jack managed to trace the source of the mysterious cosmic rays Hardy had been investigating by a system of triangulation. Thinking it probable that Hardy would be taken to this location, Jack and the three Fairfields took off for the spot in Uncle Jim's new jet-propelled airplane (replacing the old Silver Albatross amphibian of early radio days).

As for Hardy, he had arrived at the strange Point X, and met Professor Zorn (Wheeler Oakman), an individual clearly up to no good. Then Hardy heard the voice of the unseen "Ruler." They were developing a cosmic ray weapon with which to dominate the entire world. Will Hardy co-operate? Or will he die? Uncharacteristically, Hardy chickened out and agreed to work on the project. (However, we never doubted him. Vic Hardy was only stalling for time.)

Apparently, his rescue was imminent. The jet plane bearing Jack Armstrong and his friends was drawing near. Alerted to this fact, Zorn turned on a complicated electronic gadget that froze the controls of the plane. The jet went crashing into a mountainside with disastrous results.

Chapter Three, "Island of Deception," revealed a cheat. Seen from another angle, the plane only made a forced belly landing after Jack managed to regain the use of the controls. ("Fake! Fake!" screamed the audience.)

The group finally managed to reach the island's trading post, and there met the brooding Jason Grood (Charles Middleton), the man behind the voice of the unseen "Ruler." When a native was killed by a Grood henchman, Blair (the "infamous" Jack Ingram), the Fairfield party was held responsible by the island's ruler, Princess Alura (Clair James), really only a puppet of Grood's.

There was only one thing a group of natives could do in a situation like this in a serial. They took the four foreigners to the Temple of Xalta, to be thrown into the Pit of Everlasting Fire.

Uncle Jim managed to escape (after all, he had been going through things like this on the radio since 1933), taking Billy along with him. Jack and Betty were not so fortunate. (Their luck had been like that since 1933, too.) The two slightly post-teen-agers were tossed into the pit of bubbling fire.

Naturally, a helping hand from a friendly native, Umala (Russ Vincent), saved Jack and Betty in Chapter Four, "Into the Chasm." Umala had realized that Grood and his bunch meant no good for his people. (His trust in Jack Armstrong was well-placed, but would be surprising from a minority representative in today's less trusting world.)

The group of Americans was reunited and Umala directed them across a rickety suspension bridge to the relative safety of his village. There is only one thing a rope suspension bridge is good for (as the present writer always thinks as he crosses one to a friend's mountain home)—being cut down by the villains as one gets halfway across!

It is Chapter Five, "The Space Ship," that offered a really significant plot development. Not, of course, in the method of escape from the hazard. Jack and his band land on a rocky ledge "almost miraculously" as even the pressbook admitted.

The significant development was Grood's demonstration of his "aeroglobe," which was in reality an artificial satellite put into orbit outside the Earth's atmosphere. The man-made satellite was old in science-fiction novels, but this 1947 serial offered one of the earliest screen demonstrations of the concept.

After the extra-atmospheric test of the craft, the aeroglobe began settling back toward its launching pad concealed in the apparently volcanic Fire Pit. The luck of Jack Armstrong was infallible. He and the Fairfields had chosen this very moment to investigate the inside of the Fire Pit, just as one hundred seventy tons of space ship started to sink down on top of them.

However, the sixth episode, "Tunnels of Treachery," revealed that the Americans saved themselves by flattening their bodies against the sides of the pit and letting the aeroglobe slide past them. No rocket-blast burns? Apparently not.

The adventurers were on the island of Jason Grood for the rest of the serial, alternating between the menaces of a jungle island, and those of the superscience of the pioneering (but evil) astronauts. The jungle menaces included a quicksand pit, a native spear attack, and a plunge from a cliff. The superscience cliffhangers included poison gas, the deathrays of the Cosmic Beam Annihilator in one episode and of the Tanilic Light in another.

Finally, by the next-to-last episode, "Journey into Space," the aeroglobe had been equipped with a giant Cosmic Beam Annihilator. Grood planned to take the craft up and use the Beam to wipe out an entire city, only a sample of what the planet had in store if they did not accede to his plans.

Vic Hardy was to go along on the flight, and even though he appeared to be working hand in glove with the aeroglobe gang, Grood planned to dispose of him (in a matter fitting Middleton's Ming the Merciless image from *Flash Gordon,* where he got farther out into space).

Hardy was dressed in a flightsuit (which also protected him from the cosmic rays generated by the weapon) when Jack confronted him. Before Hardy could explain his innocence, that he was only playing for time, Jack Armstrong displayed a trace of youthful impulsiveness and knocked the older man cold, taking his flightsuit and going aboard the aeroglobe in Hardy's place.

As the flight began, Jack was discovered by Professor Zorn. During the fight that followed, the aeroglobe went out of control, heading for destruction.

Chapter Fifteen promised "Retribution."

Jack Armstrong evaded Zorn and managed to parachute to safety before the aeroglobe exploded into fragments, destroying Professor Zorn and the other henchmen of Jason Grood.

Back on the ground, Vic Hardy had recovered and showed the stuff we always knew he had. He got the drop on Grood, and demanded that the mastermind sign a full confession. However, Hardy must still have been groggy from the earlier punch delivered by Wheaties-eating champion athlete, Jack Armstrong. Grood managed to overpower Hardy, just as Jack with Billy and Uncle Jim arrived on the scene.

Grood attempted to escape to a waiting airplane, but Jack followed him and engaged him in a hand-to-hand struggle. Stooping to his usual evil ends, Jason Grood tried to kill young Armstrong with a hand grenade but only got blown up himself.

Jack, Billy, Betty, and Uncle Jim were now able to leave the island, no doubt taking some small satisfaction in having saved the world from destruction (at least, temporarily).

As "The End" credit came up, Jack Armstrong must have said: "It was only what would be done by any All-American boy who got plenty of fresh air and exercise, used lots of soap and water, and ate three hearty meals daily, beginning with *Wheaties,* Breakfast of Champions!"

As for Uncle Jim, he must have muttered, "I'm getting too old for this sort of thing."

While it was his *first* screen adventure, it was the final adventure of all for the character Uncle Jim Fairfield, who had already departed the radio show, replaced by Vic Hardy. As evidenced by his actions in the movie serial, Vic Hardy never seemed quite so trustworthy as good old Uncle Jim.

A BOY IN THE ORIENT

Milton Caniff's newspaper comic strip, *Terry and the Pirates*, which began in 1934, was made into a movie serial by Columbia Pictures in 1940. James W. Horne directed the fifteen chapters, which starred young William Tracy as teen-aged soldier of fortune Terry Lee. (Years later, Tracy, too old for the title role, played Terry's sidekick in a television series based on the cartoon strip.) Coming along with Terry from the printed page were his friends Pat Ryan (Granville Owens), faithful Chinese servant Connie (Allen Jung), and giant magician Big Stoop (Victor De Camp).

Dr. Herbert Lee (John Paul Jones) went to Asia in the first chapter, "Into the Great Unknown," to uncover the secrets of a lost civilization of that enormous continent. This particular lost civilization (there were so many serials) was ruled by the half-breed warlord, Fang (Dick Curtis), who terrorized both natives and white men. The jungle housed the sacred temple of the god Mara. And the temple housed another great treasure which was naturally coveted by the greedy tyrant.

Some of the natives, however, were not under the domination of Fang. These had given their loyalty to a beautiful and mysterious woman known as the Dragon Lady (Sheila Darcy), and were at odds against the tyrannical Fang.

Dr. Lee's son, Terry, and Pat Ryan, the doctor's assistant, marched into the jungle with important papers required by the former. Everywhere they went, Terry and his friend were shunned. The only persons who gave them any consideration were trader Allen Drake (Forrest Taylor) and his pretty blond daughter Normandie (Joyce Bryant).

Disaster struck in many forms that night. While Terry was ape-handled by a monstrous gorilla, the documents were stolen and the Lee party raided by Fang's Tiger Men. Terry and Pat, with Big Stoop and Connie, then journeyed into the jungle in search of Dr. Lee. During the night, their hut was set aflame by Fang's murderous Tiger Men.

A convenient tunnel at the rear of the hut provided an escape for the four heroes in the next episode.

In "The Mountain of Death," the third chapter, Terry and Pat decided to make an alliance with the exotic Dragon Lady in order to battle the terrible Fang and his Tiger Men. As they ventured to the Dragon Lady's lair, the Temple of the Dawn, they found a secret hideaway where they interrupted the sacrifice of a young maiden, saving her life. For their sacrilege, they were approached by the irate high priest who prepared to run them through with his sword. At the opening of the next installment, "The Dragon Queen Threatens," they were saved by Connie and Big Stoop, who entered the temple with blasting guns. The priests followed the intruders to the Temple of the Dawn, where they fled before the mercy of the Dragon Lady. The beautiful woman was about to execute Terry and his pals when his explanation of how they prevented a pagan ritual from claiming a human life made her realize they were on the same side. But when the Dragon Lady learned that Terry's father was trying to uncover the secrets concerning her own people, she acted not like a jungle queen but as a real woman, and changed her mind. Terry and the others *would* be executed. But suddenly the Tiger Men attacked, and in the confusion, Terry, Pat, Connie, and Big Stoop fled the Temple of the Dawn.

Terry was trapped on a bridge blown up by Fang's henchmen, was nearly drowned in an underground jail cell, was attacked by a hungry alligator, and was blown up in a power boat. But he lived through all of these perils, until victory came his way in the last segment of the serial, "The Secret of the Temple."

Terry and the Dragon Lady were friends again. In the temple

of the god Mara, Fang had finally uncovered the sacred treasure —an enormous diamond. But his chances were diminishing. The jungle drums beat out the message that the soldiers of the Viceroy were closing in on him to bring him to justice (of course, we all know that the really big trouble never came until the drums stopped!). The real homicidal fiend began murdering his own people to get at the diamond. But a gorilla, chained in the temple, seeing his master killed by Fang, broke free and slew the evil tyrant. Pat returned the diamond to the Dragon Lady, who now regained her rightful place in the temple of Mara. In return, she granted Dr. Lee the liberty to enter the temple at his leisure and study the past records of her people.

Other serials with boyhood heroes were Universal's *Tim Tyler's Luck,* also based on a comic strip hero, and starring Frankie Thomas (later Tom Corbett, Space Cadet on television) and *Junior G-Men of the Air,* one of the serials featuring the more-or-less reformed Dead End Kids, as related elsewhere. Mascot made numerous serials starring the perpetually youthful Frankie Darro. The last serial to have a boy in the title role was *Cody of the Pony Express* (Columbia 1950) which featured Dickie Moore as young William F. Cody, later Buffalo Bill. However, he was eclipsed in the credits and footage by Jock O'Mahoney (later Jack Mahoney) as Lieutenant Jim Archer.

The era of the boy hero was growing to an end. The "boy" hero of literature and movies had generally been really a teen-ager, *not* a small boy of eight or ten. By the fifties, the teen-aged boy was no longer regarded as a developing child, but as a young adult. "Teen-age" problems were by then the problems of a sex life, getting a job, and going into the Army. Far behind lay the world of Frank Merriwell and Huck Finn and Jack Armstrong —the world of boyhood pirates, airplanes, treasure maps, winning touchdowns. It was a lost world, but perhaps not a world totally well lost.

5

Real Life Heroes   "Just Strangle
the Lion in Your Usual Way"

THE GREAT HOUDINI

Since it was sometimes difficult to fully accept the heroics performed by serial stars, the studios often cast real life heroes to show audiences that such activities were possible and believable. The practice of starring popular heroes, who would normally be facing death in their own walks of life, in cliffhangers, began during the silent era. In each instance, these silent serial stars essentially played themselves on the screen, which made their filmed exploits even more credible. Audiences seemed to regard such casting as if a newsreel cameraman, employed by the studio making the serial, just happened to be in the vicinity while their idol faced death in one ingenious form or another.

Harry Houdini, the stage magician and escape artist who became legendary as the greatest in his profession for all time, was hired by Octagon Films Incorporated to star in a fifteen-chapter silent serial, *The Master Mystery,* directed by Burton King, and scheduled for release in 1919. Houdini was unfortunately stocky, and coarse featured, totally unlike the satanic magician image. Unlike many stage performers who looked down on movies as crude entertainment, he gladly accepted the part of Quentin Locke of the Justice Department to bolster his career. He even lent his literary talents to helping writer Arthur B. Reeve create the script.

In the first episode, International Patents, Inc. was revealed as a vast organization attempting to stop progress from ruining its own business ventures. An evil genius and big name in the business world controlled the organization from his castle retreat. Under the castle, in a cellar carved from solid rock, was the Graveyard of Genius, where the prototypes of futuristic inventions were kept after being purchased from their inventors.

The main strength in the combine lay in its most powerful agent, a towering robot named Q, the Automaton, one of the inventions held by the organization. The creature (supposedly possessing a human brain) was a distant cry from the robots later used in serials by master villains Bela Lugosi and Eduardo Ciannelli. It barely looked more than an assembly of round cans, with an oil drum waist, and a happily smiling face. The manner in which it walked, raising one arm with each step, made it appear as menacing as a toy robot that any kid's parent can purchase today in a department store. Floyd Buckley portrayed the automaton, showing superstrength and invulnerability (or near invulnerability, since the brilliant Quentin Locke later invented a special exploding bullet that was able to pierce the metal skin of the monster).

Quentin Locke began investigating the secretive organization, encountering Eva (Marguerite Marsh), the pretty daughter of the scheming mastermind. But he also met the lumbering Q, the Automaton which was hidden behind a secret door, and appeared in every chapter to smash its way through the prop sets.

But the good agent survived the attacks by the robot, plus a number of other dangers resulting from his investigation. He was almost burned by deadly acid, poisoned with noxious gas, and even entangled with barbed wire. But in reality being the world's greatest escape artist, Locke freed himself from every predicament. His escapes from such mundane entrapments as ropes which were tied around his entire body gave his fans an opportunity to view his talents at closer range than the stage permitted, watching him use his toes and fingers and teeth to unravel and cut his bonds.

The Master Mystery concluded with an episode titled "Unmasking of the Automaton," with Quentin Locke's fabulous bullet putting an end to the powerful creation (exposed as a human being wearing a costume). The chapter also concluded Harry Houdini's association with serials. Since he insisted upon making his exploits on the screen as realistic as possible, his audience, expecting to see more spectacular and unbelievable escapes, did not hold the chapterplay among their favorites. He later starred in some feature length productions, where he could be more himself, since these films were aimed at a different audience. But Harry Houdini being himself—even in the most extraordinary plots—was a bit spectacular.

THE LEATHERPUSHERS

Many youngsters have idolized the heroes of the sports world, especially the fighters who went on to glory in the championship boxing ring. Just preceding Houdini's serial, Universal in 1919 starred boxing champion James J. Corbett in an eighteen-episode chapterplay, *The Midnight Man,* directed by James W. Horne.

Corbett, older than most serial heroes of the era, still managed to do some quite spectacular feats in *The Midnight Man.* But the serial did not have the thrills of some of its contemporary episodic rivals. In effect, *The Midnight Man* was more a melodrama than an action epic, going in for the heavy-handedness of serials of earlier years.

Heavyweight boxing champion of the world, Jack Dempsey, fared better than Corbett in his only movie serial, *Daredevil Jack,* a 1920 Pathé chapterplay, with fifteen installments directed by W. S. Van Dyke.

Jack Dempsey exhibited a surprisingly capable acting ability in *Daredevil Jack,* portraying the hero, Jack Derry. The character was a college sports star who also managed to become involved in a mystery. He met a pretty girl played by Josie Sedgwick, whose deceased father had discovered a hidden oil basin.

Derry finally located the oil basin and won the girl by the fade-out of the last chapter, "The Triple Chase," but not before being shanghaied, clubbed, and almost incinerated. Amid the action of the serial, a young actor performed with Jack Dempsey who would one day be one of the greatest stars of the silent cinema, the "Man of a Thousand Faces," Lon Chaney.

Daredevil Jack increased Jack Dempsey's popularity as a pugilist, but he never made another cliffhanger, returning to his main love, boxing. In Philadelphia, on September 23, 1926, Dempsey was defeated in the ring by Gene Tunney. Before that historic bout, Tunney was given a rest from his boxing activities and hired by the same studio, Pathé, to slug his way through ten episodes of *The Fighting Marine,* directed by Spencer G. Bennet. Tunney was glad to take a vacation from the ring, since his acting would gain him the then tremendous and previously unheard of purse of $24,000, plus one-fourth of the total gross of the serial. Pathé gambled that Gene Tunney would beat Jack Dempsey in the ring, since it had scheduled the release of the serial the same month as the bout. Had Tunney lost to his opponent, his value as a chapterplay hero would have been a box-office knockout.

Tunney's serial role required more than fighting in the ring, although he did show off his boxing skills in the chapters. As a punching Marine, he also found himself entombed alive, engaged in furious horseback riding, and even trapped by a falling tower. *The Fighting Marine* was well-received, but it did not inspire Gene Tunney to make any more cliffhangers.

The serials would soon be made with full audio tracks. The coming of sound would mysteriously see an end to professional pugilists boxing their way across the screen, week after week. But there were other real life heroes from other walks of life to thrill their fans and thwart the villains.

WILD ANIMAL TRAINER SUPREME

The curly-haired man in the garb of a wild animal trainer clung with sweating hands from the rough stone rim overlooking the pit of growling, hungry alligators. He wasn't tremendously handsome, but his steel-hard face and almost hypnotic eyes told that his terrible predicament might well have been a newsreel of an actual real-life encounter with Death.

The man was Clyde Beatty, whose name was the same whether on or off the screen.

He grunted heroically, hearing the scaly reptilian throwbacks to the dinosaur age splashing and snapping and roaring—and waiting for him. There seemed little hope of escaping the doom which would shred him into a snack for the alligators, for his every effort to clutch the stone rim was thwarted by the grinding foot of his human enemy. More, more, Clyde Beatty slipped, until . . .

Clyde Beatty, whose name was pronounced to rhyme with "bait" and not "beat," has become known as "the world's greatest wild animal trainer" and "wild animal trainer supreme." He left home and joined a traveling circus at the appropriate and impressionable age of fifteen in 1920; working his way to the position of assistant animal trainer with Howe's Great London Shows. Within three years, Gollmer Brothers Circus had made him a star. In later years, he acquired his own show, the Clyde Beatty Circus. The almost hypnotic mastery he had over the wild beasts of his center ring—including the natural enemies, lions and tigers—has since become almost legend.

Clyde Beatty's workings with the big cats, whose jungle might seem to go dormant under his staring command, was the greatest and most dynamic wild animal trainer of them all. It was only natural that he should spread his stardom into the movies.

Taking with him his whip, chair, and gun, Beatty went to Hollywood and starred in a number of action-packed motion pictures. The first of these was a feature for Universal titled *The Big Cage* in 1933, a picture that was extremely well received, and proved that Beatty's ticket sales potential went beyond the big tent's turnstile.

Since Clyde Beatty's very life centered upon action and death-defying thrills, it was only natural that he be cast in the type of film especially created to convey such excitement. Understandably, his next two ventures into celluloid would be on the serial screen.

Clyde Beatty seemed only seconds away from death. Within moments, those enormous fangs would lock into his flesh, rip him to shreds. But the last time we saw the hero was one week ago—and a lot can happen in seven days!

Somehow, Beatty's perspiring fingers did not seem as near the rim of the alligator pit as they did the week before. Miraculously, the time that transpired between episodes of this serial, *The Lost Jungle,* had allotted him the hairbreadth ability to pull himself an extra inch or two away from immediate death. But there was yet a stomping, burly heavy looming like a monster above him, grinning fiendishly as he again brought down his foot. What Beatty may have lacked in looks, height, and in sheer brute power, he had in pure determination. With muscles straining, and despite the tremendous odds that should have tolled his death a week ago, he managed to pull himself out of the alligator pit and defeat his opponent.

The Lost Jungle was released in 1934 as a twelve-chapter

cliffhanger by Mascot, produced by the mastermind behind that
studio's list of action films, Nat Levine.[1]

Armand Schaefer and David Howard directed the screenplay
by veterans Barney Sarecky, Wyndham Gittens, and themselves,
in taking the circus star out of the big city and placing him in
the savage environment of the great cats.

The first episode of *The Lost Jungle* brought Clyde Beatty's
circus and his cage filled with the Hagenbeck-Wallace Wild Animals to the winter months, when the tents of the big top were
closed to the public. Due to the carelessness of his jealous assistant Sharkey (played by the leering Warner Richmond)
Beatty's young friend, played by then child star, Mickey
Rooney, was killed by an escaped cat. Beatty then rushed in to
restore the brute to its cage, realizing that the suspicious
Sharkey would probably bear close watching.

Capitalizing on the time during which the circus would be
closed for the winter, Beatty decided to journey to Africa in
search of new animals to tame. Sharkey, Beatty, and his sidekick press agent Larry (Syd Saylor)[2] set out for Africa in a fantastic dirigible, courtesy of the studio's miniature workshop.
Beatty, however, had neglected to check the weather reports
before starting his aerial voyage to Africa. The dirigible was
hurled into the furies of a tremendous electrical storm, sending
its occupants crashing on an uncharted South Seas jungle
island, and ending Chapter One. Among the following week's
survivors were Clyde Beatty, Larry, and Sharkey.

[1] Like many other serials, *The Lost Jungle* was also released in an
edited feature length version. However, unlike most feature condensations
of serials, *The Lost Jungle* motion picture was released simultaneously
with the chapterplay instead of years or decades later. Levine stated that
the feature length version contained considerable footage that did not
appear in the serial.

[2] Comic relief characters were very much a part of serials of the early
talkie era. Syd Saylor's particular trademark was the manipulation of his
bow tie due to a large and maneuverable Adam's apple.

Once Clyde Beatty became orientated to his new life away from civilization, he found himself confronted with a number of conditions familiar to discoverers of "lost jungles." There was stranded Captain Robinson (Maston Williams) and his lovely daughter (Cecilia Parker), and Robinson's mutinous and murderous crew who had been scouring the island for buried treasure. Robinson had been forced to build a fort-like stockade to protect his daughter and himself from the renegades. Recognizing the good guys, Beatty discovered a staggering iron door, leading to a buried city lost to the centuries. It was inside this city that the treasure lay buried.

The lost city itself showed that its inhabitants, having devised the numerous trapdoors and secret passageways, and designed the overhanging chandeliers, had been of considerable social sophistication. However, despite their former greatness, the one-time inhabitants no longer existed. The only resident of the lost city now was a lumbering and savage gorilla. Even as Sharkey gave his allegiance to the villainous crew in hopes of attaining the treasure for himself, it was the gorilla who provided many of the cliffhangers for Clyde Beatty and his friends. At one point Larry ended a chapter while hanging from a loose chandelier over the alligator pit, each moment pulling him closer to death amid a puff of shattering ceiling. Even if he managed to leap to shore before his own weight sent him plunging down into hungry mouths, Larry would not have found safety. For waiting only several feet away, arms extended for the kill, was the ape of the lost city. It was only the gunshots fired by Clyde Beatty at the monster that saved the press agent and gave him time to jump away from the alligator pit.

Clyde Beatty's heroics carried him through the dozen episodes, pitting him against angry sailors anxious to steal the treasure which he discovered, from a variety of starved jungle cats, including lions and tigers, and from the monstrous gorilla who seemed to have a personal desire to stop the intruders from defiling his buried domain. But in the last episode, unable to fulfill his own dream of capturing the ape alive and returning him to the circus, Beatty was forced to blast the bullets that ended the animal's life. Then, digging his way through a wall of the lost city, Clyde Beatty led his friends to freedom.

Only four Mascot serials followed the *Lost Jungle: Phantom Empire, The Miracle Rider, Adventures of Rex and Rinty,* and *Fighting Marines,* all released in 1935. The studio had been the primary factory for action features and serials through the late 1920s and early '30s. Nat Levine felt the time had arrived to move on to bigger, better film enterprises. The head of the little studio with the tiger "mascot" began the changeover by first leasing the vacant Sennett Studio in North Hollywood, absent from the cameras since 1933. Levine then merged Mascot with Consolidated Film Laboratories and Monogram, a small studio notorious for low budget program features accepting an offer made by the laboratory's chief Herbert J. Yates. Later, Monogram was bought out by the other two companies, and Republic Pictures was created.

Levine decided that his new Republic serials would be vast improvements upon those turned out under the Mascot trademark. Analyzing his past products, he realized that perhaps the old Mascot plots were at times too involved. The Republic plots would be simple, so that an adequate synopsis (for people who had missed the previous episodes) could be imprinted beneath still photographs of the characters at the opening of each chapter, in as few sentences as possible. (In later Republic serials, there would be only one title or "recap" card, hopefully explaining all that was required to newcomers.) The absence of music, such a hazard for the Mascot chapterplays especially in the action scenes, would be corrected with powerful scores to accompany all moods and situations. Furthermore, comic relief characters would be played down in future scripts.

When Republic premiered its very first serial, *Darkest Africa* in 1936, the movie posters tacked outside the theatre that Saturday afternoon again publicized the name of the greatest wild animal trainer of them all, Clyde Beatty.

In *Darkest Africa,* which was directed by B. Reeves Eason and Joseph Kane, Clyde Beatty found himself in many of the same jungle situations as in *The Lost Jungle.* That was not surprising, however, since one of the scriptwriters of *Darkest Africa* was Barney Sarecky, who took Beatty to that unnamed South Seas island. There was a gorilla, Bongo, played by "Naba" (actually Ray "Crash" Corrigan, whose film roles fluctuated between handsome hero and shaggy ape), not a vicious killer this time, but the pet of a jungle boy, Baru (played by Manuel King, a budding and overweight rival to Beatty himself, as he was billed "the World's Youngest Wild Animal Trainer"). There was also another lost city, called Joba. This time, however, the forgotten city was not inhabited only by a lonesome gorilla, but by a strange race of white men, throwbacks to another civilized age, and their warriors, the weird, flying, winged Bat-Men.

These Bat-Men literally flew, by life-size, lightweight dummies soaring with the aid of unseen piano wire, a process developed by Republic special effects man Howard Lydecker, and later brought to perfection in that studio's Captain Marvel and Rocket Man serials. The scenes wherein the Bat-Men flew were totally convincing and satisfying, vastly superior to the tiny Hawkmen fliers in Universal's *Flash Gordon* released that same year. Sometimes, they would be seen gliding near the ground as a fellow Bat-Man walking only several feet below would motion directions to his airborne comrade. At other times, through the use of miniatures, the Bat-Men entered and left the city of Joba in large flocks.

Even though the Bat-Men of Joba were an impressive sight, flying with their spears and clad in their ancient costumes and bird beaked metal helmets, the real star of *Darkest Africa* was

Clyde Beatty. Though admittedly a wild animal trainer and not a full-time actor, Beatty played his role with a conviction and honesty that overshadowed any lack of thespian training. He was entirely believable at all times. When Clyde Beatty appeared on the serial screen, there was no doubting that this was a real hero—involved in real (albeit scripted) heroics.

In the first of fifteen episodes, "Baru, Son of the Jungle," Clyde Beatty, investigating the strange appearance of an Indian tiger in darkest Africa, met the juvenile animal trainer. Although Spanish, Baru's blond and fair-skinned sister Valerie (Elaine Shepard) was a captive in Joba, where the evil high priest Dagna (Lucien Prival) had presented her as a goddess. As long as the people of Joba accepted her as such, Dagna could control them.

Naturally, the situation was of the type that Clyde Beatty could not refuse. Braving the dangers of irate natives, untamed lions and tigers, and the down-swooping Bat-Men, Beatty, Baru, Bonga, and a reasonably sized safari, set out for the lost city of Joba.

Beatty and his partners, human and inhuman, arrived in Joba where they were subjected to a number of perils that were spectacular enough to end the episodes and to summon us back the following week. Clyde was tossed into a tiger pit, where only his own long-developed skill as a wild animal trainer saved him. At another point, he and Baru nearly fed a giant lizard and an enormous centipede. But the cliffhanger that made us wonder if perhaps there was no possible escape was that climaxing Chapter Fourteen, "The Divine Sacrifice." The divine one sacrificed was goddess Valerie, who in order to save Clyde and her brother Baru, had agreed to Dagna's demand to leap to her death from Pinnacle Rock. At the end of the episode, we saw the white dressed figure plunge from the edge of the cliff and smack with crushing impact amid the rocks below!

As the last episode, "Prophecy of Gorn," opened, we were

permitted a gasp of relief, for we learned that someone else had replaced the girl so that she never leaped from the cliffside.

Clyde Beatty, Valerie, and Baru then prepared to leave the city, when nature, as she always does when lost cities and evil tyrants near the end of an adventure, erupted in a violent earthquake, killing Dagna and his army of killer Bat-Men. Naturally, only Clyde Beatty and his friends escaped the holocaust.

Darkest Africa although still crude when compared to the later, more polished, Republic serials of the early 1940s, showed a definite improvement over those predecessors filmed at Mascot. For Levine and Republic Pictures, the art of the motion picture serial was only beginning to mature. For Clyde Beatty, the motion picture industry was to be only a hobby, his main interests still locked within the protective bars of the big cage. *Darkest Africa* was his second and final serial. His acting talents were seen later in several feature length films, including John Wayne's production of *Ring of Fear,* 1954, in color and Cinemascope, and starring the Clyde Beatty Circus.

In 1949, *Darkest Africa* was rereleased under the typically Republic title of *King of Jungleland.* Many of the studio's chapterplays began with *"King of . . . ,"* but in the case of Clyde Beatty, Wild Animal Trainer Supreme, the title was most appropriate.

"BRING 'EM BACK ALIVE!"

Frank Buck, the red-blooded adventurer (and somewhat cold-blooded businessman) who didn't kill wild animals but instead captured them for zoos, thus gaining his nickname of "Bring 'Em Back Alive," starred in *Jungle Menace,* a movie serial made by Columbia Pictures in 1937. *Jungle Menace* was significant for two reasons. It was the only chapterplay to star Frank Buck (who had produced his own semi-documentary film from books he had authored, *Bring 'Em Back Alive* and *Fang and Claw*), putting the true life hero through fifteen exciting fictional installments. Also, it was the very first motion picture serial ever made by Columbia.

The fast-talking, mustached hero put on his jungle civvies, complete with pith helmet and holstered revolver, to play the part of Frank Hardy in the serial. Hardy performed his heroics in the Asian jungles of Malay. The location was ideal for a serial. At last no one would question the appearance of a tiger (an animal which constantly turned up in cliffhangers set in Africa).

The first episode of the serial was suitably titled "River Pirates." The Banning plantation had been exporting vast shipments of rubber. The shipments had fallen under the greedy glances of a band of river pirates, led by two sinister characters. These were Murphy (LeRoy Mason), who killed on a whim, and a mysterious character known as the Tiger Man (Sasha Siemel). The Tiger Man was so named because of his skill in hunting down tigers and other ferocious jungle cats with only a spear. Actually Siemel was as much a real life hero (though not as well known) as Frank Buck. What he did on the screen, he also did in real life.

The pirate band had been attacking the boats that carried the rubber away from the plantation. The raids were finally brought to the attention of Tom Banning (William Bakewell), the son of the plantation owner, and the nephew of one of the local businessmen. On the ship that would take him to the vicinity of his home, Tom met a wild animal trapper and explorer named Frank Hardy (essentially Frank Buck with a slightly different name), who was transporting a shipment of savage animals. During the unloading of the animals, a number of growling lions broke loose, and it looked like Frank and his friends were about to serve the beasts as meals.

"Frank Hardy" used all the skills he learned as Frank Buck to recapture the lions at the opening of Chapter Two, "Deadly Enemies."

Later, Frank was a guest at the plantation. One of his caged animals had again gotten loose and was prowling about. Tom's father had already been killed during one of the numerous pirate raids, and Marshall (played by the distinguished English actor, Reginald Denny), the foreman of the plantation, began to track down the cutthroat Murphy. In the pursuit, Marshall had been seriously wounded. Frank, and Tom's girl friend Dorothy (Charlotte Henry) and her Aunt Valerie (Esther Ralston), found the wounded foreman while searching the jungle for the stray cat. Frank immediately sent for a doctor. But in a movie serial, doctors were not always to be trusted, some of them hypocrites when it came to their Hippocratic Oath. This physician was a member of the gang and proceeded to silence Marshall, who knew too much.

Together, Frank and Tom decided to track down the pirates and bring them to justice. They were helped in their attempts by Police Inspector MacLeod (Robert Warwick). But even with the law on their side, the two heroes did not suspect that Tom's uncle was really the leader of the gang and was also in partnership with Armand Rogers (played by a young Duncan Renaldo), who operated a swank nightclub.

Frank Hardy was becoming too involved in matters that didn't concern him. The pirates knew that he had to be eliminated, this time with a double threat. First, a fire was started in the plantation's compound. Then his wild animals were released from their cages. Again, Frank Hardy's knowledge of animals (which was as authoritative as Buck's) enabled him to subdue the monsters, including a vicious tiger.

When Murphy decided to double-cross his gang of killers, he was wounded. Meanwhile, Frank, Dorothy, Valerie, plus some members of their crew, were shipwrecked during a severe storm on an island. The Tiger Man, who had become discouraged by the gang's villainy, was also one of the survivors. Again, death roamed the jungle in the form of two escaped cats, tigers this time. The natives of the island were petrified by the carnivorous monsters, calling them "devil beasts." Frank again brought his jungle skills into flamboyant exhibition. For his deed, he was told by a renegade white man living amongst the natives that the lives of him and his friends would be spared.

Finally the rubber pirates knew that their evil ways would soon be ended. Murphy was being hunted down by both the police and Tom's uncle. Murphy broke into Roger's office just as the police, with Frank and Tom, encountered him in the act. But they were not quick enough to stop the murderous pirate from killing Rogers in revenge.

Frank Hardy and Tom Banning brought the rest of the cutthroats to justice. Tom and Dorothy announced their wedding plans, and Frank returned to the cages of his beloved "friends," the animals. Then the concluding chapter, "Give 'Em Rope," faded out.

Jungle Menace, which was produced by Jack Fier and directed by George M. Melford and Harry Fraser, put Frank Buck through perils that he could have encountered during his exciting life, much of which was spent in the jungles of the world. In the serial, there were typhoons, stampeding animals, and bone-crushing jungle snakes to face and overcome. But Frank "Bring 'Em Back Alive" Buck defeated the countless jungle menaces, proving that he was as much a hero on as off the screen.

Whether he was an actor or not was another question. Still, he was intelligent enough to deliver lines with some feeling, though his inexperience showed. All in all, this pioneering Columbia serial was better than many that followed.

AMERICA'S ACE FLIER

The Mysterious Pilot was the second movie serial made by Columbia Pictures, directly following Frank Buck's *Jungle Menace* in 1937. The fifteen-chapter cliffhanger starred a man who was handsome in a way unlike that of the assembly line serial heroes of later years. He was Captain Frank Hawks, known as the fastest airman in the world, an aviator idolized by boys of all ages. In *The Mysterious Pilot,* Captain Hawks took a brief rest from the actual dangers of flying, and turned himself over to the perils of the screen and the direction of Spencer Gordon Bennet.

The serial was adapted from the novel *The Silver Hawk* (coincidentally using Captain Hawks's name in the title), written by William Byron Mowery. The first installment, "The Howl of the Wolf," commenced with pilot Jim Dorn (Frank Hawks) on assignment for the Royal Canadian Air Force. Dorn was camped near the Titan Pass railroad station and was mapping the Canadian wilderness for that government.

Meanwhile, on a train nearing the station, Jean McNain (played by Dorothy Sebastian), a guest of Carter Snowden (played by Guy Bates Post), overheard him accused by a stranger of murder. Afraid that the accusation might be true, the girl fled from the train to take refuge in the woods. Later, the train collided with another, with Snowden surviving. The mysterious stranger was found dead, a bullet lodged in his skull. Suspiciously, Carter Snowden had disappeared.

But Snowden had an ace up his sleeve. Two of his gangster friends, Kilgour (played by reliable old Tom London) and Carlson (Ted Adams), had been following the train from the sky. Snowden and his bodyguard, Soft Shoe Cardigan (Harry Harvey), were picked up by the two villainous pilots, and taken to a lodge near Titan Pass. There, safe for the moment, Snowden announced that the girl Jean knew too much and must be found right away.

Jean had meanwhile encountered Jim Dorn, who agreed to fly her to her father. But Dorn's craft, the Silver Hawk, was spotted and pursued by the crook's plane. Dorn then served a double purpose by doing some stunt flying. He evaded the gangsters for a while, and at the same time was able to show off for his pretty passenger. Then, following her directions, the pilot landed the plane near the cabin supposedly occupied by her father. The place, though, was deserted. Jean asked his forgiveness, for she had lied in order to escape the wrath of Carter Snowden. But Jim Dorn knew that he was now in the middle of a baffling mystery and a war against crime. He had to protect Jean McNain no matter what the cost.

In the second episode, "The Web Tangles," Jim Dorn's plane flew through a dangerously narrow mountain pass. Powerful air currents took control of the plane, sucking it into a perilous spin. The following week, Dorn managed to regain control of his craft and pull it out of the hazardous chasm.

Other chapters had Jim Dorn lying unconscious in a burning tent, tied to a log and sent downstream, and trapped in a room with a gang of murderous woodsmen.

The chapters, set among Canadian forests and lumber camps, centered on that element for which Frank Hawks's fans went to see *The Mysterious Pilot*—fantastic aviation. There were numerous dogfights in the air, with Dorn soaring off after Snowden and his thugs. At the climax of Chapter Three, "Enemies of the Air," Dorn flew off with guns reporting at Snowden's craft, blasting off the tail, and sending the enemy ship into a down spin. The gangsters saved themselves from cracking up with their plane by parachuting to safety. In other episodes, Jim Dorn was lowered from a plane into a speedboat, while the gangster plane followed with blazing guns; he descended via rope from the Silver Hawk to Jean's plane; and was attacked and apparently doomed to crash after a machine-gun dogfight sent his ship into a tailspin.

"Retribution" was a suitable title for the fifteenth installment. Jean had been kidnapped by Snowden, and was taken away by transport plane. Dorn, and his pal Kansas Eby (played by Western movie star Rex Lease), learned of the abduction and chased after them in their plane. Attempting to force down the transport plane they were attacked by another ship, flown by the gangster Carlson. Finally, after an exciting battle in the air, Dorn blasted Carlson's plane from the sky. Soft Shoe became panicky over the death of the other pilot, and his fear revealed itself in some hazardous flying. Snowden, infuriated at his pilot, knocked him cold. The transport plane went into a spin and crashed. Jim Dorn, not to be evaded so easily, bailed out after them, his parachute becoming entangled in the treetops. Meanwhile, Soft Shoe had been blinded and maddened by the fire burning the transport plane. In his crazed state, he accidentally plunged off the side of a cliff, eliminating another of Dorn's opponents. Jim, though also temporarily blind, had freed himself from the trees, and Jean managed to escape from the wreckage of the transport plane. She was able to find Jim who was also about to stumble off the edge of a cliff and save him from death. Kansas found Snowden dying amid the wreckage of his plane. In his final moments, the villain confessed that he was in truth the murderer of the man on the train. With the mystery solved, Jim Dorn regained his eyesight with the nursing of Jean, their future marriage more than a thought.

Although the hero of *The Mysterious Pilot* was named Jim Dorn, there was no doubt in anyone's mind that the character was essentially the same as the star playing the part, Captain Frank Hawks. With his leather aviator's cap and goggles, and his long-barreled .38 revolver, Hawks appeared on the screen in heroics that were in character with his real life activities. Most serials of contemporary setting used aerial footage. But those stunts could always be attributed to miniatures photographed to look full size, doubles skilled in performing fantastic aerial feats, and the use of old newsreel footage. Frank Hawks gave credibility to the thrills in *The Mysterious Pilot*. Audiences knew that what they saw him do on screen he probably could do—and might have already done—in real life.

FROM PIGSKINS TO PERILS

A man was plummeting to his death from the cockpit of a biplane. Below, the ground moved with dizzy speed. If the apparently doomed man could be seen a bit closer he would be immediately recognizable to sports fans as football hero Harold "Red" Grange, the famous number 77 on the University of Illinois team. He continued to fall, and there was little hope of escape as this chapter of *The Galloping Ghost* reached the climax.

The Galloping Ghost was a twelve-installment chapterplay, one of the earliest talking serials to come out of the Mascot studios. The story involved football only as a starting premise. The central storyline concerned the war-like rivalry between opposing taxi cab companies. Grange, naturally, was on the side of the righteous cab company. And because he was a good guy, he found himself most often at the mercy of the villains.

When you are a serial hero, you seem to develop a special kind of luck that almost makes you wonder if Fate is pulling some strings on your behalf. Coincidences seemed to happen at the most unnatural, unpredictable places and times in chapterplays. So it was with "Red" Grange. As he fell from that airplane, plunging through what should have been miles of empty space, another plane flew beneath him. The football star-turned-movie hero caught onto the wing of the second craft, landing safely, and escaped splattering the countryside with "Red."

In *The Galloping Ghost,* "Red" Grange was accused—wrongfully of course—of accepting a bribe given by a gambling ring. Actually Grange took the blame to cover up for a teammate on his football squad, Buddy Courtland (played by tall, husky Francis X. Bushman, Jr.). Buddy was meanwhile recovering in a hospital.

"Red" had been taken off the football team because of his supposed crooked actions. He turned to Buddy's sister Barbara (Dorothy Gulliver), attempting to convince her that he wasn't guilty of taking the bribe. But Barbara did not believe him. Instead she drove away with James Elton (Walter Miller) who, unknown to her, was the boss of the gambling ring.

The football hero was attacked at the Mogul Taxi Garage by the cabmen, actually members of Elton's gambling ring. This garage was, in truth, their secret headquarters. "Red" was saved by the intervention of another group of cabmen. But during the conflict, the hero was knocked out—and beneath a descending elevator car.

Someone pulled "Red" out the following week, saving him from being permanently shafted.

In Chapter Nine, "The Sign in the Sky," Grange was in a house that was bombed by Elton, who decided that the meddling ex-football player had interfered once too much. Needless to add, Grange escaped.

Harold "Red" Grange received the starring role in *The Galloping Ghost* through the efforts of his business manager, a theatre owner named Frank Zambrino. The man had seen Grange act in films before, in two silent feature length films, *One Minute to Play* (1926) and *Racing Romeo* (1927). Returning exclusively to football, Grange avoided the movies until Zambrino recognized his athletic client serial star potential. Zambrino then contacted Mascot chief Nat Levine and convinced him that "Red" Grange should star in one of his chapter-plays. Levine agreed, placing Grange on a weekly salary, and turned out *The Galloping Ghost* in three weeks. When the production was finished, the gridiron star had $4500 to his credit.

But that money was not easily earned. Serials were made for action, and in those early days before stuntmen did mostly everything but the close-ups and dialogue for the star, actors were required to work hard for their pay.

And so "Red" Grange, and his partner played by a very young Creighton Chaney (later Lon Chaney, Jr.), engaged in some furious outdoor antics, including a warehouse fight almost forty feet above a hard concrete floor without benefit of a net to stop anyone who might be careless enough to fall off, and numerous chases and hazards with speedboats weaving and careening under and between the San Pedro piers off the Pacific coast.

The Galloping Ghost was directed by Mascot veteran B. Reeves "Breezy" Eason, who also filmed some fast action in *Law of the Wild* with Rex, King of the Wild Horses, *Mystery Mountain* (both 1934), starring Western immortal Ken Maynard, *Adventures of Rex and Rinty,* also with Rin-Tin-Tin, *Fighting Marines,* with Grant Withers, *Phantom Empire,* with Gene Autry, Frankie Darro, and Betsy King Ross, and *The Miracle Rider,* with Tom Mix (all 1935), for Levine's Mascot Pictures. He also directed *Darkest Africa* and *Undersea Kingdom* in 1936 for Republic.

Eason might not have been the greatest director of heavy drama, but for action scenes he was one of the best, ranking alongside Academy Award-winning second unit director Yakima Canutt. (To prove that action directors who obviously loved their work were not necessarily doomed to chapterplay oblivion, "Breezy" Eason directed such historically memorable sequences as the chariot race in the silent *Ben-Hur* (1926), the charge in *The Charge of the Light Brigade* (1936), and the burning of Atlanta in *Gone with the Wind* (1939).) He put "Red" Grange through some hazardous ordeals—some downright terrifying, as perilous off as on the screen.

But in those early days of the talkies, it sometimes took a real-life hero from sports, aviation, or wild-animal business to perform all the dangerous feats demanded by imaginative and impractical writers—a real hero like Harold "Red" Grange.

"Red" Grange was not the first football hero to be featured in a movie serial. Nor was he the last.

Years before the filming of *The Galloping Ghost,* All-American football star Ernie Nevers was featured with Frank Albertson and heroine Cecilia Parker in a 1932 chapterplay based on a story by the creator of Sherlock Holmes, Sir Arthur Conan Doyle. The cliffhanger was Universal's *The Lost Special,* and spread the action and intrigue of a railroad setting through a dozen episodes.

Director Henry MacRae, who brought Flash Gordon and his science-fiction friends to serial life, placed his characters in numerous perils in *The Lost Special.* In one chapter, he had stars Albertson and Parker bound to the cowcatcher of a runaway locomotive.

Much of the thrills of *The Lost Special* were attributed to its source, Sir Arthur Conan Doyle, and the fact that the serial had such a sophisticated origin was played up in the advertising:

> Another BIG-AUTHOR serial from the same studios that gave you Peter B. Kyne's *Heroes of the West* and Talbot Mundy's *Jungle Mystery* . . . Terrifically fast, tremendously thrilling, and packed right with the sort of mystery that only the touch of a master writer can give!

Republic Pictures topped all other serials starring football heroes with its 1941 production of *King of the Texas Rangers,* using "Slingin'" Sammy Baugh. (Again, the theme of the serial was not centered on football, although there were shots of

Baugh on the playing field before he graduated to Ranger work. Obviously, the studios figured that there weren't enough thrills on a football field to satisfy an audience of chiffhanger fans for over three months' worth of Saturday afternoons.)

King of the Texas Rangers was to be a twelve-episode cliffhanger set in modern times, involving spies and saboteurs working their evils in Texas. Since the Japanese had not yet bombed Pearl Harbor, and the United States was not in the war, the name of the country operating with secret agents on our free soil was not disclosed. But there was no confusion as to the true identity of the homeland of the mysterious "Excellency" who commanded a huge Zeppelin that floated over Texas for weeks.

When news reached some of the Republic contract players, many of whom were as suited to a horse as they were to a studio set, that a football star was given the lead role in a Western serial, there were more than a few snickers. Obviously, they thought, "Slingin'" Sammy Baugh had been selected for the role of Texas Ranger Tom King because of his sports popularity and his looks. He was tall, rugged, and bore a striking resemblance to that greatest of cowboy heroes, Tom Mix, another real life hero covered elsewhere. (Baugh was given a large white hat such as Mix wore to make him look even more like him.)

When "Slingin'" Sammy arrived in Hollywood, the whispers about another city slicker donning a cowboy outfit failed to bother him. In fact he had a surprise in store for everyone.

Kenne Duncan, the movie bad guy who made audiences do double takes since he resembled a villainous Hopalong Cassidy and who played a crook named Nick in *King of the Texas Rangers,* told this writer: "Everybody wondered what a football player would be able to do in a Western. But you should have seen him handle a horse. He'd been raised in Texas, on a ranch. He'd forgotten more about horses than most guys will ever know. He could take direction well, too, and he learned a lot about acting very quickly. If he had stayed in the business, he could have been as big as John Wayne."

Duncan's fellow villain in the chapterplay, Roy Barcroft who played Ross, replied with: "This was a pleasure, to have a man come in and do the lead who was a real horseman. He became a coach in later years, and has a big ranch now in Texas."

There was no more doubting that Baugh had the proper qualifications for braving the Axis perils thrust on him in *King of the Texas Rangers*.

Ranger King was predictably introduced on the football field.

25. EXTERIOR: FOOTBALL FIELD: LONG DOWN
on players in huddle. Second team at left lined up. First team moves to line of scrimmage.
ANNOUNCER'S VOICE: They're back in the huddle. King looks over the defense. Center's down over the ball.

26. MEDIUM CLOSE
TOM KING *kneeling, ready for punt.*
ANNOUNCER'S VOICE: They shift over to the right, King and Ellsworth back.

27. LONG DOWN
on football field. Ball is flipped to KING.
ANNOUNCER'S VOICE: Here comes the pass from center.

28. LONG MED.
KING *catches ball and runs to the left background, then starts to throw ball.*
ANNOUNCER'S VOICE: The ball goes back to King. He's following one . . .

29. LONG DOWN
on football field as ball is passed from KING *to another player.*
ANNOUNCER'S VOICE: . . . man around. He's going to throw a forward pass . . . he does. Ellsworth takes it on the side lines. He's coming up there.

30. VERY LONG FULL
Down angle on crowd in grandstand.
ANNOUNCER'S VOICE: Five . . . ten . . . fifteen and he's driven
out of bounds.

31. LONG DOWN
Players on football field.
ANNOUNCER'S VOICE: Another first down for Texas. They're
marching goalward. Here's the . . .

32. MED. DOWN
KING *and referee.*
ANNOUNCER'S VOICE: . . . shift to right again. King is back . . .
the ball goes back . . .

33. LONG DOWN
Players on the field.
ANNOUNCER'S VOICE: . . . to Slingin' Tom. He tries to throw a
forward. No, he changes his mind. It's a running play . . .
up the side line . . .

King's playing days were soon over with the grim fact of
his father's death. He was shortly off on a mission to Old
Mexico.

INTERIOR CANTINA
KING: I'm Tom King of the Texas Rangers.
PEDRO: I should like to be certain you are a Texas Ranger,
senor. I am Pedro Gracia, Lieutenant of Rurales.

CLOSE
PEDRO *covering* KING *with gun.* KING *takes out his wallet and
opens it.* PEDRO *taking it and examining card and photo. He
hands the wallet to* KING.
PEDRO: Bueno, and who are these men?
KING: That man killed my father, Ranger Tom King, while he
was working on a sabotage case.
PEDRO: Sabotage! Oh, now I see.
KING: I don't understand.
PEDRO: I am investigating some of your countrymen who are
suspected of sabotaging American oil properties in Mexico.

I have a tip they are hiding back in the hills in an abandoned olive oil plant. Come, we'll go together, eh?

KING: I have no authority south of the border.

PEDRO: You have two guns which I may need. I have the authority which you may need. It's what you call, fifty-fifty, eh?

But Sergeant King survived all of these perils with an assist from lanky stuntman Tom Steele and, when more spectacular acrobatics were required, Dave Sharpe.

One of the greatest cliffhangers of all time was featured in *King of the Texas Rangers*. Barton's gang of cowboy saboteurs was blowing up the mountainside in order to catch a valuable train in an avalanche of rock and debris. Only one man could save the train, Sergeant King. The Ranger waited on the hillside until the mighty locomotive thundered by. Then he leaped, landing atop the fast-moving train, and made his way inside the engine cab. The locomotive chugged into the tunnel carved through the mountainside. Another blast went off, burying the train in a torrent of rubble. Only a miracle could save King of the Texas Rangers.

A ranger like Tom King needed no miracles. He had his own courage—and the talents of merciful scriptwriters—to get him out of any predicament, regardless of the hazard. "Open up that throttle!" he ordered the engineer, his voice barely carrying over the sounds of the locomotive and the exploding tunnel. The engineer did as he was told, and in one of the most spectacular scenes ever to appear in a serial (even though this was really a stock shot from an earlier Republic feature length movie), the great engine shot like a torpedo from the mountainside, bursting free of the fallen rocks, saving everyone who would otherwise have been killed through the machinations of Barton.

In the last installment, "Code of the Rangers," Sergeant King finally learned that Barton was a fifth columnist, and the brains behind all the attempts at sabotage that he had been thwarting. Barton had stolen a secret American aviation gasoline formula and was fleeing to the giant Zeppelin wherein his "Excellency" gave his nefarious commands. Getting into their own airplane, King and Pedro soared after them. There was but one thought in King's mind, one way to end the threat of the fifth column in Texas. "Bail out!" he ordered his partner. Then he guided the controls so that his plane aimed right for the gigantic cigar-shaped craft. Sergeant King then bailed out after Pedro, precious seconds before his plane crashed into the Zeppelin, which erupted in a tremendous gush of flame, destroying Barton, his "Excellency," and the saboteurs.

King of the Texas Rangers was Sammy Baugh's only serial. After its completion, he returned to the sports world and his beloved game of football. He could have done more serials, for he had the makings of a true action star. Strong, capable of handling the demands imposed by scriptwriters, he suffered only from having had absolutely no previous experience in acting. But his acting ability was better than that of many leading men of cliffhangers and action features. In serials, it was the ability to ride and fight that counted. "Slingin'" Sammy Baugh could do both. On the strength of this single production, he has joined the ranks of the screen's foremost men of action in the minds of many.

6

Jungle "Look Out
The Elephants Are Coming!"

THE APE MAN

Korak, the son of Tarzan, was helplessly tied to a wooden post in the jungle. He had been captured by hostile savages, residents of the Village of Death. Korak tried to loosen his bonds, but failed. It was obvious that the jungle boy needed help—big help. From the youth's mouth came the fearsome cry of a human ape. Within moments, aid arrived in the lumbering form of Tantor the elephant.

Tantor's snake-like trunk wrapped itself around Korak, then pulled him up into the air, stake and all. This was "An Amazing Denouncement," a chapter of the silent serial, *Son of Tarzan,* made with fifteen episodes by National Film Corporation in 1920.

Korak was portrayed by young Kamuela Searle, a Hawaiian, with a muscular frame and hair that hung almost to his chest. Searle was less fortunate than most serial heroes who could escape from any predicament. For Tantor the elephant thrust both him and the stake hard against the ground with a force not written into the script. As a result, Searle died in real life as a result of the injuries before the serial's completion. A double later assumed the role of Korak to finish the chapter-play. Since installments of *Son of Tarzan* were being released to theatres as they were being shot—not after the entire serial had been completed—the publicity regarding the actor's death lured many people of morbid tastes to the theatre, hopefully to see him actually die on screen.

Son of Tarzan also featured Korak's immortal father, the creation of Edgar Rice Burroughs in the first of his famous series of novels, *Tarzan of the Apes,* first published in the October 1912 issue of the periodical, *All Story.* Tarzan really an Englishman, Lord Greystoke, had been raised from infancy in the jungle by the great apes and eventually became a "civilized savage," speaking a number of languages fluently, and possessing the keenest of minds and strongest of bodies. The Ape Man was played in *Son of Tarzan* (which was based on the fourth in the series of Burroughs' novels, *The Son of Tarzan,*) by the grimacing actor P. Dempsey Tabler, a husky man who had been an athlete in Tennessee. Since Tabler was losing his hair at the time he was selected for the part of Tarzan, he was given a rather unconvincing wig to give him some authenticity. His performance as the Ape Man was not popular. It was Tabler's final performance in a film. Dark-haired Karla Schramm, who had played Tarzan's mate Jane in a previous feature, *The Revenge of Tarzan* (1920) for Numa Pictures Corporation, re-created the role in *Son of Tarzan.* Korak as a small boy was played by Gordon Griffith, who had portrayed the youthful Tarzan himself in the full length *Tarzan of the Apes,* made in 1918 by National.

The serial opened with Korak's (Jack in English) encounter with Ivan Paulovich (played by leering, dark-eyed Eugene Barr), one of Tarzan's former opponents. Paulovich was as evil as his name sounded, and promptly kidnapped the boy. Seizing upon his first opportunity, the son of Tarzan escaped, helped by Akut, the pet ape of his own abductor. Back in the jungles of Africa, Korak freed a white girl named Meriem (played by Mae Giraci and as an adult by Manilla Martan) from her own captors, a horde of evil Arabs. Korak took the girl, in reality an heiress as were most silent serial heroines, to the jungle estate of his father, Lord Greystoke. There Korak and Tarzan protected Meriem from the nefarious Ivan Paulovich, who, in the tradition of the silents, wanted her inheritance for himself.

Son of Tarzan established a precedent for movie serials. Previously, there had been no pictorial retelling of earlier chapters, orienting the viewers who had not seen those installments as to the plot development. In *Son of Tarzan,* a pictorial recounting of the entire Tarzan legend preceded the first chapter's action. Producers immediately realized the potential in this technique created by director Harry Revier and continued it in future serials.

Numa Pictures returned to the Edgar Rice Burroughs character in 1921 with a fifteen-episode serial titled *Adventures of Tarzan.* It was what the studio considered to be the greatest Tarzan adventure ever made, including a prologue featuring Edgar Rice Burroughs himself, and starring Elmo Lincoln, the first actor to ever play the part, in *Tarzan of the Apes.* Lincoln, a huge man with an enormous barrel chest who made Tarzan's savagery believable when he howled the cry of the great apes, played the role with a fur jungle outfit draped over one shoulder, and an Indian-like band around his long black hair.

Advertising for *Adventures of Tarzan* boasted the return of Lincoln, plus a long list of other elements that would make this the most exciting screen version yet based on Burroughs' character:

"*Adventures of Tarzan* stars Elmo Lincoln, the greatest Tarzan of them all.

"It is a real wild animal serial—jammed with lions, leopards, apes, elephants, crocodiles, and other jungle beasts in scene after scene of excitement and thrill.

"Joe Martin, famous screen ape, plays a leading part.

"*Adventures of Tarzan* is censor-proof.

"Tarzan, plus Lincoln, plus wild animals, plus serial, gives you the record breaking State Right production of all time."

The story, filmed in California and, in part, in the desert regions of Arizona, was based on Burroughs's novel, *Tarzan and the Jewels of Opar*. The fabulous lost city of prehistoric men was ruled by the beautiful Queen La (played by Lillian Worth), who openly proclaimed her love for the Ape Man. But Tarzan was not the type to be untrue to his mate Jane (now played by leopard-attired Louise Lorraine) and rejected the tempting La, an act which resulted in many conflicts. During the chapters directed by Robert F. Hill, the plot was furthered by Tarzan's battles with Clayton (played by Percy Pembroke), in line for the Greystoke title and fortune, and Rukoff (played by Frank Whitson), a Bolshevik attempting to keep them away from Opar.

Tarzan of the Apes met perils of the spectacular variety in this serial. An erupting volcano and earthquake, sacrifice by superstitious natives of the Sun God, a boat plunging below the surface of the water, and attacking jungle cats were only some of the perils faced by Elmo Lincoln in *Adventures of Tarzan*. Though the most popular film Tarzan up until that time, Lincoln finally hung up his loin cloth, retired from the part of the Ape Man, yet continued acting in motion pictures.[1]

Tarzan's screen image was revamped for the 1928 Universal serial *Tarzan the Mighty*, loosely based on Burroughs' *Jungle Tales of Tarzan*. Gone was the Elmo Lincoln-type Tarzan that resembled a shaved ape who expanded to resemble a human balloon when he beat his chest and roared after each

[1] Elmo Lincoln starred in other silent serials, including three made by Universal Film Manufacturing Company: *Elmo the Mighty* (1919), *The Flaming Disk* (1920), and *Elmo the Fearless* (1920). In the first two, Lincoln was co-starred with Louise Lorraine, Jane of *Adventures of Tarzan*. In 1927, Lincoln did another jungle serial, *King of the Jungle* for Rayart. In this picture, he played a white hunter. Again, the perils of the silent serial days took effect when Gordon Standing, a friend of Lincoln, was killed by an angry lion in reality.

kill. The new Tarzan, the hero of this fifteen-installment chapterplay, was played by former champion gymnast Frank Merrill. He was a tall, perfectly muscled actor who replaced an injured Joe Bonomo, the original selection for the part. Merrill who doubled for Lincoln in *Adventures of Tarzan,* had been in *Perils of the Jungle,* a 1927 serial directed by Jack Nelson. Also directing—with Ray Taylor—*Tarzan the Mighty,* Nelson regarded Merrill as the logical replacement. Frank Merrill's Tarzan wore leopard skins, plus a leopard hide scalp band.

The Ape Man made friends with two castaways, the pretty Mary Trevor (played by brunette Natalie Kingston), a role substituted for Jane, and her brother Bobby (played by young Bobby Nelson). Lost races of various sorts were always turning up in Edgar Rice Burroughs' Tarzan novels. In *Tarzan the Mighty,* the lord of the jungle discovered a lost race of pirates who now lived like savages. Tarzan battled the pirates led by Black John (played by bearded Al Ferguson), using his own natural strength to pick the pirate up and hurl him through the air in one scene.

During the filming of *Tarzan the Mighty,* Frank Merrill, the second runner-up in the World's Most Perfectly Developed Man contest (to Charles Atlas, of course), actually perfected the art of swinging from tree to tree on long vines. Or to be exact, the vine was a disguised rope. His own strength allowed him to swing through the trees grasping his pretty co-star in one arm. Footage of Merrill soaring amidst the treetops was later studied by Metro-Goldwyn-Mayer executives for application to their upcoming feature of 1932, *Tarzan the Ape Man,* starring Johnny Weissmuller.

Black John later pretended to be a lost heir of Lord Greystoke, Tarzan's uncle. The scheming pirate's objective was to eventually marry Miss Trevor. The wedding was scheduled to take place in England. Suddenly, Tarzan appeared on European soil, saved the day, and took Mary as his wife. (Tarzan was not a bigamist in this serial. According to this story, Jane never existed. *Tarzan the Mighty* showed the progression of the Ape Man's origin, culminating with his marriage to a different woman.)

Tarzan the Mighty was a profitable serial; so much, in fact, that Universal made a sequel, *Tarzan the Tiger,* the following year. Frank Merrill again appeared as the Ape Man in this fifteen-chapter cliffhanger, following the direction of Henry MacRae, who would produce *Flash Gordon* for that studio seven years later. Jane was reinstated in the cast of the new Tarzan serial, portrayed by Natalie Kingston who married the Ape Man in the previous chapterplay under a different name. And Al Ferguson returned as the villain. This time he masqueraded as a prominent scientist who used his position to capture Jane and make her a product on the slave market.

Tarzan's African estate had been attacked by a horde of Arabs. The Ape Man went through two chapters trying to save his wife and estate. Then, in the third installment, he was struck on the head. The result was that durable plot device—amnesia. During the time in which he knew none of his friends—or enemies—Tarzan of the Apes was tied to a tree and used by spear-throwing natives for target practice, mauled by a hungry lion, was surrounded by attacking jungle savages, and rescued Jane from a lecherous gorilla and snapping crocodiles.

The serial was based on Burroughs' *Tarzan and the Jewels of Opar,* as had *Adventures of Tarzan.* Lillian Worth played Queen La of Opar, wearing scant and be-jeweled jungle attire. Again, she ruled over a primitive civilization, and possessed a hidden trove of treasure desired by the evil Ferguson.

In Chapter Thirteen, Tarzan was again struck on the head. And, in the tradition of all such second blows in motion pictures, his memory was miraculously restored. Now aware who he was and learning what had traversed for the past ten weeks, Tarzan devoted his full time in tracking down the villain, triumphing over him, saving Jane from a fate worse than death, and gaining possession of the Oparian jewels.

When Tarzan, the Ape Man, accomplished his mighty feats in the serial, audiences for the first time in cinema history actually got to hear him yell. Sound films were already the vogue by the time *Tarzan the Tiger* was released. Primarily a silent picture, this serial was issued simultaneously with and without sound. The talking version of the chapterplay was barely more than crudely dubbed music and audio effects, with a minimum of dialogue and the cry of the Ape Man so familiar to readers of Burroughs' novels. Frank Merrill did his own victory cry in *Tarzan the Tiger,* the only production ever to use his version of the yell.

Universal had planned to do a follow-up to *Tarzan the Tiger,* Edgar Rice Burroughs' *Tarzan the Terrible,* again with Merrill who was already wrongly known as "the original Tarzan." But Merrill suffered the fate of many silent film stars. His voice was not suited to the talkies. He retired from his movie career to work with children as an athletic director. *Tarzan the Terrible* was never filmed.

Sound films were, as Tarzan was with the M-G-M features, in full swing in the 1930s. With the complexities of legal contracts on his side, motion picture producer Sol Lesser had acquired the rights to make five Tarzan movies completely separated from the Weissmuller adventures of M-G-M.

Lesser's first venture into Tarzan's jungle was in 1933, in a twelve-part serial, *Tarzan the Fearless.* Casting the role of the jungle king was of immediate importance, since Lesser wanted to star an actor who could follow the image established by Weissmuller—an illiterate, monosyllabic tree-swinger relying on savage heroics, brute strength, and a zoo full of animal friends to survive the perils of the jungle. That same year Paramount had released a film which was a direct imitation of Tarzan. It was *King of the Jungle* and featured a Tarzan-type hero raised by lions in Africa. The character was Kaspa, the Lion Man. He was portrayed by Olympic swimming champion Buster Crabbe.

Crabbe seemed the most logical choice for the new Tarzan serial. His athletic career corresponded closely to that of Weissmuller. He had a powerful physique and was perfectly capable of enacting the heroics necessary for a movie Tarzan.

Tarzan the Fearless was scripted by Basil Dickey and George Plympton, who went on to write many serials for Universal, Columbia, and Republic. It was directed by another veteran, Robert F. Hill.

Lesser's Tarzan chapterplay was scheduled for a rather unique type of release. It was issued as both a feature-length film and a serial, simultaneously. The feature ran a total of seventy-one minutes. The serial had an hour-long first installment, virtually a film by itself. The chapterplay was designed so that eight episodes could follow the feature version with barely a break in continuity.

In the serial, Jane had again been ignored. The female lead who would eventually fall under the savage glance of fearless, leopard-clad Tarzan was blond Mary Brooks (Jacqueline Wells), who was looking for her missing father, Dr. Brooks (E. Alyn Warren), who had, like many fathers of lovely girls, gotten lost in the African jungle. During her search, Mary was captured by another lost race, worshippers of Zar, the god of the Emerald Fingers (an idol that seemed to have been borrowed from the the Universal horror feature of 1932, *The Mummy*). Leading the jungle cult was the expected high priest (played by pop-eyed Mischa Auer). Aiding the unnamed high priest was his assistant Abdul (Frank Lackteen), and Nick (Matthew Betz) and Jeff (Philo McCullough), two crooked jungle guides. To capitalize on the M-G-M Tarzans, Lesser included Cheetah the chimpanzee in his cast.

Through the dozen installments, Tarzan encountered such

perils as a charging rhinoceros, a snarling gorilla that sought to attack him and Mary Brooks, the hungry appetites of cannibals, and a death fall through space. He still had time to save Mary, find her father, and defeat the savage religious fanatics and their white cohorts.

This Tarzan spoke even less than Weissmuller's. He did barely more than smack his chest, say "Unngghh!" or point to a picture of an elephant in a book and tell Mary, "Tantor!" When he yelled, it was not his own victory cry, but one cribbed from the Tarzan radio serial, in which former movie Ape Man James Pierce did the screaming.

Tarzan the Fearless was Lesser's first attempt at making a Tarzan film. Despite Crabbe's tremendous athletic prowess, wherein he rode elephants, was carried off to safety in Tantor's coiling trunk, swung from vine to vine high above the ground, and saved the girl from stampeding animals, the serial was extremely crude. Almost devoid of music, it was later given a score taken from old Westerns; good action music, but hardly appropriate for a jungle chapterplay. Before this addition, *minutes* passed with views of distant animals and no music, no sound effects, no dialogue, no sound whatsoever. It was about the most silent "talkie" ever made.

For Buster Crabbe, *Tarzan the Fearless* was the end of his association with the Ape Man. It was his third major film, but the beginning of a career that would take him to outer space, the Old West, the big city of gangsters, and even back to the jungle in almost one hundred films and serials. He would one day be identified as the dashing heroes of several worlds, Flash Gordon and Buck Rogers, and eventually return to sports as athletic director for a resort hotel.

For Sol Lesser, the serial was the beginning of a long association with the Ape Man. The producer would never make another Tarzan serial, but would number a lengthy list of feature length movies about the character, running through the late 1950s.

Edgar Rice Burroughs himself, seeing the money made by other producers in filming the exploits of his jungle lord, turned to films in 1935. The author had been approached by George W. Stout, Aston Dearholt, and Ben S. Cohen who had proposed forming a company to mostly film Burroughs' stories. He accepted the offer, and the newly formed Burroughs-Tarzan Enterprises proceeded to make a serial. It was *The New Adventures of Tarzan,* and was based on a story hastily written by Burroughs called *Tarzan and The Green Goddess.*

The New Adventures of Tarzan, a serial with twelve installments, went the route of *Tarzan the Fearless* in regards release. Only while the Buster Crabbe serial had two forms, the new chapterplay would have three. It could be booked as a seven-reel full-length movie, a complete serial with twelve episodes, or the feature with a following of seven installments.

There was more confusion, however, in the very casting and conception of the Tarzan character. Audiences now had yet another Ape Man to somehow place with his predecessors, and he was the most "different" talking Tarzan yet to swing across the screen.

This latest of Tarzans was selected by Burroughs himself. He was an actor by the name of Herman Brix, a champion Olympic shotputter in 1928, and one of the actors originally considered for the lead in the 1932 *Tarzan the Ape Man* from M-G-M. Brix was a tall athlete with a slim yet perfect build, capable of appearing the way Burroughs envisioned Tarzan. But there was yet another difference in this Tarzan. Since Burroughs was finally personally involved with the production of a Tarzan film, he wanted to make the character think and behave —including speech—the way he intended. Brix's Ape Man would not grunt and use the "Me Tarzan, you Jane" dialogue popularized by Weissmuller. Tarzan in his new adventures would be cultured and speaking complex and compound sentences befitting an English nobleman. Some of Brix's scenes in *The New*

Adventures of Tarzan had him walking through the city fully dressed. One scene aboard a ship even allowed him to wear a dinner jacket, black bow tie, tailored pants, and black shoes. But in the jungle, clad in a loincloth, Tarzan was the savage fighter with which his movie fans had become accustomed. To further give authenticity to Tarzan, Burroughs rejected the name Cheetah and gave the little ape the name Nkima, which was that of the chimpanzee in his novels. Surprisingly, Jane was omitted from the story.

The New Adventures of Tarzan was filmed in the jungles of Guatemala. The location, plus footage of the natives, gave the serial authenticity—and a terrible sound track, actually apologized for in the credits. No apology is needed now. For TV, it has been redubbed by a modern cast as in foreign films. More important, Brix's portrayal of the Ape Man was the most realistic of all actors to that date to take on the role. In one chapter, Tarzan was tied to a post. He escaped by expanding his muscles with terrible strain until his bulging sinews gradually pulled the ropes apart. The feat was believable because Herman Brix actually did free himself with his own strength. For such reasons, and the fact that he was portrayed as Burroughs wrote about him, many Tarzan fans favor Brix's version above all others, bar none.

The story showed Tarzan going away from his jungle estate to locate a missing friend taken from the Burroughs books, D'Arnot. His search took the Ape Man to savage Guatemala. Meanwhile, Alice Martling (Dale Walsh) and her father (Frank Baker) had been looking for a stone idol—the Green Goddess—which contained the secret for a high explosive. There was also the matter of a lost Mayan treasure that whetted their fancy. D'Arnot had been captured and imprisoned, coincidentally, in the lost city which was also the home of the legendary Green Goddess. Tarzan, who had met Alice and her father, accompanied them to the lost city, where they saved D'Arnot. But the Green Goddess had been stolen by a scoundrel named Raglan (Ashton Dearholt). Tarzan stalked the villain through jungle and city until he was able to get back the idol, restore peace to the wilds of Guatemala, and return with his new friends to his luxurious African estate.

Herman Brix fought many dangerous creatures in *The New Adventures of Tarzan,* both animal and human. He was attacked by natives out for vengenace because their idol had been stolen, and by the civilized man who stole it. And he was caught in the spike of a tiger trap; almost sacrificed to the Green Goddess; attacked by a lion that he wrestled armed only with a knife, which, needless to mention, found its place beneath the feline's golden hide, and hurled over a gushing waterfall. Brix never made another Tarzan film. Later changing his name to Bruce Bennett, which had a nicer sound and more box office appeal than Herman Brix, the actor continued performing in serials and features, and still appears on TV looking 30 years younger than his true age.

The New Adventures of Tarzan was the last serial made to use the character. The Ape Man had swung out of Burroughs' novels and onto the silent screens. And when the movies gained a voice, Tarzan gained his yell. He had retired from the serial screen, but swung through feature length movies and television episodes. But even though the name "Tarzan" never again appeared in a cliffhanger title, other characters wearing loincloths and braving the perils of the jungle made us think that perhaps the Ape Man was still with us on a weekly basis.

MORE LORDS OF THE JUNGLE

Jan, the jungle boy, was a junior version of Tarzan of the Apes in Universal's 1935 serial, *Call of the Savage.* The chapterplay was based on a novel, *Jan of the Jungle,* written by

Burroughs' acknowledged literary rival, Otis Adelbert Kline, and published in a 1931 issue of *Argosy*. Since Jan was a successful competitor to Tarzan on the printed page, it was only logical that he'd give the Ape Man some more friction by appearing on the screen.

In the first chapter of *Call of the Savage,* an American company called the Carnafellow Foundation believed that the cure to infantile paralysis existed in the jungles of Africa. Two American specialists, Dr. Trevor and his assistant Carl, concerned with the boon to mankind resulting from such a discovery, were stationed by the company in the dark continent. Their two colleagues, Bracken and Phillips, however, were not quite as humanitarian as they were, and only wanted the half-million-dollar reward offered for the cure. In the jungle, Trevor discovered the cure. But aware of the schemings of Bracken and Phillips, the doctor wrote half the formula on a piece of parchment, and engraved the second half on a wrist band which he attached to his young son, Jan. During the night, tragedy occurred. The experimental test animals broke out of their cages, smashing everyone and everything, including Dr. Trevor's wife. During the confusion, Jan and his pet chimpanzee Chicma fled to the jungle. Trevor, still alive, went in search of the boy. Also saved from death were the two scoundrels, Bracken and Phillips.

Fifteen years later, the two crooks who had been relaxing in the United States, heard that Dr. Trevor had appeared in the home of a trader in Africa named Andrews. Trevor had lost his memory and would be fair game for the two villains. Returning to Africa, they immediately sought Andrews and the doctor.

Meanwhile, Jan, now grown to young manhood and capable of battling jungle beasts with the skill of the Ape Man himself, and his chimpanzee friend were captured by the crew of a tramp steamer, where he met a young girl named Mona, coincidentally claiming to be the daughter of Andrews. Disaster struck as the ship was tossed violently by a raging storm. In the conflict, Jan was befriended by a mysterious sailor named Borno. Suddenly the boiler room exploded, and Jan and his new friends were apparently killed.

They escaped the following week when a second explosion threw them into the water, clear of the danger.

The jungle has always been a breeding ground for perils. Jan of the Jungle was captured by cannibals when a split tree branch dropped him right before their salivating jaws. He was required to fight a man-eating lion when Mona clumsily fell into a trap set for the beast. He was shot from a tree and left for dead. And Mona was menaced by a grinning (and obviously phony) gorilla and a river filled with approaching crocodiles.

In the twelfth and final chapter, "The Pit of Flame," Jan, Mona, Andrews, and Dr. Trevor were prisoners in the legendary city of Mu. Escaping from their prison, they were nearly incinerated by fire issuing from a pit, a trap which killed the villains Bracken and Phillips. Borno, Jan's mysterious friend, now revealed as a former resident of Mu, convinced the lost city's emperor that Mona was actually his missing daughter. For that reason, orders were given to turn off the flames. The last chapter faded out with Jan and Mona remaining together in the lost city of Mu.

Call of the Savage was a popular serial, though not using the real Tarzan character. Jan was played by a very young Noah Beery, Jr., who continued acting in serials and feature length films for decades.

A far better serial than *Call of the Savage* capitalizing on Tarzan was made by Republic Pictures in 1938. It was *Hawk of the Wilderness,* and like the chapterplay adventures of Jan, was based on a novel of the same name by yet another Burroughs imitator, William L. Chester. The book, *Hawk of the Wilderness,* was serialized in *Blue Book* magazine in 1936. Africa was not the locale of this Tarzan-like adventure. Chester changed the setting to a lost island, north of the Bering Strait, ruled by a hero much in the likeness of the Ape Man. He was Kioga, the white son of a shipwrecked husband wife team of explorers, and raised to manhood by the animals and a primitive tribe of Indians.

Kioga, wearing long pants, moccasins, and a headband, was portrayed in the twelve-chapter serial by former movie Tarzan, Herman Brix. His portrayal of Kioga equaled his performance as the Ape Man. And since *Hawk of the Wilderness* was directed by two of the best serial directors in the business, William Witney and John English, his acting was enhanced by a better production than *The New Adventures of Tarzan.*

Many years after Kioga was raised by the Indians of the island, the small body of land was discovered by Dr. Munro (Tom Chatterton), one-time friend of Kioga's father Lincoln Rand, and his daughter Beth (Jill Martin) and other explorers. On the island, the group discovered the grown-up Kioga—and also a fantastic treasure.

The island held many perils for the explorers, including an attacking tiger, a crushing avalanche, and hostile Indians. Kioga heroically rescued them again and again.

A bit of racism entered the plot when the explorers were captured by the Indians and tied to a stake. The savages fearfully marveled at one of the members of the party, a Negro named George (played by "Snowflake" in the days when such derogatory names were "in"), since black skin was something they had never viewed before. One of the party used this as an opportunity of escape. "If you don't free us," he warned the redman, "we'll turn your skin black, too!"

The last chapter, "Trails End," was one of the most action-jammed final episodes in the history of serials. The Indians were attacking. A group of pirate cutthroats, after the explorers and the treasure, engaged the Indians in a battle to the death. The explorers were being menaced by a strange wolf-headed villain. Over all of this action, the volcano was erupting and blasting the island apart. As the Indians and pirates finished each other off, the explorers learned that their escape plane was not large enough to take them all away from the doomed island. Then one of the party showed his true WASP colors by refusing to take Kias (played by Mala), Kioga's Indian friend, with them because of his "ethnic inferiority." While the island was cracked by earthquake and melted by lava, Kioga rushed the others into their airplane, which flew away from the island before it was completely destroyed, soaring with a treasure of diamonds toward Alaska.

Hawk of the Wilderness was a great serial, one of the best to be made by Republic Pictures. Although most hard-core Republic devotees scoff at the chapterplay for its lack of stamped-out automobile chases and carbon copy fist fights, the serial featured some of the studio's finest action. It was photographed by William Nobles against a gorgeous setting of untarnished mountains and unpolluted forests. The serial screamed with the grandeur of nature at her finest. For Herman Brix, who swung through the trees of the island wilderness, it was his finest contribution to the cliffhangers.

Another former serial Tarzan, the one and only Buster Crabbe, returned in a loincloth to fight wild animals with his bare hands in 1952 for Columbia's jungle chapterplay of fifteen episodes, *King of the Kongo*. Though two decades had elapsed since he played Tarzan, Crabbe's superb physical appearance made his wrestling with the jungle cats as believable in the 1950s as in the 1930s. His face was a trifle lined after the years, but not enough to make a difference—and not enough to conflict with his mighty physique.

Buster Crabbe played Thunda, a Tarzan-like jungle man in *King of the Kongo*. Thunda was really Captain Roger Drum of the United States Air Force, bound for Africa to expose a group of subversives. His plane crashed in the jungle in the first episode, "Mission of Menace," where he was rescued by a primitive band of rock people, led by the sexy jungle woman Pha (Gloria Dea).

King of the Congo was based on a Thunda comic book drawn by Frank Frazetta, a critically acclaimed artist now associated with the Ace Books paperback editions of Tarzan novels. In the comic book, the jungle lord cavorted in a prehistoric land, complete with gigantic dinosaurs. In the serial, with a limited budget, Thunda was given only the usual menaces to handle. With a producer like Sam Katzman, the serial, directed by Spencer G. Bennet and Wallace A. Grissell, was given less, with barely more extravagancies than a studio jungle set, prefabricated ancient temple, and a number of "wild" animals.

Drum had been taken to the temple by Pha. Suddenly, the subversives appeared, led by a villain named Boris (Leonard Penn). The primitives immediately sounded the temple gong, clanging the alarm. But the ancient temple crumbled at the powerful vibrations of sound, burying Captain Drum alive.

With the prowess of Flash Gordon and Tarzan, Captain Drum emerged alive from the debris. The natives, amazed by his stamina and strength, named him Thunda, the King of the Congo. Thunda had become their champion, and he used his superb physical shape to fight off a tribe of prehistoric cavemen armed with crude weapons of the past, to save Pha from a herd of stampeding animals, and perform other tasks of jungle valor. Thunda himself was attacked by a full-grown gorilla, thrown into a pool of quicksand, hung upside down from a tree and left for leopard bait, and run down by a truck loaded with ammunition.

In the fourteenth episode, "Savage Vengeance," the mighty Thunda was about to be beheaded by the cavemen. Tied, unable to move, he watched the descent of the primitive ax. The following week, the hatchet sliced through the jungle man's bonds, and he escaped. After some furious action in which subversives were bombed to splattering deaths, and Boris was chewed up by the jungle beasts, Thunda united the cavemen and the rock tribe, bringing peace to the jungle.

King of the Kongo was the last serial to be made featuring an imitation Tarzan. It was also the last cliffhanger to star the King of the Chapterplays, Buster Crabbe. The athletic star continued performing in action features. And despite his age, he maintained the image of the hero. Even in his films of the 1960s, Buster Crabbe looked like he could strangle a lion with his bare hands.

THE GREAT WHITE HUNTERS

Serial heroes like Jungle Jim and Congo Bill proved that you didn't have to be raised by the Apes to battle the terrors of half-starved animals and bloodthirsty savages. The great white hunters and safari guides only had to squint their eyes beneath the brims of their pith helmets and fire a few rifle shots over the heads of the superstitious natives until they hollered "Bwana!"

Universal's *Jungle Jim* was a twelve-episode serial made in 1937. It was based on King Features' newspaper strip, written and drawn by Alex Raymond, the great craftsman who also created *Flash Gordon*.

The chapterplay starred Grant Withers as Jungle Jim, with his female admirer from the comic strip, Shanghai Lil, played by Evelyn Brent. His native friend Kolu was played by Al Duralle.

"Into the Lion's Den," the first episode of *Jungle Jim,* began with a safari of villains, led by Bruce Redmond (Bryant Washburn) and his henchman Slade (Al Bridge), who were in the jungle to locate another strange white jungle girl supposedly heir to a large fortune. She was the Lion Goddess, the ruler of another tribe of primitives, and hopefully heir Joan Redmond.

Jungle Jim, however, was trekking through the flora with his own safari. He wanted to locate the heiress so that she could rightfully claim what was hers, and to take revenge on Redmond and Slade who had murdered one of his friends. The two safaris encountered the natives ruled by the Lion Goddess, who attacked the white intruders. Suddenly, the beauteous Lion Goddess appeared and commanded her feline subjects to strike at the invaders. Jungle Jim was attacked by an obedient lion and forced into a pit at the mercy of the beast.

Only a change of heart on the part of the Lion Goddess saved Jungle Jim from death by fang and claw.

Later, the Lion Goddess—Joan Redmond—sentenced Jim to die for killing one of her beloved cats. The method of execution was consistent with Joan's jungle role. She released another of her cats, this time a tiger of which Jim made short work. This act of valor surprisingly had the opposite effect on the jungle queen. Now she admired Jungle Jim enough to grant him freedom.

In the eleventh installment, "In the Cobra's Coils," the archfiend known as the Cobra (played with demoniac fervor by Henry Brandon) joined forces with Slade. The Cobra trapped Jungle Jim and his partner, Malay Mike (played by the perennial "old-timer" sidekick, Raymond Hatton) and ordered his men to spear the two to death. They were saved by Joan in the concluding episode, "The Last Safari," who commanded the native assassins to stop. The Cobra then made an effort to escape in his plane. Jungle Jim rushed after the villain, hanging on the craft's tail. While the airplane rose into the sky, Jungle Jim made his way into the cockpit, where he threatened the Cobra at gunpoint. With the situation under Jim's control, the Cobra could do nothing save obey. He landed the plane safely and realized that he would soon be jailed. Jungle Jim and Joan Redmond then left for the United States, presumably to be married.

Jungle Jim was directed by Ford Beebe, who also handled

the screen's *Flash Gordon,* and by Cliff Smith. The hero fared
well in his dozen episodes—better than Congo Bill did in 1948.

Congo Bill was another Sam Katzman production for Columbia, directed by Spencer Bennet and Thomas Carr. Katzman
brought a number of comic book heroes to the serial screen,
always with the same "quickie" and inexpensive results. He
seemed to get the best characters—including Superman and
Batman—and do the worst with them.

The chapterplay was based on an adventure strip beginning
in the early 1940s, in National's *Action Comics,* created by
executive editor, Whitney Ellsworth. Congo Bill strongly resembled Alex Raymond's creation, with a name lacking any
originality. (It could have been worse. He might have been
given the alliterative name of Congo Connie.)

Congo Bill had a total of fifteen chapters to act in the serial.
In the first episode, "The Untamed Beast," we again were given
the standard plot of the typical jungle chapterplay. A trust fund
held a half million dollars for any surviving heir of Les Culver,
original founder of the Culver Circus. Ruth, Culver's daughter,
was lost in the jungle as a baby. According to the terms of the
trust fund, two scoundrels Tom (Stephen Carr) and Bernie
MacGraw (I. Stanford Jolley) would receive the money unless
a real heir showed up within the year. Meanwhile, Tom had
learned of—yes—*another* strange white jungle goddess in Africa
who might be Ruth Culver. Bernie, sure that she is Ruth, apparently because he'd seen a number of jungle serials, and fear-
ing that Tom would try to locate the girl, clubbed him and placed
him near the cage of a killer gorilla. Congo Bill (played by a
mustached Don McGuire) saw what had transpired and rushed
to the rescue, only to be attacked by two thugs. In the next episode, "Jungle Gold," Congo Bill managed to revive and rescue
Tom MacGraw from the snorting ape.

The cliffhangers in *Congo Bill* were mild compared to some
of those faced by Tarzan, Kioga, and even Jungle Jim. A boul-

der was rolled down on him, he was shot, and stabbed. Some imagination went into the climax of Chapter Eight, "Sinister Schemes," wherein a device with revolving blades was lowered toward his reclining frame.

In the last chapter, "The Missing Letter," Congo Bill overpowered the villains and rescued jungle girl Lureen (played by blond and buxom Cleo Moore). Together, they left for America where his skill with training wild animals—and her money—would make the greatest circus of them all.

7

The Aviators "Land That Plane at Once, You Crazy Fool!"

"SPIN THE PROP, PARTNER."

The heroic exploits of pilots, zooming off on secret missions and engaging enemy aircraft in ear-shattering dogfights, have always fascinated kids. The thrills of flying were incorporated into virtually all serials whose setting did not predate the invention of the airplane. Many sound chapterplays, in fact, were devoted primarily to the courageous pilots whose planes roared through the skies with double or single wings so that villains might be thwarted and justice restored to the land.

Mystery Squadron, a 1933 Mascot serial in twelve episodes, starred two actors identified on the screen, not with flying, but with riding horses and shooting outlaws. Short, curly-haired Bob Steele, and the contrasting giant, Guinn "Big Boy" Williams. Together, using the old formula of opposites making a commercially acceptable team (like the thin Stan Laurel or Bud Abbott with the rotund Oliver Hardy or Lou Costello), the two left their Western gear and secured flier's outfits from the studio wardrobe department.

Directed by Colbert Clark and David Howard, *Mystery Squadron* introduced stunt fliers Fred Cromwell (Bob Steele) and Bill Cook ("Big Boy" Williams). The two daredevils were hired to guard a large dam, which had been used as a target by a mysterious airplane that had repeatedly shown up and then vanished into the sky. As the duo watched for the arrival of the plane, they were surprised to see a miniature craft fly into the area, bringing a message. The Mystery Squadron, the message warned, had been toying with them long enough and would soon give an all-out attack on the dam. Things looked gloomy. And to make matters worse, Fred and Bill's flying skills made them appear to be working for the Mystery Squadron. The workmen laboring at the damsite immediately went into action by a form of justice that seemed to suit the occasion—they wanted to lynch the two flyboys. Escaping from the angry mob, Fred and Bill decided that they must find and defeat the Mystery Squadron singlehanded, relying only on their fists and their ability to fly planes better than anyone else.

After many instances of near death, Fred and Bill finally tracked down the sinister Black Ace, the leader of Mystery Squadron. Fred was held at rifle-point by members of the Mystery Squadron, decked out in silvery flight togs and aviator's caps. Then he was confronted by the Black Ace himself, who wore similar garb except for a black flight cap. Fred finally got the opportunity to unmask the fiend. His face nearly shattered with surprise to learn that the Black Ace was not one of Mascot Pictures' usual stock company of mastermind villains, but perennial hero Jack Mulhall! With the knowledge of the Black Ace's true identity, Fred and Bill defeated the Mystery Squadron and proved their innocence.

By 1936, the formula for the air story of the thirties had been finalized by many serials, feature films like *Hell's Angels,* books, pulp magazines, comic strips, and radio programs.

The *Tailspin Tommy* newspaper strip by Hal Forrest and the *Jimmie Allen* radio series seemed to be mutually inspired by one another. The same things were always happening in both. (Jimmie Allen was the main character of a better-than-B feature from Paramount, *Sky Parade,* but never made it into a serial. Interestingly, Grant Withers played the boy aviator's sidekick both in this film and the *Tommy* serials.)

The movie serial of *Tailspin Tommy* followed earlier events in the Allen radio show with amazing fidelity.

In the aptly named town of Littleville, Tommy Tompkins (Maurice Murphy) worked as a garage mechanic but dreamed of a life in aviation. His friends were fellow mechanic Skeeter Mulligan (Noah Beery, Jr.) and Betty Lou Barnes (Patricia Farr) who ran a cafe at the airport at Three Point. The teenager's life was changed by the dramatic appearance of dashing Milt Howe (Grant Withers) who made a crash landing at the airport, during a competition flight for an important mail contract for the Three Point Airline, run by Paul Smith (Charles Browne). Their competition was Taggart Airlines, owned by ruthless "Tiger" Taggart (oily John Davidson) who had the secret help of the apparently sympathetic Bruce Hoyt (silent serial hero, Walter Miller, fallen onto evil days).

Unknowingly, Smith sent the treacherous Hoyt to replace the injured Howe in the vital race. Deliberately, Hoyt stalled for time. Disgusted, Howe decided to get the plane through, despite the small matter of having a broken arm. (Someone—at least the audience—must have gasped: "The crazy fool! He'll never make it!") Sure enough, Howe never made it. During a storm, the pilot was thrown against the side of the plane and knocked out. Fortunately, he had taken mechanic Tommy Tompkins along with him to work the throttle. Even though the plane had slipped into a deadly tailspin, the boy managed to get the older pilot off the controls and to pull the ship out in the nick of time. As the story was repeated, so grew the fame of "Tailspin Tommy."

As a reward for his heroic intervention, Tommy was given a job as mechanic with Three Point Airlines, and Skeeter (who had stowed away on that perilous flight) was made his assistant. The airline pilots gave the eager teen-ager lessons in flying.

Later, after several dangerous experiences in the air, Tommy took over for a grounded pilot to fly the Atlas Mine payroll through. Taggart, embittered over losing the mail contract to the rival Three Point lines, determined to destroy his competition and sent out a ship to shoot down Tommy's craft. The boy and the inevitable girl stowaway, Betty Lou, bailed out of the damaged plane before the crash, and on the ground, engaged in a battle of wits to keep the crooks from stealing the payroll from the wrecked plane. They held out until Milt Howe arrived on the scene.

As the chapterplay unfolded, other sequences involved Tommy flying Skeeter through to Denver for a critical operation after the young mechanic's eyes had been burned by exploding oil; Tommy and Milt Howe, rescuing another pilot, Speed Walton (Edmund Cobb, usually a villain in other roles) and a shipment of gems, both captured by Taggart men; and a big national air race in Los Angeles.

During the race, Taggart, out to ruin Three Point and collect on his bets, made several attempts on the life of Tommy, who of course was racing for Three Point. In the most spectacular attempt, the double-dealing Hoyt took off at the controls of a ship Tommy was pumping gas into, dragging the boy up in the air with the ship, leaving him dangling from the fuel hose he was desperately hanging on to. Skeeter, now recovered from his injury, took off in another ship and flew under the plane from which Tommy dangled, just as the hose broke, sending Tommy hurtling through the air, but only to land on Skeeter's ship a few feet below.

Although the Three Point crew was beginning to get just a wee bit suspicious of Bruce Hoyt, Betty attempted to prove her suspicions, and got herself kidnapped for her trouble. Tommy and Skeeter managed to trail her to the Shoreham Hotel and rescue her, just before a disastrous earthquake destroyed the hotel and much of the resort town.

By this time Tommy's heroic actions had brought him to the attention of movie producer Arthur Grant (Bryant Washburn).

Grant put Tommy to work in an air epic on the scale of *Hell's Angels*.

The producer entered in partnership with Three Points Airlines owner Smith to get the money to complete the film. Smith mortgaged his airline to back the project (naturally, he had faith in Tommy Tompkins as a movie star as well as a pilot). As always, the scheming Taggart was in the background; it was *his* representative who bought the vital mortgage on the Three Points line. Taggart's next move was to see that the movie production company went broke, so he would gain control of the mortgaged airline. (It was fairly complicated finance for kids to follow on a Saturday afternoon.) With the ever-willing Hoyt, he arranged for the double-crossing pilot to bomb an expensive set prematurely, so that the explosion would not be filmed and the cost of the set lost. Betty, still suspicious of Hoyt, overheard the plan and warned Tommy, so that he flew behind Hoyt and successfully photographed the bombing of the set so that the money was not lost. (Apparently, these producers had never heard of the *miniatures* actually used in the serial footage.)

The exposed Hoyt panicked. In an attempt to escape Tommy, Hoyt went into a fatal tailspin and was killed.

His problems never seemingly over, Tommy had to crash his plane on the tracks ahead of a train carrying his mother among other passengers headed for their doom on a flooded-out bridge. Finally, Tommy was able to turn the confession of Taggart's business and his henchmen tried to escape the pursuing Los Angeles police in a furious car chase. But the crooks wound up in a flaming crash that claimed their lives as they had so often tried to take the life of Tailspin Tommy.

Following this first serial directed by Louis Friedlander, Universal offered a 1936 sequel called *Tailspin Tommy in the Great Air Mystery*. The second photoplay was directed by Ray Taylor, and brought back Noah Beery, Jr. as Skeeter and Grant Withers as Milt Howe, but presented a new, more mature

Tommy—Clark Williams—and a sexier Betty Lou—Jean Rogers. Withers' role was severely reduced (as was his billing) since he was the mysterious Eagle who piloted a sometimes *invisible* plane, although his mysterious origin was not revealed until the closing chapters. The first serial had made a number of attempts at "realism" (in *serial* terms) but the second was more typical of the hokum of the medium.

In one especially interesting chapter Tommy and Skeeter were streaking through the stratosphere in a stolen enemy bomber when suddenly Skeeter got conked by a flying monkey wrench, tossed through the air by friend McGuire who was in an airship piloted by Betty. The girl was skillfully maneuvering her ship near Tommy's bomber and . . .

EXT. BOMBER COCKPIT—NIGHT—MED. TWO SHOT—TOMMY, SKEETER
> *as* MC GUIRE's *hand-thrown monkey wrench crashes through the cockpit window and strikes* SKEETER *on the shoulder.* SKEETER *reacts with sudden surprise.*

SKEETER: That guy McGuire's gone batty!
> *Then he sees there's a note wrapped around the wrench.*

MED. SHOT—SKEETER
> *as he picks up the wrench, unties the note and reads it. He reacts to the note's alarming message.*

SKEETER (*yelling to* TOMMY): There's a time bomb on this ship! We've got two minutes to bail out!

BACK TO MED. TWO SHOT—TOMMY, SKEETER
> *as* TOMMY *replies.*

TOMMY (*casually*): Go to it, Skeeter.
SKEETER: But what about you?
TOMMY: Get out first—I'll follow you! Jump!
> SKEETER *leaps out of the bomber. As soon as he clears the wings* TOMMY *leaps out after him.*

EXT. NIGHT SKY—FULL SHOT
> *Their parachutes open and they float down to the dark ground. A bit later there's a deafening roar and the blind-*

*ing flash of light as the time bomb explodes and rends the
giant bomber into a thousand pieces.*

Tommy and Skeeter rode the high winds safely back down
to Earth of course, thanks to the timely intervention of Betty
and McGuire, then went on to more rather typical serial stunts
as they attempted to save Don Alvarado Casmetto (Pablo Al-
verex) and his daughter Inez (Delphine Drew) from the designs on their wealth drawn by the Don's renegade half brother
Manuel (Herbert Haywood). They encountered such dangers
as the crash of giant Dirigible 76; a series of explosions; and
a repetitive number of airplane crashes. However, the serial
was well made, with some of the more-or-less "adult" story and
production values Universal supplied in their serials.

CAPTAIN EDDIE'S BOY

Ace Drummond, a serial of thirteen episodes made by Universal in 1936, was based on the King Features comic strip of
the same title created during the 1930s by real life flying ace,
Captain Eddie Rickenbacker. The legendary World War I pilot
who had soared through the sky establishing his own transcontinental speed record two years before the serial was made,
had based the strip on his own action-filled life. Therefore, the
Ace Drummond movie serial might be interpreted as an exaggerated dramatization of Rickenbacker himself, had the flier
ever encountered the many threats and science fictional elements written into the script. Rickenbacker even appeared in
an iris shot in the credits, smiling and nodding.

The chapterplay dealt with the attempts of several countries
to form a world-wide Clipper Ship air service. In Mongolia,
however, a murderous organization, led by a sinister mastermind known only as the Dragon, tried to destroy the final link

in the project. It was the mission of the heroic pilot Ace Drummond to stop the dangerous Dragon.

In the role of Ace Drummond was a former singer with Ben Bernie's band, John King (later to star in Western movies as "Dusty" King). The actor was suitably cast as the flying hero, and was also commissioned to sing *Give Me a Ship and a Song,* the serial's theme, at the opening of each episode. Ace's girl friend, Peggy Trainer, was played by lovely Jean Rogers, who was no novice to the art of movie flying. That same year she had starred in *Tailspin Tommy,* and in that studio's *Flash Gordon,* where, as Dale Arden, she rocketed through space to the planet Mongo. A youthful Lon Chaney, Jr., was cast as Ivan, a typical hired crook.

In the first episode, "Where East Meets West," Ace Drummond was investigating the destruction of airplanes by mysterious forces, including supercharges of electricity. To avoid being shot down by one of the Dragon's ships, Ace bailed out. Then he was captured by the nefarious Dr. Bauer (Fredrik Vogeding), who had been holding Peggy Trainer hostage. But the dynamic hero escaped with the girl in a plane. During their flight to freedom, an antiaircraft gun blasted the ship, forcing it to plummet downward and smash into the wall of a Buddhist temple.

That crack-up was but the first serial hazard to be faced in the serial by Ace Drummond. In trying to find the Dragon, the hero engaged in a furious dogfight ordered by the fiend. Ace's plane caught fire, apparently roasting him alive. This cliffhanger, culminating Chapter Two, "Invisible Enemy," had the distinction of being witnessed by another flier, Amelia Earhart Putnam. Hearing that Rickenbacker's character was about to be filmed in the action of serial combat, she took a drive out to the San Fernando Valley in California where that sequence of the serial was being shot. It gave the actors an ego boost and helped the studio publicize the serial. This was "hot copy" when a real life flier visited the set of a film character created by another real life flier.

In the fourth installment, "The Radio Riddle," Ace Drummond was the victim of an air attack. He had been pursuing Peggy's father (played by distinguished character actor, Montague Shaw) in his car. The enemy planes swooped down toward their speeding target and blasted it apart with their bombs. The following week it was shown that Ace, only slightly injured, was pulled from the wreckage by his friends Jerry (Noah Beery, Jr.) and Billy Meredith (Jackie Morrow).

"The Sign in the Sky" had Ace Drummond attempting to rescue a Clipper plane which was about to be destroyed in midair by the Dragon's powerful deathray weapon. Ace tried warning it by broadcasting his voice over a radio. Suddenly the heroic pilot was blasted by an electric flash which shot from the radio board. He fell to the floor . . . Dead?

No, Ace was only stunned, and the Clipper ship was saved before the deathray could do its damage.

Kai-Chek (Chester Gan) was rescued by Ace from the sadistic death of a collapsing room of a monastery. In return, the Oriental informed Ace that the Dragon was going to destroy the airport from the sky. In an attempt to prevent the disaster, Ace Drummond took off in his plane, but was shot down by the Dragon at the end of Chapter Twelve, "Squadron of Death."

Ace Drummond emerged with only a few scratches from the crashed plane in the last installment, "The World Akin," with a luck possessed only by chapterplay heroes. While Jerry proceeded to blow up the Dragon's squadron of doom, Ace chased the master criminal to the monastery from which he had saved Kai-Chek. Ace proved that he could aim a gun as well as he could pilot a plane and shot the Dragon's weapon out of his hand. Unmasking the fiend, Ace learned that the Dragon was really Chang-Ho (Arthur Loft), a Chinese who had been believed to be on the side of the law, and who had even been the "victim" of his own poison gas to avoid suspicion. In a last effort to escape, the unmasked villain stole Ace's plane, but crashed instead, ending his evil influence, and allowing for the success of the world system of Clipper planes.

All of the chapters of *Ace Drummond* were introduced by recap titles in the form of comic strips, to re-create the feeling of the medium from which the serial was adapted. This was new to Universal. The studio then used similar gimmicks in their succeeding serials.[1]

Ace Drummond left the serials and returned to the pages of the funny papers. But there were other daring pilots that would make exciting chapterplay heroes waiting in the hangars.

Another famous aviation strip was *Smilin' Jack,* written and drawn by another real life pilot, Zack Mosely. The strip had the unique stylization of such strips of the '30s as *Dick Tracy* and *Little Orphan Annie*—not good representational art, but possessed of an absolutely distinctive quality almost totally missing from the bland product of today. As usual, the movie serial from Universal in 1942 reflected almost none of these values, but was only a wartime spy and pilot thriller using the name of Smilin' Jack Martin for the lead character. Tom Brown did not even wear a mustache such as Smilin' Jack had in the comics, and had the help of none of the supporting characters from the strip (such as Downwind, who always faced "downwind" so that you never saw his face).

Strangely, Edgar Barrier played a friend of Jack's called Tommy Thompson—certainly very close to Tommy Tomkins of the *Tailspin Tommy* comic strip. Some younger fans must have thought this was a "crossover" (in comic collector's terms) of one hero to another's story.

[1] Republic Pictures continued the practice of giving the recap with text printed below a photograph of one or more of the characters. Columbia used their own identifying technique of having an announcer tell the audience what had happened during the previous installments. The latter was a carry-over from the announcer's role on dramatic radio.

Basically, the photoplay concerned the efforts of Smilin' Jack, an American flier working with the Chinese forces shortly before Pearl Harbor, to rescue his friend, Tommy Thompson of the Australian Secret Service, from a prison in Northern China. Tommy had been trying to find the route of a secret road between China and India, vital information in wartime, when he had been captured by Japanese agents. Gertrude Miller (Rose Hobart), a supposed war correspondent, but really an Axis spy, also sought the information with the help of her henchman, Kageyama (Turhan Bey, a handsome minor star in a surprising come-down as a spearhead heavy).

The secret was known to Mah Ling, governor of the Chinese province of Mandon (Cyril Delevanti). Also in the cast was General Kai Ling (Sidney Toler, one-time Charlie Chan, another surprising serial performer).

Smilin' Jack took off in his plane in an attempt to rescue Tommy, along with Tommy's pretty sister, Janet (Marjorie Lord). Suddenly, a sneaky Japanese plane attacked them, and despite all Jack could do, his plane was sent spinning down in flames.

The preordained bail-out saved Jack and Janet. They finally reached the Mandon temple where the friendly priest, Lo Parr (Nigel de Brulier, who also hung around temples as old Shazam in *Captain Marvel*) helped them rescue Tommy from the Japanese.

One of the interesting gadgets of the serial was a device that when fitted over one person's throat could let him speak whatever he wanted to, and turn a phonograph record of another person's voice into the entirely different words of the device-wearer. (This one was used to discredit Smilin' Jack and temporarily turn his own allies against him.) Another was a mechanical pencil used by female spy Gertrude Miller to fire fatal poison darts.

The serial included some interesting cliffhangers: Jack being thrown into the ocean in a weighted box; the flier and his friends in a submarine being rammed by a ship; and Smilin' Jack being forced to walk across a fiery pit of red-hot coals to prove his worthiness to possess the secret of the hidden road to temple priests. He did prove worthy to be granted the secret, as Gertrude Miller and her spy ring were accidentally bombed by Japanese airplanes tricked by Smilin' Jack.

SECRET SQUADRON LEADER

Captain Albright walked into the office of his friend Major Steele and looked with concern as his superior told him that the nation was facing its greatest threats. Ivan Shark, a traitor and one of the worst villains the world had ever known, was attacking the United States with a fleet of enemy bombers. Captain Albright knew what he had to do. But he could accomplish a quicker defeat over Ivan Shark under the identity the free world had come to know and respect—Captain Midnight.

That was the opening of "Mysterious Pilot," the initial episode of Columbia's fifteen-chapter serial, *Captain Midnight,* directed by James W. Horne and released in 1942. This was a war year, and to instill a sense of patriotism in the young viewers who would come to the movie theatre on Saturday afternoons, Columbia based the serial on the single most popular aviator on radio, Captain Midnight, so named because of a mission he completed during World War I precisely at the hour of twelve. Since he was always battling the evil Ivan Shark on his radio program, it was only logical that the perpetual battle would be carried over the screen.

In the serial, Captain Midnight was portrayed by Dave O'Brien (who played both Tex Ritter's co-star in Westerns and comedy leads in *Pete Smith Specialties,* and later became a writer for television's *Red Skelton Show*). O'Brien wore a black leather uniform, with his insignia (a winged clock showing the hour of midnight) over his heart, and an aviator's cap with goggles all but concealing his features.

After Captain Midnight accepted the assignment to thwart his inevitable foe, Ivan Shark (played by James Craven, who made the perfect movie traitor) ordered one of his agents, Martel (Charles Hamilton), to heist an invention that could aid him in his attacks (a recurring serial theme). It was a new type of range finder, perfected by inventor John Edwards (Bryant Washburn). But Edwards had anticipated Shark's plans and given his device to Joyce (Dorothy Short), his daughter. There was only one man to whom she should give the range finder, he instructed. That man was Captain Albright. Shortly afterwards, the inventor was taken away by Ivan Shark's agents.

Captain Albright learned of the kidnapping and immediately switched his identity to that of Captain Midnight. Edwards had been taken to a cabin hideaway. But finding the place was simple for a man of Captain Midnight's abilities. The dynamic hero arrived at the cabin, where he leaped into a fight with the enemy agents. Ivan Shark, realizing that this was his opportunity to get rid of his archenemy for good, ordered his pilots to bomb the cabin. It appeared as if Ivan Shark had erased his enemy in a furious explosion.

But Captain Midnight jumped to safety in time to avoid being blown to his constituent minutes. He had survived with enough energy to continue falling into the death traps arranged by Ivan Shark. At the culmination of Chapter Two, "The Stolen Range Finder," Captain Midnight's sleek airplane taxied into an approaching truck, placed on the landing field by the crooks. The following week, we learned that the plane suffered only minor damage, as the hero in black jumped out with his guns speaking with rapid bursts. "Mistaken Identity," the fourth episode, presented the Captain with that most classic of all cliffhangers. He was on a moving platform headed straight for the teeth of a whirring buzz saw. The next week, Edwards acted in time to turn off the deadly machine. But at the climax of that episode, "Ambushed Ambulance," Midnight stumbled into a rotating airplane propeller. He escaped that form of death by skillfully turning his body with just seconds to spare.

In "Shells of Evil," Chapter Eight, Captain Midnight was able to reveal the skills in the art of dogfighting that made him a legend of the First World War. Ivan Shark had fled in his plane, and the hero in the black uniform flew off after him. But despite Captain Midnight's maneuvering, his plane was damaged by Ivan Shark's savage blasting. The ship of the valiant crusader went into a death spin and crashed in an eruption of flames.

Captain Midnight did not escape the crash. But Midnight's assistants, Chuck (Sam Edwards) and Ichabod Mudd (Guy Wilkerson), two characters also taken from the radio program,[2] saw the disaster and pulled him from the wreckage. They were happy to learn that he survived with only a scratch or two. The crash would have killed a lesser hero.

Many of the succeeding cliffhangers in *Captain Midnight* continued to center upon the perils of aviation. Captain Midnight was riddled with bullets (in the fashion of Japanese fighter pilots strafing helpless Yanks as shown in American wartime movies) as he parachuted from Ivan Shark's plane and was caught in a burning, exploding bomber.

Finally, in "The Fatal Hour," Ivan Shark had captured Joyce and her father and locked them and Major Steele (Joe Girard) in an underground jail cell. The range finder was in his possession, and now, he thought, nothing could stop him. But first, his prisoners had to be eliminated. Ivan Shark was about to electrocute the three when Captain Midnight and a squad of policemen raided the house. During the confusion the master

[2] The radio character "Joyce" was altered to that of the scientist's daughter.

villain accidentally touched a crowbar into the electrical wiring, destroying himself by his own evil device.

Hop Harrigan was flying blindfolded toward a rocky mountain wall! His heavyset pal, Tank Tinker, peeking out from his own blindfold, exclaimed that they, and their passenger Dr. Tobor would be killed unless Hop did something quick. But it seemed too late. Hop's plane shot directly for the mountain!

So ended the first chapter, suitably titled "A Mad Mission," of Columbia's 1946 serial, *Hop Harrigan*. Like *Captain Midnight,* the *Hop Harrigan* chapterplay was adapted from a radio program heard over the Mutual Network, and also from the cartoon strip by Jon Blummer that ran during the 1940s in *All American Comics*.

Hop Harrigan (played by William Bakewell) operated a small airfield. The business had been leased to him by Gail Nolan (Jennifer Holt) and her All-American younger brother, Jackie (Robert "Buzz" Henry). From this airfield, Hop and Tank became involved with many airborne mysteries and adventures. One of these involvements occurred in the first episode.

When J. Westly Arnold was saved from death by Hop Harrigan, he commissioned the young pilot to fly a friend of his to a secret destination. The friend was an eccentric scientist, Dr. Tobor (played by burly John Merton, who usually enacted the part of a Western bad guy), who had invented a motor which he claimed to be better than even those powered by atomic energy. Dr. Tobor wanted to return to his hidden laboratory, and Hop accepted the offer.

During the flight, Hop's plane was tailed by one of the planes in the fleet of the Chief Pilot, a mysterious villain desiring the sensational motor. Though not in a fighter plane, Hop performed some fabulous maneuvers with his ship and escaped the bullets of the enemy plane.

Dr. Tobor was grateful to Hop Harrigan for saving his life—but not grateful enough to divulge the location of his hidden laboratory. He compelled Hop and Tank to don blindfolds and sightlessly guide the plane's controls, while he told them what adjustments to make. Thus, the pair of aviators found themselves headed for certain death.

Hop finally yanked off his blindfold and swerved his plane, missing the mountain wall by perilously few inches.

Derwin Abrahams directed *Hop Harrigan*. And during the fifteen chapters allotted him by Columbia Pictures, he saw to it that the young flier was kept busy, protecting Dr. Tobor and battling the sinister Chief Pilot. When Tobor suspected Hop and Tank of purposely leading him into the Chief Pilot's death-ray, he hurled a gas bomb at them in their plane, then bailed out. Luckily, they revived in time from the effects of the gas and landed the plane without a single dent. Later, the deathray was turned on Hop, who leaped away from its beam the following week. And Hop was knocked off a roof saving himself by luckily landing on a fire escape.

In the final episode, the Chief Pilot was killed by one of his own men, ending a major threat to Hop Harrigan and the good guys. But now they were faced with a far worse menace than the Chief Pilot, a menace that threatened every living creature, according to the chapter's title, "The Fate of the World." Dr. Tobor had gone totally insane, announcing that he planned to destroy the entire planet at an ordained hour. Hop battled time to get to Dr. Tobor's hideout before the Earth was blown to debris that would circle silently in space forever. Surprised at his hideous work, Tobor and his assistant Retner (played by Ernie Adams, the ideal "stoolpidgin" of movies) turned to face the fury of Hop Harrigan. But the villains were defeated by a minor explosion that did not wreck the world, but destroyed Dr. Tobor and the results of his twisted mind.

Hop Harrigan was not a supercrusader such as Captain

Midnight. He wore no distinctive uniform and was satisfied with his flying jacket. He was only an ex-serviceman, like the brothers and fathers of his young audience. He was a celebration of the "average man" as hero, but he and his kind would lose their popularity to the "superhero" like the mysterious leader of the Secret Squadron.

Bruce Gentry was another "normal guy" hero of somewhat fleeting fame, who originated in the New York Post Syndicate cartoon feature. Bruce, like Hop, was a private pilot without any type of military uniform. A leather jacket and cap were enough to distinguish the mustached flier who soared and slugged his way through fifteen installments of Columbia's 1949 cliffhanger, *Bruce Gentry,* produced by Sam Katzman, directed by Spencer G. Bennet.

Bruce Gentry was played by Tom Neal, in the days before his real-life prison conviction for a tragic act of violence. Neal's features were of the typical chapterplay mold, his face being average enough to allow doubling by stuntman Dale Van Sickel in the more hazardous scenes.

"The Mysterious Disc," the first chapter took off with handsome Bruce Gentry about to embark on a mission to Los Angeles. Bruce's plane was buzzed by a flying disc (in reality an embarrassingly bad animated cartoon drawn over the action scenes by Columbia's special effects department). After some fancy maneuvering, Bruce evaded the saucer which blew up in midair. After he landed in Los Angeles and began conferring with Benson, the scientist was kidnapped by three crooks, and taken to the secret headquarters of an unseen villain known as the Recorder. The mastermind questioned Benson, speaking only via recordings which gave him his name. Bruce Gentry had meanwhile taken a job offered by Paul Radcliffe (Hugh Prosser) to track down the flying discs, the latter wanting them for use in commerce. Taking off in the direction from which the saucers seemed to originate, the heroic pilot encountered another whizzing disc which struck his plane right on target (he didn't learn his lesson from the previous time) and burst it into flame and bits of metal.

A quick parachute jump from the plane before the flying disc struck saved Bruce Gentry in the second installment.

Later in the serial, Bruce again encountered one of the deadly discs. He had gone to a shack in a far-off canyon to examine a fragment of another disc that he had acquired. Meanwhile, a saucer was launched toward the shack, apparently killing Bruce and his friends as it made explosive impact. The title of the chapter was the less than spectacular, "The Flying Disc." In the eighth installment, we saw Bruce and the others escape through a trap door. In Chapter Twelve, "Parachute to Peril," his plane was struck by a disc *again*. And in the following episode, Bruce *again* cheated death by bailing out before the explosion. This cliffhanger and its solution made many viewers suspect that Columbia was sparing their budgets—and the time of scriptwriters George H. Plympton, Joseph F. Poland, and Lewis Clay—by just reprinting the footage at the end of Chapter One and the beginning of Chapter Two.

Perhaps the most inane solution to any cliffhanger in *Bruce Gentry* was in Chapter Fourteen. In the previous episode, the leather-jacketed hero soared off a cliff on a miniature motorcycle. Other studios would have resolved the cliffhanger by showing the mini-bike and rider land in a body of water, so often at the base of such drop-offs. But things were different in this Katzman serial. Bruce survived the plunge by being transformed into an animated cartoon in midair, while a parachute flopped out from under his jacket and broke his fall.

Despite such ridiculous situations as the motorcycle fall, *Bruce Gentry* was one of Columbia's closest attempts at imitating the serials of Republic, a studio known for superbly staged action sequences. It was directed by Spencer G. Bennet, a veteran of many of Republic's better serials. And it featured the stunting teamwork of Tom Steele and Dale Van Sickel, who "fought" each other so many times at Republic with a rhythm rarely achieved by other teams. Still, the serial was produced during the last days of Columbia serials and could not equal the standards of the prime years of Republic.

In the final episode, appropriately labeled "The Final Disc," the Recorder finally appeared, wearing a black mask that covered his head in the fashion of an executioner. Bruce entered the Recorder's shack and unmasked him. He then realized why Benson was interrogated by a recorded voice. Benson couldn't be in two places at the same time, for he was the Recorder. Meanwhile, Krendon (Tristram Coffin), Benson's evil assistant, released a disc to blow up the Panama Canal. The famous pilot took off in his plane and overtook the disc and—*again!*—bailed out, allowing his ship to crash into the devious device. Suddenly, the control apparatus for the discs blew up, dooming Krendon and his criminal friends, and sparing Bruce Gentry from going through the saucer ordeal for a fourth time.

Columbia Pictures seemed to have all the best aviators signed to their studio. They had Captain Midnight, Hop Harrigan, Bruce Gentry, plus the dynamic star born in the first issue of *Military Comics* in 1941, the famous Blackhawk.

The motion picture version of *Blackhawk* was made in fifteen chapters in 1952. Again, like *Bruce Gentry,* the serial was produced by Sam Katzman and directed by Spencer G. Bennet, this time in association with Fred F. Sears.

For the part of Blackhawk, Katzman and Bennet decided to hire none other than Superman himself, or at least Kirk Alyn, the actor who had played the Man of Steel in their two previous chapterplays, *Superman* and *Atom Man vs. Superman*. Surprisingly, the actor looked as much like Blackhawk, with his blue military uniform and black hawk insignia over a yellow background, as he did like Superman. Alyn, who had resolved never again to put on the red and blue outfit of the Man of To-morrow for fear of the type-casting hurting his acting career, agreed to play Blackhawk in the chapterplay.

According to his comic book origin, Blackhawk was an American pilot who joined the Polish Air Force in 1939 to fight the Germans. When Blackhawk's brother and sister were killed by a bomb set off by his archenemy, Captain von Tepp, the hero swore to avenge their deaths. To track down the German villain, Blackhawk organized his own small army, consisting of similarly uniformed (but without Blackhawk's characteristic chest emblem) crusaders for freedom, the memberships vary-ing. When Blackhawk made it to the movies, he took along with him Chuck, the American (John Crawford), Olaf, the Teuton (Don C. Harvey), Stanislaus, the Swede (Rick Vallin), André, the Frenchman (Larry Stewart), Hendrickson, the Pole (Frank Ellis), and Chop Chop, of obvious origin (Weaver Levy). Unfortunately, all of these "Blackhawks" appeared to be red-blooded Americans and did not speak with the accents so familiar to the readers of the comic book adventures. (Scripter George Plympton told of a production staff meeting in which all were aghast at the confusing babel of accents from a recording of the short-lived *Blackhawk* radio series.)

Stanislaus was approached by the evil organization, the In-ternational Brotherhood, in the first chapter of the movie serial, "Distress Call from Space!", to take on a job of sabotage. Naturally, Stanislaus refused the offer made by the group's top agent, Laska (played by the luscious Carol Forman), to the delight of Blackhawk and Chuck who were eavesdropping. Laska retaliated by substituting an exact double for Stan who was exposed by Hendrickson. Boris, the imposter, overpowered Hendrickson and was about to mine the airfield, when Chop Chop demonstrated his own brand of heroism by attacking the saboteur. But he too fell to the evil Boris, who set off the explosives, dooming the mighty Blackhawk.

The explosions had gone off prematurely, as seen the following week. And Blackhawk escaped.

Chapter Three, "In the Enemy's Hideout," placed Stan masquerading as his menacing double. When his true identity was learned, the hero was bound to a post on a landing strip, directly in the path of a taxiing plane. But the following week, he was rescued by a feat performed by Blackhawk as dangerous in real life for Kirk Alyn as it was for the military crusader. Without the use of a stunt double, Alyn rushed up to the plane, grabbed it by the wing, and turned it out of Stan's path. The feat was a dangerous one, especially with those rotating propellers that could slice off an arm or worse. However, a hidden pilot helped guide the heavy metal plane. (The scriptwriters were thinking of the old wood and canvas planes of the thirties which really could be so guided by a single man.)

Blackhawk was called by elderly Professor Rolph (William Fawcett) to see the deadly electronic ray he had invented. After a demonstration of its power, the scientist was kidnapped by Laska's henchmen. Blackhawk pursued the villains in his car. But the automobile was bumped from the rear by the crooks' vehicle and onto the railroad tracks. Needless to say, a train was happening along! But Blackhawk jumped to safety the following week before his car was sideswiped by the speeding locomotive.

In the fifth chapter, "Human Targets!" (this was a favorite title that kept appearing in many sound serials, especially those made by Republic) Blackhawk was blasted by Rolph's death-ray. In other episodes, he nearly met his demise when his parachute failed to open, when his plane was intercepted by a superscientific flying disc and blown to pieces (which made *Bruce Gentry* fans cast looks of weary awareness at each other), and when an explosive planted in his plane blew the craft apart in midair.

Laska decided to renounce her allegiance to the Leader, the real head of the International Brotherhood in the last installment, "The Leader Unmasked!" The Leader had decided to destroy his beautiful agent, which gave her a good reason to oppose him. But the Blackhawks had been trailing her in their automobile. As the valiant heroes in uniform stormed into the office of the Leader, Laska killed her former master and then fell into the clutches of Blackhawk. He smiled, knowing that he and his men had stopped the activities of the sabotage ring.

The final episode of *Blackhawk* had come to an end. There were no other serials made by any studio following *Blackhawk* that were based solely on the exploits of a famous flying hero from comics or radio, (although some serials like Republic's *Flying Disc Man from Mars* in 1951 featured heroes who soared through the heavens in privately owned planes as minor plot elements). The world of popular entertainment was gradually coming to replace the pilots who zoomed from country to country with space pilots rocketing from planet to planet. But during the years when a trip to Los Angeles via air could be an exciting adventure, with attacking biplanes and parachutes that failed to open, the aviators were heroes to respect and envy.

8

The Detectives   "Gangbusters!"

HARDBOILED DICK

Dick Tracy proved to be the most popular detective to appear in a movie serial. The character was so well-received, in fact, that Republic Pictures starred him in a quartet of some of the most popular chapterplays of the era—*Dick Tracy* (1937), *Dick Tracy Returns* (1938), *Dick Tracy's G-Men* (1939), and the last of the series, *Dick Tracy vs. Crime, Inc.* (1941).

These serials were based on the strip created by cartoonist Chester Gould for the Chicago Tribune–New York News Syndicate, beginning October 12, 1931. The title, *Dick Tracy,* came from the colloquial term "dick" which referred to any plain-clothes detective, and the fact a "dick" did a lot of "tracing" of people.

The *Dick Tracy* strip was unique. The villains were bizarre monstrosities, far surpassing the usual caricatures. They were unbelievable creatures that could not possibly have existed anywhere on this planet, even in the wildest freak show. There was a flat, two-dimensional feel about the strip, which lent even more unreality to *Dick Tracy*. But Gould offset this unbelievability by introducing such authentic crime-stopping techniques and well-conceived plotting and characterization that *Dick Tracy* was accepted as a new and totally serious newspaper serial.

Some of the bizarre elements of the newspaper strip were retained when Republic decided to make the serial *Dick Tracy*. The villain was as monstrous as many of the archfiends of the comic strip. Tracy's chief opponent in the cliffhanger was known both as the Spider and the Lame One, a sinister character with a great dome of a head surrounded by a band of hair and with bushy, meeting eyebrows. Aiding him in his crimes was a dwarfish hunchback named Dr. Moloch (John Piccori). Aside from this pair of fiends, the serial kept the characters more credible. In subsequent Dick Tracy serials, such bizarre characterizations were omitted in favor of more human villains.

The casting of the role of Dick Tracy was perfect. Naturally no one really had an angular face like the one drawn in the comic strip.[1] Republic's casting office was, however, able to find a handsome young actor who managed to "suggest" the comic strip features of Dick Tracy, in the line of the jaw, especially, although his nose was not at all angular. He was Ralph Byrd, recently out of a Universal feature, *Chinatown Squad* (1935). Byrd accepted the role and as a result was to be associated with the character of Dick Tracy even after his death in 1952 of a heart attack when only forty-three years of age.

Dick Tracy's brother Gordon was abducted by the Lame One's thugs in the first serial's initial chapter, "The Spider Strikes." Moloch, a mad doctor in his own right, performed a sinister gland-changing operation on Gordon Tracy, wiping out his past memories and preventing him from knowing right from wrong.

MEDIUM SHOT

> *Two henchmen hold up the unconscious form of* GORDON TRACY *before* MOLOCH, *a gargoyle-eyed hunchback, seated before the room's fireplace.*

FIRST HENCHMAN: Tell the Lame One we brought Gordon Tracy here.

SHOTS TO COVER

> *All the men except the unconscious* GORDON *turn to follow*

[1] In an hour-long color *Dick Tracy* television pilot made in the late 1960s to hopefully launch a new series based on the character, actors were made up to look *exactly* like the comic strip versions of Dick Tracy and his band of enemies. The result was most unpleasant.

the approaching shadow and dragging footsteps of the
SPIDER, *also known as the* LAME ONE.
The SPIDER *enters.*

MOLOCH: He's hurt, but if he's not gone too far, I might do
more than you can imagine . . . by means of this operation,
a simple altering of certain glands, he will be unable to distinguish between right and wrong.

SPIDER: He can be useful to me, Moloch, very useful.

Republic insured that Gordon's personality would be completely altered by having two different actors play the part. Before the operation, Gordon was portrayed by Richard Beach;
after, he was played by Carleton Young. (Young certainly was
right to play Dick Tracy's brother. He played the role of another famous detective, Ellery Queen, on radio.)

Gordon Tracy had been transformed into an agent of the
Lame One, and his detective brother had no way of knowing
the true identity of this latest villain. The Lame One then placed
Gordon at the controls of his Flying Wing, an airstrip of the
future, which was the ideal craft for making raids from the sky,
especially since it carried a powerful raygun and frequently
used it.

MEDIUM SHOT
TRACY *is talking into microphone as* GORDON *and several*
henchmen as before enter quietly through the door behind
the detective.

TRACY: Get a squad—

GORDON: Too late, Tracy!

SHOTS TO COVER
TRACY *whirls to confront* TRACY. *Keeping him covered,* GOR-
DON *goes to the radio, snaps it off. He searches* TRACY, *re-*
moves the detective's gun from his pocket. As GORDON *pulls*
out the gun, the genuine Morga necklace falls to the floor.

GORDON: Why were you so anxious to get the imitation—or
were you trying to fool us?

TRACY: I did fool you.
GORDON: A lot of good it did you.

SHOTS TO COVER
> TRACY's *hand goes to his other pocket and pulls out a small bottle; the men react to his words.*
TRACY: I wouldn't be too sure. Nitroglycerine, gentlemen! I'll take both necklaces now!

Also in opposition to the villains were Tracy's young adopted son Junior (Lee Van Atta), the lovely Gwen (Kay Hughes), and for comedy relief Mike McGurk (played by Gene Autry's sidekick, Smiley Burnette). Other actors who appeared in *Dick Tracy* were the familiar Byron Foulger (then using the middle initial "K") and one of the greatest stars of the silent era, Francis X. Bushman. For a serial, the cast of *Dick Tracy* was impressive.

As Dick Tracy continued to battle the vicious Lame One and his Spider Gang, he was required to prove himself as a worthy hero in his first serial. At one point he was bound and left to die in a burning building (Chapter Thirteen, "The Fire Trap"). In another episode, Tracy barely escaped being operated upon by the hunchbacked Molach (Chapter Fourteen, "The Devil in White").

In the fifteenth and final chapter, "Brothers United," Dick Tracy was struggling with the Lame One when the villain's entire face slipped away to reveal another! He had been wearing a mask and now stood revealed as the man Tracy had least suspected. The unmasked archfiend managed to escape in an automobile driven by Gordon until the speeding vehicle went off an embankment, dooming its occupants. Tracy hurried to the scene to find the dead heap that had once been his worst enemy, and also his dying brother whose final moments brought back his memory.

Dick Tracy was directed by Ray Taylor, who had made numerous silent chapterplays, and Alan James. The serial, rarely seen today, was just the beginning for the character and for Ralph Byrd. Immediately the actor was identified with the role of the comic strip detective so that, as far as the fans were concerned, Ralph Byrd *was* Dick Tracy. He would continue his role in the next three Republic Dick Tracy chapterplays.

The same leading characters from the first serial returned in *Dick Tracy Returns,* but with changes in casting. Jerry Tucker was the new Junior, while Lynne Roberts portrayed Gwen and Lee Ford played Mike McGurk.

The story was basically a rewriting of the real life Ma Barker story. Only in the serial a quick sex change by the writers altered the character to Pa Stark (played by that most evil of all cliffhanger villains, Charles Middleton), aided in his criminal acts by his five nearly-as-bad-as-he-was sons—Champ (John Merton), Slasher (Jack Ingram), Dude (Jack Roberts), Trigger (Raphael Bennett), and The Kid (Ned Glass), all with appearances befitting their names.

Pa Stark and his notorious family had just held up an armored bank truck when Dick Tracy arrived with the police. The gang managed to escape with half a million dollars. Tracy captured The Kid and planned to place a witness to the crime on a transport plane which would fly him to a new location where he would testify. Pa Stark, knowing of the flight, used a radio beam to guide the plane toward the mountains. Dick Tracy went after the transport plane in his own ship to save it from being destroyed, but suffered himself the fate of crashing into the mountain, apparently undergoing immediate cremation, and ending the first installment, "The Sky Wreckers."

Naturally a hero with fourteen chapters ahead of him could not be eliminated by a mere crashing plane. He was thrown clear of the wreck the following week, and managed to survive all of the hazards originating in the evil mind of Pa Stark.

An unconscious Tracy was placed in an automobile by Stark.

Then the vehicle was rolled down a ramp and into an onrushing truck in Chapter Two, "The Runaway of Death." He leaped out just before the fatal collision.

In Chapter Three, "Handcuffed to Doom," Tracy's assistant Steve (Michael Kent) had been knocked out and handcuffed to the top of a wild-running freight car. Luckily, however, Dick Tracy managed to find an old "unused army tank" and drove it alongside the track until its speed matched that of the boxcar. With the tank still going at top speed, Tracy boarded the freight car and climbed to the top of it. Futilely he attempted to halt the car with the hand brake. He was too late! The boxcar shot off the end of the track to sail into space and crash in the ravine below. Next week, Steve regained consciousness in time and both he and Tracy dove to safety. This cliffhanger proved extremely popular with the writers when the Republic executives told them to ease the budgets by writing in scenes that could be lifted out of the stock footage library. Among other Republic serials using the sequence was the later *Dick Tracy vs. Crime, Inc.*

Dick Tracy Returns was a more polished serial than its predecessor, because it was made a crucial year after *Dick Tracy,* and primarily due to the directing team of William Witney and John English. It provided much action that could be later reused in the further serial adventures of Dick Tracy. Its main drawback was in the use of economy chapters.

An economy chapter in a serial was an episode in which virtually nothing happened other than the savings of dollars by the studio. Generally the economy chapter showed the hero and his confederates sitting around a table discussing what had already happened, while the scene dissolved to a series of flashbacks. At times, as in Mascot's *The Miracle Rider,* this technique was limited to only a few scenes. Most times, unfortunately, the flashbacks over, someone would inadvertently rush into the room with a bomb or other diversion to lure the hero into another cliffhanger.

While most serials using economy chapters were satisfied with one, *Dick Tracy Returns* foisted two Saturday afternoons of reruns on the audience.

In the fifteenth episode, "G-Men's Dragnet," Dick was captured by Pa Stark and his killer brood, taking him to their hideout, an old rock crusher plant. Suddenly an entire force of G-men arrived at the scene and after a wild gun battle killed off all the Starks except their evil Pa. Concealing two vials of nitroglycerin on his person, Pa Stark feigned surrender by emerging from the hideout with raised hands. With the advantage of the explosives, the villain forced Tracy into an airplane and took off wanting the detective to take him out of the United States to freedom. But Tracy was not one to be told what to do by a scoundrel like Stark, regardless of two vials of nitroglycerin. In a fateful attempt, Tracy turned the plane over and bailed out, leaving Pa Stark to die in a blinding flash of fire and debris.

Dick Tracy left the police department to join the Federal Bureau of Investigation in *Dick Tracy's G-Men*. In this fifteen-chapter serial, Dick was alone as far as characters adapted from the comic strip were concerned. Junior and the others had been eliminated from this latest script.

Opposing Dick Tracy this time was the leader of a spy ring, the bearded, mustached master spy, Zarnoff, played by Irving Pichel, a good actor who later became a notable motion picture director. Zarnoff had been convicted of numerous crimes including murder and was sentenced to die in the gas chamber. The sentence was carried out. It was just the beginning of Chapter One, "The Master Spy," and already the villain had been killed. What would happen during the next fourteen episodes?

Zarnoff had apparently had dealings with some member of

1. Flash Gordon (Buster Crabbe) protects Dale Arden (Jean Rogers) from a fate worse than death at the hands of the off-screen Ming in the first of three serials based on *Flash Gordon*, 1936.

2. (Below) Buster Crabbe let his hair go to its natural brunette for the 1936 *Buck Rogers* as he leads a band of supposed Saturnian extras. While Buck was first in the comics, the film version copied the successful Flash Gordon movie series.

3. Helmeted Ray "Crash" Corrigan shows the broken works of a robot to young Lee Van Atta in *Undersea Kingdom*, Republic's upside-down take off on Universal's *Flash Gordon*.

4. Gene Autry, still in cowboy togs, is placed on an operating table in *The Phantom Empire*, Mascot 1935, by a group of Lemurians. A wild combination of Western and science fiction elements, there never has been a film quite like this, before or since.

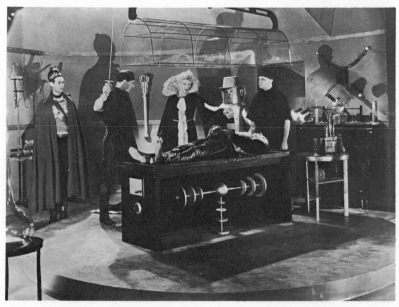

5. Tom Mix, the screen's legendary Western hero, found himself in a mysterious cobweb-strung tunnel in *The Miracle Rider*, Mascot 1935, his final film. Heroine Joan Gale and the other Ravenhead Indians were being frightened by superscientific devices, like the web-spinning gun in Tom's hand.

6. In a more conventional Western role, Buck Jones has his back to the wall—or rather, the table—as he shoves back Kenne Duncan and wards off a flailing chair from George Chesebro in *White Eagle*, Columbia 1941. Buck played a supposed Indian by that name, with the final familiar cop-out that he had been a white lad captured by the redskins.

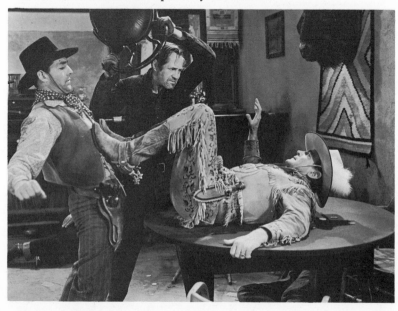

7. The Lone Ranger (Bob Livingston) has the drop on the bad guys in the second Republic serial based on the famous radio character, *The Lone Ranger Rides Again*, 1939.

8. Bob Livingston has his mask lowered in *The Lone Ranger Rides Again* as he prepares to go into action with Chief Thunder Cloud as Tonto and Duncan Renaldo as Vasques.

9. (Above) *Clancy of the Mounted*, Universal 1933, was one of the many serials about the heroic Mounties and one of many starring serial roles for Tom Tyler, who with his own slight German accent played Clancy.

10. Tom Tyler takes stock of the trouble in front of him, before flying into action in *Captain Marvel*, Republic 1941. Tyler looked exactly as the captain did in the earliest issues of *Whiz Comics*, although the comic character eventually gained an alarming amount of weight.

11. (Above) Tom Tyler as Captain Marvel, the World's Mightiest Mortal, lifts a tree out of the road. In a number of ways *Adventures of Captain Marvel* was the best made of all movie serials.

12. Tom Tyler played another costumed hero in *The Phantom*, Columbia 1943. Devil the dog was played by Fang, the dog.

13. (Above) Kenne Duncan cautions the Scorpion (the voice, at least, belonged to Gerald Mohr) as henchmen prepare the strange Golden Scorpion ray machine in Republic's *Adventures of Captain Marvel*.

14. A rare art still from *The Adventures of Captain Africa*, Columbia 1955, illustrating John Hart in a costume similar enough to that of the Phantom so that a vast amount of stock footage from the earlier serial could be used.

15. Kirk Alyn as Superman watches carefully for a chance to grab a high pressure air-drill running wild, before it can harm the unconscious Lois Lane (Noel Neill) in the first serial of *Superman*, Columbia 1948.

16. Superman (Kirk Alyn) is placed into a disintegration machine by the strange Atom Man (supposedly actor Lyle Talbot, or a stuntman) and his henchmen Terry Frost and Jack Ingram.

the Frankenstein household, for death was unable to keep him in the grave. A combination of Pulmotor and secret drugs literally brought the villain back to life to renew his crimes against the United States.

Dick Tracy learned of Zarnoff's resurrection and his nefarious plot to blow up the Panama Canal by sending a speed boat filled with explosives into the locks. There followed a furious boat chase, Dick after the explosives-laden craft. The chapter ended with a tremendous explosion.

"Captured," the second installment, showed Tracy divert the unmanned ship from its course in time to save most of the canal. Again the Witney-English team had provided another cliffhanger to enliven future serials, again including *Dick Tracy vs. Crime, Inc.* This chapter was climaxed with a favorite type of non-spectacular cliffhanger. Tracy had been overpowered and tied to a chair by Zarnoff. The master spy then rigged up a gun to fire at Tracy the moment anyone opened the door. The chapter ended with some of Tracy's G-men assistants coming toward the door.

At the opening of the next episode, Dick Tracy freed himself in time to avoid the deadly bullet.

Dick Tracy went below the sea in a diving suit to capture a criminal in a diving bell toward the end of Chapter Six, "Sunken Peril." Then someone cut his airline! It was the diving bell itself that provided Tracy's escape in the following week's installment.

The last chapter of *Dick Tracy's G-Men* featured a rather unique climax to a serial. Instead of pursuing the villain during a frantic chase that resulted in a great explosion, Tracy was captured by Zarnoff and tied to a tree in the desert. The chapter was appropriately titled "The Last Stand," as Tracy had been bound before a water hole and dying of thirst. Satisfying his sadistic nature, Zarnoff drank greedily of the water, then left the G-man to die. Zarnoff was no longer laughing when the water proved to be poisoned, letting him die alone in the middle of the desert. Tracy himself really had little to worry about as he was soon rescued by his own men.

Dick Tracy (again the only character from the cartoon strip) was back as a police detective in the final entry into the series, *Dick Tracy vs. Crime, Inc.* Again directed by Witney and English, this fifteen-chapter epic was the best of the Tracy serials. That was not surprising. By 1941, Republic had reached its golden years and would soon release some of its greatest chapterplays, including *Spy Smasher, Perils of Nyoka,* and *Adventures of Captain Marvel.* If one were to make a list of the very best Republic serials ever made, *Dick Tracy vs. Crime, Inc.* would be near the top of that list. The action sequences were superb and were complemented by an intelligently written script and a terrific musical score credited to Cy Feuer. There was a decisive attempt to give audiences more than the usual, expected serial entertainment consisting of several fist fights and a cliffhanger. Some chapters went by in *Dick Tracy vs. Crime, Inc.* without *any* major fist fights and there was still no letup to the interest or action.

Another reason for the high quality of this serial was the fact that it was in great part made up of the best sequences from earlier Dick Tracy serials. *Dick Tracy vs. Crime, Inc.* was almost a survey serial—showing the "Best of Dick Tracy." The new footage mixed beautifully with the old making the ultimate entry into the series.

Dick Tracy met his most powerful screen adversary in the fourth serial. That was the mystery villain known only as the Ghost, whose trademark was the thumbprint of "Rackets" Reagan (no relation, hopefully, to the Governor of California), one-time crime czar. Reagan had been executed at Sing Sing through the efforts of Dick Tracy. Thus, the detective was summoned to New York from Washington to stop the unknown Ghost.

The Ghost was a diabolically clever villain who wore a black mask in the form of a human head and possessed a weirdly humming device that made him invisible. He could then dispose of his enemies at his own convenience. These enemies consisted of seven members of the Council of Eight, a group of influential citizens bent on ridding the city of the current crime wave. The Ghost himself was the eighth member of the council.

With the help of Lucifer (John Davidson), the satanic inventor of the invisibility device, the Ghost learned that by bombing a volcanic fault in New York's harbor, a tidal wave and earthquake would result. The first chapter, "The Fatal Hour," showed New York City apparently doomed as gigantic waves swept away buildings (the destructive scenes from an old feature *Deluge,* made by RKO) and leveled the once-mighty city. But what remained of New York was saved by the intervention of Dick Tracy and his latest assistant, Billy Carr (Michael Owen).

Many of the cliffhangers in *Dick Tracy vs. Crime, Inc.* were stock shots from the earlier Tracy chapterplays. Nevertheless, regardless if they were or were not seen before, most of them were exciting. Chapter Eight, "Train of Doom," ended with Tracy parachuting onto the tracks just in front of an onrushing locomotive. He nearly lost his head to a heavy ax in Chapter Nine, "Beheaded." And in Chapter Twelve, "Trial by Fire," the detective was carried by a conveyor to a huge incinerator.

All the while the eight suspects, any one of which could be the Ghost, were being eliminated, so that all the previous evidence ascertaining their guilt had become worthless.

There were only two suspects left by the last chapter, "Retribution," so that at least one other man knew the true identity of the Ghost. Dick Tracy had discovered a ray which would interfere with the Ghost's invisibility device. The unseen villain was lured to the ray by Tracy and a slamming fight commenced

—photographed completely in the negative to show the effects of the counterray. Now able to see his enemy, Tracy fought him until the Ghost managed to destroy the new invention and fled to a nearby powerhouse. Tracked by Tracy's barking bloodhounds, the Ghost attempted crossing the high-tension wires but was electrocuted. Visible again, the Ghost was discovered to be the brother of "Rackets" Reagan and the meek character played in the serial by Ralph Morgan.

Actually there was no reason to suspect anyone except Morgan right from the first chapter. His make-up as the kindliest, most inoffensive member of the Council of Eight was hardly believable. The voice of the Ghost had not been changed like the voices of most of Republic's mystery villains; anyone hearing both Morgan and the Ghost speak knew who wore the black headpiece. Furthermore, Ralph Morgan's name was so high up in the cast credits that the Ghost could be none other than this actor so identified with villainous roles.

The serial was a popular one and was later reissued under the title *Dick Tracy vs. Phantom Empire*. The title was misleading, especially for anyone who might have believed this to be a new chapterplay pitting Dick Tracy against Gene Autry's subterranean world of Murania.

Dick Tracy vs. Crime, Inc. ended Republic's association with the live action character. It was not, however, the end of Dick Tracy or of Ralph Byrd's association with the role.

In 1945, RKO acquired the rights to make feature-length films using Dick Tracy. The first of these was simply called *Dick Tracy* (1945) and starred Morgan Conway instead of Byrd. Conway did a second film the following year, *Dick Tracy vs. Cueball*. Although a good actor, Conway did not click with the audience as did Ralph Byrd. Succumbing to the demands of the public, RKO reinstated Byrd in the last two films in the series, *Dick Tracy's Dilemma* and *Dick Tracy Meets Gruesome*, both made in 1947. The RKO films relied more on mystery and crime deduction and less on action than did the serials. They were well done in their own right presenting the other side of Dick Tracy's character—the side that did not necessarily rely upon flailing fists or Republic stuntmen.

Ralph Byrd's association with Dick Tracy continued into the next decade as, from 1951–52, he starred in the original *Dick Tracy* television series. Joe Devlin played his partner Sam Catchem, while the villains came straight from the mind and brush of Chester Gould. The television bad guys included Diet Smith, Breathless Mahoney, and the Mole, all familiar to the many readers of the cartoon strip.

Dick Tracy has been brought to life in other forms, including a poorly done series of cartoons featuring talking animals and other nonsense, and also in an unsold television pilot which was to be a hopeful competitor to the Caped Crusader during the already legendary *Batman* craze. But it was Republic's Dick Tracy movie serials that fans most appreciated.

THE INSIDIOUS FU MANCHU

The most diabolical, sinister, and all-around un-nice Oriental mastermind of all time was Dr. Fu Manchu. Bald as a Chinese eggroll, with Satanic eyebrows that jutted upward and a mustache that made his mouth seem always to sneer, the robed Fu Manchu was a genius at devising the cruelest of tortures. He had good reason for becoming the epitome of the Oriental mastermind. Fu Manchu wanted to conquer the world.

When a man as deadly as Fu Manchu exists there must logically be a hero in the world to balance such ambitious power. When Sax Rohmer created the character of the insidious Fu Manchu for a series of adventurous novels beginning with *The Insidious Dr. Fu Manchu* in 1913, he gave the terrible Oriental a most worthy opponent—Sir Nayland Smith of Scotland Yard, whose main goal in life was to rid the earth of the menace of Fu Manchu.

Sir Nayland Smith was a relentless detective not unlike Sir Arthur Conan Doyle's private investigator, Sherlock Holmes. He was courageous and nearly as intelligent as Holmes. Like Holmes, Sir Nayland was given his own version of Dr. Watson in the person of Dr. Petrie.

Fu Manchu and his archenemies, Sir Nayland Smith and Dr. Petrie, starred in motion pictures of both the silent and talkie eras. The mysterious villain was portrayed in features by such notable screen bad guys as Warner Oland and Boris Karloff, cackling maniacally over the elaborate devices that would slowly kill Sir Nayland, apparently the only man who could stop the archfiend from conquering the entire world.

Republic Pictures decided to make an updated chapterplay version of one of Sax Rohmer's Fu Manchu novels in 1940. It was titled *Drums of Fu Manchu,* the name of one of the books in the long-running series. The serial was filmed during the Republic peak years and the quality was evident in every capacity.

William Witney and John English, mentioned throughout this book as the most professional directors of movie serials, directed *Drums of Fu Manchu.* Working with photographer William Nobels, the directing team stressed the *mystery* elements inherent in the Fu Manchu novels, unlike most of their action-oriented photoplays. Most of their serial was photographed in shadows with the eeriest lighting possible falling upon Fu. Before he made his appearance the almost supernatural drums of Fu Manchu began to sound from nowhere. There was no denying the fact that the Witney-English Fu Manchu was more than human and possessed weird powers not even hinted at in the novels.

A young Caucasian actor named Henry Brandon played the part of Fu Manchu in the fifteen-chapter cliffhanger. He played the role with extreme relish, gloating over his every new method of inflicting horrible death.

Sir Nayland Smith was portrayed by distinguished and middle-aged William Royle and given second billing only to Brandon. Olaf Hytten's name was placed fifth in the serial's credits for his enactment of the role of Dr. Petrie.

Naturally, when Republic adapted a serial from some previously existing work, the studio felt the need to make changes. Luckily for Sax Rohmer's ego *Drums of Fu Manchu* retained most of the elements of the original. The primary change was in the role of the hero.

Young heroes usually fought the villains in Republic chapterplays. The Fu Manchu cliffhanger followed serials from that studio with youthful Zorros, Lone Rangers, and Dick Tracy. There was nothing wrong with a middle-aged detective like Sir Nayland Smith battling his Oriental adversary and his bloodthirsty hordes. Nevertheless Republic seemed to believe that the Saturday matinee crowd might not accept a hero with mature character—like Harry Carey, Tom Mix, and others who fought the baddies in the older Mascot days.

Sir Nayland, then, was made the secondary hero. Although his name was given second place stature in the credits, the real hero of *Drums of Fu Manchu* was a typically Republic Allan Parker (played by dark-haired Robert Kellard). It was Allan who was given the privilege of falling victim most often to the evil plotting of the Chinese master villain.

In the first chapter, "Fu Manchu Strikes," Sir Nayland Smith and Dr. Petrie were almost killed as a knife whizzed through the air, barely missing them as it thudded into a door. The stalwart heroes evaluated the situation, shown in the following text from the script:

PETRIE: A Dacoit knife. Then Fu Manchu is here in California.
SMITH: Precisely.

PETRIE: But Nayland, I thought you'd run him to earth in
    Burma.
SMITH: So did I, and so did the Foreign Office. But I failed.
PETRIE: But I don't understand. What deviltry is he up to now?
SMITH: The most stupendous crime of his career. Nothing
    less than the conquest of Asia and the annihilation of every
    man who does not bow to his will.

Fu Manchu's current ultimate goal was a bit less distressing
than setting himself up as ruler of the world. Fu Manchu wanted
to cause a revolution in Central Asia. To do this he required the
control of the Dalai Plaque, an artifact owned by Professor
Parker (played by character actor George Cleveland). This
plaque told the location of the lost sceptre of Genghis Khan.
Once Fu Manchu possessed the sceptre, he would be established
as ruler of the superstitious hill people of that area of Asia.

Sir Dennis Nayland Smith, now a special agent of the British
Foreign Office, pursued Fu Manchu to California. But he had
not figured that Fu Manchu's army would be composed of creatures slightly less than human. They were the *Dacoits,* the zombie products of Fu's own sinister surgery, an operation which
somehow not only reduced them to brainless robots, but also
gave them vampire-like fangs.

With the aid of his Dacoit slaves, Fu Manchu managed to
kidnap Professor Parker and his colleague, Professor Randolph
(Tom Chatterton).

Allan, the son of Professor Parker, and Mary (Luana Wal-
ters), daughter of Professor Randolph, allied themselves with
the detective, Nayland Smith.

Near the climax of the first installment, Mary had seized the
Dalai Plaque and was attempting to escape Fu Manchu on a
speeding night train. What she did not know was that the villain
had arranged for a second train to chug down the same track
but from the opposite direction! At the climax, the night became
illuminated as two powerful locomotives collided and exploded
in one of the most shattering cliffhangers in serial history.

Only the heroics of young Allan rescued her, pulling the girl off the train, before the head-on collision.

There were more perils in *Drums of Fu Manchu,* but of a nature that really seemed strange for a Republic serial. The studio always relied on action, much of it routine and, after a while, even boring. In the Fu Manchu cliffhanger, great emphasis was placed upon the mystery surrounding the diabolical Oriental, and much of this feeling became manifest in the chapter endings.

Of course, there was the usual airplane crash (apparently dooming Allan and Mary in Chapter Three, "Ransom in the Sky"), the car plunging off the cliffside (seemingly crunching Smith and Allan in Chapter Eight, "Danger Trail"), and the customary exploding dynamite trap (blowing Allan to bits, or so it appeared, in Chapter Eleven, "The Tomb of Genghis Khan").

But there were other, highly imaginative cliffhangers, so unlike the usual Republic fare. The second episode had Allan plunge through a trap door where an octopus waited with anxious tentacles. It was an installment suitably titled "The Monster." Chapter Five, "The House of Terror," had a very strange cliffhanger, in that it created a mood rather than a terrific explosion or fall through space. With the heroes unconscious in the terror house, Fu Manchu stalked menacingly through the rain, as eerily lit as possible, entered the house, stood over his fallen enemies, and grinned. There was more feeling of the foreboding in that grin than in the deathray that Fu Manchu later used to sacrifice Mary on the altar and in his arsenal of time bombs, machine guns, and an Edgar Allan Poe inspired swinging knife.

Perhaps the most sinister of Fu Manchu's attempts to eliminate his detective archenemy was in the fourteenth chapter, wherein the Oriental mastermind assumed the role of "Satan's Surgeon." Sir Nayland Smith had been captured, while Allan Parker was left for dead. The courageous British crimefighter had been laid out on an operating table. Over his motionless body stood Fu Manchu and his army of mindless Dacoits. The drums of Fu Manchu began to pound with their horrible rhythm—the sound that always seemed to trigger one of Fu Manchu's traps. The evil villain brought his scalpel to the forehead of the unconscious detective. Fu Manchu grinned ghoulishly and jerked his hand over the man's head—*pressed down!* "Sir Nayland Smith!" said Fu Manchu. "Dacoit!"

Things had never looked grimmer for Sir Nayland Smith. However, he was spared from an existence as a mindless Dacoit slave by the sudden intrusion of Allan, who was still alive and fighting.

It was Allan Parker and not the more appropriate Sir Nayland Smith who helped provide the exciting climax to the final episode, "Revolt." Allan and Fu Manchu were struggling to the death while the station wagon they were in sped precariously toward an embankment. Heroically, Allan leaped aside, leaving the helpless Fu Manchu to meet an explosive demise as the car slid off the embankment, rolled over, and blew up.

It appeared as though the insidious Fu Manchu was dead. However, in the final moments of the last chapter, the evil mastermind returned, heavily bandaged, to swear that he would strike again at his greatest enemy, Sir Nayland Smith. That was the ending of the serial version.

Years after its original serialized release, *Drums of Fu Manchu* was re-edited into a compact feature length film, complete in itself. In this version Fu Manchu never escaped that fatal car crash,[2] although readers of the Sax Rohmer novels knew that such a world-conquering fiend could not really be eliminated by so mundane a death.

[2] Republic did a similar bit of rewriting when it released a feature length version of *King of the Rocket Men* with the new title *Lost Planet Airmen*. The serial version clearly showed New York City reduced to rubble by a great deluge; the feature explained that the flood never took place but was the imagined dream of a madman.

Drums of Fu Manchu remains as one of Republic's best movie serials. For once the six screenplay writers—Ronald Davidson, Franklyn Adrean, Morgan Cox, Sol Shor, Barney Sarecky, and Norman S. Hall—attempted to re-create the true feeling of the original property within the framework of fifteen chapters. Like *Dick Tracy vs. Crime, Inc.,* the Fu Manchu chapterplay provided more than the usual formula slugfests and explosions. Unfortunately, as with many Republic serials adapted from other sources, copyright clauses prohibit the authorized screening any more of *Drums of Fu Manchu.*

Years later, Republic secured the rights to film a *Fu Manchu* half-hour television series. The productions were inexpensive and generally uninteresting, failing to compete with the original serial.

"THEREFORE, THE MURDERER CAN ONLY BE . . ."

Charlie Chan, that paternal detective who combined modern crime-fighting techniques with the wisdom of the Orient, solved his first crime on the motion picture screen in a serial.

House Without a Key, a silent chapterplay made by Pathé in 1926 with a total of ten episodes, was not a Charlie Chan serial per se. The production, based upon the very first Charlie Chan novel, could be more accurately described as an Allene Ray-Walter Miller vehicle that happened to include the Oriental detective in its cast of characters. Both Ray and Miller were extremely popular during the era of silent serials. Apparently the executives at Pathé attributed more value to their names than to that of Charlie Chan.

In "The Spite Fence," the first chapter which was considerably longer than any of the following nine parts, the plot of a standard murder mystery unfolded. The serial was set in Hawaii, where Charlie Chan was employed as a plainclothesman on the

Honolulu police force. Twenty years before, the wealthier of two brothers supposedly committed a crime. A mysterious treasure chest was reputed to contain evidence pertaining to the crime. The treasure chest was supposed to be destroyed by Miller, but it inadvertently fell into the hands of the villains, led by the ever-reliable Frank Lackteen.

The remaining chapters of the serial showed the attempts of the good guys, including the played down Charlie Chan, to retrieve the treasure chest.

Spencer G. Bennet directed *House Without a Key* and took his characters through an adventure with intriguing chapter titles like "The Mystery Box," "The Death Buoy," "The Mystery Man," and "The Spotted Menace." It was only in the final installment that "The Culprit" was exposed.

In the later Charlie Chan features, a good deal of the footage involved his American-born number-one son.

The "World's Greatest Detective," Nick Carter, a hero of mystery novels since the turn of the century and still the subject of James Bond-type fiction, never made it to the movie serial screen. Adapting the character would have proved too expensive for a studio like Columbia Pictures who made their chapterplays as cheaply as possible. When Columbia decided to film a movie serial based upon the Nick Carter character the studio found it more practical to turn to Carter's own "number-one son."

Chick Carter, the youthful son of Nick Carter, began to help his famous father solve crimes in the days of the dime novels. He was, at youngest, in his late teens, but might have been barely of voting age. The character, though not as popular as father Nick, was eventually given his own radio program called *Chick Carter, Boy Detective*. If the studio could not obtain the rights to Nick Carter, Chick Carter was the logical alternate choice.

The character was given fifteen episodes to prove himself worthy of his father's reputation in Columbia's 1946 serial, *Chick Carter, Detective,* directed by Derwin Abrahams. Like many serials adapted from other media, this cliffhanger proved that once again the writers (this time George H. Plympton and Harry Fraser) either were unfamiliar with their source or merely enjoyed making significant changes. The result was that Chick Carter was no longer a boy detective, but a decisively older grownup, played by Lyle Talbot. Though more than a competent actor, Talbot just was *not* a boy detective. He played the part as if he were the original Carter—old Nick himself.

Like *House Without a Key,* the Chick Carter serial ignored the direction of so many serials that played up fantastic weapons and bizarre villains, and remained a relatively straight crime drama.

In the first chapter, "Chick Carter Takes Over," Joe Carney (played by the most familiar heavy of the B Westerns, Charles King), owner of the famed Blue Diamond, planned to have the jewel stolen by hired thugs in order to collect $100,000 insurance and pay back a debt to gangster Nick Pollo (George Meeker). Sherry Marvin (Julie Gibson), a singer in a nightclub run by Carney, learned of the plot and hid the diamond in a cotton snowball. The result was that an imitation Blue Diamond was heisted by the crooks. Spud Warner (sometimes comical Eddie Acuff), a news photographer, and a reporter named Rusty Farrell (Douglas Fowley) attended Sherry's performance. Playfully taking one of the snowballs away from the singer, Spud caused her to toss Nick the wrong one. An alarm was given and police Lieutenant Chick Carter arrived with a squad of patrolmen. One of Nick's gunmen, Vasky (Leonard Penn), forced Rusty and jewel expert Jules Hoyt (Joel Friedkin) to drive off in a squad car. The initial episode ended with the careening automobile crashing into a gas pump and erupting into flames.

A quick leap in the nick of time saved Rusty and established a rather strange precedent for any movie serial. The chapterplay was titled *Chick Carter, Detective*. And yet the detective was rarely involved in any of the cliffhangers. These perils were usually survived by other characters. Like Charlie Chan, Chick Carter had been reduced to a secondary character in his own serial. At least he was allowed top billing, with his name in the title.

Chick Carter was given dangers to end only two chapters. In the eighth episode, "Chick Carter Gives Chase," he was nearly electrocuted by a short-circuited switchboard. In Chapter Twelve, "Chick Carter Faces Death," the detective was knocked into a rock-crusher.

Two cliffhangers for the serial's star were not much to demonstrate many heroics, but the detective did manage to occupy considerable footage rescuing the other characters. With so few perils to worry about, it was not surprising that Chick Carter managed to round up the gang and the Blue Diamond was recovered.

Almost as popular a serial detective as Dick Tracy was a Scotland Yard plainclothesman named Blake. While Dick Tracy starred in four motion picture chapterplays, Blake was featured in three.

Blake of Scotland Yard introduced the character of Angus Blake in a silent 1927 adventure. The serial was made by Universal in twelve episodes and directed by Robert F. Hill.

In the first episode, "The Castle of Fear," Angus Blake (Hayden Stevenson) was introduced as a retired criminologist. He did not remain inactive for long. A mysterious villain known as the Spider (no relation of Dick Tracy's enemy or to the hero of the same name) was attempting to steal a secret formula that could change ordinary ore into gold. When Lady Diana Blanton's (Gloria Gray) father was confronted by the Spider, Lady

Diana persuaded Blake to renew his past association with Scotland Yard. Aided by a woman in white (Grace Cunard), Blake was finally able to defeat the Spider in the last chapter, "The Final Reckoning."

Blake of Scotland Yard was a popular serial, and a sequel, *Ace of Scotland Yard,* was made in 1929 by the same studio. Crauford Kent played the new Blake, who came out of retirement a second time when his girl friend, played by Florence Allen, became a target of the villains who wanted to use her to get an artifact known as the Love Ring. This "MacGuffin"[3] was uncovered by her father during an expedition to Egypt.

Ace of Scotland Yard was directed by Ray Taylor, later to direct *Dick Tracy.* Taylor emphasized eerie atmosphere and plotting. The fifth chapter was titled "Menace of the Mummy," which was indeed a weird title for a serial installment.

By the time *Ace of Scotland Yard* was completed, sound films had already come into their own. There were still theatres booking only silent films. Since the serial was Universal's first made in sound, with dialogue, music, and sound effects, and because the studio did not want to lose the lingering silent market, additional scenes were shot for the sake of clarity and simultaneously a non-talkie version was issued.

The character was not revived until 1937, when Sam Katzman's Victory Pictures decided to remake *Blake of Scotland Yard.* Now, however, he was known as Sir James Blake (silent movie actor Herbert Rawlinson), formerly a Scotland Yard C.I.D. inspector, now retired and involved with more enterprising pastimes. His latest endeavor was financing an invention made by the real star of the serial, young Jerry Sheehan (played by Ralph Byrd, fresh out of his first performance as Dick Tracy). The invention was a deathray, a device coveted by a

[3] The term "MacGuffin" was popularized by Alfred Hitchcock and refers to the object of "shtick" around which the plot revolves. Treasure maps, coveted deathray devices, and secret formulas were popular "MacGuffins" in the movie serials.

sinister mystery villain known as the Scorpion, who skulked about London with a slouch hat, mask, long black cloak, and a glove shaped like the pincer of a great anthropod. Thus, the Scorpion had a motive to strike, and Blake and Jerry had good reason to attempt thwarting the fiend.

The cliffhangers in the sound *Blake of Scotland Yard* were sometimes unique and took advantage of the European settings. In Chapter Two, "Death in the Laboratory," Jerry was beaten up and tossed into the sewers of Paris. Similarly, Blake (who had become a secondary hero, like Sir Nayland, Charlie Chan, and Chick Carter in their serials in favor of the younger Jerry Sheehan) was knocked out and thrown into the Thames in Chapter Five, "Death in the River." The seventh episode, "Face to Face," provided an unusual climax. Blake had been masquerading as the Scorpion. When the real Scorpion confronted him, in the presence of another villain, *that* was the cliffhanger. Such cliffhangers as this irritated the fans of more spectacular climaxes of other studios, primarily those of Republic. But when we all knew that the Republic hero would leap out of the car just before it exploded, or revive in time to escape the barn before that exploded, it was the more mysterious cliffhanger as the confrontation between the two Scorpions that kept fans guessing between Saturdays.

In Chapter Fifteen, "The Trap is Sprung," Blake was able to show that a more mature hero could indeed bypass the heroics of the younger man and triumph over the villain. Blake himself recovered the deathray machine, captured the Scorpion (who was unmasked in the previous installment), and was again able to return to a more quiet life.

OUT OF THIN AIR

The masked avenger known as the Green Hornet appeared in the color comics and on the radio, much as Dick Tracy did.

However, the Hornet originated on the radio, and was later adopted to comics and the screen; Dick Tracy was pure cartoon in origin. Both made good characters for more than one movie serial.

Another radio creation, *Gangbusters,* only had a very minor span as a comic book adaptation (as a supporting feature in *Popular Comics*) but critics were often given to pointing out that radio producer Phillips H. Lord turned allegedly "true" crime stories into straight comic book stuff. The movie serial made not the slightest pretense of being true, and was only the usual chapterplay fantasy.

The serials of the Green Hornet were much closer to the image of the broadcast series.

Alan Ladd appeared in the first of these serials titled *The Green Hornet* in 1939. The actor was blond, cool, self-contained, and obviously heroic, just like the Green Hornet. However, Alan Ladd did *not* play the part of the masked avenger. This was before even *This Gun for Hire,* much less *Shane;* Ladd played a minor supporting role, but a somewhat dashing one as a young pilot named Gilpin.

The role of newspaper publisher Britt Reid, who was secretly the mysterious Green Hornet, fell to Gordon Jones. Jones was a good-looking dark-haired young man of the type who dimpled when he smiled. Yet he seemed more at ease in later years when after becoming only moderately chubby he became a comedy relief in Western features starring Roy Rogers and others.

Keye Luke was perfect as the houseboy-scientific genius-masked helper, Kato. Anne Nagel proved an attractive Lenore Case, Britt Reid's secretary, and Wade Boteler was a serviceable Mike Axford, the dumb Irish assistant (a role somewhat resented by smart Irishmen like one of the present writers).

These characters, and several other minor ones, all were taken from the radio series created by George W. Trendle and written by Fran Striker for Station WXYZ, Detroit. Al Hodge, the radio actor in the role of the Hornet, could easily have done the movie serial as satisfactorily as he did the later television role of Captain Video. Reportedly, Hodge did supply the dubbed voice of the masked Green Hornet on the screen, but not that of Britt Reid (Gordon Jones, of course).

The script by George H. Plympton, Basil Dickey, Morrison C. Wood, and Lyonel Margolies was directed by veterans Ford Beebe and Ray Taylor.

The photoplay began with *Daily Sentinel* publisher Britt Reid learning from one of his reporters of a graft-ridden dam project, one of the many rackets plaguing the city, all of which the *Sentinel* was pledged to fight. Before the day was out, the mysterious Chief of the Crime Syndicate issued orders through Curtis Monroe (Cy Kendall) for a Syndicate lawyer, Felix Grant (Edward Earle) to attempt to buy out the *Sentinel* to get rid of its crime exposés. Naturally, Reid scorned the offer.

As the crooked attorney left, Reid sent his bodyguard, ex-policeman Mike Axford, to trail the man. But Grant evaded the Irishman. However, the unseen Syndicate Chief told him that since he had aroused suspicions, the lawyer had to get out of town.

Before Grant could finish destroying papers that might incriminate him, he received a visit from Britt Reid who now wore the insect-insignia mask of the Green Hornet over the lower part of his face. The world thought that the Hornet was a crook and a killer who would do anything to serve his own ends, which probably meant cutting in on the Syndicate's racket. Grant was terrified, but before he could talk, two Syndicate crooks, Dean (Walter McGrail) and Corey (Gene Rizzi) burst into the room. In the fight that followed, Grant was killed and the Hornet fired his unique gas gun at the two crooks, knocking them unconscious for several minutes. With the police on the way, the Hornet left, racing into the night beside Kato as the

Oriental drove the Black Beauty, "sleek, super-powered car of the Green Hornet," which according to the movie serial, could travel at "over two hundred miles per hour" thanks to Kato's revolutionary new "energizer."

But the Hornet's plans were foiled by another crook, Ogden (Arthur Loft), who revived the two men and arranged things to look as if the Hornet had murdered the lawyer, using the seal of the Hornet that Reid had left behind. (This paper seal was the counterpart of the Lone Ranger's silver bullet.)

Later, the Green Hornet visited the graft-corrupted construction site that figured in the Syndicate's plans. He forced a crooked contractor named Markheim (Don Rowan) to lead him down into a faulty underwater tunnel (a foolhardy but courageous act). Sure enough, just as the Hornet and Markheim went through the airlock, the inadequate air compressor failed. The Hornet gruffly forced the crooked builder to remain with him in the tunnel as the workers fled for their lives. Finally, the two men started to follow the workers, when Markheim stumbled and fell. In terror of his life and of the Hornet, Markheim blurted out the vital information that there were twelve top bosses in the Syndicate. Then, as the Hornet bent to help Markheim, the whole tunnel collapsed, apparently burying both men under tons of debris. Thus ended Chapter One, "Tunnel of Terror."

In the second episode, "Thundering Terror," the Green Hornet managed to grab one of the fallen timbers as the rushing waters carried him to a safe location. Markheim was carried away, and fatally injured.

At the *Sentinel* offices, ace reporter Jasper Jenks (Phillip Trent) reported to Reid that all of the construction workers were insured by one broker named Mortinson (Douglas Evans) and that those policies were all payable to the late Mr. Markheim's construction company.

Suspecting the insurance broker of being in the Syndicate,

the Green Hornet began an investigation of Mortinson. He and Kato narrowly missed being blown to bits by a bomb planted in the crook's safe to catch them. With no doubt remaining in his mind, Reid pursued the car of Mortinson. Running low on gas, the racketeer made a daring leap from his speeding automobile to a chugging locomotive, slowing down to take on water. Naturally, the Green Hornet could make no less a spectacular transfer from car to train. Entering the engineer's cab, the Hornet found himself in a fist fight with the desperate Mortinson. The two men struggled furiously, then fell from the cab, apparently beneath the ever-clicking wheels of the racing train.

In the third episode, "Flying Coffins," we found the Hornet and the crook, Mortinson, rolling down an embankment, not seriously hurt.

After turning the unco-operative Mortinson over to the District Attorney, Britt Reid and the *Sentinel* began the investigation of another Syndicate racket, the Bartlett Flying School.

Jenks, the reporter, watched the solo flight of an eager young pilot named Gilpin (yes, Alan Ladd). Gilpin was soloing after only four hours of instruction. Apparently, his own natural flying skill (the skill Alan Ladd would demonstrate so many times again) enabled Gilpin to barely bring in the plane without cracking up.

Shortly, Reid was involved in a complicated investigation of the school (this single chapter of the Universal serial had more plot than many complete serials from Republic in later years). Another student pilot was less lucky than Gilpin; he was killed in a Bartlett plane. His insurance claim intended for his fiancée was collected by another girl, posing as the fiancée. When confronted by the Hornet, the imposter admitted she had kicked back most of the money she claimed to the Syndicate. Before the Hornet could make use of her testimony, the girl swindler was abducted by two Syndicate crooks, and when they crashed in an attempt to escape the pursuing Hornet, the girl was killed, although the crooks walked away from the wreck. (The good die young.)

Meanwhile, Gilpin had become suspicious and he was about to take off in a plane that the crooked school had rigged to crash. However, the faithful Kato had overheard the crooks' plan and informed the Hornet. At first, the Hornet tried to reason with the headstrong Gilpin not to fly the plane. (Once again the audience yelled, "Don't take off in that plane, you crazy fool!") The youthful pilot would not listen to reason and the Hornet had to apply his final persuasion—he knocked Gilpin out with a blast from his gas gun.

One of the crooks, Bart (Ben Taggart), came into the hangar and was overpowered by the Hornet and loaded into the sabotaged plane. Then, the Green Hornet did what any serial hero would do if he knew an airplane had been booby-trapped. The Hornet took off in that plane.

Regaining consciousness, Bart began whining in terror and told the masked man what he wanted to know. He admitted being involved in the Syndicate, helping collect insurance on both the pilot and the planes in the wrecks that were carefully arranged. That information looked as if it were going to do the Hornet a lot of good. At that moment, the bomb went off, engulfing the plane in flames. There was only one parachute and the crook tried to grab it all for himself. The Green Hornet, chivalrous but disposed to save his own life, struggled with the racketeer for possession of the parachute as the plane went into a tumbling tailspin toward the ground and certain destruction.

Naturally, "The Pillar of Flame," the fourth episode, revealed that the Green Hornet would not let even a crook die in his place. A final punch from the gloved fist of the masked man subdued Bart, and the Hornet bailed out of the doomed airplane, carrying Bart along with him to safety.

The fourth chapter followed the example established by the

first three episodes: the Green Hornet investigated another racket run by the Syndicate (this time a stolen car ring) and narrowly escaped death when a car he was in went out of control and crashed into the pump standards of a gas station, setting off a spectacular fountain of fire.

In the succeeding installments, Britt Reid and his *Daily Sentinel* employees exposed a crooked junk yard, an attempt by bus passengers to victimize the bus line (known in the trade as a "real switch"), another plot to swindle a trucking company, a protection racket against dry cleaners, and a rigged election.

In defeating these schemes, the Green Hornet faced such perils as being caught in a truck crashing through the guard rail of a bridge, being shot down out of a window, being bathed in a downpour of acid, and in the next-to-final episode being trapped in a hazard somewhat more appropriate for Tarzan than the Green Hornet—caught in an elephant stampede (at the local zoo)!

The thirteenth and final episode, "Doom of the Underworld," showed the Hornet crashing through a wall (it was only a thin wall) to save himself from the thundering herd of enraged elephants.

Later, the Syndicate, finally driven nearly out of business, determined to *blow up* one source of agitation to themselves— the *Daily Sentinel*.

As the Hornet, Reid arrived in time to stop the bomb plot and to trail two of the crooks involved in the scheme—Dean and Corey who have carried through all the various rackets of the serial.

At long last, the Green Hornet was led to the headquarters of the Syndicate, the offices of Curtis Monroe. During his usual bit of Hornet snooping, Reid discovered a secret room with a recorded message from the mysterious Chief on a turntable. He found that the message could be activated by Monroe himself. Monroe was really the Chief, who listened along with the others to a message he had recorded earlier for play at a more convenient time.

When Dean and Corey came back to the office, the Hornet, hidden in the secret room, imitated the voice of the Chief and gave instructions to *Monroe* (who was not there) to kill Dean and Corey before clearing out.

Monroe finally returned, along with the thug, Ogden, and found himself in a shoot-out with the waiting pair who expected him to try to kill them. After the smoke cleared, only Monroe survived, just long enough for the Hornet to get a signed confession out of him.

Later the City Council presented an embossed resolution of commendation to the *Daily Sentinel* for its efforts in wiping out the Crime Syndicate. When Britt Reid pinned it up in the city room, Miss Case defiantly added the seal of the Green Hornet (obtained in an earlier adventure).

The Hornet imitating the voice of the Chief in the last episode was not a ringer. He had imitated the voices of minor crooks all through the serial to lure them into traps, etc. He did those voices perfectly too. Since all of the masked Hornet's dialogue was dubbed, it was a simple matter for the actor he was supposed to be impersonating to dub in his own voice, simulating a perfect "imitation."

Universal followed *The Green Hornet* with a 1944 sequel, *The Green Hornet Strikes Again* following the same crime exposé pattern, but presenting a new Britt Reid, the handsome and always professional, Warren Hull.

Universal's other serial borrowed from the radio airwaves *Gang Busters,* 1942, presented another dependable leading man, Kent Taylor (later Boston Blackie in the early television series). The mustached Taylor played Detective Lieutenant Bill Bannister, a character entirely original to the screen, since the radio series only presented real-life policemen such as Commissioner Lewis J. Valentine of New York detailing actual crime cases.

Even the youngest audience member could hardly be expected to think that the events of the photoplay were anything but contrived in Hollywood. Ralph Morgan (comedian Frank Morgan's brother) as Dr. Mortis had assembled a League of Murdered Men—men he had apparently risen from the dead—so that Mortis could seize power and wealth from a helpless city. Against him were pitted the police—the fearless Gang Busters of the title—led by Lieutenant Bannister and his assistant, Tim Nolan (Robert Armstrong, looking a bit more tired than when he had brought back that "Eighth Wonder of the World," *King Kong* in the 1933 feature). They received somewhat dubious aid from newspaper photographer Vicky Logan (Irene Hervey).

Aside from Dr. Mortis reviving the dead—apparently only those dead by a mysterious poison of his own making—performed with only the most meager use of mad scientist props Universal must have had left over from its series of Frankenstein features, there was very little of a science fiction or fantasy element to the well made, and interesting serial. It stuck to the usual cops and robbers element of car chases, gun fights and fisticuffs in old warehouses.

Finally in the twelfth chapter, "The Long Chance," Bannister was captured by the Mortis gang and as the episode ended, the white-smocked Dr. Mortis leaned over the form of Bannister on the operating table, preparing to turn him into one of the living dead, forever a slave of Mortis himself.

Bill Bannister came back to consciousness and was told that he must have a renewed supply of Mortis drug if he wanted to stay alive. Besides that, Tim Nolan and Vicky were prisoners of the League of Murdered Men. Bannister's first order? Kill the Mayor and the Chief of Police. Bannister agreed, but outside of the gang's headquarters, Bannister put through a tele-

17. (Above) The gunfight behind barrels or crates, a familiar scene in many serials, with a familiar star, Kirk Alyn, with James Dale in *Federal Agents vs. Underworld, Inc.*, Republic 1949.

18. Kirk Alyn in a heroic pose in *Blackhawk*, Columbia 1952. This title role provided Alyn his sixth serial starring vehicle. Assuming a position held by Buster Crabbe in the thirties, Alyn became in the forties and fifties "The Last of the Serial Kings."

19. (Above) Kane Richmond in *Spy Smasher*, Republic 1942, another of the select group of high quality serials made between 1939 and 1942, the brief Golden Age of the sound serial.

20. Douglas Croft as Robin and Lewis Wilson as Batman climb onto a rooftop full of danger in *The Batman*, Columbia 1943. This serial, like its sequel, was notoriously bad, far worse than the average serial. Its 1965 revival inspired a new TV series for the character, and a distorted reputation for serials in general.

21. Dick Purcell has the drop on heavies George Lewis and Tom Steele (also an ace stuntman) in *Captain America*, Republic 1944.

22. That's really stuntman Dale Van Sickel delivering a right cross to the heavy in *Captain America*. While stuntmen were seldom used in close-ups, the mask and a certain facial resemblance to star Dick Purcell allowed Van Sickel to get away with it.

23. (Above) The Shadow (Victor Jory) is about to put the arm on villain Jack Ingram, who in turn has a grip on heroine Veda Ann Borg in *The Shadow*, Columbia 1940.

24. Gordon Jones in the Hornet guise cautiously turns a corner in *The Green Hornet*, Universal 1940.

25. Baddie Frank Lackteen is about to give the shaft to Tom Neal as he tries to free the bonds of happy Frances Gifford in *Jungle Girl*, Republic 1941.

26. The eternally evil Charles Middleton (more famous as Ming in *Flash Gordon*) and the always lovely Lorna Gray (à la Adrian Booth) watch the ever popular George Lewis turn the torture rack tighter on the seldom safe Kay Aldridge in *Perils of Nyoka*, Republic 1942.

27. Women hardly ever got the drop on Roy Barcroft, Republic's meanest (and most lovable) bad guy. The heroine most capable of holding a gun on the popular heavy was Linda Stirling, seen here in *Jesse James Rides Again* (1947), a serial which whitewashed the infamous outlaw.

28. The heroine Marion Shilling is menaced by the shadowy villain in *The Clutching Hand*, an independent serial of 1936. This scene is representative of many early talkie and silent serials before the development of "choreographed" fist fights drastically changed the tone and pace of serials.

29. Youthful Frankie Darro, star of many serials, shows a vital film can to flier-helmeted Jack Mulhall and two players in *Burn 'em Up Barnes*, Mascot 1934.

30. Clark Williams as Tommy points to the mysterious Eagle's helmet held by Noah Beery, Jr. in *Tailspin Tommy in the Great Air Mystery*, Universal 1935.

31. *Captain Video,* Columbia 1951, offered a different cast than the television series it adapted with Judd Holdren as the captain and Larry Stewart as the Video Ranger, about to enter their spaceship with Dr. Tobor (George Eldredge).

32. The Rocketman costume developed by Republic was used time and again during the last days of the movie serials. In this scene, the man in the rocket suit stuntman Dale Van Sickel is battling a robot, stuntman Tom Steele, originally seen in *Undersea Kingdom.* It *is* from the 1952 *Zombies of the Stratosphere,* but *could* be from a handful of other titles.

phone call to the police chemist. If a man were brought back to life, Bannister asked, would he need a supply of a certain drug to keep him from turning back into a corpse? The chemist mulled the question over, but finally spoke with authority. No, the formerly dead man would not need any further dosage. Bannister nodded. That was all he needed to know.

Bannister faked the deaths of the city officials but only so that he could lead the police to Mortis' hideout. The Frankensteinian character made a mad dash for freedom, emerging from the manhole entrance to his secret hideaway, just as a subway train roared down the tunnel and chopped him into too many pieces to be reanimated.

About the only thing the movie serial kept from the radio show was the title and a loudly narrated opening complete with machine guns, police sirens, and marching convicts. Even that was slightly paraphrased.

OUT OF THE SHADOWS

The Shadow's mocking laughter was heard for decades every Sunday afternoon on the radio, but he was equally at home in the pulp-paper fiction magazine about his exploits. Both the magazine and the radio series began in 1931, with the broadcast dramas having a small headstart. However, it was the pulp magazine version of The Shadow that was brought to the serial screen. On the air, The Shadow was totally invisible, thanks to his hypnotic power to "cloud men's minds." He needed that ability to cope with the mad scientists, zombies, and werewolves he encountered. In the magazine novels by Walter B. Gibson under the pen name of Maxwell Grant, The Shadow only dressed in a black cape and slouch hat, skulking through the darkness to be virtually—but not literally—invisible. If his

powers were less fantastic in print, so were his opponents—
mostly mundane crooks and robbers.

The 1940 Columbia serial, *The Shadow,* followed the lines
of the pulp character fairly faithfully, even though the invisible
man of radio was familiar to *millions* of fans, while the magazine
version was known only to a few hundred thousand readers.
However, Columbia had had some success with its earlier serial
about an imitation of The Shadow called the Spider (*The
Spider's Web,* 1938). The screen rights to this competitive
magazine character proved more accessible than those to The
Shadow. (Rights were also obtained for a 1941 sequel, *The
Spider Returns.*) The movie studio did what all movie studios
did and imitated success.

Special effects to simulate an invisible man were expensive
for a serial but not impossible, as Republic would prove with
the villainous Ghost in its 1941 production, *Dick Tracy vs.
Crime, Inc.*

The chief villain of the film serial of *The Shadow* was known
as the Black Tiger. Although it sometimes seemed a bit redun-
dant to have both the hero and the villain a masked mystery
man, serial makers seemed to feel that it was required. (Where
only the villain was a colorfully disguised figure—as Roy
Barcroft in the role of Captain Mephisto for *Manhunt of
Mystery Island*—he became the most interesting and memorable character of the serial.)

In the opening chapter, "The Doomed City," the Black Tiger
was spreading a wave of terror. Railroads were dynamited, airplanes wrecked, and factories were blown up. As part of his
unfathomable plans, the Tiger sent some of his thugs to invade
the private laboratory of wealthy Lamont Cranston (an excellent actor, the appropriately hawk-nosed Victor Jory). The
Tiger's agent overpowered Cranston's friend and companion
(and secretary) Margot Lane (Veda Ann Borg) and stole the
formula for a fantastic new explosive from its inventor, a

Cranston employee named Stanford Marshall (J. Paul Jones).

Lamont Cranston found himself with a very personal interest in bringing the Black Tiger and his gang to justice. He was known to the police for his "amateur detective work," but they did not know he was the phantom-like figure of the night, The Shadow, whose guns spoke from beneath his black cloak when the cause was just.

Cranston prevailed upon his friend, Police Commissioner Weston (Frank La Rue) to release a known Tiger agent so that he might be followed. Cranston succeeded in trailing the man to an old warehouse. There he performed a masterful feat of disguise and emerged in the character of a Chinese, Lin Chang. As Lin, Cranston warned the thugs that there was an impending police raid so that he might gain their confidence. The plan worked well enough that he learned the Black Tiger intended to destroy an exhibit of that revolutionary new development, television. Cranston escaped during the raid with the help of his chauffeur, Vincent. (The part was played by Roger Moore, not the younger star of *The Saint* television series. The role was a considerably down-graded one from that of the character of Harry Vincent in the magazine novels. Harry Vincent was a co-hero, at home in high society, and would have been a chauffeur only as a fleeting pose.)

In the midnight-hued garb of The Shadow, Cranston went to the television exhibit and warned the audience, including many important personages, to leave. He was immediately engaged in battle by the hoods of the Black Tiger, led by Flint (the never-reforming Jack Ingram). In the violent struggle, The Shadow was felled by a thrown chair, and left by the crooks to be blown up by the death trap composed of inventor Marshall's new nitrogen bulbs. The bomb exploded, destroying the television exhibit, and apparently The Shadow.

In the second installment, "The Shadow Attacks," it was revealed that The Shadow survived the bomb blast for no good reason except he was the hero. He climbed out from beneath the debris, dusted his cloak off, and went away into the shadows.

The film serial proceeded in singularly unimaginative fashion. All the mystery and menace of The Shadow was lost by having him often appear in broad daylight and brightly lit rooms. The weapons and schemes of the Black Tiger were far from fantastic. All in all, the serial was simply a detective story in which the hero chose to wear a black cloak and slouch hat for no justifiable motive.

The following chapters had The Shadow escaping a bursting boiler in a basement, an attack of ammonia vapor, an overdose of X rays, and an exploding radio. (These hardly seem more perilous than the dangers faced by many a housewife in the 1970s.)

The Shadow also managed to save the lovely Margot from being crushed by a descending elevator as she was trapped in the bottom of the shaft. In his role of Lin Chang, The Shadow seemingly imperiled himself by arranging to have Lamont Cranston framed for murder!

It almost was a humorous touch, as many things seemed in supposedly adventurous Columbia serials directed by James W. Horne, who was fresh from directing Laurel and Hardy comedies. *The Shadow* was scripted by Joseph Poland, Ned Dandy, and Joseph O'Donnell and produced by Larry Darmour.

In the final episode, "The Shadow's Net Closes," The Shadow and Vincent battled their way into the headquarters of the Black Tiger to rescue the industrialists the madman had kidnapped in order to force them to sign over their holdings to him. At last, The Shadow ripped the mask from the face of the Black Tiger and revealed him to be Stanford Marshall, inventor of the stolen nitrogen bulbs. In the struggle that followed, the erstwhile Black Tiger was thrown against one of his own electronic machines and electrocuted. The Shadow had the last laugh as usual.

INTO THE WEB

The Spider first spun his web to entrap gangland in the pages of *The Spider* magazine in 1933, just over two years after The Shadow first saw print. The web-spinner was an obvious imitation of The Shadow, even though the early issues were not similar enough to please the publisher. In later issues, he added a cloak and hat exactly like The Shadow's, and developed an equally haunting laugh. An added factor in the Spider's appearance was make-up that made him look like a fanged hunchback on occasion. (On still other occasions, he only affected a Domino mask—one, however, made of blue steel.)

As a literary character under the authorship of talented novelist and war correspondent Norvell Page writing under the pen name of Grant Stockbridge, the Spider was a truly multi-dimensional figure with an endlessly fascinating array of hangups. His mission in life was to *kill* criminals, placing himself entirely outside the law. Yet he wondered if his late father would approve of his bloody work, and longed for the ever-denied approval of the series' father figure, Police Commissioner Kirkpatrick. He had fantasies of himself as a Christ-like figure who received personal visits from at least an Egyptian deity—Amon-Ra. The Spider's relationship with his girl friend, Nita Van Sloan, was much weirder than that between The Shadow and Margot Lane. Their love was so deep that it was suggested that they were parts of the same being, interchangeable. Nita sometimes donned the disguise of the Spider, *becoming* the Spider. As for the Spider himself, he dealt death to criminals, and he clearly considered himself a criminal for being a murderer. There have been few characters in authentic literature as complex as this pulp hero.

Naturally, the movie serial about the Spider could catch little of this flavor. An accurate rendition of the Spider novels on screen would have been denied by the motion picture production code. Yet *The Spider's Web* in 1938 did manage to suggest the frantic pace of the novels, and the Columbia serial accurately retained many minor characters and details from the original stories in a way Republic's productions never did.

Warren Hull was a reasonable choice for the Spider's alter-ego, Richard Wentworth. His costume as the Spider was too flamboyant, with a huge cape embroidered with webbing, but Hollywood had to be granted some license, one supposes. Iris Meredith was an attractive and unusually efficient (for a serial heroine) Nita Van Sloan. Kenne Duncan in beard and turban played Wentworth's servant, Ram Singh, and Richard Fiske and Donald Douglas played two other aides, Jackson and Jenkins. With another bit of license, Commissioner Kirkpatrick became Commissioner Kirk for no apparent reason; elderly Forbes Murray played the role.

The Octopus was the villain of the piece. He had one clearly defined goal (which always proved best for a serial): he wanted to seize control of the entire transportation system of the United States—trains, planes, even buses. The Octopus wore a white outfit resembling that of a Ku Klux Klansman and delivered orders to his henchmen through a voice-distorting microphone. He also affected the use of crutches, which meant that the audience should be on the lookout for the person who was the fastest of foot (aside from the Spider, of course).

Dismayed at the acts of sabotage, the Police Commissioner gave up on his own force of men and called for help from amateur criminologist Richard Wentworth. (How many cases would it take before Wentworth and Lamont Cranston were at least recognized as *professional* criminologists?) Uncharacteristically, Wentworth refused. He and his fiancée, Nita Van Sloan, were planning on a plane trip out of town to get married.

(The *real* Spider of the novels would not have rested so long as a criminal remained alive.)

But Wentworth found he could not turn his back on danger. Crooks, not knowing of his reluctance to get involved, had rigged wires across the landing strip to cause the crash of Wentworth's ship. He narrowly avoided the trap, and climbing from the plane, engaged the thugs in a gun fight, killing three of them and managing to capture a fourth. This man was killed in the prison hospital by tentacles of the Octopus before he could talk.

Knowing that his life was in danger, Wentworth sent his fiancée, Nita, out of town to supposed safety in the protection of faithful Ram Singh. Hardly had she left, however, than Wentworth learned that the Octopus planned to blow up a bridge over which Nita's auto would cross. In a wild chase, Wentworth overtook her car in his own, and forced Nita's vehicle off the road before it could drive straight into the disaster.

Later, the criminologist deftly disguised himself as a squint-eyed, lumpy jawed crook known as Blinky McQuade and went out to hang around barrooms to gather information. (He seemed to enjoy the task fully as much as Tonto did in *The Lone Ranger*.) He came back loaded with information. The Octopus planned to blow up a certain passenger bus set to leave from the city terminal.

Wentworth changed his disguise to that of the Spider, "dreaded scourge of the underworld." Racing to the terminal, the Spider engaged the mobsters in a furious gun battle. Forcing the crooks back, the hooded phantom got aboard the booby-trapped bus and drove it away from the crowds in the terminal. As the Spider steered the bus into the street, there was a thunderous blast and smoke obscured the scene.

So ended Chapter One, "Night of Terror," and so began

Chapter Two, "Death Below," except, of course, for the inevitable shot of the Spider leaping to safety that proverbial split-second before the explosion. In a bit of a departure, the police blamed the bombing on the Spider as one of many crimes they believed him responsible for, and gave chase to the mysterious "Master of Men" who eluded them as always.

The serial developed interestingly with the use of gas-filled rooms, television spy pick-ups, and a deathray gun. The plot used such elements as the Octopus pretending to be the Spider, and at one point, apparently learning the Spider's true identity.

The cliffhangers included one where the Spider and Nita were hanging from the chain lift of a tall crane and sent hurtling toward the ground when the chain was allowed to run through completely free; the Spider caught between the crushing jaws of electric-powered vault doors; plus the usual assortment of fires, explosions, and car crashes.

The effect of the cliffhanger was always spoiled by Columbia's practice of showing preview scenes from the following chapter in which the Spider (or whatever their hero) was clearly shown to have survived.

Finally, the Spider came face to face with the Octopus in Chapter Fifteen, "The Octopus Unmasked." In order to save the captured Nita and Jackson, the Spider shot the gang leader dead and removed the hood, revealing the Octopus to really be a banker named Chase (actor Charles C. Wilson). No relation to the Chase Manhattan, one is confident.

The Spider's Web was scripted by Robert E. Kent, Basil Dickey, George H. Plympton, and Martie Ramson, and was directed by Ray Taylor and James W. Horne.

In 1941, Columbia offered *The Spider Returns* directed by Horne alone from a script by Plympton and a new collaborator, Jesse A. Duffy. Warren Hull and Kenne Duncan returned as the Spider and Ram Singh, but with new aides: Mary Ainslee as Nita, Dave O'Brien as Jackson, and Joe Girard as the Commissioner. This time a new wave of sabotage being spread by the dread Gargoyle was no more a match for the Spider than the Octopus.

The detectives booked and fingerprinted in this chapter are only a representative selection of the many sleuths who have prowled through chapterplays. In the sound era, the serial screen also offered two serials about *Secret Agent X-9*, (starring Scott Kolk and Lloyd Bridges respectively), as well as *G-Men vs. The Black Dragon* (young Rod Cameron), *Federal Operator 99, Flying G-Men, Who's Guilty?, Red Barry* (Buster Crabbe), *G-Men Never Forget* (Clayton Moore), *Federal Agents vs. Underworld, Inc., Radar Patrol vs. Spy King* (both starring Kirk Alyn), and others.

Almost *every* serial was a *mystery* story.

You waited all through the weekly episodes to find out who was the villain at the end. Or sometimes for a switch, as in *The Lone Ranger* and *The Masked Marvel,* you waited to find out who was the hero.

The game may not have been played as scrupulously fair as an Ellery Queen novel, but it was usually fun.

9

The Superheroes   "Could Superman Knock Out Captain Marvel?"

THE MAN OF STEEL

Superman, the flying strong man from another planet, has been one of the most fantastically successful fictional characters in history, in every medium from his original source, the comic books, to the movie screen. In 1948 the Columbia serial, *Superman,* became the top money-making serial of all time.

The basic premise of the Superman character is so classic it seems almost consciously contrived by a psychologist to appeal to the wish-fulfillment fantasies of youngsters, and perhaps even those not so young.

Clark Kent is a rather ineffectual young man, barely holding onto his job as a reporter for the *Daily Planet.* He is scorned by his fellow employee, the beautiful and daring Lois Lane, as a fool and a weakling. But she is unaware that Kent hides his true self, that beneath his shell—that is, a drab business suit and horn-rimmed glasses—he is virtually a god, the symbol of absolute virility, *Superman!* Discarding his ordinary clothes, Kent stands revealed in a skin-tight blue costume, enhanced by a red cape, red shorts, red boots, and red monogram "S" over a yellow shield on his muscular chest. Even his hair is no longer neatly combed, but wind-tossed and showing a spit-curl.[1]

In this role, his *true* self (the powerless weakling is the sham,

[1] This may be one of the earliest examples in recent times symbolizing freedom and power through "wild" hair.

the pose) Superman can take such gigantic leaps that he seems to *fly,* bend iron bars in his bare hands, lift an automobile over his head, and let bullets bounce off his skin, which is "invulnerable."

The source of all these powers was described in the first issue of *Action Comics* in 1938, which first presented Superman to the world. Writer Jerry Seigel and artist Joe Shuster created the comic strip several years before while in their teens, had tried vainly to sell it into newspaper syndication, but finally sold it to the National line of comics, for whom they had done other strips. They received $200 and ultimately lost all their rights in the multi-million dollar creation.

The comic book origin was followed with relative fidelity in the 1948 movie serial.

"In the far reaches of space, like a pinpoint at infinity, there once was a tiny blue star . . ." the off-screen narrator's voice droned, " . . . in reality a planet like our own. This was the ill-fated planet Krypton, which revolved around the brilliant sun of its own solar system."

The jagged, mountainous terrain of the alien world came into view, and then the capital of the planet, the center of a race of people, quite like human beings in appearance but possessed of unearthly abilities.

Within the futuristic Kryptonian city was Jor-El, the planet's foremost scientist, clad in flowing white garments not unlike those of ancient Greece. (In serials, the more futuristic civilizations inevitably seemed to adopt more primitive styles.) Suddenly there was a sizable tremor—a Kryptonquake—and Jor-El realized that he could no longer delay in his plan to shoot his doomed race off to the livable planet Earth in spaceships of his own invention.

Later in the great council hall of Krypton, Jor-El revealed his findings that their world was doomed to be drawn into the sun.

JOR-EL: We must flee Krypton. I urge that an army of laborers
be drafted to construct a fleet of spaceships to transport our
people to Earth. There we will find an atmosphere similar
to ours.

COUNCILMAN: Krypton has undergone quakes in the past and has
survived. You challenge credulity by claiming our planet is
being drawn into the sun's orbit. The doom of Krypton! Escape through the air! Are these not the utterances of a man
whose mind perhaps has begun to wander?

The councilmen only laughed at the greatest of scientists.
Ridiculed, Jor-El returned to his laboratory and completed
work on the silver-gray rocket model which could at least save
his wife Lara and their infant son.

Another tremor shook the planet, so violent that Jor-El was
thrown to the floor. Eruptions of mighty volcanoes added to
the horror of the dying planet. Jor-El, working against the time
of his own death motioned for Lara to enter the rocket model
with their child. But the lovely young woman refused, realizing
her place lay with her husband. Placing his son inside the protective space craft, Jor-El released the firing switch and the
shiny projectile blasted off its launching platform, dwindling to
a dot in space as the planet Krypton exploded to dust.

"And as Krypton and all its people perished," came the voice
of the narrator, "the infant son of Jor-El and Lara hurled
through the infinite reaches of space toward distant Earth."

The flight of the rocket proved true, but the sizzling craft
landed with a destructive impact in a rural area of the planet
Earth. There, it was spotted by a passing motorist, Eben Kent,
and his wife Sarah who rescued the tiny infant, wrapped in red
and blue blankets, just before the rocket blew up.

The baby was later adopted from an orphanage by the Kents
and given the name Clark Kent, and a home on their farm.

As young Clark grew older, he learned that he was not like
other boys. His speed was greater than that of a speeding auto-

mobile. He could leap over the barn on the farm, see farther than others could with a telescope and even look through solid objects like a human X-ray machine. His skin seemed impervious to harm or pain. His strength was enough to lift a tractor from the fields.

When he reached manhood, Clark realized that he was no ordinary human being. His foster parents told him the strange story of where he came from, and his mother gave him a uniform she had fashioned from the red and blue blankets he had been wrapped in as a baby. He must use his great powers to help those weaker than himself, to fight all the forces of evil and destruction in the world. Clark Kent was—and must be— *Superman!*

PA KENT: You came to us out of the sky, from what distant planet we can't even imagine. You are different from other people. Your unique abilities make you a kind of Superman . . . Because of these great powers—your speed and strength, your X-ray vision and supersensitive hearing—you have a great responsibility.

MA KENT: Here's a uniform I made for you out of the blankets you were wrapped in when we found you. The cloth is a strange kind that resists both fire and acid. I hope it will protect you, always.

CLARK KENT: I'll wear it only when I'm . . . I'm . . . Superman. It will be better if no one knows he and Clark Kent are the same.

The 1948 film followed the slight name changes already made in the comics for the two sets of parents for the mighty Superman. His natural parents were originally Jor-L and Lora, which were changed to Jor-El and Lara, and his foster parents were first John and Mary Kent of Ohio, but were changed to Eben and Sarah Kent of Smallville.

There had also been changes in the character and abilities of Superman himself.

Originally, in 1938, Superman was the *sole* survivor of the destroyed planet Krypton, and only able to leap through the air for a mere eighth of a mile, and his hide was so thick it could be penetrated by "nothing less than a bursting shell." By 1948 when the film serial was made, Superman's powers had increased enormously. He could fly around the world in one bound if necessary, and absolutely nothing could damage his skin.

Today, in the comics, not only Superman, but virtually half the population of Krypton seems to have survived in some manner or other, in artificial satellites, cities shrunk down to fit into a gallon jar, another dimensional "Phantom Zone," *ad infinitum*. Not only the people of Krypton have survived, but a whole menagerie of superanimals, including dogs, cats, horses, monkeys, and even a turtle. Fortunately, these innovations were not introduced into the movie serial.

When the adult Superman in his guise of Clark Kent first accepted the uniform from his foster mother on the screen, it was the culmination of years of effort to bring a "live" Superman to motion pictures.

Movie studios were interested in the phenomenally successful character of Superman soon after his first appearance. Republic Studios was dickering with the publishers for several years for rights to make a Superman serial. One of the problems seems to have been the publishers' insistence on *absolute* control over the script and production. Twice, Republic announced that they would make *Superman*. In 1940, the studio announced that it had been considering a Superman serial, but instead would make *The Mysterious Dr. Satan,* featuring a comic book-like hero, the Copperhead, to battle the evil doctor. In 1941, in a promotional publication sent to film distributors, *Republic Pictures Advance Serial Promotion Book,* the studio announced with a two-page advertisement complete with story-board type drawings of some proposed scenes that the *Superman* epic would be released that same year.

However, it turned out that Republic was not the only studio negotiating with the National comic line. Superman came to the screen in 1941, but in the form of an animated color cartoon from Paramount Pictures, the first of a series of seventeen. These cartoons were excellent, not humorous in intent, but a wonderful showcase for animation, with Superman's voice being supplied by the Superman of the radio series, Bud Collyer. However, the Paramount cartoons apparently tied up the exclusive use of Superman on the screen. Undismayed, Republic turned from making a Superman serial, to doing one of his chief comic book rivals, the equally superhuman Captain Marvel (and employed several of their plans for Superman in the Marvel chapterplay).

Seven years passed before Superman was again scheduled to be brought to the screen.

Producer Sam Katzman, chiefly noted for never having lost money on any film bearing his name, acquired the live action rights to the Man of Steel and tried selling the property to both Universal and, again, Republic in 1947. Universal turned it down on the basis that the company had not made a cliffhanger since 1946 and preferred to leave that phase of their history in the past. Republic renounced the Superman concept with the statement that a superpowerful flying hero would be impossible to adapt to the screen, apparently forgetting about their own *Captain Marvel* serial of 1941. (Of course, by this time, Republic was no longer buying the rights to famous characters, but creating their own, such as the flying hero of *King of the Rocket Men* who would soar into theatres in 1948.)

Finally, it was Columbia, the studio whose serials were all produced by Katzman since the mid-1940s, who agreed to pay the price for the rights to make a serial of *Superman*.

The choice of *who* would play the part of a live Superman next came to the fore.

Numerous actors were considered for the role, both well known and unknown. Reportedly, Buster Crabbe was considered for the part, but he was not happy with the idea of doing another comic-strip hero such as the Flash Gordon and Tarzan roles he had been type-cast in, and the producers must have decided that he was a bit too mature, and of course little resembled the cartoon drawings of Superman. Some one else had to be found.

Sam Katzman looked over photos of actors he had previously employed in consultation with the National Comics line representative, Whitney Ellsworth. Finally, one actor's face seemed perfectly suited for the part, a young man with long experience on the stage and in films by the name of Kirk Alyn.

The energetic producer tried selling the exacting publishers' representatives on how well-suited Alyn would be in the part of the Man of Steel—his handsome face with the slightly aristocratic nose and clean jawline would be perfect as Superman. Finally, Kirk Alyn walked into the producer's office—wearing a goatee and mustache grown for a part in an historical film. His reception as a potential Superman was lukewarm.

However, studio portraits and a later shave convinced all concerned that Kirk Alyn was right to play the part of Superman.

Of course, this was *not* what the studio announced to the world.

The solemn announcement came that trying to find a suitable actor to play Superman was a hopeless quest, and that no one but the *real* Superman would be convincing in the part. The Real, authentic Superman was to come to the screen himself! It was too much for any but the youngest fan to accept, but Columbia's press releases had it that the true Superman was flying to Hollywood to star as himself in the most anticipated cliffhanger since *Flash Gordon*.

Even the colorful posters outside the theatres and the credits of the film had it featuring "SUPERMAN, Kirk Alyn, Noel Neill, Tommy Bond, Carol Forman . . ." The cast listings did admit to Kirk Alyn playing Clark Kent, although not Superman.

Alyn was a trained actor, in athletic condition, and he had even had experience as a reporter for a newspaper published by Columbia University's School of Journalism to add authenticity to his role of Clark Kent. Perhaps his muscles were not super-human enough to satisfy everyone, but millions of fans did accept him as *being* Superman. For years, he was so identified with the role that it interfered with his career, and only lately has he been able to escape the image enough to play such roles as a crook in features like *Banning*.

Producer Katzman hired Spencer Bennet to direct the *Superman* chapterplay. Bennet was not the most art-conscious of directors for features or even serials, but he was prolific, economical, and absolutely professional. His films were virtually edited in his mind before a frame of film had been before the lens. He knew exactly what to shoot and how to shoot it, thus in effect editing the film in the camera, so that the film editor's job was one of making physical splices, not of creative selection. This method saved the studios enormous sums of money.

The writing staff was headed by George H. Plympton, another veteran of Katzman serials. Although a thorough professional, Plympton did enjoy exasperating the publishing company's representatives by having Superman cry in the script, "Hi-Yo Silver!" instead of "Up, Up and Away!" (The joke never got to the screen.) The official credits gave the adaptation to Plympton and Joseph F. Poland, with the screenplay by Arthur Hoerl, Lewis Clay, and Royal Cole. However, Plympton supervised all the writing.

After the origin of Superman was explained to the audience, the first chapter of the serial continued with Clark Kent leaving the home of his late foster parents, and heading for the big city of Metropolis where he planned to get a job with a newspaper, which would help him keep aware of people who needed his superhuman services.

Near the railroad station, Kent spotted a damaged track, its rails twisted out of shape. The speeding express on that track was carrying important government officials, and two reporters, Lois Lane (played by pert Noel Neill) and young Jimmy Olsen (snub-nosed Tommy Bond). The train would soon speed across the break in the tracks to a horrible wreck, dooming all the passengers.

The station agent yelled to Kent. "The Express has already passed the last station! I couldn't stop it!"

Slipping away from the agent and vanishing behind a clump of bushes, the soft-spoken young man removed his glasses and the business suit, revealing the startling red and blue costume of *Superman!*[2]

The first episode concluded after twenty-six and a half minutes with the doomed train rushing down on Superman. (Possibly the less initiated of the audience was supposed to fear that the Man of Steel himself might also be in danger.)

Of course, Chapter Two began with Superman twisting the rails back into place, and holding them secure as the train sped safely by.

Later, Kent formally met the two reporters and did get a probational job from editor Perry White (white-haired Pierre Watkin) on the *Daily Planet*.

The greatest danger the city of Metropolis seemed to face came from the Spider Lady (blond, faintly foreign Carol Forman), and her gang of henchmen which included such serial regulars as Jack Ingram, George Meeker, Terry Frost, Rusty Westcott, ex-hero Charles Quigley, and that most durable of Western bad guys, the heavy-set heavy, Charles King.

[2] The costume was really gray (for blue) and brown (for red). Those colors photographed better in black and white.

Lois soon learned that Superman was a handy fellow to have around when he rescued her from a mine-cave-in, the climax of Chapter Two.

The cliffhanger of Chapter Three was one of the most unusual. Kent had gone to interview a professor who had found a strange meteor. When the professor showed the meteor fragment to Kent, the reporter collapsed.

The following chapter revealed that Kent recovered when the meteor fragment was replaced in its lead box, and that the fragment came from Superman's home planet. The radioactive substance, Kryptonite, was the only thing that could rob Superman of his powers, or even kill him if he were exposed to it long enough. (This concept was first used by the comic-strip originators, Siegel and Shuster for a special edition comic book in 1940, but the book was never published. Apparently by spontaneous coincidence, the radio series' scripters also later introduced Kryptonite and played it up before it became commonplace in the comic magazines.)

The Spider Lady learned of the substance that could rid her of Superman so that her one-woman crime wave could go on, unhindered. In her quest of the rare element, she sought to learn what knowledge Lois Lane and Jimmy Olsen had of it. Lois narrowly escaped an electrically charged death trap (Chapter Four), another elaborate trap in a museum (Chapter Five), and a plunge from a cliff in a car (Chapter Six).

To save her from going over the cliff, Superman arrived in the nick of time, scooped her up and flew away with her.

Here, it must be noted, was the weakest point of the serial— Superman turned into an animated cartoon when he flew. Even the smallest child could see it was a cartoon. The effects created by Republic for Captain Marvel were very convincing; even the more routine ones for the Superman television series always showing the TV actor, George Reeves, in the same flying pose, were better. Kirk Alyn subjected himself to more than discomfort—downright agony—suspended by supposedly invisible wires before a rear projection screen of moving clouds, suspended there for an entire work day. Producer Katzman fired all the production employees connected with the fiasco, and went to the animated concept he later used (equally unsuccessfully) for the flying saucers in *Bruce Gentry*. (The animating artist also did the one flying scene in the George Reeves feature film of 1951, *Superman and the Mole Men*.)

In the subsequent chapters, the Spider Lady's mob continued to threaten Lois and Jimmy. Superman had to save the boy reporter from being carried to his death by a conveyor belt leading to an electric furnace (Chapter Seven), rescue Lois from fires in both Chapters Nine and Ten. Even elderly editor Perry White was menaced in the cliffhanger for Chapter Thirteen when one of the Spider Lady's thugs threw the newspaperman out of the window of his skyscraper office. (White managed to save himself, by grabbing the heavy cords of the venetian blinds.)

In the showdown, the Spider Lady attempted to destroy her supposedly invincible foe with *two* weapons—the Kryptonite and the marvelous Reducer Ray, a disintegrator weapon she had sought to obtain all through the serial and now at last had in her possession. Lois and Jimmy were helpless in the hands of the female mastermind and her thugs when Superman darted onto the scene. Sensing victory, the Spider Lady ordered the Reducer Ray turned full blast onto the Man of Steel. He took the deadly ray and remained unharmed. As for the Kryptonite, he had neutralized its effect by a lead lining beneath his uniform. The Reducer Ray continued to build up fantastic energies, until it exploded, destroying forever the menace of the Spider Lady and her henchmen.

During these chapters, Superman performed many effective stunts. He bent the iron bars of a jail cell and the bumper off a car with his bare hands. He stopped a train by bracing his hands against its impact, crashed through walls of stone and of wood. Most often, he would take two crooks, one in either hand, pick them up off the floor and crack their heads together. All of these were done relatively convincingly, but the special effects were marred by the flying scenes. A typical sequence would show the cartoon Superman on a downward flight, disappearing behind a building. From the other side of the wall would emerge the live-action actor, Kirk Alyn.

Kirk Alyn performed many graceful leaps of his own, which, if combined with good special effects, would have produced an excellent flying effect. As it was, Alyn did many dangerous and arduous tasks in the serial. He had a stuntman, Paul Stader, who did not really look much like him. (The skin-tight uniform offered better comparisons than the hats and business suits worn by many serial heroes and their stuntmen doubles.) Stader performed only one stunt in the whole serial—a leap from the back of a truck—and nearly broke his leg, taking him off the production.

Despite the flaws in the special effects, the cast and director managed to make the whole thing come off. The serial became a tremendous financial success, playing first-run theatres that had never before booked a serial.

A sequel was called for and it was released in 1950, a second serial of fifteen chapters, *Atom Man vs. Superman*. The casting and production team were virtually the same as the first serial. The most significant addition was that of the Man of Steel's bald archenemy from the comics, Luthor, played by Lyle Talbot, once a star of Broadway and the screen, who now was doing character roles. Talbot wore a rubber scalp to simulate baldness for the role of the diabolical scientist, and spent most of his off-screen moments exchanging cooking recipes with Kirk Alyn who shared his hobby.

Luthor had adopted the second identity of Atom Man, wearing flowing black robes and an all-concealing helmet of lead to repel Superman's X-ray vision. After attempting to blackmail Metropolis with a threat to destroy the city, Luthor and his men were captured by Superman and imprisoned. Utilizing a device by which the atoms of the human body could be separated and reassembled in a different location, Luthor helped his hench-man, Lawson (stuntman Paul Stader), escape jail. Luthor, us-ing his device, was able to remain in prison while doubling on the outside world as the unknown Atom Man.

In the course of the serial, Luthor designed several other fantastic inventions. He perfected a *synthetic* Kryptonite that made Superman unconscious and "At the Mercy of Atom Man" in Chapter Seven.

Using the same method as his jail-escape device, Luthor, alias Atom Man, reduced Superman to only a semi-tangible ghostly figure unable to prevent the archcriminal's deeds. (Finally, Superman transmitted instructions for his rescue to Lois Lane by barely being able to work the keys of her typewriter.)

Later, a paroled Luthor soon attacked Metropolis full force with flying saucers (poorly animated) that destroyed airplanes and finally another cartoon device, a torpedo that threatened the entire city.

Superman streaked through the air, red cape streaming be-hind him, to overtake the "Rocket of Vengeance" in the four-teenth segment of the serial. Apparently, as the chapter ended, Superman had failed and Metropolis and all his friends in the city were destroyed.

In the last chapter, "Superman Saves the Universe," it was revealed that the Man of Steel did manage to divert the torpedo and sent it into the ocean where its explosive fury did no serious harm. Meanwhile, Luthor had turned another device, a sonic vibrator upon the city, causing a new wave of destruction. With the captured Lois Lane as hostage, Luthor escaped in his spaceship.

After doing his share to avert more wreckage and to save victims of Luthor's inventions, Superman took off after the spacecraft, smashing in through the hull, and carrying both Lois and the criminal scientist away, saving Luthor for jail and Lois for further adventures.

Atom Man vs. Superman was far more gimmicky and gadget-prone than the first serial, *Superman,* but was flawed by the same Katzman cheapness in production values, despite the cast and crew.

The star of both serials, Kirk Alyn, had an active career in other serials, including roles in *Daughter of Don Q* (1946); *Federal Agents vs. Underworld, Inc.* (1949); *Radar Patrol vs. Spy King* (1950); all Republic; and Columbia's *Blackhawk* (1952). At various times in his career, Alyn was considered to play the parts of Batman, Captain America, Rocket Man, and Flash Gordon (for a TV series) due to his typical heroic features. He was offered the role of the Man of Steel on television at one point, but refused it. Since the days of the serials, he has appeared in the legitimate theatre in many stage plays, in feature films, and on television. As a hobby, he has been a food columnist and photographer for a smaller newspaper than the *Daily Planet*—the real-life *Canyon Crier.*

THE OTHER WORLD'S MIGHTIEST MORTAL

Captain Marvel could fly like Superman, and he was as strong, fast, and as impervious to harm from bullets. But he came second. Perhaps because he was number two, he tried harder. In many respects, the comics and the movie serial of *Captain Marvel* were superior to the inspiration, Superman.

The Marvel serial did get to the screen first, but only because of legal difficulties in obtaining the film rights to *Superman.* Since Captain Marvel only came in off the bench as a substitute for the original Man of Steel, he must be considered second even though the fifteen chapters of *Adventures of Captain Marvel* were released in 1941, seven years before the live-action serial of *Superman* appeared.

After the success of Superman in the comics field, Fawcett Publications introduced a competitor, Captain Marvel, in the February 1940 issue of *Whiz Comics*. (There was an earlier experimental issue with sort of a trial balloon called Captain Thunder.) The red-suited character had most of Superman's powers (the most obviously missing: his X-ray vision) and another attribute (perhaps a power, perhaps a weakness): his secret identity was that of a non-superpowered small boy. The boy, Billy Batson, became Captain Marvel by shouting the magic world "Shazam" and becoming, in a stroke of enchanted lightning, the World's Mightiest Mortal, Captain Marvel. When there was no pressing danger, Billy remained a normal human being, prey to ordinary human frailties.

Billy Batson had been granted this miraculous gift by an old wizard named Shazam. He took his name from the initials of the six great heroes of legend, each one famous for a different virtue or power—Solomon (wisdom), Hercules (strength), Atlas (stamina), Zeus (power), Achilles (courage), and Mercury (speed). When Billy spoke the word, he gained all of those abilities, and was transformed into a grown man in an outfit resembling that of a *general* of some Eastern principality—red tights and shirt, trimmed with gold braid, with a white cape similarly trimmed, and flop-topped gold boots.

A gold sash and lightning bolt chest emblem completed the picture.

This was the basic premise of both the comics and the movie serial, but they diverged in the details of the origin.

The Marvel comics were the most *simplistic* of all superhero strips. It was as if *Peanuts* were used to tell the adventures of some dashing, superpowerful idol (other than Snoopy, of course). The line drawings were simple, not merely approaching the cartoon but entering well into that field, as apart from representational illustration. The storylines were parodies, satires, extravaganzas. (In fact, the comic book Captain Marvel may be regarded as a *satire* on all such similar comic heroes.) The comics were drawn from the first by C. C. Beck and written by Otto Binder during their best period. Naturally, the origin given Captain Marvel for this style of comic book story would be starkly fundamental. Billy Batson was led down into an abandoned subway tunnel in the heart of some great city by a figure with his face masked in the shadows of his hat brim. There, Billy saw an old magician on a throne who told him that because he was good at heart he was to be granted the power to become the superpowerful Captain Marvel by speaking the magician's name, Shazam.

The Republic serial modified this concept quite a bit, and made it somehow more acceptable. The changes they made also reflected the movie's basic divergence from the comics—the film serial almost completely eliminated the elements of wit and humor that made the comics memorable. However, Republic Studios replaced the humorous element with a serious, dedicated professionalism.

Bringing a superhuman hero to the screen in a manner that the audience would accept was a difficult business, and Republic brought all their powers to bear in filming *Adventures of Captain Marvel*. The result is unquestionably one of the finest movie serials ever made, possibly *the* best with the exception of the three Flash Gordon epics (which are somehow in a class all by themselves).

In the first chapter of the photoplay, Billy Batson was an assistant radio operator with the Malcolm archaeological expedition in the Far Eastern land known as the Valley of the Tombs. Billy appeared to be a young man of perhaps sixteen (played by the perennially youthful Frank Coghlan, Jr.), looking a few years older "in person" than he did on the comics page.

The expedition was besieged by a band of hostile natives until their guide, Tal Chotali (sly John Davidson), went out under a flag of truce to parley with the chieftain, Rahman Bar (virile Reed Hadley). There would be no true desecration of sacred places unless the volcano, Scorpio, roared back to life—thus spake the sacred legend. Having lost the religious argument, Rahman Bar reluctantly withdrew.

The expedition's distinguished leader, John Malcolm (played by Robert Strange) told his associates the story of the Scorpion's Curse, but nevertheless led them into the main tomb. Billy refused to go into the innermost tomb, not wishing to desecrate anyone's religious beliefs. Instead, the boy went down another passage to help pack some incidental pottery. Malcolm, along with Professor Luther Bentley (Harry Worth), Dwight Fisher (Peter George Lynn), and Dr. Stephen Lang (George Pembroke), entered through a small opening, finding inside the fabulous idol of a Golden Scorpion, each of its arms set with a lens. When the arms of the figure were moved into line, the lenses produced an explosion that sent a great stone slab falling across the entrance of the tomb, sealing the scientists inside.

The same shock wave in the other passage opened a hidden door before Billy's startled eyes. Cautiously, he entered. Inside, an ancient sarcophagus parted and revealed the standing figure of old Shazam. The commanding, bearded figure (played by Nigel de Brulier to perfection) told the boy that he had been selected to receive superhuman powers to see that the secrets of the Scorpion Dynasty were not put to evil use.

INT. TOMB OF SHAZAM—DAY
> *The dust of centuries fills the air as* BILLY *gapes in awe at the towering figure of* SHAZAM.

SHAZAM: I—am—Shazam!
BILLY: My name is—

SHAZAM: Ah, it is known to me. Your name is Billy Batson. You did not pry into the secret of the Scorpion. That is why I am here.

BILLY: But where did you come from?

SHAZAM: Out of the past, my son, down through the ages to guard the secret of the Scorpion.

BILLY (*incredulously*): You've been alive all these years?

SHAZAM: What you call "life" returned to me when your friends violated the tomb of the Scorpion.

BILLY: But they meant no harm!

SHAZAM: Then they should obey the inscription written on the tomb. The harm is being done. It is your duty to see that the curse of the Scorpion is not visited upon innocent people.

BILLY: My duty?

SHAZAM: Yes. So long as the Golden Scorpion may fall into the hands of selfish men it is the duty of Captain Marvel to protect the innocent from its evil use.

BILLY: But who is Captain Marvel?

SHAZAM: You are, my son. All that is necessary is to repeat my name—Shazam. By its repetition you will become Captain Marvel and take on the virtues you see recorded there . . . SHAZAM *indicates a large slab of rock upon which are carved out the powers of* CAPTAIN MARVEL. SOLOMON, *wisdom.* HERCULES, *strength. And the others.* BILLY *reads them silently, impressed. Then he turns back to* SHAZAM.

SHAZAM: You must never call on these powers except in the service of right. To do so would bring the Scorpion's curse upon you.

(*beat*)

And now, my son, repeat my name and return to the service of your friends!

BILLY *takes a deep breath. Then:*

BILLY: *Shazam!*

There is the clap of sudden thunder. A burst of smoke. And where BILLY *once stood now stands for the first time the figure of* CAPTAIN MARVEL.

Captain Marvel was played by Tom Tyler. His angular face, piercing eyes, and slender frame perfectly matched the very *first* appearance of Captain Marvel in the comics. Even his costume was exactly like that in the very early issues of *Whiz Comics* with a red shirt with one triangular flap that fastened with a single button on the right shoulder. The red tights and the white cape, both trimmed in the gold braid to match the lightning emblem on the chest, the sash, and boots were the same. Actually, by the time the movie serial appeared, there had been modifications made in the cartoon character. On the comics page, Captain Marvel had grown much heavier, appearing a bit oafish at times, and his shirt had lost the buttoned-down flap, becoming one piece. (Comic book publishers seemed to make it a habit to send movie producers only the very first issues for samples—the first screen *Batman* wore a costume patterned after the first experimental design for comics, which was rapidly replaced by a more streamlined version.)

While the stern-faced Tom Tyler did not reflect the good-humored do-gooder Captain Marvel was in cartoon panels, he seemed perfect for the screen. He was holder of a world weight-lifting championship, making him *literally* one of the strongest men in the world. Although identified primarily with Westerns, he was not so much a cowboy but simply a *hero* type. Tyler was believable as an explorer in *Jungle Mystery* (a 1932 Universal serial) and an aviator in *Phantom of the Air* (another Universal serial, 1933) as well as Bill Cody in *Battling with Buffalo Bill* (a 1931 Universal chapterplay). After leaving Detroit in 1924, known as Vincent Markowski, Tyler got his first film work in the silent *Ben-Hur* but his first starring role was in the 1925 Western, *Let's Go, Gallagher*. His first talking Western was *West of Cheyenne* in 1931, and he made countless others, becoming one of the ever-changing cast of the "Three Mesquiteers" series of the '40s. He occasionally played a villain, such as opposite John Wayne in that landmark film, *Stagecoach,* 1939. That villainy was topped in 1940 when he played one of the classic monsters, Kharis, the living mummy of *The Mummy's Hand.*

Whether he was seeking a wider range of roles or just was financially desperate when he accepted the role of the Mummy, Tyler may have placed himself in line more prominently to play Captain Marvel, who shared with Kharis the quality of being weirdly superhuman.

The one criticism his co-workers always make about Tom Tyler was he was clumsy. His lanky arms were always knocking over props, and in the fight scenes, many times Tyler would accidentally connect with a punch that was, of course, supposed to narrowly miss. While he was magnificent for looking heroic in the close-ups (no one but the most hardened cynic could say Tom Tyler looked silly in that red outfit) much of the action, particularly the flying scenes that looked absolutely *real,* were performed by stuntman Dave Sharpe, another of those ever-recurring names that made the serials possible.

Immediately after Billy first became Captain Marvel, the red-uniformed hero hurried out of Shazam's chamber and lifted the huge stone slab that sealed the archaeologists in the tomb. Becoming Billy Batson again by repeating the magic word as he had been instructed, he joined the others and helped them bring out the figure of the Golden Scorpion—fortunately, sort of a portable-sized idol.

The Golden Scorpion proved a handy gadget—by arranging the lenses set in each of its arms one way, it became a deathray. Arranged another way, the lenses turned common materials to gold.

The diverse powers of the Golden Scorpion figure were deemed too powerful to be placed in the hands of any one man, so the lenses that produced the supernatural effects were divided among the various members of the expedition—the group of five middle-aged scientists. (Presumably at some future time, proper disposition of the complete Scorpion idol would be figured out.)

Through the behind-the-scenes exhortations of the black-robed and masked human Scorpion (if so dastardly a villain could be called human!) and the eruption of the sacred volcano of Scorpio, Rahman Bar and his native horde attacked the encampment. Troopers from Fort Mooltan answered a call for help but were trapped under a hail of arrows, spears, and rifle bullets.

All the Malcolm expedition were faced with death. They left in two automobiles, as Billy Batson mysteriously stayed behind. Firing one last pistol shot at the invaders of the camp, Billy holstered his gun and cried, "Shazam!" Captain Marvel appeared in a burst of magic smoke, his cape lifting in the breeze.

The scene that followed is one of the most exciting in any serial, or any action feature film. It was a combination of breathtaking stunt work, acrobatics, special effects, direction, editing, and acting. Everything was absolutely *professional* to bring to the live action screen that most difficult of subjects—the comic book superhero.

Captain Marvel had made one brief earlier appearance when he appeared for the first time and lifted a massive stone slab, but this was really his first appearance in action. Republic went all out.

The World's Mightiest Mortal seemed to sense his superhuman powers, without yet fully knowing their extent. Seeing some hostile natives operating a machine gun below him, Captain Marvel took a graceful dive off a 30-foot cliff and landed on top of them. He seized one turbaned native and lifted him over his head, throwing him at another death-lusting marauder. The killers quickly saw that this was no ordinary infidel, and ran full speed from the scene.

With his friends in danger still from the murdering tribesmen, Captain Marvel kneeled at the belt-fed machine gun and fired a burst of bullets that felled several of the running men. It may not have been chivalrous, but it was certainly justifiable homicide among the litter of corpses the tribesmen had created.

But Captain Marvel found shooting and killing distasteful

and lifted the heavy field piece, hurling it from him, smashing it. He went after the other killers with his bare hands.

From a slight rise, the natives opened up on the red-uniformed figure with rifle fire. With obvious surprise, Captain Marvel looked down at the bullets bouncing from his own chest, and first learned he was invulnerable to almost all mortal harm.

The caped figure sprang up, his heels knocking two natives sprawling, and performed a complete back flip to land on his feet again. He seized up a rifle, but now he knew he would never have to use any weapon other than his own superhuman body. He broke the long-barreled gun across his knee like a stick of kindling, and smiled in grim satisfaction as the tribesmen ran in terror from this red-garbed demon.

Meanwhile, the first car carrying the five distinguished scientists had crossed safely a bridge spanning a deep gorge, but the station wagon with pretty, firm-jawed Betty Wallace (Louise Currie) and youthful Whitey (played by Billy Benedict), who seemed even lower in seniority on the expedition than even teen-aged Billy Batson, was headed into trouble. The natives had set dynamite under the bridge, and sure enough, it went off just as the station wagon was crossing. The bridge broke like a matchstick but held together for a moment. Whitey frantically attempted to back up, to get back on solid ground, but it was too late. The bridge and the car plunged toward the bottom of the gorge.

Back at the camp, the natives had regrouped and were riding down on Captain Marvel, attempting to trample him beneath the flashing hooves of their steeds!

It was a double cliffhanger, but the moviegoer could hardly be expected to believe that Captain Marvel himself could be hurt by being trampled in a mere horse stampede. Not after seeing him impervious to harm as he performed superhuman feats.

How did Captain Marvel do it all?

A lot of the effects were due to the acrobatics of stunt expert, Dave Sharpe. He took terrific leaps off high points, holding his body straight as if he could actually fly, only rolling to land as softly as possible at the last split second. (He did the back flip, knocking the two natives down with his feet, without any trickery at all.)

The rest of the flying effect was due to the special effects genius of Howard Lydecker. In an interview with one of the present writers, he told how a dummy was made, slightly better than life-size (seven feet from head to toe), constructed of lightweight papier-mâché, so that it totaled only fifteen pounds. The prototype had been of the character, Superman, but was discarded when Republic canceled plans to film that serial. The red-and-gold Captain Marvel uniform was made of thin silk and cotton jersey. The figure was made in the form of a man flying with outstretched arms and arched back after the drawings of artist Mac Raboy (who sometimes did Captain Marvel, Sr., but was more identified with the *Captain Marvel, Jr.* strip about the World's Mightiest Boy, sort of an adopted son). Four tiny pulley wheels were connected to each shoulder and leg calf and strung on wires between two mountain ridges, various buildings, etc. The dummy was weighted perfectly so it would move on the two wires without any propulsion other than its own weight. When the figure was supposed to fly *up,* the cape was weighted down, the figure slid backward, feet first, but then the film was reversed so that it seemed to fly upward.

When this figure was used in conjunction with the obviously real man, stuntman Sharpe, leaping or jumping into the air off a hidden trampoline, it looked very real indeed. When Captain Marvel landed, Sharpe would jump from a considerable height in slow motion, land, and start to turn. After a quick cut, Tom Tyler would complete the turn, staring down the evil-doers with his piercing gaze.

Some of the spectacular flying scenes had Captain Marvel

flying "up" from the street level to the roof of the Biltmore Hotel garage located in the downtown section of Los Angeles, flying after two running men and overtaking them, and winging after a man riding away from him on a horse. The figure was obviously real and solid, not superimposed or matted in. The only trouble in the special effects was that some—but only some— of the insert shots of Tyler "flying" against the clouds of a rear projection screen showed the wires supporting the star. It is unfortunate that these shots could not have been eliminated by the film editor.

As the second episode began, Captain Marvel took to the air again, simply flying away from the path of galloping horsemen. He flew to the gorge, dived into the water, and pulled Betty and Whitey to safety before magically changing back to the boy, Billy Batson.

Safe from the tribesmen, the expedition returned to the United States where Billy resumed his job at a radio station (the call letters from the comics, W-H-I-Z, were never mentioned).

Billy broadcasted that the whole Malcolm expedition was grateful to be beyond the reach of the menacing Scorpion at last. At that moment, the robed figure of the human villain, the Scorpion, was showing the Scorpion idol to his big city chief henchman, Barnett (Kenne Duncan). His plan was to get the lenses one by one and restore them to the idol, to then use its wealth and power for his own ends.

Captain Marvel would attempt to thwart each of the Scorpion's attempts to gain the lenses. As the second chapter ended, the red-uniformed hero burst through the window of the laboratory belonging to one of the Malcolm Expedition scientists, Carlyle, when Barnett and his hirelings were trying to steal one of the vital lenses. The bullets of the thugs had no effect on Captain Marvel, but Barnett managed to catch him off balance when he struck him with a chair. The Captain stumbled backward into arcing beams of powerful electricity which seemed to render him unconscious. He fell onto the conveyor belt of a deadly contrivance set for intruders and was carried into the path of a falling guillotine!

It was a nice touch, demonstrating that Captain Marvel *could* be harmed by some mortal agency (the electric arc), but although we could see that Captain Marvel could be *temporarily stunned,* no true fan could fail to believe that the deadly, descending blade would not be shattered on Captain Marvel's superhuman body, as indeed it was in the beginning of Chapter Three.

Only two other chapters of the serial would have Captain Marvel himself placed in "danger." Chapter Five, "The Scorpion Strikes," had him apparently in concern over being boiled in molten lava in an old tunnel (but simply flying away from it in the next episode). The next installment, Chapter Six, "Lens of Death," had the costumed hero falling from another surge of powerful electricity—but simply reviving from it in the next solution.

As the fight continued against the Scorpion's plan to seize all the lenses (and apparently kill off all the expedition scientists in the process), Captain Marvel in his vulnerable human form of Billy Batson found himself in trouble from a time bomb in an airplane; a time bomb in an automobile; from non-time (aerial) bombs as he lay tied in a target shack; from a trap set with automatically firing machine guns; and a sinking ship at sea. The heroine, Betty, was the object of two cliffhangers as she lay unconscious at the wheel of a careening automobile in one, and in another, clutched at faithful Whitey as the roof of a stone temple fell in on them. Billy, Betty, and Whitey all survived, usually by Billy changing to Captain Marvel in the nick of time.

Each of the scientists had hidden his lens in a different location. It developed that Lang murdered by the Scorpion, left his lens near its original location in the Valley of the Tombs. His map showing the exact spot was torn into sections and divided

among Billy, Betty, and the archaeologists: Malcolm, Tal Chotali, and Bentley had shifty, ominous gazes.

The new, abbreviated expedition set sail for the Valley of
the Tombs. Aside from a shipwreck, and attempted murder by
the Scorpion, the trip was uneventful.

Rahman Bar and his tribesmen, not seen since the first chapter, were still on hand in the Valley of the Tombs. The natives
captured the party from America, but Billy changed to Captain
Marvel in time to rescue them—and to be seen in the act of his
magical change by the Scorpion himself. The unlucky expedition was captured once again, this time including a bound—*and
gagged*—Billy Batson.

The robed and hooded Scorpion demanded of the tied Billy
his secret for becoming Captain Marvel. Was it some "powerful drug?" Would he talk, or—? Billy nodded. His gag was removed. "I'll not only tell you—*I'll show ya!*" Billy told him.
"Shazam!"

After the cloud of magical smoke, Captain Marvel easily
broke the ropes that had held him powerless as Billy, knocked
Rahman Bar sprawling, and tore the hood from the Scorpion
revealing him to be—the mustached Bentley! (Actually, actor
Gerald Mohr did the voice of the Scorpion. In one misleading
scene Robert Strange dashed through the shadows unmasked,
wearing the Scorpion costume.)

Snarling, Bentley pulled a gun, and held Betty as his hostage,
backing away from both Captain Marvel and the angry natives,
disillusioned to find that the Scorpion was only another masquerading infidel. Covertly, Rahman Bar stole to the device the
Scorpion had built from the lenses he had stolen—a powerful
"atom smasher." Using it, the native chieftain disintegrated the
scheming Bentley where he stood.

Captain Marvel had one final task—he lifted the Scorpion idol
and hurled it into the volcanic depths of Scorpio, where it would
rest until men could use its knowledge wisely. Then—without

speaking the magic word—Captain Marvel suddenly reverted without the customary puff of smoke and *boom!* to the form of Billy Batson. The spectral voice of the old wizard, Shazam, told him that the work of Captain Marvel was done, that Billy, Betty, and Whitey could now leave the Valley of Tombs in peace.

It was a mildly disturbing note to young fans who knew that Captain Marvel's powers were not taken from him, that he still fought other evils in the color pages of the comics. Only in later years was Captain Marvel forced into retirement—by Superman's lawyers.

Only the movie serial of the great Captain still perpetuates his fame, still in release under its misleading 1953 rerelease title, *Return of Captain Marvel,* for those few dingy theatres showing serials for kids, and for the appreciative audiences of some art theatres. Republic Pictures Corporation also has on sale three 8mm home movie titles of Captain Marvel, offering in effect an hour and a half featurization of the serial.

The photoplay was directed by that near faultless action film team, John English and William Witney, written by Ronald Davidson, Norman S. Hall, Arch B. Herth, Joseph Poland, and Sol Shor, with music composed by a staff headed by Cy Feuer, who later produced such Broadway hits as *Guys and Dolls.* The result of their work is a wonderful film with serious intentions, not the easy ridicule cynical adults brought to costume hero films in later years. The saving grace is the near absence of what many serial devotees most like about Republic Serials—the stuntwork fist fights. Captain Marvel was too superpowerful to take more than one punch to subdue an ordinary mortal. The screen time *had* to be filled with something other than punches. This serial had time for plot and characterization, as well as action. The result was what may well be the world's mightiest movie serial.

10

The Long-Underwear Boys
"You've Met Me, Now Meet My Fist!"

THE CAPED CRUSADER

The cowled and caped Batman sat alone at an ornate desk in the shadowy recesses of the subterranean Bat's Cave, unperturbed by the various winged forms flitting about the rocky walls, obviously lost in a brown study (or at least, lost in a black cave). Suddenly, another masked and caped figure entered the scene. It was Robin, the Boy Wonder. Batman looked up, his eyes widening beneath the mask, a broad grin splitting across his face. Arising, the older man placed one hand on the boy's shoulder, and they exchanged friendly smiles. Then the two skipped out of the picture, off to strike a blow against the underworld. Or something.

This is how the first chapter, "The Electrical Brain," of the serial, *The Batman,* began. There would be too much mayhem and murder to follow to give Batman and Robin much time for further smiles, but audiences might find a few laughs for themselves, whether planned or not.

The relentlessly grown-up world has always been slightly amused by the costume figures that appeal so strongly to children, and even to many college-age or older people. To those who completely reject the element of fantasy from their life and thought, the masked "mystery man" will forever seem silly. Yet to those frustrated by being a child caught in an adult world, or by being a dreamer in a world sitting tight on its "practicality," the costumed hero represents a vicarious exercise of *power* to accomplish secret wishes by superhuman means.

There are many obscure sources for the masked crimefighter, but the first on the scene in terms of popular culture was Johnston McCulley's Zorro, the colorful swordsman of the novel, *Mark of Zorro,* published at the time of the First World War, and given vitality on the screen by Douglas Fairbanks, Sr. Many of the creators of the famous characters to follow openly admit their debt to Zorro, including cartoonist Bob Kane, originator of Batman.

The essential factor of all these mysterious figures is a private self that appears weak and powerless, but that is a mask for the true self, the colorfully costumed and titled figure who can achieve virtually anything. It is always the everyday, civilian self that is only a pose, and the powerful, heroic alter ego the true self. The comic books achieved the perfect schism in 1938 with the creation of *Superman.* In the original stories, at least, his workaday pose of reporter Clark Kent was the total ineffectual boob, in *absolute* contrast to his near godlike powers as the Man of Steel. The movies, unlike the comics, in both serials and features, often seemed to miss the whole point of the double-identity figure and have the hero in ordinary clothing doing virtually anything he could do in his heroic costume. In the second Batman serial, at least, Bruce Wayne got into almost as many fights as his alter ego, Batman, and in the Durango Kid features, Charles Starrett could fight and shoot as well as an ordinary cowpoke as he could in the black outfit of Durango. Under these circumstances, there was simply no *point* to these competent, openly declared crime-fighters arbitrarily deciding to put on a mask and cape at some given point.

Often in the comics, and sometimes in the movies, the heroes had to disguise not only their identity but the fact that they had literally superhuman abilities to leap tall buildings in one bound, or to let bullets bounce off of them. The popularity of these superheroes has continued, but from the first, there has been a vocal faction who preferred their heroes not quite so Olympian.

As kids, we could duplicate Superman's uniform by dyeing a pair of old longjohns blue (or leaving them red for Captain Marvel), but we could not fly off the garage. We never even *tried* to fly off it (more than once). No matter how much exercise we took or how many bowls of prescribed breakfast cereal we ate, we could never stop a mighty locomotive in its tracks, or burst steel chains by lung expansion. We were human, and we would remain in that pitifully mundane condition, while the Man of Steel and his rival, the red-suited world's Mightiest Man, laughed down at us from the sky.

Our need for closer identification with the dynamic figures who wore flashy outfits and shadowy masks was better realized in another type of hero, first developed in the pages of such pulp fiction magazines as *The Shadow* and adapted to the more colorful comic book pages early in the evolution of that medium. This type of character, wearing the familiar full-length leotards and usually, a flamboyantly flowing cape, was not superhuman at all. Rather, he was a normal human being—like us—who became a crime-crushing lawman of spectacular talents through the rigid training of his own mind and body, and perhaps through the invention of certain invaluable gadgets. Through the characters of this sub-genre, we knew that if we worked hard enough at it, we too might at least have the *hope* of someday becoming a dashing hero.

The most enduring of these more human costumed heroes is The Batman. The pulps gave us The Shadow, and newspaper comic pages offered us The Phantom earlier, but no other such character has had such great and sustained popularity. Batman ties with Superman as the most popular comic book figure of all time.

Batman was created by a teen-aged artist, Bob Kane, in the pages of *Detective Comics,* beginning in No. 27, 1939. Kane has admitted his debt to Fairbanks' portrayal of Zorro and to The Shadow of fiction fame. In the early stories especially, Batman closely resembled The Shadow as a creature of shadows, able to terrify criminals with a single strain of chilling laughter. He haunted the night, his weird attire able to evoke fear in the hearts of evil-doers.

By day, the Batman is really Bruce Wayne, a wealthy playboy known to the outside world as a benefactor and humanitarian, but hardly capable of athletic heroics. As a boy, Bruce had witnessed the murder of his parents by a petty crook who attempted to rob them on a darkened street. As could be easily believed, the event significantly affected the whole life of young Bruce. He swore on their graves that he would devote his life to warring on criminals, and as the years passed, trained his body and mind to the limits of human skill. Ready to emerge upon the world, Bruce Wayne decided that he must adopt a guise so terrifying that his very appearance would instill fear into the hearts of the underworld.

"Criminals are a superstitious, cowardly lot," Wayne reasoned to himself, "so my disguise must be able to strike terror into their hearts. I must be a creature of the night. Black, terrible . . . a . . . a bat!"

The costume he chose was not quite as somber as The Shadow's solemn black cloak and clothes. As the Batman, Wayne wore a basic overall garment of blue-gray, over which he donned midnight blue trunks, gloves and boots, and added a flowing cape in the design of batwings, and a cowl with slanted eyes and sharpened ears. The last part of the costume was a gold-colored "Utility Belt" with a seemingly endless number of compartments housing tiny gas bombs, a miniature blowtorch, two-way radio, etc., etc., etc.

Later, in Detective Comics No. 38, 1940, Batman got his famous partner, Robin, the Boy Wonder. Robin was originally a boy named Dick Grayson, the youngest member of the Flying

Graysons, a family trapeze act with the circus. After Dick's parents were killed in a fake trapeze accident arranged by protection racketeers, Batman arranged to adopt the boy, revealing to him that his (Bruce Wayne's) parents were also killed by the underworld, and swearing the boy in as a junior partner. "And swear that we two will fight together against crime and corruption and never to swerve from the path of righteousness . . ." Batman intoned. "I swear it!" the boy responded. The costume he adopted was more colorful than his guardian's. Robin wore a gold cape, green shorts, and a red leather vest with an "R" over the heart. Cartoonist Kane revealed that there were several sources for Robin and his costume. He would be sort of a young, laughing Robin Hood (again inspired by a Fairbanks screen portrayal); he took his name and red vest from the bird, the robin, who would join the bat in flight; and an assistant of Kane's at the time was named Robinson.

From the mysterious Batcave, Batman and Robin darted out to fight crime, frequently summoned to action by Police Commissioner Gordon, aided by their faithful butler, Alfred. Together the Dynamic Duo fought such reoccurring menaces as the sinister clown-faced Joker, the pompous (but deadly) Penguin, the beautiful (but deadly) Catwoman, and won millions of readers in comic books and in newspaper comic sections.

In 1943, Batman and Robin finally made it into the movies. Columbia Pictures offered us a fifteen-chapter serial, *The Batman*. It was produced by Rudolph C. Flothow and directed by Lambert Hillyear, and while Bob Kane was given a credit line for having "created" the property, it was the concoction of a Hollywood staff of writers.

Bruce Wayne (alias Batman) and Dick Grayson (Robin) were played by a pair of relative unknowns, Lewis Wilson and Douglas Croft. Wilson's face did resemble the comic book Bruce Wayne's, but he was too thick in the middle and very unathletic in appearance. Croft was a bit too old for the part, and looked even older, when a hairy-legged stuntman doubled for the bare-legged "boy" in the fights. The costumes of both Batman and Robin closely followed those in the comics, but were unconvincing. In tight close-ups, one could see ragged cloth edges to the eye-holes merely poked in the masks. Neither Wilson nor Croft, nor their stunt doubles, had the style and grace of the comic book version, or of the action men in the competing serials from Republic Pictures. The final misfortune, one which adds to the hilarity of modern audiences watching a revival, was Lewis Wilson's voice. It was not deep, and was touched with something resembling a Boston accent, making for rather peculiar affectations. Despite it all, Wilson played the part of Batman with a not-uningratiating sincerity.

Receiving third billing in the serial was character actor, J. Carrol Naish, as Dr. Daka, the Japanese superspy in America trying to seize control of the entire nation. Naish was the true star of the chapterplay, hamming it up with old "sinister Oriental" techniques from the silent films. One ghoulish scene was Dr. Daka taking delight in feeding the alligators that lived beneath the trap door of his secret lair. Naish milked the scene, chortling and rubbing his hands. After the alligators consumed all the raw meat (where could even a Japanese spy get enough ration stamps for all that meat?) Daka talked to his pets, apologizing for not having any more. Then his eyes shifted toward a man under his control standing off to one side. Daka grinned sadistically. But he was interrupted by one of his henchmen, failing to complete his ghoulish act.

As usual, motion picture producers played fast and loose in adapting famous characters to the screen. Characters who had established a basic appeal to millions were "improved" almost out of recognition in some cases. Batman fared better than most. The Caped Crusader exchanged his superpowered automobile, the Batmobile (complete with distinctive bat-like grill), for a mundane limousine. He retained his Utility Belt, but never

once in the entire fifteen chapters of the 1943 serial did he use
it—for anything except to hold up his tights. The picture did
use the Batcave from the comics, only changing the form of the
name slightly to the Bat's Cave. There was, moreover, a subtle
but significant alteration in the basic concept of Batman; he was
no longer the lone, unauthorized gangbuster of the comic books,
but on the screen he was a secret agent working from confiden-
tial orders supplied by the United States government.[1]

With his status officially sanctioned by the government, Batman set out to round up the enemy sabotage ring, operated by
Dr. Daka and the rest of those "shifty-eyed Japs!" (Not one
racial slur was missed—"You're as yellow as your skin!" "Little
imps of Satan!" etc., etc.) As Daka chortled over his pet alligator in his secret headquarters located behind a Chamber of Hor-

---

[1] Serials were subjected to rigid censorship. Since they were aimed at
the younger audience, producers were forced to stay within certain bounds
that would not be objectionable to parents. A hero could not take the law
into his own hands in most cases. When caught in time, such characters
were changed in the scripts to official secret agents before being granted
approval by the censorship board. Heroes should not drink or smoke,
although as part of his disguise as a crook in one scene, Bruce Wayne
did puff on a cigarette. Bullets could not be shown striking a man's body;
the gun and the human target had to be separated by cuts from one
camera angle to another. (This meaningless cop-out devised by some
bureaucratic mind was also later applied to comic books, where the gun
and the victim had to be in separate panels.) The same rule held true for
a man being struck with a club; the swing of the gun butt or blackjack
had to be shown from one angle, the victim falling from another.

Another rule of the censoring body spelled out that the hero could kill
more villains than the crooks could kill good guys, but the hero had to
accomplish the slaughter through the use of fewer bullets. (Remember—
the only crime is inefficiency.) The censors were squeamish about the
details of how murder was done being shown. Care had to be taken so
as not to show the youthful audience how to actually do away with their
parents (or maybe even the censors). For example, you could show a
close-up of a fuse sizzling toward a dynamite keg set to blow some good
guy to Kingdom Come; but you could not show a close-up of the match
lighting the fuse. If kids ever found out how to strike a match, the Establishment seemed to feel it was in big trouble.

rors side show, elderly Martin Warren (Gus Glassmire), the uncle of Bruce's girl friend, Linda Paige (Shirley Patterson, a rather sexy redhead) was captured by Daka's henchmen as he was released from prison and brought to the secret location of the archfiend. The master spy immediately turned Warren into a zombie, by placing a weird device over his head which made him subject to whoever's voice sounded through the special microphone. The whole contraption literally resembled a partially disassembled juke-box, a Wurlitzer gone mad.

This terrible hokey scene, like the rest of the serial, was done by a director who should have known better. Years before, in 1934, Lambert Hillyear had directed a feature film about a different type of "bat-man," although this vampire bat was offstage most of the time in difference to his offspring, *Dracula's Daughter*. Unlike most sequels, *Dracula's Daughter* is regarded by many as superior to the original *Dracula*. From this sensitive, moody horror classic, Hillyear had gone to directing one of the most ludicrous serials ever made. Even considering the quality of the material given him to work with, Hillyear showed a total lack of interest or imagination in making the film.

Typical of the "silliness" of the serial was the cheap gimcrack device Dr. Daka had his zombies, like old Martin Warren, wear on their skulls. It was apparently made from odds and ends of an Erector set. Daka sent one of his zombies, wearing this "cap," along with two more alert gangster types, to a hospital to steal radium, needed to power one of his superweapons, a raygun. But the Batman and Robin intercepted the thieves on the hospital rooftop. During the fist fight between the Dynamic Duo on one side, the two crooks and one zombie on the other, Batman was hurled off the roof, to seeming death many stories below.

At the opening of the second episode, "The Bat's Cave," the Batman luckily landed on a painter's scaffolding, knocking off one of the workmen. As the painter dangled helplessly, clawing for life, Batman single-mindedly began climbing up the scaffolding's ropes, to reach the roof again.

As the episodes rolled on, week after week, audiences were greeted with equally incredulous sights. In one scene, the Batman and Robin battled a group of thugs inside a building while the faithful Alfred (played by the painfully proper Britisher, William Austin) waited outside. During the fight, Batman's cape fell from his shoulders and landed in a pile on the floor. The fight went on and on, with Batman's cape lying on the floor in plain view. The scene cut to a quick shot of Alfred looking concerned as he waited outside, and then back to the fight. Batman was again wearing his cloak, swinging away at his adversaries. Was the audience supposed to think the Batman had picked up the cape and put it back on in the middle of the fight? Was it assumed that the dumb kids wouldn't even have noticed such a "minor" error? Probably the only logic involved was the logic of cheapie-quickie films of the '30s and '40s: it would cost too much to shoot the scene over.

As Batman and Robin thwarted Daka's spies on land, sea, and the air, all the time trying to rescue Linda's uncle, they were subjected to the usual perils of fire, explosions, bullets, and near fatal plunges. As Chapter Ten, "Flying Spies," drew to an end, Batman alone was fighting two zombie pilots (Kenne Duncan and George Lewis) as the plane flew wild with no one at the controls, and finally entered a power dive that took it slowly, ever so slowly as Batman fought on against the zombies, slowly to a blinding crash into the earth.

Would the next chapter reveal that Batman had parachuted out in time? Would it be one of those terrible cheats where the next chapter falsified things and had the plane pulling out of the dive safely? Neither was the case. As the next episode, "A Nipponese Trap," opened, we saw the plane crash with Batman still on board. There was a terrific explosion, smoke, fire, and . . . Batman came staggering out of the wreck, slightly dazed by the whole thing. The audience was equally dazed by disbelief. It might as well have been a silent comedy where Larry Semon fell off a cliff and merely got up and brushed himself off.

Although Batman and Robin had been fighting his agents for fourteen chapters, the first face-to-face confrontation with Dr. Daka came in the fifteenth and final episode, "Doom of the Rising Sun." The supposedly captured Batman was to be thrown to Daka's reptilian pets in a coffin-like crate, but unknown to Daka and the audience for Chapter Fourteen, Batman had escaped the box and substituted one of the thugs for himself. (The "recap" of these events was one of the longest stagewaits to the original cliffhanger in serial history.) When at last the Dynamic Duo confronted Daka, Robin gasped "A Jap!" Linda, like her uncle, had been turned into a zombie by a session under the master spy's futuristic hair drier. Batman threatened Daka himself with being turned into one of his mindless creatures, and naturally the "yellow" Japanese removed the electronic spell from the girl. Dr. Daka knew better than to take on the fists of Batman, but he did make one last desperate dash to escape. But any effort to escape the Batman was foredoomed. Dr. Daka, the madman who tried to subjugate all of wartime America, fell to a gnashing, grisly death within the jaws of his own half-starved alligators.

Later, with her uncle restored to Linda, Bruce Wayne and Dick Grayson arrived on the scene, too late for the action as usual.

The serial proved popular enough, despite its limitations, to have a sequel, although it was to be six years later.

New Adventures of Batman and Robin appeared in 1949, produced by quickie-king Sam Katzman, and his favorite director, Spencer G. Bennet. As usual on a Katzman production, the low budget showed everywhere in money-saving shortcuts, and inadequacies.

Even Batman's costume was so cheap it looked as if it might

have been made by his grandmother for a Halloween party. The cowl or hood fitted so poorly, it was obvious that the actor beneath it could neither see nor breathe very well. The only addition on the costume line was pink tights to cover the hairy legs of Robin, and the stuntman who doubled for him.

The man actually beneath the painfully cheap mask of Batman this time was curly-haired Robert Lowery, familiar from an endless string of B features. The second Robin (who now sported a dark-colored cape) was portrayed by John Duncan, whose rather surly expression and the tattoo on his arm (from the actor's private life, certainly inappropriate for Robin) made him look more like he should play the part of a character you might find lifting hub caps off a car, than one trying to capture a car thief.

The fabled Batmobile was in for the lowest level casting of all. No longer even impersonated by a limousine, it was replaced by a 1949 Mercury.

As the second serial opened, Batman and Robin were called upon by Commissioner Gordon (Lyle Talbot) to recover a stolen remote-control device, invented by scrawny old Professor Hammil (William Fawcett), an eccentric scientist confined to a wheelchair. The machine had been stolen by a strange man in a dark cloak and hood, known as the Wizard, who planned to use the gadget in a complicated scheme to steal a priceless hoard of diamonds.

By the infallible circumstance that served all serial heroes, the jewel robbery was witnessed by Bruce Wayne and Dick Grayson, along with magazine photographer Vicki Vale (square-chinned Jane Adams). After loosing the girl long enough to change clothes, the two crime-fighters entered the scene as Batman and Robin, engaging in a somewhat clumsy fist fight with several crooks, and surprisingly enough, capturing them. (Crooks usually managed to escape in serials, at least, until the final chapter.)

As this chapter neared its climax, Batman and Robin were caught in a grounded airplane under the guidance of the remote-control device operated by the Wizard. The Dynamic Duo were told that either they toss out the jewels where the Wizard could find them, or he would wreck the plane, sending them to their doom. Again surprisingly, Batman turned chicken (perhaps on behalf of Robin) and complied. He should have known better. The Wizard pushed a button and the plane exploded with smoke and fire.

Next week, we found out that Batman and Robin escaped from the exploding plane by leaping to safety only seconds before the blast.

In another situation in which the Dynamic Duo was trapped, this time inside a steel vault, Batman turned his back to the camera discretely and reached into his Utility Belt (which was a plain strip of cloth without any compartments whatsoever) and pulled out a blowtorch—a foot-long, ten-pound blowtorch! (The scriptwriters had probably called for the miniaturized, three-inch blowtorch carried in the comic books, but the film-makers had followed literally the call for a prop "blowtorch.")

The film also confused the use of another piece of Batman's hardware. The Bat Signal, a searchlight with a bat emblem darkening part of the circle of light it cast, was shown brightly projected on convenient clouds in broad daylight whenever Commissioner Gordon needed help.

One of the weirdest episodes of the second serial was Chapter Four, "Batman Trapped," in which the Batman spent half of the episode climbing up the side of a cliff, while Robin, in his stocking feet, successfully followed a speeding truck back to the Wizard's secret hideout.

In Chapter Fifteen, Batman and Robin (footsore and weary) succeeded in learning the true identity of the Wizard—the eccentric, supposedly crippled scientist, Hammil. The old man and his thugs put up a pretty good fight with the costumed crime-fighters in the scientist's study, but fell under the fists of the Dynamic Duo.

In the customary epilogue, Bruce Wayne used a phonograph record of Batman's voice played on the other end of a telephone connection to convince Vicki Vale that Wayne was *not* the Batman, a growing suspicion in her mind. Batman and Robin were free to continue their war on the underworld.

Seeing either of the Batman serials, either the first in 1943 or the second in 1949, produced a quite different effect on audiences then, than when both of these productions were revived, each in a four-hour "camp" marathon, to capitalize on the popularity of the character, both before and after the appearance of Twentieth Century-Fox's television program. (One reason for the TV series was the popularity of these serials when revived.) During the initial release of the cliffhanger, the serials did seem to have a certain charm and wonder, and even contemporary pertinence. Audiences did have some awe for this larger than life hero. And the first serial, particularly, despite its poorly constructed script, crude action scenes, and other flaws, had an honesty about it, a forthright simplicity. Different colored capes suggested varying lighting effects, caused by exteriors, interiors, and the Bat's Cave, just as in comic strip panels. The two heroes also worked within their definitely human abilities. There was no cheating, like climbing up a wall with a camera turned sideways as in the television show. And the roles were played with earnest seriousness, without the apparent contempt the TV producers had for their audiences and their own product.

The children of today, reared on a constant bombardment of mediocre, predigested television programs, are nearly incapable of accepting fantasy or using imagination. (One cause of the wide-spread use of hallucinatory drugs by young people has been attributed to their lack of ability to fantasize without them.) Elements contributing to a lively imagination—listening to stories told by grown-ups or on dramatized radio, reading, or simply playing cowboys and Indians—are missing from the lives of many children today. If every nail isn't driven into place on every piece of stage furniture, if any imagination is required or any concesson of a few extra pounds or gray hairs of an aging hero has to be made, it all seems silly and phony. The children of today, and their parents, caught in the same TV-orientated culture, can only laugh at *Batman*. The gap is too wide. The present writers can only feebly protest that Batman and the other old serials did have *"something."*

THE SUBVERSIVES' DREAD

Spy Smasher was to Captain Marvel what Batman was to Superman in the pages of the comic magazines. That is, both Spy Smasher and Batman were normal human beings who wore fancy outfits to fight crime in contrast to the literally superhuman heroes published by their respective magazine chains.

When he came to the motion picture screen, Spy Smasher fared far better than his rival, Batman. *Spy Smasher* was made by Republic in 1942. The studio was better at action, and in this case, acting, writing, and general production. The screen offering is made available today to TV stations as an edited-down feature film, *Spy Smasher Returns,* and holds up remarkably well as a nicely done B feature of the '40s—a major accomplishment for any serial.

The chapterplay revolved around Alan Armstrong, who was secretly Spy Smasher, and his identical twin, Jack. (The use of the name "Jack Armstrong," already famous as the All-American Boy of radio, was probably the writers' little "In" joke.) Both roles were played by actor Kane Richmond with a subtlety often missing from such "split-screen" offerings in major A productions. Alan and Jack were not *absolutely* identical. Although, of course, exactly the same age, Jack seemed to be the younger brother with a lighter voice and more boyish mannerisms. That was only natural. Alan Armstrong had no doubt been aged by going through hell, in perilous missions and, at least once, torture at the hands of the Gestapo.

As the mysterious foe of all spies, Alan Armstrong wore a dark uniform very similar to the one in the comics pages. There was a flowing cape, a diamond-shaped chest emblem, and gloves. (In the comic magazine, the outfit had originally been a brown aviator's uniform. Later, the costume seemed to shrink to standard tight-fitting long underwear and to turn bright green, all due to wartime soap substitutes, one might suppose.) Centered on Spy Smasher's belt was a large "V" for victory, and the Morse code symbol for the letter, three dots and a dash. Mort Glickman's powerful musical score echoed the "V for Victory" theme adapted from Beethoven's *Fifth Symphony* that was familiar from countless movie and radio patriotic appeals: *"Da-da-da-daaaa."*

The movie studio was not done with its tinkering. Besides minor costume changes and the addition of a brother, Spy Smasher's famous flying craft, the Gyrosub, appeared on the screen but according to the scenario it was not the mystery man's own ship, but was the craft of the enemy agents, now re-christened "The Bat Plane" in Chapter Four, "Stratosphere Invaders."

Several of the comic strip characters were retained in the movie version: Admiral Corby (portrayed by distinguished white-haired character actor, Sam Flint, who is still called on to autograph *Spy Smasher* stills nearly thirty years later) and the admiral's daughter, Eve (Marguerite Chapman, one of the many beauties discovered by Howard Hughes and taken from a modeling career in New York to Hollywood films).

The final carryover from the comics was "the Mask," a Nazi villain who appeared in the very early episodes of *Spy Smasher* in *Whiz Comics* (when the strip was in such a formative stage that even the readers were not let in on the secret that Alan Armstrong was really Spy Smasher, although he was the only reasonable suspect for the role). In the chapterplay, hissable actor Hans Schumm hid behind a flimsy handkerchief with eyeholes that a sneeze might easily dislodge as he captained a sinister U-boat. Since he appeared as often without the disguise as with it, the only purpose of the mask seemed to be to make him familiar to comic book fans.

At the head of the cast, Kane Richmond brought a great deal of experience in action roles. He had graduated from selling theatre films to appearing in them, beginning with a series of prize-fighting *Leather Pusher* movies. He appeared in many other features, usually as a Mountie or a detective, most prominently as The Shadow in three Monogram feature films of the 1940s. In cliffhangers, he appeared in Mascot's *Adventures of Rex and Rinty,* 1935, getting third billing under a horse and a dog; as a Martian guardsman in *Flash Gordon's Trip to Mars,* 1938; and as a supporting player in the independent *Lost City.* Following *Spy Smasher,* he was to be the star of several other serials; *Haunted Harbor,* Republic, 1944, *Brenda Starr, Reporter* (not the title role) and *Jungle Raiders,* both 1945, and *Brick Bradford,* 1947, all three from Columbia. Today, Kane Richmond reports he has retired from films. "I'm a businessman now. I deal in women's clothes . . . I wouldn't go back unless I was offered a really good series," Richmond reported to the present writer. "It was hard work in those days. I used to do a lot of my own stunts . . . You know, I still get fan mail . . ."

More than any other production, it is *Spy Smasher* that elicits that fan mail for Kane Richmond.

The story opened in Nazi-occupied France where the mystery man was captured and sentenced to die by a firing squad.

A fussilade of shots cracked out and the costumed hero dropped to the ground. The smug Germans placed him into a coffin and gave him over to the French to bury. The patriots of the Underground had arranged for the American to fake death. Resistance leader Pierre Durand (Frank Corsaro) smuggled Armstrong by railroad and plane, finally into the United States.

Meanwhile, the Mask in his Nazi submarine headquarters plotted to disrupt the economy of the United States through his master plan of flooding the country with counterfeit currency.

On a speeding train, an enemy agent spotted a man he thought he recognized as his hated enemy, Spy Smasher. The Nazi attacked, trying to throw the American off the train, under the grinding wheels. But even as the Nazi struggled with the Yank, the real Spy Smasher was skirmishing across the tops of the moving passenger cars to swing down and to hurl the spy from the train. Spy Smasher removed his masking headgear and greeted his twin brother, Jack, who was gratifyingly surprised to find his brother, Alan, still alive.

Jack also learned that his brother, Alan, was the secret lone wolf agent who was world famous as Spy Smasher. With boyish eagerness, Jack agreed to help Spy Smasher in his battle against the Mask and all his Nazi agents.

Later, Spy Smasher parachuted from an airplane piloted by Jack, landing on the property of Admiral Corby, head of naval intelligence, and his daughter, Eve (Jack's fiancée). The hero's timing was perfect, as his landing coincided exactly with an attack by the Mask's henchmen. Battling them off, Spy Smasher removed his cap and goggles and went inside the house where the admiral and Eve mistook him for his twin, Jack. Corby speedily swore "Jack" in as a deputized government agent.

The Mask's chief henchman, or "spearhead villain" in trade terms, was Drake (the suavely mustached Tristram Coffin), who worked for the Ocean-Wide Television Network and who had insinuated himself as Jack's friend. Drake's methods of broadcasting seem of dubious practicality by today's standards but were actually far more advanced than television was in reality during World War II. His simple espionage technique was to casually leave the camera inside Corby's office—still switched on—after one of his many routine interviews for genuine broadcast. The camera piped the vital security information directly into the Mask's receiving screen in his submarine—and presumably into the sets of any home viewer tuned into the proper channel. (Of course, there weren't *many* viewers back then.)

Drake's men picked up a supply of the counterfeit bills, left them by the Mask's U-boat. But Spy Smasher and Jack spotted them from their speedboat and took off after them through the spray, but lost them after the usual serial perils of gunshots and explosions.

A twisted cellophane cigar wrapper marked "Acme Cafe" proved a valuable clue. Spy Smasher patronized the cafe in his civvies as Alan Armstrong, where he saw a dark-looking character twist a cigar wrapper in the same manner, then disappear inside a telephone booth, without ever coming out.

Casually, Alan entered the booth and called Admiral Corby, telling him to raid the establishment. Then he switched outfits to become Spy Smasher (pulling the telephone booth switch so enjoyed by Superman), and located the hidden panel in the booth, going through it into a wine cellar connected to an old railway tunnel.

His cigar-smoking quarry was below, counting some of the phony money stacked on the table.

"Got change for a five?" Spy Smasher quipped with typical costumed hero jocularity, his gun drawn.

"Spy Smasher!" gasped the crook. (Somehow, the crooks always cry out the name of the costumed heroes.) The heavy raised his hands at the sight of the aimed weapon.

Upstairs, Admiral Corby's men raided the restaurant, while the waiter escaped through the secret phone booth exit. Down in the wine cellar, the waiter leaped on Spy Smasher from behind, starting a slam-bang fight. Chairs and bottles crashed to the floor amidst flying fists and falling bodies. Then stored explosives were set off in the middle of the turmoil. The darkness was split with the searing light.

Spy Smasher darted away from the flaming barrage, boarded a railway handcar loaded with hand grenades and started down the tunnel, only to find his way blocked by a wall of burning oil.

A tremendous blast brought down the curtain on "America Beware," the first installment of *Spy Smasher*.

Luckily, the second chapter revealed that Spy Smasher escaped the flaming oil by hurling one of the grenades into the holocaust, blasting down an avalance of debris to smother the fire.

Meanwhile, Corby had discovered the origin of the counterfeit money—the French island of Martinidad, also ruled by the Nazis. Dispatched on his mission, Spy Smasher arrived on Martinidad in time to save his former ally, Durand, from a public hanging, expose the island's governor (George Renarent) as an agent of the Mask, and to end up as a captive inside the flooded torpedo room of the Mask's U-boat which seemed destined to be a watery grave for the costumed secret agent at the climax of Chapter Three, "Iron Coffin."

The unconscious Spy Smasher was rescued in the following episode by his friend, the noble Durand, who fired the American out a torpedo tube to surface safely. The Frenchman died with a contented smile on his lips as the sheet of water rose over him.

In the succeeding episodes, Spy Smasher learned of the weird "Bat Plane" used by the crooks employed by the Mask, and climbed aboard as the craft took off. Inside, he fought the pilot back and parachuted to safety as the ship crashed in a terrific explosion. (Explosions are a big part of serials. Dedicated fans will rave over the "great explosions" by the special effects men.)

Another time, the costumed hero escaped being crushed to death by a descending elevator. In other chapters, Spy Smasher avoided death in an exploding water tower; from the blast of underwater mines; an automobile plunging from a great height; and in the classic serial cliffhanger, he was nearly carried to his death on a conveyor belt leading to a chewing buzz saw.

The most unique chapter ending of them all was that of Chapter Eleven, "Hero's Death." The familiar figure of Spy Smasher, in his helmet and cape, was gunned down by an armed mob of enemy agents, his body splattered with bullets at point-blank range. He wobbled, swayed, and toppled from the rooftop of a tall office building, smashing lifelessly against the pavement of the dark street below. No one—not even the mighty, yet mortal, Spy Smasher—could escape from such a "hazard." (It might be a hazard in the terminology of the film-makers, but it could prove fatal for anyone else!)

In the twelfth and final chapter, "V . . . —", it was revealed that the victim did *not* escape death. But it was brother Jack, not Alan, the *real* Spy Smasher, who wore the costume of the secret agent and who died from the hail of bullets. Of course, one might observe, it was unnecessary for the spies to shoot him—the fall alone would have been enough to kill him.

Alan Armstrong became even more dedicated, bent on avenging his brother's death. He learned that the television reporter, Drake, was working with the Nazis. After engaging Drake in a fist fight inside a houseboat tied up at the docks, Spy Smasher was slowed down long enough for Drake to escape in a nearby speedboat. The mystery man dived into the water, grasping a rope trailing from the boat, and hauled himself hand over hand up into the fleeing craft. Once again, Spy Smasher and Drake exchanged punches in a furious fight for survival. Meanwhile, the Mask inside his U-boat was preparing to tor-pedo the coastline defense plants. The torpedoes struck, and the sea erupted in a spreading mass of flaming fuel. The careening speedboat struck the periscope of the submarine. Blinded, the submarine desperately tried to avoid the sea of fire, but ran into a network of deadly, exploding mines.

With one final, decisive blow, Spy Smasher knocked Drake unconscious amid the weird patterns of dancing flames, and leaped overboard to precarious safety as the U-boat descended, struck a mine, and was blown to smithereens along with the Mask and all his band of Nazis.

Although a competitor to *Batman* in the comics, *Spy Smasher* could hardly be called a competitor to *Batman* in the movie serial field. There is *no* comparison. *Batman* was one of the worst serials ever made, and *Spy Smasher* was one of the best—*the* best serial in the opinion of those aficionadoes especially admiring the Republic school of special effects and stunt work action. In any art form—even as primitive a one as movie serials—there can be no one single best example. It depends on varying taste and opinion which is best in some particular area. Although lacking the beauty and imagination that appeals to a kind of racial unconscious in the Jungian sense that is found in *Flash Gordon;* the evocation of the most fundamental of childhood fantasies that is in *Captain Marvel;* or the work of truly great men of the films as evidenced by Karloff in *King of the Wild* or Tom Mix in *The Miracle Rider;* the serial, *Spy Smasher* emerges in a class by itself, the foremost cliffhanger example of a whole school of Hollywood film-making in the '40s that gloried in matchless pure entertainment.

The script by a staff headed by Ronald Davidson, with Norman S. Hall, Joseph Poland, William Lively, and Joseph O'Donnell was consistently logical and well-constructed, with credible dialogue and good characterization. The cinematography of Reggie Lanning is not merely adequate, as was the case with most chapterplays, but atmospheric and often artistic. Howard Lydecker's miniatures in his special effects work provided many "great explosions" and a thoroughly realistic "Bat Plane." The

stunt work was exceptional, some of it done by star Kane Richmond himself, but with the most spectacular feats being
performed by his double, Dave Sharpe, who rolled from an
overturning motorcycle to leap atop a careening auto that
plunged from a cliff, and did countless other flamboyantly acrobatic stunts.

Director William Witney, formerly of the Witney-English
team of serial-makers, extracted the most from his actors and
his settings, particularly good exterior locations at brick foundries, weird construction sites, prison yards, road underpasses, mountains, and prairies.

Today, *Spy Smasher* remains one of the few movie serials
that can be enjoyed simply *as a film* by an adult audience, without emerging as "camp."

THE STAR-SPANGLED AVENGER

Captain America was fighting two desperate gangsters in
hand-to-hand combat while a skyscraper began collapsing
around him, caused by the man-made earthquake of the
Scarab's Dynamic Vibrator. The red-white-and-blue garbed
Captain threw punch after punch at the two thugs in drab business suits. Even so, it appeared the face beneath the blue hood
was taking a painful battering from the fists of gangland. Then
a gloved *punch* sent one of the crooks out the skyscraper window to a screaming, plunging death. Meanwhile, the Dynamic
Vibrator had begun to climax, generating a tremendous amount
of electricity, the arrow of its indicator telling that total destruction was near for the two fighters—and the group of people
trapped in the room-size vault, including Captain America's
girlfriend, Gail Richards. At last, the hired thug fell under the
fists of the star-spangled hero. But then, it hardly seemed to
matter who won the fist fight. After Captain America rescued

his friends from the locked safe, the towering office building collapsed in on itself in a thunderous disaster, no doubt taking whoever was left inside to their doom.

Well, there might be *some* doubt that Captain America had been killed. At least, enough for us to come back the following week to see how the escape might be accomplished.

Captain America was one of the most popular costumed crusaders in the early '40s. His red-white-and-blue uniform was more colorful than the gray hues of Batman (whom he most closely resembled) and more patriotic than the blue, red, and yellow of Superman (who wasn't even a native born American but a visitor from another planet with more than human powers). Like Batman and Superman, Captain America wished to hide his true civilian identity beneath his flamboyant uniform. Once again, we were told only the secret self has power, only the side apparent to the world is weak.

In the 1944 Republic serial *Captain America,* District Attorney Grant Gardner (Dick Purcell) entered the office of the distinguished Commissioner Dryden (Charles Trowbridge) who was seated uncomfortably behind his desk in the presence of Mayor Randolph (Russell Hicks). The mayor disdainfully reminded Dryden of the long series of unsolved Purple Death murders, a type of killing apparently borrowed from Ming the Merciless who attacked Earth with his own Purple Death dust in *Flash Gordon Conquers the Universe* several years earlier.

At this point, Gardner interjected: "You'll remember the Commissioner and I have cleared up crime waves in this town before."

"Yes," the mayor agreed, "but that mysterious Captain America did most of your work for you. If only we could contact him now."

"I feel certain that this new crime wave will bring him out of hiding to help us," Gardner assured him.

Gardner's words were prophetic. That night, the star-spangled crusader once again appeared, to strike fear into the hearts of evil-doers and in general to drive the agents of the mysterious Scarab buggy.

The district attorney had inside information—he was, himself, Captain America. Like so many law-enforcement officials, Gardner had dreamed of a way of fighting crime outside the hampering restraints of the law.

Certainly, the insidious Scarab was creating enough of a crime wave to dampen the bleeding heart of any apologist for criminals. His Purple Death had claimed the lives of more than one of the city's leading citizens.

The doomed man marked for the Purple Death first received a valuable Scarab jewel that, when grasped firmly, emitted a poison that dulled the will so that the radioed voice of the Scarab himself could control him as a puppet.

As Wilson, his first victim, drove his sedan along a mountain road, he heard the words of doom seemingly out of empty air. "This is the voice of the Scarab, Wilson. I command you to drive your car over the cliff." Wilson turned the wheel as he was commanded and ended his life in a flaming, tumbling crash.

Shortly afterward, the second entranced victim was told, "The Scarab is speaking to you, Evans. You have reached the end. You will walk to the window and step out . . . into eternity." The order was obeyed.

The man who spoke those commands was really monocled Dr. Maldor (Lionel Atwill), curator of the Drummond Museum. Embittered by others claiming the priceless artifacts and scientific discoveries of an archaeological expedition he had headed years before, Maldor had decided to take his revenge as the sinister Scarab. Apparently, more than one side can hide behind a secret identity to obtain what it considers "justice."

As the Scarab, the museum curator put Captain America through enough perils to test his stripes for certain. The cos-

tumed avenger was only able to leap to safety a scant second
before the floor and roof collapsed in that skyscraper doomed
by the mastermind's Dynamic Vibrator. At other times, Captain America avoided being burned alive in a huge packing
crate by accurately blasting the fastening nails with his revolver
so that his flaming prison almost miraculously parted; being
smashed beneath tractor treads by luckily reviving from a head
injury in time to roll aside sparing only seconds; and being done
in by an exploding barn while fighting a crook, an exploding
machine while fighting a crook, and an exploding boiler room
while fighting a crook. In each instance, Captain America managed to subdue his opponent within enough time to flee the
doomed structure before the fuse sizzled into the explosives or
before the gauge indicator moved all the way from *safety* to
fire.

Through all of these perils, and a good helping more, Captain America fought valiantly, and it wasn't easy. Grant
Gardner-Captain America was played by actor Dick Purcell,
who was a veteran actor of numerous B features, a bit overage
and overweight. While younger men were in the Armed Services, Purcell played the hero with considerable competence,
though his voice suggested a bit of a so-called "whiskey" rasp.
Purcell did his best. His stuntman, Dale Van Sickel, did even
better in the action scenes. As in many serials, it was only when
the stuntman took over that the character really seemed to come
to life. In the midst of one of those fabulous brawls, we forgot
defects of the actor and thought of the stuntman (unknowingly,
of course), "Maybe he really *is* Captain America!"

Certainly, it was difficult for faithful comic magazine readers
to accept the movie serial version of Captain America at all,
whether it was in the person of actor Purcell or stuntman Van
Sickel. The original version of Captain America in the comics
was far different.

In 1941, with war looming on the horizon, the time was ripe for an overtly patriotic hero. The first issue of *Captain America* was published that year by the Timely (now Marvel) comics group. Created by the team of Joe Simon and Jack Kirby, both of whom wrote and illustrated, the flag-draped hero was a man of his time. He became a hit.

In the first story, a man who could only be President Franklin D. Roosevelt pondered in his office a new method of combating the spies and traitors in our midst. Going into action, the President introduced his generals to "J. Arthur Grover," head of the Federal Bureau of Investigation. Grover led the military men in disguise to a tenement district curio shop. Inside, they were taken by an apparently elderly woman up a rickety staircase and into a laboratory worthy of the maddest of scientists.

The "old" woman unmasked to reveal the lovely young face of an American girl, a secret agent. Following her directions, the spectators peered through a quartz-like glass to observe the experiment the President felt would change history.

Inside the laboratory stood Steve Rogers, a skeletal stripling with wispy blond hair, obviously in need of Ironized Yeast, Ovaltine, Wheaties, and the other miracle cures of the era. Rogers had been deemed too puny for active military service, we learned, but had volunteered for this special service. The experiment, it was hoped, would fulfill Rogers' dream—to be physically able to fight the Nazi devils who were already infiltrating America even without declaration of war.

An elderly scientist gave Rogers a hypodermic injection of a new serum. As the miracle drug shot through his bloodstream, the skimpy physique of Steve Rogers filled out, new blood, bone, and muscle growing faster than if he had only answered a Charles Atlas ad. Rogers stood aglow with sheer power.

"Behold!" the scientist exclaimed, his head well below the

shoulder of the newly born giant. "The crowning achievement of all my years of hard work! The first of a corps of superagents whose mental and physical ability will make them a terror to spies and saboteurs! We shall call you *Captain America,* son! Because—like you—America shall gain the strength and the will to safeguard our shores!"

Yet fate decreed that there would be no more superagents following the prototype. A Nazi spy was in the laboratory among the spectators. He boldy revealed his true allegiance and began blasting away with his luger. The genius who had invented the formula (and apparently had neglected to write it down with the typical absent-mindedness of comic book scientists) fell victim to the spy's bullets. Outraged, Captain America ignored the hail of lead and hurled the spy to his doom among electric-charged laboratory apparatus.

With bureaucratic inefficiency, Steve Rogers found himself a private in the Regular Army. Yet, he moonlighted on his true mission by capturing Nazi spies secreted about the nation, clad in a costume that makes one wonder why Captain America was never arrested for defacing an American flag. The leotard-tight uniform was blue, with red and white stripes across the abdomen and back,[2] large white star on chest and black and white sleeves. A blue hood covered the upper portion of his face and head, adorned with tiny white wings, suggesting those of an American eagle, above his exposed ears, and with a bold A stamped on his forehead. His red boots and gauntlets suggested a buccaneer of the seas and the chain mail of his blue shirt hinted of a knight on solemn errand. Like a knight, he also carried a shield of mysterious origin and construction. This had circular stripes with a star in the middle. The captain could do a lot of amazing feats, maneuvering the shield, but the most

[2] With the second issue of *Captain America,* the stripes only covered the abdomen. In the current comic book revival, again the stripes go all the way around, giving the impression of a patriotic merry-go-round.

amazing was the way he could strap it to his back beneath a standard Army blouse without it showing a trace, keeping his colorful identity secret.

Yet in the comic book pages, his secret was not safe from at least one other. One fateful night, when Steve Rogers was discovered in the act of becoming "Cap" by young Bucky Barnes, he was forced to admit his other identity and he took the boy under his shield, so to speak, as an apprentice in the war on spies and criminals. Bucky must have been a likable lad. Although too young to enlist, the whole regiment accepted him as a sort of unofficial mascot and he hung around the base in an Army uniform. As Captain America's partner, he changed his uniform for a more picturesque one of red and blue, but kept the same name: Bucky. (But then, it might be reasoned, lots of people have the same first name.)

The ageless duo smashed their way through comic books for decades, undergoing periodic changes and revivals. Today, Captain America is still the foe of evil-doers, even "self-styled superpatriots," proving that time may mellow zealots, perhaps. Bucky was "killed," or is at least "missing in action" from the days of World War II. (Dedicated fans hope he may be discovered still alive.)

Republic Pictures killed off Bucky even before the comic books, and they wounded the good Captain in the same sally. The studio was notorious (to fans, at least) for making arbitrary changes in the characters they adapted from other media. The Lone Ranger, Captain Marvel, even the venerable Zorro (who underwent a change of sex when played by Linda Stirling in *Zorro's Black Whip*) were subjected to alterations. Few, if any, of the changes made in these characters were for the better. Many fans were actually offended by these affronts to their heroes.

Captain America suffered more amputations than any other such character so brusquely handled by Republic. His shield was yanked off his arm and discarded for a more mundane .38 revolver. The wings were clipped off his hood, and he was stripped of his blue chain-mail armor and white sleeves, while the pirate boots were replaced with high shoes. If one got down to a technicality, the plain cloth that remained was not even really bright red and blue, but a dull gray and dark blue, which photographed better in black and white. The addition of miniature flags to his gloves and a small shield to his belt did not help to restore the glory of the original star-spangled outfit.

His character was as hacked upon as his uniform. Not only did he lose his junior partner Bucky, he lost his own "private" name—Private Steve Rogers. He was kicked out of the Army and made a district attorney (rated an "essential" civilian job, no doubt—enough to get anyone out of the Army). His new name was Grant Gardner, apparently chosen at random by the Republic staff. The movie serial never offered any competing version of how Grant Gardner became Captain America. He just *was,* that's all.

Chaos struck when the heads of Timely Comics learned of the changes in their character that would burst on the screen in the 1944 release of the serial. They could overlook the absence of Bucky and the differences in their hero's costume, but the omission of Steve Rogers, the Army setting especially during the middle of World War II, and the use of a gun was intolerable.

In a letter seen by the present writers, Republic coldly informed Timely that the sample comic book pages sent them by the publishers in no way indicated that Captain America was a soldier named Steve Rogers and that he did not carry a revolver. Furthermore, since the serial was well into production, they could not and would not return to the original concept through costly retakes, nor undergo expensive and unsatisfactory dubbing in of the name of Steve Rogers over Grant

Gardner. Since Republic was under no contractual obligations to do any of these things, the matter was closed.

As the crime-fighting D.A., Grant Gardner in his secret identity, Captain America continued his war on crime in the Republic serial.

The Scarab was an insidious enough enemy himself, and he was backed up by a particularly formidable chief henchman or "spearhead heavy" as the type was referred to on the studio lots, Matson (George Lewis). It was Matson's job to hire the thugs to do the Scarab's dirty work and to see that the master villain's deadly plots were carried out. The Scarab, like most serial masterminds, found simple explosions too simple. He relied on special timing devices which served no function other than to stretch out the action and increase the suspense. Matson's (and other bad guys in other serials) explanations of the timers were always the same. In "Wholesale Destruction," Chapter Seven, Matson and one of his men, Barton (stuntman Duke Green) had rigged a Nitrogas explosion to destroy the Tec-Ni-Gas Oil Company.

MATSON: The steam will carry the Nitrogas to every building in the plant. As soon as the pressure hits three hundred and fifty pounds, the gas'll ignite and the whole place will blow up.
BARTON: Well, let's get out of here.

Naturally the gauge slowly moved toward the 350 lbs. number while Captain America charged into a furious battle. As always he left the building before the fatal explosion.

The next episode, "Cremation in the Clouds," featured a similar method of destruction. Two of Matson's men, Blain and Stark, had placed a time bomb in the plane of Gardner's girlfriend, Gail Richards (played by Lorna Grey, who was more exotically beautiful than many major stars). Blain and Stark reviewed (for the benefit of the audience) the workings of the bomb from their safe position in the airport workshop.

BLAIN: As soon as the motor starts, that bomb mechanism starts operating.

STARK: And when the clock makes ten revolutions, everything will blow up.

BLAIN: Come on, we've got to look busy.

Ten revolutions gave Blain and Stark time to look busy and to engage in a fist fight with Captain America. A cliffhanger was approaching, which meant plenty of fast cutting from scene to scene to increase the tension and overall feeling of imminent doom. The following excerpt from the "cutting continuity," the script compiled after the film had been edited, illustrates the typical progression of shots in a Republic chapter climax:

190. LONG MED.
 CAPTAIN AMERICA *and* STARK *fighting. Camera pans to right as they fight.*

191. EXT. SKY: LONG MED. TRAVEL
 GAIL *piloting plane right to left.*

192. INT. PLANE: C.U.
 On clock dial attached to bomb. Sweep hand is revolving and smaller dial hand is at Eight. As sweep hand continues to revolve, smaller dial hand jumps to Nine.

193. CLOSE
 GAIL *at plane controls.*

194. EXT. SKY: LONG TRAVEL
 Plane flying right to left.

195. LONG MED. TRAVEL
 GAIL *piloting plane right to left.*

196. INT. PLANE: C.U.
 On clock dial attached to bomb. Sweep hand is revolving and smaller dial hand is at Nine.

197. CLOSE
GAIL *at plane controls.*

198. C.U.
On clock dial attached to bomb. Sweep hand is revolving and smaller dial hand is at Nine. As sweep hand continues to revolve, smaller dial hand jumps to Ten.

199. EXT. SKY: LONG TRAVEL
Plane flying right to left suddenly explodes.

SOUND: EXPLOSION

FADE OUT:

Captain America managed to conquer his opponents and radio Gail to bail out before her plane erupted in flames.

Time after time, Captain America would stop the Italian-looking Matson and one or two of his thugs from one of their thefts or murders in the name of the Scarab and engage them in a rousing, smashing (and well "choreographed") fist fight from which the crooks barely escaped, even though they outnumbered the costumed avenger. But finally, there came a fight from which Matson did not escape. In Chapter Eleven, Matson was knocked off a high railing by Captain America into a stone quarry far below. Fatally injured, the criminal died in the hospital.

However, apparently not even the spectre of Death could stay the plans of the Scarab, the fanatical Dr. Maldor. The doctor's thugs hijacked the corpse of Matson and secreted it to the Electronic Researches Ltd. building, where Dr. Clinton Lyman (Robert Frazer) had invented a life-restoring machine. There, amid a barrage of one million volts of electricity, enough to spark even Dr. Frankenstein's interest, Matson was brought back to a new, second life of violence. Once again, Captain America intervened, but unsuccessfully. Matson escaped, and Dr. Lyman and his machine, not unlike the incident in the hero's comic book origin, were destroyed. The episode had lived up to its title: "The Dead Man Returns."

Those fight scenes, though repetitious and often predictable as to when they would appear, were the highlights of the film. Directed by John English and Elmer Clifton, but largely staged by the stuntmen themselves, these celluloid battles were equal to those in any action film. Stuntman-actor Dale Van Sickel[3] doubled Dick Purcell as the Captain, immediately slimming a few pounds off the waistline. Van Sickel was the "ramrod" of the crew of stuntmen, leading Ken Terrell (doubling George J. Lewis as henchman Matson), Fred Graham (doubling Lionel Atwill as the Scarab), Duke Green, Joe Yrigoyen and Tom Steele (who only appeared in the first episode, since most of his time during the filming of *Captain America* was captured by his own ramrod job in *The Masked Marvel*), fighting them in such diverse settings as a mine, an antique-decorated study, a warehouse boasting an enormous guillotine-like paper cutter, and an aircraft garage.

Captain America represented the apex of the traditional action film fight, in the opinion of many cliffhanger enthusiasts, but followed the long-dictated formula. Dale Van Sickel and his stunt squad would walk through the fight, careful not to smash any of the numerous props[4] designed to breakaway

[3] Dale Van Sickel's handsome features, fellow stuntman Tom Steele related, added to the workings of a few friends handling the studio lighting, resulted in a "heavy" that appeared better looking than the star and hero.

[4] Breakaway glassware, such as bottles and windows, were then made from sugar (now a plastic is used), and breakaway furniture from lightweight yucca wood. However, despite the precautions, accidents would happen during stunt fights. Serial bad guy Kenne Duncan, who was in *Captain America,* related, "You've got to pick up a breakaway chair by the back or they'll break the back off." Equally villainous Roy Barcroft added, "Let me tell you, the hardest I was ever hit was with a breakaway chair. And let me tell you something about a breakaway chair. If they don't hit you right with it—if they hit you with the edge of the seat—he'll knock your brains out. This happened to me with Allan Lane. I came the closest to being knocked out as I ever have in my life with a chair he hit me with, on the edge." It was not infrequent for the breakaway props to shatter in the hands of the actors when they forgot the nature of the fragile objects.

painlessly on collision. Once the key actions were known by Van Sickel and the two stuntmen doubling the heavies (the time-honored two-against-one-hero odds of the serials), they would enact the choreography while wearing padding beneath their clothes on the elbows, knees, and back, in front of the camera which photographed the battle in a master longshot, "undercranking" so that the action would appear slightly faster than in reality on the screen. Almost always in serial fights, the stuntmen wore hats, fastened to their heads by elastic bands, screening their faces so that telling them from the actors they represented was difficult. (That also answers the question: Why don't their hats fall off during a fight?) In this serial, a slight variation was that the hero wore a mask, even better than a hat for hiding his identity.

The punches thrown by the stuntmen were broad, exaggerated roundhouse swings, missing the face by at least a five-inch safety margin. A real punch, as would be thrown in a boxing ring, would go unnoticed by the camera lens. At the point the stuntmen's punch "struck," his opponent's head would snap back, he would stagger backward, or fall into a breakaway chair that would crash under him, or he would tumble over a table or desk. The camera photographed the blow at such an angle that it looked like the fist really connected. Later in the sound mixing room, a loud *smack!* and a grunt or groan would be added for realistic effect.

The fights were photographed, ranging from the extreme long or "master" shot to full and medium shots. There were never any extreme close-ups in serial fights where a man's face would be seen being brutally pounded by his opponent's fists. And blood was almost nonexistent in movie serials. A hero would step out of a fight with two heavies without even a slight headache, let alone a minor cut, bruise, or loose tooth. Emphasis was placed on the sheer beauty of the flow of action—primarily due to the extraordinary performances of the stuntmen.

With today's society condemning violence in any form, especially that seen in motion pictures and on television, it is easy to watch a seven- or eight-minute brawl in a revived episode of *Captain America* or other serial, to see a countless barrage of socks and kicks and clobberings, and, due to the way in which it was photographed, forget even the word "violence." In the serials, a fight wasn't realism and violence—it was excitement and action.

After the entire master shot was filmed with the stuntmen, the principle actors would imitate some of the struggle at points called "bridges," for close-ups or medium shots to be intercut with the main action. Stuntman Dale Van Sickel threw the punch but you saw star Dick Purcell landing it on the crook's chin, with the film editor cutting right on the action so that it seemed one man was carrying through one movement. This method of stunt fighting was—and is today—successful with audiences who never notice it is not the same man, or who suspend their disbelief.

After many such fights, Captain America came to the ultimate showdown with the Scarab in Chapter Fifteen. Gail Richards, Grant Gardner's assistant and the only person who knew to whom the flag of the mysterious Captain America belonged, was kidnapped by the Scarab. But first, she managed to get a message to D.A. Gardner in which the name, "Rodlam Baracs," when spelled backwards by the perceptive investigator, revealed that the Scarab was actually Dr. Maldor.

Meanwhile, back at the museum, Maldor had placed Gail in a glass coffin and had turned on a gas which would shrivel her to the appearance of an ancient Egyptian mummy. Maldor chortled that he had even discovered the true identity of Captain America, when the costumed avenger arrived on the scene. As the gas rose higher in the case containing the helpless girl, there ensued a terrific fist fight between the near-superhuman Captain and the elderly museum curator. Finally, with a punch that started on one side of the room, traveled across it, and landed on Maldor's jaw, Captain America defeated the Scarab. Then he saved Gail from the horrible, shriveling doom of the mummy case, and together they disappeared into the night ahead of the arriving police.

In the last scene, Grant Gardner, Gail Richards, and the other good guys, cheerfully awaited the tolling of midnight on a clock down in the street (suspiciously looking like London's Big Ben) which would mark the time of execution for the Scarab. The hour came, fulfilling the chapter's title, "The Toll of Doom."

Although the serial was later rereleased as *Return of Captain America,* there was only one motion picture version of the Star-Spangled Avenger. A lot of us missed his shield, his boy sidekick, and the rest of it from the comic pages, but apparently, he—or his fists—made quite an impression on some.

THE GHOST WHO WALKS

The Phantom, mysterious costumed avenger of the African jungle, was fatally wounded in the first chapter of the movie serial devoted to his exploits. He was carried to the ancient Skull Cave, where he lay on his deathbed. It looked like a short serial.

There had to be a catch to it, and there was.

The Phantom was more than one man. In each generation of an old and honorable family the eldest son donned a skin-tight costume of royal purple and forever masked his features to become an eerie menace to all evil-doers—the Ghost Who Walks, *The Phantom!*

To the side of the failing hero came his adult son, Godfrey Prescott (Tom Tyler). As it must in every generation, it was time for the torch of justice to be passed on. After the final shadows fell that night, there would be a new Phantom—yet as far as the jungle world would know, still the same Ghost Who Walks.

The history of The Phantom goes back four centuries. In that time, the man who would become the first Phantom was marooned on a jungle shore by pirates, he being more dead than alive. Through his knowledge of gunpowder and skills of civilization, he became ruler of the Bandar tribe of pygmies in the Deep Woods of Africa. There, he swore by the Oath of the Skull to devote his life to destroying piracy and all other forces of evil.

Then for the first time, The Phantom put on his purple-hued garments and the Skull Ring that would leave its imprint in the cheek of many a killer down through the generations. The ring and the design for the costume were passed on, father to son, until they reached our own era. The present Phantom had added a brace of forty-five automatics to the outfit but all else was the same. As his forefathers had before him, he sat on the great Skull Throne, his wolf-dog, Devil, at his side, dispensing justice.

As a movie serial, *The Phantom* followed *Batman* from the same studio, Columbia, in 1943. The producer was the same, Rudolph C. Flothow, but it had a better director of serials, B. Reeves Eason. The script by Morgan B. Cox, Victor Mcleod, Sherman Lowe, and Leslie J. Swabacker was a considerable improvement over what had been done to the previous mystery man hero.

Despite following Batman to the screen, The Phantom was an older character, the *first* popular figure in a mask and costume in comics. However, *The Phantom* was a syndicated newspaper comic strip, and such newspaper strips are generally better written and illustrated since they are in a more highly competitive, better paid field than that of inexpensively produced comic magazines. The Phantom was appealing to a general audience, including many adults, in various newspapers long before kids discovered Batman in the comic books.

Lee Falk, who has been described as a man of such magnetic, dynamic personality and sleek good looks to be a movie star himself, created the comic strip of *The Phantom* and continued to write the stories. The year was 1936, and during the same era he developed his *Mandrake the Magician* as well. Creator of two landmark comic strips, Falk could not draw a straight line himself. He has survived two artists on *The Phantom*— Ray Moore, followed by Wilson McCoy—and today he works with artist Sy Barry. Falk once described his Ghost Who Walks as "a combination of Robinson Crusoe, Tarzan, and Superman." That was a charitable description since The Phantom came *before* Superman, and that strip owes something to The Phantom, in point of fact, as does Batman and all the "long-underwear" boys discussed in this chapter.

When the movies finally got around to The Phantom, they did him justice with a fine action star, Tom Tyler. At that time, he was known primarily for Westerns, but he projected such a quality of unshakable heroism, he proved well-suited to play a larger-than-life costumed character, even the literally superhuman Captain Marvel, his Republic serial role of 1941. Though he is sometimes accused of being "wooden" in speech and movements, he might well be described as the Gary Cooper of B films, both features and serials.

After the first chapter of the movie serial revealed the origin of the present Phantom (The Phantom is dead; long live The Phantom), we learned of the lost city of Zoloz, which housed considerable archaeological and monetary wealth. The location of this sacred citadel could be deciphered by the manipulation of seven pieces of ivory. The first three of these was owned by Professor Davidson (Frank Shannon); the next three by Singapore Smith (Joe Devlin), a small-time hoodlum; and the last, and most important, was missing from the puzzle.

Davidson, with his pretty brunette niece Diana (Jeanne Bates) planned to obtain the help of Byron Andrews (Guy Kingsford) for an expedition into the jungle, in search for the city of Zoloz. But his three keys were stolen first by the crafty Singapore Smith.

The Phantom comes to the aid of all who need his help. His smashing fists and flaming guns took their toll. The stolen keys were returned to their owner, but there were many perils ahead in the search for the still missing seventh key. At the heart of the tangled web was Dr. Bremmer (raw-boned Kenneth McDonald) who was behind the murder of the present Phantom's father. It was his plan to make Zoloz into a secret air base for enemy nations. Naturally, he would do anything to protect this secret work. He would set any trap, sink to any villainy, to destroy the one man who stood in his way—the Ghost Who Walks, The Phantom.

As the masked jungleman tried to aid Davidson and his daughter and to prevent the evil work of Bremmer, he was thrown into danger after danger as each chapter built to its climax.

Time and again, The Phantom and his Allies were threatened by attack from savage jungle beasts, by the firearms and fireworks-like explosions of the evil doctor's henchmen, and nearly had their hopes (as well as their lives) dashed by a falling suspension bridge. All in all, it was a good thing The Phantom was "immortal."

Finally, the Ghost Who Walks and his less spooky friends were taken prisoner by the man who was supposedly the owner of the seventh key—the tyrannical chieftain, Tarter. After sly deliberation, Tarter agreed to surrender the final key, only providing that The Phantom could wrestle it from a chain around the neck of his pet gorilla. Such a task could even give pause to a living legend; but The Phantom took on the shaggy beast.

(Movie gorillas are somehow always shaggy, although the actual primates have short fur.)

After an exchange of holds and furious blows, The Phantom bested the huge beast and had the final key for his prize.

The group of white men finally reached the lost city of Zoloz. At the city, Dr. Bremmer had attempted to trick the natives into working on his air base project by dressing one of his own agents as the fabled jungle hero, believing the real Phantom had been killed in an explosion. However, The Phantom had emerged from the clouds left by the explosion with a seeming ghostly invulnerability. He went on to expose the impostor and to turn the natives against Bremmer and his spies. Once aroused, not even the Ghost Who Walks could prevent the duped natives of Zoloz from extracting final and terrible vengeance from Bremmer and all his band.

While *The Phantom* has not been seen generally since its initial release, existing still photographs reveal a care in production, a taste in casting, settings, and mood totally missing in such disasters as *Batman* from the same studio. Unquestionably, *The Phantom* was one of Columbia's better serials, although beginning to show that studio's notorious low budget defects.

It was over ten years before Columbia considered making a sequel to *The Phantom*. By this time, Sam Katzman was in charge of serials, and he was making them cheaper than anybody had ever produced union-made theatrical movies. One story has it that Katzman's company had actually begun filming the serial before negotiations with King Features, owners of *The Phantom* comic strip, were completed. In any case, either before or during production, the King Syndicate wanted too much money, and The Phantom could not be used again on the screen.

At least, not *exactly*.

In these closing days of theatrical serials, both of the remaining producers, Columbia and Republic, were using *vast* amounts of stock footage from previous serials for every "new" production. Some chapters would consist of only three or four minutes of new material to tie together a reel of stock footage. In all cases, it would have been better to simply rerelease the old serial intact instead of butchering it into an allegedly "new" production to offer theatres. Television offered a more lucrative field of employment to the production crews and actors than the few days work to match up some new shots with the old material. Each studio *did* rerelease two of the old serials each year to a new generation, as well as providing two of these makeshift conglomerations, during this period of the mid-'50s.

Even without use of the name and exact costume of The Phantom, Columbia did use a great deal of stock footage from the original serial for this psuedo-sequel.

The hero's name was changed to *Captain Africa* (which might make you suspect the use of the first Negro serial star, but such was not the case). The new hero, Captain Africa, wore a costume only slightly different than The Phantom. He wore a leather aviator's cap in place of a cloth hood and a pair of riding britches in place of the cloth leotards, but the black mask, form-fitting shirt, belted guns, and boots were the same. Most importantly, *from a distance,* the costume changes were hardly apparent at all.

The new star was youthful John Hart, who had played Jack Armstrong in the earlier Columbia serial, and who played the Lone Ranger on television for one season only, while Clayton Moore was on strike. He was a collar-ad type, little resembling the angular-faced Tom Tyler, but again, in long shots or even *quick* medium shots the difference was not that apparent. (Of course, by this time, the producers must not have cared too much if you did notice.)

If you squinted your eyes, and checked the contents level of your popcorn box often enough, you might think you were seeing The Phantom. (Kids are pretty sharp about such things. When Bob Livingston, star of the second Lone Ranger serial, appeared in several later feature films as the "Masked Rider," the young fans of the present writer's generation simply referred to him by the name of the character he continued to imitate—the "Lone Ranger.")

The official title of this "Columbia Super-Serial," was *The Adventures of Captain Africa,* fifteen episodes, directed by Spencer G. Bennet, and scripted by a single writer, George H. Plympton, since a large staff was not required to write the smaller number of new sequences.

Once again, serial fans were treated to a story of a lost civilization, crocodiles, slavers, and a gorilla, which seemed destined to be engaged in a fight with Captain Africa. There was, of course, a faithful Wolf Dog (like The Phantom's own "Devil") and Captain Africa appeared with him in a cloud of smoke on his great stone throne. Once again, a masked jungle avenger faced doom on a collapsing suspension bridge.

Captain Africa, trying to be The Phantom, faced the perils of an attacking lion, the near-drowning in an abandoned well, the narrow escape from the spikes of a crashing castle gate, the chomping jaws of crocodiles, and a plunge into a tiger pit. (Somehow Asian tigers were always turning up in the African jungles in serials and other B thrillers. Sometimes some excuse would be made about an escape from a trapper's ship, sometimes not.)

Just how closely Captain Africa followed in The Phantom's footsteps can be judged from the various chapter titles. Chapter Nine of *The Phantom* was "The Fire Princess," and Chapter Ten of *Captain Africa* was "The Vanishing Princess" (who vanished in a burst of fire). Chapter Twelve of *both* serials was called "Fangs of the Beast."

In the final episode, "Captain Africa's Final Move," the masked man saved his friends and brought the wicked to justice

—but not without the help from twelve years earlier of the Ghost Who Walks. Truly, The Phantom never dies.

Columbia offered only one other "original" costumed hero such as Captain Africa, a character who seemed to have originated in the comic books, but did not. Again, this serial was something of a "sequel"—a sequel to a serial that Columbia never made.

The Black Commando was patterned very much after Republic's Spy Smasher, in a serial made the same wartime year of 1942. The serial was actually titled *The Secret Code,* but fans simply referred to it as "The Black Commando." Beneath his solid black outfit, complete with black hood and gloves, the Commando was really Police Lieutenant Dan Barton (played by Paul Kelly), who donned the costume to smash an enemy spy ring. On at least one occasion, he varied his costume with an aviator's cap and goggles such as Spy Smasher wore. Advertising posters proclaimed "Smash spies with the Secret Service!" and most blatantly of all, "Thrill again to spy smashers' biggest chase!"

Fortunately, this was not the era of *massive* use of stock footage (and anyway, Columbia did not own *Spy Smasher*). Most of *The Secret Code* was new material.

Lieutenant Dan Barton arranged for himself to be thrown off the police force, so he could work more effectively in secret against the spy ring. Feldon (Gregory Gay) arrived from Berlin with a secret spy code. He informed the leader of the alien agents in America, Thyssen (Robert O. Davis), that the United States Government scientists had discovered a method of producing synthetic rubber. Ex-Lieutenant Barton arranged a ruse to trap the spies into trying to steal the secret formula, and was captured by the enemy agents. In their custody, Barton learned the plans of the spy ring. He managed to make an escape, and shortly returned in his bizarre guise of the Black Commando.

In this and succeeding chapters, the Black Commando braved a usual assortment of serial perils: an exploding building; a plunging airplane; bolts of dancing electricity; an inferno of blazing oil; poison gas; and an entire shipyard exploding around his ears.

In Chapter Fifteen, "The Secret Code Smashed," Dan Barton finally decoded the prime secret message, using such weird objects as a list of names, a square of celluloid, and clothes hanging on a line to simulate Roman numerals. The secret code told of an enemy submarine that would rescue the crew of saboteurs in less than half an hour. After contacting his former teammates on the police force for aid, the Black Commando and the authorities rounded up the spies, and a U.S. destroyer sunk the U-boat which was to rescue the enemy agents. The Black Commando's career ended in a burst of glory.

The Secret Code was an above average serial for Columbia Pictures, produced by Larry Darmour and directed by the ever faithful Spencer G. Bennet. There were three writers on the script, Leighton Brill, Robert Beche, and Basil Dickey. Of the three, Basil Dickey went on to write many scripts for the other major serial studio, Republic, including *The Masked Marvel, Captain America,* and *Zorro's Black Whip.* As it was, *The Secret Code* closely resembled the typical Republic product, such as *Spy Smasher* which was such an inspiration to the exploits of the Black Commando.

11

New Masks for New Heroes
"Get That Masked Trouble-Maker"

Some select few of the flamboyant mystery man heroes who lurked behind concealing masks and costumes in movie serials were not adapted from the comic books where they would have been at home. Besides Columbia's Black Commando in answer to Republic's *Spy Smasher,* the Republic Pictures Corporation, home of action films, also created a number of superheroes especially for the screen.

The Masked Marvel (1943) featured a hero in the simplest of all crime fighting disguises (bearing some similarity to Will Eisner's cartoon hero, *The Spirit*)—a form-fitting mask worn over the face, concealing all but the wearer's mouth and chin. He wore a standard gray business suit, a white, black-brimmed hat, and dark gloves.

The serial was a reverse upon the old mystery villain theme. In *The Masked Marvel,* the nefarious Sakima (played by Caucasian actor Johnny Arthur, as was common during wartime), a former Japanese envoy now responsible for sabotaging American war industries, was known right from the first episode, "The Masked Crusader." Rather, it was the hero whose identity was secreted from the audience. To complicate matters even more, The Masked Marvel was one of four investigators— Bob Barton (David Bacon), Frank Jeffers (Richard Clarke), Terry Morton (Bill Healy), and Jim Arnold (Rod Bacon, David's real-life brother). And all four wore gray business suits, and white, black-brimmed hat, probably to inflate their egos. It was *something* to be suspected of being the Masked Marvel, a title usually reserved for wrestlers. Certainly their identical garb was not meant to dupe pretty Alice Hamilton (Louise Currie), for she was the only person aware of the Marvel's real identity. This was just another attempt by the studio to confuse the audience, so that the wrong man seen in long shots could fall off a rooftop and end one of the chapters. (The whole situation of various suspects for the masked hero dated back to Republic's first Lone Ranger serial.)

The Masked Marvel was called by Warren Hamilton (Howard Hickman) and Martin Crane (William Forrest), the heads of the World-Wide Insurance Company, to investigate and halt the sabotage work done by Sakima. Hamilton was unaware of Crane's allegiance to the Japanese villain and became an easy murder target.

Alice, Warren's daughter, was not passive concerning her father's death. She courageously joined the four gray-clad investigators in their war against Sakima. After the quartet of heroes left the room in which they had been assembled, Alice learned to her surprise that one of them had returned.

ALICE: The Masked Marvel!
MASKED MARVEL: Yes, Miss Hamilton, I'm sorry I startled you. We've met before. I'm one of the four men who just left here.
ALICE: But your voice?
MASKED MARVEL: That is part of my disguise. Before I remove my mask, I want your promise never to reveal my identity to anyone.
ALICE: You have my word.

Alice's word was enough. Serial heroines were as trustworthy as the heroes.

Mace (Anthony Warde), Sakima's number-one henchman with a name befitting his cruel and blunt personality, was ordered to contaminate airplane fuel with a liquid which would cause the fuel to explode in midair.

But the Masked Marvel learned of the plot against his country and trailed Kline and Spike (stuntmen Dale Van Sickel and Duke Green), two of Mace's hired thugs, to the top of an enormous oil tank, where they were pouring the liquid into the gasoline.

"Hold it," the deep voice of the Masked Marvel commanded.

Surprised, the two heavies looked up. Spike hurled the empty liquid container hard against the Marvel, knocking him off balance. Together, Kline and Spike rushed the hero, beginning a terrific fight. During the battle, Kline managed to escape down the ladder to where Mace was waiting.

"The Masked Marvel!" Kline exclaimed.

The fight atop the gasoline tank had not subsided. As they rolled to the guide rail, a gun fired.

"Those guns will bring the cops," Mace yelled. "We'd better finish off the Marvel and get away quick!" Mace rushed to a canvas-topped truck (which seemed to be the favorite type of truck used by villains in serials) containing a number of gasoline cylinders. With a flick of his cigarette lighter, he ignited their contents into a lake of dancing flames. "That'll take care of him and the lend-lease gasoline too."

The crook started to run as Kline grabbed him. "You can't do that. Spike's up there."

"Run, you fool!" Mace shouted with a sneer.

The truck continued to burn as Mace and Kline tried to escape. A bullet fired by the momentarily free Masked Marvel buried itself deep into Kline's back. (It was never murder when a serial hero gunned down a villain in the back.) But Spike attacked with full force from behind. The fight raged until the masked crusader was pushed off the edge of the tank. The fall was more hazardous than even Spike suspected, for the audience could see one arm of the Masked Marvel literally torn from its socket to remain stuck to the side of the tank, imparting a faint suspicion of the use of a dummy.

Flames raged like the inside of an erupting volcano as the Masked Marvel, miraculously whole and entire again, plummeted through the canvas topping of the truck. He gaped around at the cremating doom that awaited him.

At last the flames penetrated the cylinders of gasoline!

The truck exploded with blinding, deafening violence!

In another instant the entire gasoline tank belched apart in an encompassing mountain of flame and debris!

We were left with but one phrase of assurance: "Next week . . . Chapter Two—Death Takes the Helm."

The Masked Marvel had to survive somehow as there were eleven chapters yet to come. Luckily at the beginning of the next installment the Marvel regained enough of his sense to jump from the blazing truck seconds before it erupted into oblivion.

Sakima's plans did not stop with the first interference of the Masked Marvel. The next stages in the villain's scheme to disrupt American defenses were to hijack a shipment of valuable industrial diamonds, to explode a bomb (with the usual timing device to prolong the action) under the storm drain of an aircraft plant, and to steal a new model periscope. The Masked Marvel and his aides were always there to thwart Sakima's thugs, but only after risking falls down elevator shafts, from rooftops, surviving exploding automobiles and speedboats, and the worst fate of all, the threat of being unmasked. Chapter Four, "Suspense at Midnight," was a unique episode especially for Republic, in that it did not climax with a spectacular "death." The cliffhanger went as recorded in the serial's cutting continuity:

177. EXT. CRANE'S ESTATE: MED. LONG (NITE)
On investigator as he runs to left to house, camera panning.
Another investigator enters at camera left and runs to house.
Another investigator enters at camera right to house.

178. INT. CRANE'S STUDY: MED. (NITE)
  BOB *enters study door at right.*
BOB: Well, what happened?
  He walks to left to CRANE *at desk, camera panning.*
CRANE: Well, I just received some important information. Where are the others?
BOB: Why, they're . . .

179. MED. CLOSE (NITE)
  On study door as TERRY *enters.*
BOB: (O.S.)
  Where are Jim and Frank?
  TERRY *walks to left to* BOB *and* CRANE *at desk, camera panning.*
TERRY: Frank's just coming in.

180. MED. (NITE)
  On Study Door as FRANK *enters.*
FRANK: What's up?
BOB: Well where's Jim?
  Camera pans to left as FRANK *walks to desk.*

181. INT. SECRET BASEMENT: CLOSE (NITE)
  On SAKIMA *seated at desk listening to dictograph. Camera moves in to closer shot as he smiles.*
FRANK: (O.S.)
  Why, I . . . I haven't seen him.
SAKIMA: So Jim Arnold is the Masked Marvel.

FADE OUT:

Naturally Sakima's deduction was premature and inevitably wrong.

By the last installment, "The Man Behind the Mask," two of the gray-suited investigators, Frank and Jim, had been killed off, narrowing down the possibilities of the Marvel's secret identity. At least one other person, the second surviving investigator, knew the Masked Marvel's identity by process of elimination. But he didn't tell. In the serial he played dumb and silent, unless he never did figure out the double identity of his partner.

Suspecting Crane of working with Sakima, the Masked Marvel overheard him contact the Japanese mastermind. Exposed, Crane tried to escape but perished in the flames of his own exploding getaway car. Now the unidentified hero was free to pursue the leader himself. Meanwhile, the cunning Sakima was readying a time bomb to destroy his house and any incriminating evidence after he had safely escaped. But he had not calculated the sudden appearance of the Masked Marvel who entered into battle with Meggs (Eddie Parker), the butler, whose fighting ability made it appear as if he moonlighted as a bodyguard . . . or a stuntman. After the fight, Sakima was wounded by a bullet, and the battered Meggs turned on the bomb. Only the lightning reflexes of the Masked Marvel (as usual) allowed him to safely exit through the French windows before the entire structure was blown apart destroying the menace of Sakima forever.

The Masked Marvel decided to keep his identity a secret from the public in case a sequel were ever made. For a while it seemed as if even the audience was to be kept in the dark. Finally, the Marvel appeared unmasked, as the youngest of the four investigators, Bob Barton. At least, Chapter Twelve stated that the Masked Marvel was actually the character portrayed in the serial by David Bacon.

In truth, however, he was not. Except for the final scene in which Barton admitted his identity, the Masked Marvel was played in every scene by stuntman Tom Steele. The mask itself was made to only fit a blade-thin Steele, molded directly from his own face. His natural voice unsuited for heroic parts, Steele mouthed the words of a deep-voiced radio actor, Gayne Whitman (one of the actors to play Chandu the Magician on radio). But *all* the visuals, including close-ups and some of the most thrilling, elaborately choreographed stunt fights of all time, were performed by Tom Steele.

What is particularly interesting about *The Masked Marvel* is that Tom Steele, despite his starring in the serial, was given absolutely no screen credit whatsoever. While Duke Green, Dale Van Sickel, and Eddie Parker, all stuntmen, received screen credit for even small parts, Steele was granted none. Apparently, Republic decided not to give any indication that the Masked Marvel was not, in fact, David Bacon. But why was Tom Steele not credited for his *other* roles in the serial? He not only played the Masked Marvel, but also various crooks that were killed off only to reappear later with a mustache and new name. At one point in *The Masked Marvel,* Steele actually chased himself up the stairs. Such was an easy way to hire actors. Most of Republic's stuntmen resembled typical movie heavies.[1] Surely, the studio chiefs reasoned, no one would recognize a typical film tough who had been killed off several weeks before.

The Masked Marvel was directed by the Dean of serial directors, Spencer G. Bennet. With the screenplay by seven writers—Royal Cole, Ronald Davidson, Basil Dickey, Jesse Duffy, Grant Nelso, George Plympton, and Joseph Poland—and a terrific music score by a staff headed by Mort Glickman, Bennet made an exciting serial, one of Republic's best, with some of the most beautifully photographed and edited action

---

[1] Since Republic serials and features were more oriented toward action than script and characterization, many of the leading men at that studio were chosen on the basis of their resemblance to the stuntmen who would double them in the more strenuous scenes—usually Dale Van Sickel or Tom Steele. The stuntmen's measurements were posted in the Republic casting office. And the stars were picked on the basis of their matching those statistics. Players like Allan Lane, Rod Cameron, Larry Thompson, Clayton Moore, George Turner, Kirk Alyn, Bruce Edwards, Jim Bannon, and others were at least partially hired for their resemblances to Steele and "doubled" him in the closer shots and dialogue scenes. Dick Purcell, Charles Quigley, and others followed suit with Dale Van Sickel.

sequences in the history of cliffhangers. Of particular significance was the conclusion of Chapter Ten, "Suicide Sacrifice," wherein the Masked Marvel sped through the night in pursuit of an electrically controlled railroad handcar, filled with explosives. The handcar was sent by Mace to collide with a train transporting vital airplane parts. The only way the Masked Marvel could save the train was to crash his own car into the small rolling platform of destruction. Only a split-moment leap from his automobile saved him from annihilation. The sequence was both thrilling and perfect craftsmanship.

The most popular original costumed hero to roar out of Republic Pictures' North Hollywood studio lot was Rocket Man, whose initial appearance was in *King of the Rocket Men* (1949).

Rocket Man, of which there was only one despite the misleading title, surpassed the Masked Marvel in his ability to thwart criminals because he could fly. And with that added ability came a new outfit and new gimmickry, inspired by the *Buck Rogers* cartoon strip.

The uniform of Rocket Man was beautifully simple, a characteristic which contributed tremendously to the character's appeal. He wore a simple leather jacket (the kind any kid might own), topped with a silver-gray bullet-shaped helmet, which had a visor perforated with three openings for the eyes and mouth. A silvery rocket pack with twin tanks was attached to his back and buckled around the jacket with a belt. (The helmet and rocket pack were a bit more difficult for a kid to acquire. The many smooth curves prevented an accurate homemade version fashioned out of cardboard or other available material, though we did our best.) On his chest was the control panel devoid of all the complications of modern inventions, including the similar rocket belt developed by the United States Air Force. Rocket Man's controls consisted of a small platform with three simple dials (the kind you could buy in any radio repair shop) and the stampings, ON-OFF, UP-DOWN, and SPEED CONTROL—FAST SLOW. Those were controls that even the youngest audiences could understand. That's the way Rocket Man's fans would have made the flying belt themselves.

Flight and a cruising outfit were not Rocket Man's only advantages over his adversaries. He carried a raygun that appeared to be a German Luger (acceptable in this post-wartime serial) with a silvery cone propped over the barrel. This weapon could blast apart any object of reasonable size at the mere squeeze of the trigger. Unfortunately, Rocket Man rarely got a chance to use the raygun.

The rocket suit was developed by Professor Millard (James Craven playing a good guy for a change), a scientist believed killed by the serial's mystery villain, Dr. Vulcan. Millard, having survived a laboratory explosion triggered by Dr. Vulcan, retreated to an isolated cave where he completed the flight suit which he had previously described to hero Jeff King[2] (played by mustached Tristram Coffin).

After Dr. Vulcan successfully killed a number of members of Science Associates, an organization to which it was apparent that the master villain belonged, Jeff King visited the exiled Professor Millard, who handed him the flight suit. King regarded the assuming of this second identity with incredulity. But Millard assured him that his own confidence in the apparatus by which King would soar through the heavens was absolute.

Jeff King accepted the garb and gadgets of Rocket Man and agreed to undergo a test cruise. Millard warned him to stay close

[2] Republic delighted in naming their heroes "King." This provided a convenient way to legitimately name their serials after the leading man with a formula title that seemed to please the fans. Similarly, the studio released *King of the Royal Mounted* (1940) and *King of the Texas Rangers* (1941) with Sammy Baugh as Sergeant Tom King, *King of the Forest Rangers* (1946) with Larry Thompson as Steve King, and Republic's final serial, *King of the Carnival* (1955), with their last serial star, Harry Lauter, as Bert King.

to the ground during the virgin flight. This seemed a bit curious. Just what did Millard mean by staying close to the ground? Five hundred feet or five miles, a fall in that tin helmet would permanently impair one's health.

With the rocket suit hidden in his automobile trunk, Jeff King learned that Dr. Vulcan's men were speeding away in a canvas-topped truck with a stolen missile which the fiend planned to launch in destruction of an entire community.

It was nearly the end of Chapter One, "Dr. Vulcan—Traitor," when the great moment finally arrived—the first screen appearance of Rocket Man. Jeff King removed the leather jacket, the rocket pack, the helmet, from the car trunk. Within seconds, he snapped down the visor and became a new man—Rocket Man. Shoving the ray pistol into the belt of his jacket, he switched the control dial from OFF to ON. There followed the rising whine of atomic power. Then he turned the second switch from DOWN to UP; and the speed control from SLOW to FAST. Rocket Man rushed forward and leaped into the air (via a hidden mini-trampoline). There was a loud explosive sound and a blast of smoke as the helmeted hero cleared the top of the camera.

And Rocket Man, the screen's last great original serial hero, was soaring through the skies!

Meanwhile, in the canvas-topped truck, the three hirelings of Dr. Vulcan drove on with the stolen projectile of doom. Rocket Man was within range of the truck in moments. A quick adjustment of his chest controls from UP to DOWN, and the jet-pack hero zoomed toward the truck.

Inside, Tony Dirken (played by square-shouldered Don Haggerty), Dr. Vulcan's top gunman, and Blears (David Sharpe), guarding the gleaming missile, heard the strange, alien sound that cut through the air. Blear bit hard on his cigar as his eyes bulged to see the weird sight of a man shooting through the air toward him. In another instant, Rocket Man landed in the truck and a furious battle flared into action.

Hearing the sounds of the fight, Knox (Tom Steele),[3] the driver turned to shout, "Hey! What's going on back there?"

The fight continued. Dirken was knocked into the ON-OFF switch of the missile. The shiny projectile smoked, hummed, vibrated, and blasted out of the rear of the truck.

Rocket Man stopped in the midst of the fight to watch the missile roar through the sky. "If that torpedo explodes in any populated area," he admonished the wide-eyed Dirken, "you'll be guilty of mass murder!"

After swift adjustments were made on his control bow, Rocket Man blasted off in pursuit of the missile. Gradually, the gap between the two flying projectiles narrowed. Rocket Man took the raygun from his belt, aimed and fired as the torpedo angled over the city. There was a tremendous explosion, lighting the daylight sky. And Rocket Man fell from the smoke, unconscious, toward a pioneering "splashdown."

Fortunately, Rocket Man, after going through the same action in the next chapter's opening recap, regained full consciousness in time to reset the UP-DOWN controls and rocket away.

The third episode, "Dangerous Evidence," presented a rather unusual dilemma for the airborne hero. Jeff King learned of the existence of a photograph taken of Rocket Man in longshot flight. It was believed that the enlarging of the picture would reveal the true secret identity of Rocket Man, thereby ruining his efficiency as a mystery man. The fact that the face behind the helmet was unrecognizable even under the tightest close-up gave little credence to that development in the plot.

[3] Again we see the ubiquitous use of stuntmen. While Tom Steele was seen in the cab of the truck, he was actually doubling Tristram Coffin in the fight in the rear of the vehicle. Stuntman David Sharpe, also in that conflict, did Rocket Man's leaps into the air. Doubling for Don Haggerty was Dale Van Sickel, who donned the Rocket Man suit in scenes wherein Steele and Sharpe were unavailable or elsewhere in the shot.

But then, villains in serials were only *slightly* smarter than the heroes.

Dr. Vulcan wore no distinguishing costume in *King of the Rocket Men.* He appeared only as a shadow on the wall, giving orders to his henchmen either in person or over the telephone. The identity of villains such as Dr. Vulcan could usually be discovered by simply reading the cast credits. Even though a different actor's voice might have been dubbed in to mislead the audience, it could be logically assumed that an actor known primarily for villainous roles, listed quite prominently in the credits (usually given about fourth billing), yet having no apparent function in the story, *was* the evil mastermind. In *King of the Rocket Men,* veteran screen bad guy I. Stanford Jolley was given sixth billing, but hardly appeared in the chapterplay. It was no surprise when Jolley, in Chapter Eleven, "Secret of Dr. Vulcan," was revealed as the mysterious voice and shadow.

In the next and final installment, "Wave of Disaster," Dr. Vulcan used his stolen Decimeter, a superpowerful destructive weapon that whirred with the familiar and recognizable Republic weird machine sound effect, to blast the Amsterdam Fault from his hideout on Fisherman's Island. The crumbling of the fault produced a tremendous city-wide tidal wave courtesy of stock footage from an old RKO feature thriller, *Deluge,* to pay back the people of New York City for not meeting his maniacal demand. He wanted a billion dollar ransom, which is what organized crime must take out of the city in a year, in smaller installments.

Most of New York crumbled under the tumultuous, skyscraper-high tidal waves, while Rocket Man soared to the rescue, smashing helmet-first through the window of Dr. Vulcan's hideout. Meanwhile, the United States Air Force was nearing Fisherman's Island to obliterate it—and Rocket Man, unfortunately—with bombs.

Rocket Man zapped the Decimeter with the raygun. But

another fight commenced with Dr. Vulcan and his henchman. The frequency with which Rocket Man engaged in fist fights with his enemies revealed the stupidity of criminals. It would have been easier for a villain to tamper with Rocket Man's controls, firing him head-first into a wall or the floor, rather than risk a smashed hand by punching that solid metal helmet.

The Air Force was already dropping their explosive cargoes when Rocket Man finished his two opponents, then flew out of the window, leaving the house behind to blow up into a flying mass of smoking timber.

The serial ended without Rocket Man revealing his identity in the hope of a sequel, and on the happy note that devastated New York would be rebuilt.

King of the Rocket Men showed the downward trend of the late 1940s Republic serials, with stock footage serving most of the cliffhangers requiring miniatures (including car and plane crashes). The cast was debatable. One of the present writers (Harmon) enjoyed seeing a more mature man with some character in his face, Tristram Coffin, as King, in contrast to the bland, colorless leads in the later serials, while the other writer (Glut) can see him only as an inappropriate "thin villain type." Mae Clarke as the girl news photographer probably *was* too mature. She had been in such early talkies as *Frankenstein* and *Public Enemy* (both 1931). Nevertheless, the serial did show signs of greatness, especially because of the new special visual effects footage created by brothers Howard "Babe" and Theodore Lydecker for the flying scenes. As Howard Lydecker had done before in *Darkest Africa* and *Adventures of Captain Marvel*, a full-size, lightweight dummy was flown on wires from one hilltop to another. The final effect was unbelievably realistic. The flying scenes were not, however, as varied or as elaborate as those using the Captain Marvel dummy. There were no shots of Rocket Man swooping down upon his fleeing opponents, both seen simultaneously in the same shot without a cut. But

Rocket Man had two advantages over Captain Marvel. He wore a helmet so that there were no shots to betray a sculpted face when the dummy flew too near the camera. And there was the added element of sound, the strange rocketing noise, that gave extra realism when compared to the silent flying Captain Marvel.

The Rocket Man character and concept proved so popular that Republic revived him in three pseudo-sequels, all heavily padded in stock footage from *King* and other past chapterplay adventures. The first two, released in 1952, one right after the other, were *Radar Men from the Moon* and *Zombies of the Stratosphere*.

Radar Men from the Moon took the 1949 Rocket Man regalia, added a few minor alterations, and the titles boasted, "Introducing a New Character . . . Commando Cody, Sky Marshal of the Universe." Commando Cody (George Wallace, the actor, not the politician) sky marshaled only Earth's stratosphere and parts of the moon, where he and his confederates found no difficulty in running about bare-handed, with no protection against atmospheric conditions except the famed bullet helmet, and unaffected by the satellite's one-sixth gravity. The brilliant scientist Cody also found nothing mysterious about traversing the distance between Earth and moon through brightly lit space, which made even the General Science One dropouts in the audience snicker (only seventeen years before the first real lunar landing).

The plot involved Retik (Roy Barcroft), ambitious ruler of the moon, clad in flowing robes and the Purple Monster's hood, attempting to conquer the Earth with his own lunarians and employee terrain traitors. Gone was the double identity motif of Rocket Man and the name "Jeff King." Commando Cody was just Commando Cody, whether in flight suit or business suit. Gone also was the simply hero vs. villain plot. In its place was the complicated interjection of space ships (laughable to Wernher Von Braun, but totally convincing to fans of Lydecker special effects), repainted juggernaut tanks left over from *Undersea Kingdom,* moonmen, and other extravaganzas. The selection of cowboy villain Roy Barcroft as the moon monarch was to match stock shots from Republic's *The Purple Monster Strikes* with new scenes of the actor again wearing the old form-fitting costume. Now, however, it did not seem to fit the stocky actor as well as before.

More stock footage and more senselessness went into *Zombies of the Stratosphere.* The zombies in this instance were not the walking dead of Voodoo legend but, with Republic's propensity for changing popular myths, Martian invaders that planned to blast the Earth from its orbit with a super H-bomb, so that their own dying planet could occupy our world's desirable position around the sun. The men from Mars (apparently not related to the Martian Purple Monster) were led by Marex, played by another Western heavy, Lane Bradford (pronouncing carefully all his "ings"). Marex and his alien brood, capable of extended periods of time walking underwater, occupied a cave complete with subterranean river. Somehow, Marex had gotten hold of Dr. Satan's robot (plus considerable lengths of stock footage of it lumbering about), producing yet another obstacle for the newest Rocket Man incarnation to overcome.

Jeff King and Commando Cody had retired. Now Larry Martin (Judd Holdren) wore the jacket and helmet, battling Martians, mechanical men, hired thugs, and even a gang of cowboys out West in a raging gun battle set in the desert (with black and white-printed scenes taken from a color Roy Rogers feature). In the last part, Chapter Twelve, "Tomb of the Traitors," Larry heard the confession of a Martian whose spaceship had crashed. Narab (played by Leonard Nimoy over a decade before becoming famous as the half-alien Mr. Spock on television's *Star Trek*) told Larry the location of the cave and its hidden hydrogen bomb. The hero rocketed to the cave, removed his flying suit, dove underwater, emerged in the secret bomb chamber, and deactivated the terrible doomsday device with only seconds preceding the planet-shattering explosion, thus saving the Earth.

In 1953, Holdren returned in a uniform, a black domino mask, and regularly donned the flight outfit, in a Republic series simply entitled *Commando Cody*. The series consisted of twelve episodes, each a half hour long and complete, but strung together they followed the same general plot stream, not unlike the early silent serials. Retik from *Radar Men from the Moon* had been replaced by the Ruler (played by foreign-accented Gregory Gay), who operated from his secret base on another planet and tried to conquer our world, again using alien thugs, employed Earth gangsters, space ships and devious weapons, and even more stock footage. Produced with the same flavor as the later Republic serials, *Commando Cody* was obviously planned as a television series, but was released to theatres as a "serial," circa 1955, before its TV appearance.

When asked to comment on his rocket suit serials, Judd Holdren replied to the present writer: "There were two different helmets. A safer, lighter one was used for stuntwork. I remember the visors would always get stuck on us. I know there were a number of men doubling for me. The person who did most of my stunts was Dale Van Sickel. By the way, the outside of Cody's office was really the office of Republic."

Concerning the differences in the large rocket ship mock-ups that he and the other players entered and exited, Holdren said: "The prop men would just add attachments, transforming Cody's into one of the Ruler's ships."

The fact that Commando Cody was revived in the form of a mystery man with a mask sparked the following explanation: "I guess the producers didn't want to take any chances on my walking out of the series. They figured I might want more money and quit doing Cody. I understand that was the reason

Clayton Moore left *The Lone Ranger* TV program. The producers, thinking the mask would hide the identity well enough, put John Hart in the part of the Lone Ranger. But public opinion forced the return of Clayton Moore after about a year. The mask didn't quite work in that case."

The Rocket Man character, regardless of his name, has endured through four serials. He blasted off into the stratosphere week after week . . . year after year . . . black jets emitting searing force. And he never once burnt off his pantslegs!

The trails he blazed seem far away. Boys who followed his Saturday matinee exploits are now real "Rocket Men" involved in NASA Space Projects, less than two decades later.

12

The Westerns
"Who Was That Masked Man?"

The sleepy-eyed, mustached young man named Vega looked up at the portrait of the masked man in the dress of a Spanish don of Old California. Then, the young man pressed a hidden switch and the life-size portrait opened inward to reveal a secret passage. He went into that passage, down a stone staircase and entered an alcove where stood his faithful horse, El Rey. Swiftly, he changed his foppish garments for ones like those of the man in the portrait—he stood garbed and masked in black. Mounting his fine horse, out of his secret cave rode the avenging phantom known for the cunning and stealth of the fox— Zorro.

This was the often-repeated scene in *Zorro Rides Again,* the first *serial* about the famous character, made by Republic in 1937, but hardly the first screen appearance of Zorro.

Douglas Fairbanks, Sr., first brought Johnston McCulley's fictional avenger to the screen in the 1920 release, *The Mark of Zorro.* As the foppish Don Diego, Fairbanks was able to exercise comedy touches as had been his *main* talent up to this turning point in his career. As the masked Zorro attempted to free the people of Old California from the oppression of their corrupt governor, he occasionally displayed flashes of humor but more slashes from his dazzling blade that carved the letter "Z" on the forehead of the oppressors. The classic sequence of this feature is the one where Zorro dared a troop of soldiers to prevent him from having breakfast in a nearby mission. In the following views, Fairbanks seemed to defy gravity and virtually to *fly* as he leaped over a donkey, dove across a wagon, swung from the edges of rooftops, and completely baffled the soldiers. It was a high mark in screen action, difficult for later Zorros to match, or even Fairbanks himself in the 1925 sequel, *Don Q, Son of Zorro.*

The first talking Zorro film waited until 1936 when the famous masked man was played by Robert Livingston, destined to later play that other most famous masked rider, the Lone Ranger. The talkie in unsuccessful two-color "Natural Color" was *The Bold Caballero.* The story began with the local garrison Commandante (Sig Rumann) killing the new governor sent by the King of Spain, so that he could retain power himself. Don Diego played along with the power-seeking military man, even pretending to arrange for the Commandante to marry the Governor's orphaned daughter, Isabella (Heather Angel) so that the rights of the family would revert to him. After many chases and daring stunts, the story ended at the point of Zorro's sword. The star, Bob Livingston, has been lavish in his praise of his fencing coach, Fred Cavens, who tutored Zorro stars all the way from Fairbanks to television's Guy Williams. His stunt-man for some of the most hazardous riding and leaps was Yakima Canutt.

Canutt was again the double for Zorro when John Carroll became the star of the first serial version, *Zorro Rides Again.* Since Canutt did almost all the scenes in which Zorro wore a mask, he was on the screen easily as much as Carroll. The youthful star contributed some flair for comedy as the milk-toast descendant of the original Zorro—James Vega.

It was quite a long descent from the original Zorro since the serial was set in contemporary times with automobiles, airplanes, and trains—especially trains in almost every episode.

The California-Yucatan Railroad owned by pretty blond heroine, Joyce Andrews (actress Helen Christian), and her brother, Phillip (Reed Howes), was the subject of the sinister machinations of big city financier, Marsden's (hulking Noah Beery, Sr.). Marsden's henchmen led by rugged Westerner, El Lobo (Richard Alexander) were doing everything they could to wreck the trains, burn their buildings, kill their men, so that Marsden could buy the vital line cheaply.

A masked rider appeared, his guns and his whip striking terror among the raiders. Shortly after, the unknown avenger revealed himself to the faithful old servant, Renaldo (actually young Duncan Renaldo in character make-up for the role). He was *Zorro*—and Zorro was really James Vega, nephew of a slain co-owner of the railroad, and great-grandson of the original Zorro.

Zorro tried to protect the railroad payroll by riding the train carrying the cash, but this time the raiders did not strike from horseback, but from the air. As the first chapter ended, El Lobo's airplane seemed about to blow the whole train to bits with a holocaust of bombs. "The Wolf" was apparently vanquishing "The Fox."

The next episode revealed that the telling gunfire of Zorro forced El Lobo to land before the final bomb could be dropped. As the serial unfolded, James Vega pretended to be an ineffectual boob, good only for serenading the blond Joyce, but when danger appeared, with the aid of devoted Renaldo, he donned the black costume of Zorro and rode out to face the dangers of both the old and the modern West.

Chapter Two ended with a time bomb ticking away to "The Final Minute" for the unconscious Zorro, who, of course, recovered in time to slip away in Chapter Three. This episode ended with a memorable prototypical cliffhanger: Zorro was trapped, his foot caught by a switch rail, as "The Juggernaut" of a speeding freight train bore down on him.

The situation had been used in countless serials since the silent era. The solution was usually that the hero simply worked his foot free in time, or in the case of heroines, the leading man arrived in the nick of time and pulled her free. A bit more cleverly and logically, Zorro used his whip to lash around the handle of the switch controlling the movable rail and jerked the switch open, releasing the rail and his foot in time for him to leap out of the path of the chugging engine.

The railroad setting figured in a number of other cliffhangers. Zorro was trapped in a runaway freight car in Chapter Eight, "Plunge of Peril," uncoupled from the train and racing backwards down a huge spillway. In the chapter immediately following, "Tunnel of Terror," Zorro arrived too late to stop Joyce and her brother, Phillip, from riding the train into a tunnel loaded with dynamite set to explode. In the next to last chapter, "Right of Way," Zorro seemed to lose a race with a train to the crossing, and the puffing steam locomotive appeared about to totally demolish the truck in which the masked man was riding. (The solutions were obvious: Zorro jumped out of the runaway freight car; the good guys merely survived the explosion; and the truck braked to a stop before it could crash into the train.)

Chapter Ten, "Trapped," took an unusual turn for any Zorro film. As James Vega, the avenger went to the big, modern-day city where the big boss, Marsden, resided to search his office for important papers. There, Zorro and his faithful servant, Renaldo, resembled uncannily the Green Hornet and Kato of radio and movie fame. While searching the office for the papers (and finding them) Zorro was surprised by members of the gang of business-suited gangsters and had a running chase from them over the rooftops of the city skyscrapers. In a desperate move to escape, Zorro attempted a leap from one roof to the next—and failed. He plunged toward the street many floors below.

The next chapter revealed that even as he fell, Zorro used his trusty whip to lash around a convenient support and to swing across to the safety of a ledge. Later, James Vega appeared in the alley where Renaldo waited with their car, cheerfully tossed the costume of Zorro into the back seat, and the two drove off into the night. Of course, this resemblance to the Green Hornet only shows what a debt all double-identity costumed heroes owe to the original Zorro.

In the twelfth and final episode, "Retribution," Zorro was captured by El Lobo and his gang of rustlers and outlaws. He was unmasked and revealed to all as James Vega. Almost simultaneously, old Renaldo was forced by circumstances to reveal Zorro's identity to Joyce. The two of them led a posse of railroad men to the location of El Lobo's hideout. Zorro managed to free himself and to aid those attacking the outlaw stronghold. Climbing a high rise of rocks, he dropped down on two men operating a small *cannon* (these are well-armed militants indeed). His fists sent them to their doom off the cliff, but he took a bullet in the arm himself. El Lobo prepared to finish off the unmasked hero with another bullet when Zorro's great horse arrived on the scene. El Rey had come along with the rest of the good guys, of course, and now his flashing hoofs took their toll from the beefy El Lobo's hide. The master villain, Marsden, was *presumably* captured in the city, but strangely, we never saw for sure.

The next Zorro serial (like the first, directed by the English-Witney team) was the only *authentic* version of the original Zorro concept ever done in chapterplay form. While *Zorro Rides Again* is often confused in many minds (including those of film historians) as a sequel to this picture, the fact is that *Zorro's Fighting Legion,* made by Republic in 1939, was a sequel to the John Carroll version of 1937.

The 1939 photoplay starring Reed Hadley, mustachioed, lanky, and possessed of a magnificent voice (he played the radio Red Ryder), was set in 1824, and had the original Zorro (Hadley) in his guise of Don Diego leaving his native California for a visit to Old Mexico, then under Benito Juárez, first Presidente of the new Republic.

Juárez (Carleton Young) was attempting to strengthen the treasury of the struggling young nation with shipments of gold from the fabled San Mendolita Mines. He got little co-operation from three conniving mine officials, one of whom donned a costume with a huge mask of pure gold, masquerading as Don Del Oro, an ancient god of the Yaqui Indians. (Just which one of the three crooks was actually Don Del Oro was left as a mystery to the audience.) The golden "god" inspired the Indians to block off the shipments of bullion. One of the local gentry, Don Francisco (Guy D'Emmery) organized a band of men, a "fighting legion," to protect the shipment and aid the Republic.

Diego arrived the very day Francisco was killed, and in typical heroic fashion, assumed command of the legion (as Zorro), aided by his sidekick, Ramón (William Corson) and his servant, Juan (Budd Buster). *"We ride with the speed of the light . . ."* sang the troop as they rode out to do battle.

The Fighting Legion succeeded in getting through with a gold shipment to Juárez. The Presidente warned the band, curiously, that he could not legally recognize their existence.

The outlaw leader in the golden armor of Don Del Oro retaliated by locating the headquarters of Zorro's men and planting dynamite in the cellar of this old mission building. Fortunately, Zorro arrived in time to free his men and to drive off the outlaws with his guns and whip.

The servant, Juan, trailed the retreating outlaws to their own hideout in a supposedly abandoned mine and passed the word to Zorro. In the clothes of Don Diego, the secret avenger went down into the mine. Glancing behind him, he saw a huge skipdrum rolling down the shaft, about to crush the life from him!

That was the "Descending Doom" of Chapter Three, but the next episode revealed Don Diego escaped by clinging to the walls of the shaft as the drum hurtled past him. This fourth episode was well-named "The Bridge of Doom." When Zorro rode to warn a munitions train of an attack, he was trapped on a

suspension bridge above a high gorge as the outlaws systemati-
cally shot away the supporting ropes. He escaped only by some
fancy rope work himself, climbing up the broken bridge.

Even a huge flaming "Z" lit on a mountainside failed to warn
the munitions train in time. The train was captured, but located
by Zorro in a cave concealed behind the curtain of a waterfall.
Zorro himself was discovered in turn by his enemies and had a
burning wagon loaded with blasting powder sent rolling down on
him.

Zorro managed to escape (by changing the course of the
wagon) for still other perilous adventures. Reed Hadley was
the only *serial* Zorro to use a sword for some of his fights, as
Fairbanks had done in the original *Mark of Zorro* and as
Tyrone Power would do in the sound remake. The other stunts
involving riding, leaps, and swinging across a blazing room on a
rope were performed once again by Yakima Canutt.

The story went on to tell in subsequent episodes of how Don
Diego's friend, Ramón, and Ramón's sister, Volita (Sheila
Darcy), were captured by the outlaws, and rescued in turn by
the masked avenger. In the rescue, Zorro captured Manuel, a
military official who was suspected by members of the Fighting Legion of masquerading as Don Del Oro. Zorro began an
elaborate plan of disguising Ramón as Manuel to trick his men
into revealing the military official's guilt, but it all came to nothing when Manuel was killed, and Don Del Oro continued his
deviltry.

Finally, Don Diego announced to the Council of the region
that he could at long last unmask Don Del Oro. He saved Kala
(Paul Marian), hereditary leader of the Yaqui Indians, from a
sentence of death and tried to convince the chief that Don Del
Oro was a false god. The two men went to look for an empty
suit of golden armor, only to find it filled by the false Don Del
Oro who ordered their deaths. After another narrow escape,
Zorro finally tracked the fake god to an Indian village where he

was arming the Yaquis for an all-out attack on the San Mendolita Mines. In the furious fight that ensued, the masked avenger tore the golden helmet from Don Del Oro, revealing him to be Pablo (C. Montague Shaw), elderly chief magistrate of the mines. The disillusioned natives once again exercised their traditional vengeance on the usurper. After the official signing of a treaty between the Indians and the Mexicans, Zorro was free to return to his native California.

Strictly speaking, Zorro never returned from Old California to the serial screen, although there were a number of later chapterplays that played fast and loose with his name.

As recounted elsewhere, Linda Stirling became the star of the 1944 Republic serial, *Zorro's Black Whip,* in which she played a character called "the Black Whip." Is "the Black Whip" only another name for Zorro then? Does this make Linda Stirling a female Zorro? One may have one's own opinion. The story was set in the American Southwest of the post-Civil War period, and retained only the secret passage behind the painted portrait and the black Spanish outfit, filled in a way never approached by John Carroll or Reed Hadley.

Another even more distant female descendant of Zorro was Adrian Booth as Delores Quantaro, *Daughter of Don Q* (the Don was Zorro's son). Accompanied by dashing Kirk Alyn as Cliff Roberts, Delores played a female detective in a large modern city out to wreck the criminal plans of familiar villains LeRoy Mason and Roy Barcroft in the 1946 Republic serial.

Son of Zorro, 1947, and *Ghost of Zorro,* 1949, were two other Republic serials offering a completely Americanized Zorro with George Turner playing the alter ego role of Jeff Stewart in the first, and Clayton Moore as Ken Mason in the second. Both of these new Zorros were nothing more than black-masked cowboys, using six-guns instead of swords. Those unmasked alter egos were about all the actors did play in the photoplays.

When Zorro put on the mask, it was incomparable stunt expert, Tom Steele, beneath the black silk.

Apparently, Republic could not let Zorro alone even when they no longer cared to pay for using his name. *Don Daredevil Rides Again* starred Ken Curtis (looking considerably sloppier as Festus on television's *Gunsmoke* series). Curtis was a bit slight of frame for a Western hero, but he was all the better to match up (as did George Turner) with the stock shots of *Linda Stirling* in her outfit from *Zorro's Black Whip*.

Man with the Steel Whip, 1954, was Republic's last Western serial (third to last of all). In it, Richard Simmons (television's *Sergeant Preston of the Yukon*) played Jerry Randall, secretly El Latigo. Apparently, Republic used stock shots from everything they had ever done on Zorro with the hero's costume growing butterfly designs, losing them, with him getting stocky, slender, and even decidedly girlish in various shots. Actress Barbara Bestar added to the production values by occasionally referring to the character "Jerry" as "Dick"—Richard Simmons' real name. The mistakes were left in with all the others.

By this time, Walt Disney had bought the rights to the Zorro character and used him in a television series. The TV show layed on the comedy with a heavy hand in the person of bumptious Henry Calvin as Sergeant Garcia. Veteran serial director John English handled the early episodes, and Republic regular, stuntman Dave Sharpe, doubled handsome Guy Williams in many scenes. It should be noted that Disney's *Zorro* was the first prime-time TV series to be told in *serial* fashion, although a rambling, episodic serial, without dynamic, peril-filled cliffhangers per se. Only the *Batman* television series has employed true cliffhangers, and then, only for comic effect.

Zorro continues to pop up in films, most recently in Italian-made epics starring Frank Latimore (who?), Tony Russell, and Guy Stockwell. No doubt others will sometime be made with this classic hero. They may have better scripts and acting, but it is doubtful that any will ever have better *action* sequences than Fairbanks' original feature, or such Republic serials as *Zorro Rides Again* and *Zorro's Fighting Legion.*

HI-YO SILVER

The most famous masked hero of the West has been the Lone Ranger, chronologically second to Zorro, but winner of even more renown since his first appearance in the radio series of late 1932.[1]

The masked rider of the plains was the culmination of nearly a century of frontier fiction. He combined the qualities of Cooper's Leatherstocking, Wister's the Virginian (both men with buried, obscure pasts) and the image of masked do-gooders played in movies by William S. Hart, Tom Mix, Ken Maynard, and others. (In these films, the masked "bad man" turned out to be either a reformed or feigned crook.)

Although created for radio drama (*not* adapted from novels or comics as is sometimes reported today), the Lone Ranger nevertheless presented a vivid, memorable visual image—a tall man in a black mask on a great white horse.

Radio listeners could easily imagine such a figure, and he was easy to adapt to the pages of color comics and juvenile novels. Six years passed since his creation before the famed Masked Man appeared in movies. Naturally enough, the appearance was in a serial.

Republic Pictures produced *The Lone Ranger* film serial in 1938, but with their usual attitude, kept only the most basic elements of the character who had proven his appeal to millions.

---

[1] The first appearance is often dated January 20, 1933, the date of the first regularly scheduled broadcast, but there were earlier experimental broadcasts whose exact dates were not recorded.

The photoplay presented a story of post-Civil War lawlessness in which five Texas Rangers fought an outlaw band led by a master villain named Jeffries (Stanley Andrews, later the kindly Old Ranger of television's *Death Valley Days*). They were aided by apparently a "sixth" Ranger, a masked rider who was really one of their number. As the serial progressed, each of these heroic law men was killed in action, until there was only one left—the Lone Ranger.

The Lone Ranger himself was billed only as "A Man of Mystery." There was five Lone Ranger "suspects" listed: Bert Rogers (played by Herman Brix, later known as Bruce Bennett); Bob Stuart (Wally Wales, also known as Hal Taliaferro); Dick Forrest (Lane Chandler); Jim Clark (George Letz, later George Montgomery); and Allen King (Lee Powell). From that maze of names it might be noted that the actors were certainly prone to "double-identities" in their professional life. While only one of these actors turned out to be the "official" Lone Ranger at the end of the serial, *all* of them wore the mask at various times either for scenes in the picture or publicity shots. Any one of them might well claim to have "played the Lone Ranger" as George Montgomery does occasionally in TV interviews, although he was *not* the last remaining Ranger at the serial's end. (In a work on cliffhangers, it would be inappropriate to reveal just which one it was at this point to those who don't know.)

The mysterious masked rider was aided by his faithful stallion Silver as on the radio (on the screen, Silver was identified as being portrayed by Silver Chief) and his trusted Indian companion, Tonto (played by the somewhat stocky and glum Chief Thunder Cloud).

The basic elements were there on the screen, but changed from the truly classic stature of the radio series, created under the supervision of George W. Trendle at Radio Station WXYZ. As he recounted again for the present writer, Trendle worked with scriptwriter Fran Striker, then station manager Brace

Beemer (later actor in the title role of the series) and others to develop the character from an admitted inspiration by Fairbanks's film portrayal of Zorro.

Basically, the radio series told of how six Texas Rangers set out after one of the worst outlaws in the West, Butch Cavendish (obviously, a fictional version of the real-life bandit, Butch Cassidy), and were caught in an ambush by him and his men in a fateful place known as Bryant's Gap. After the battle, all of the Ranger band were left for dead. Yet one man still lived, a spark of life kept afire in him by the care of a wandering Indian named Tonto. The last man alive was the brother of the leader of the band, Captain Dan Reid. (The younger brother's given name was *never* revealed, despite erroneous reports that it was John.) When the wounded Ranger recovered consciousness many days later, he asked of his brother and the other lawmen. Tonto shook his head sadly. "You only Ranger left. *You lone Ranger now.*"

The youthful lawman took the name of the Lone Ranger and hid his features behind a black mask to strike the terror of the unknown into first the Butch Cavendish band he successfully tracked down and turned over to the law, and then into the hearts of all bad men of the West. Along his perilous trail, he found his great white stallion, Silver, and fashioned silver bullets for himself so that their precious metal would be a constant reminder to him of the high cost of human life.

With immortal background themes such as the *William Tell Overture* and *Les Préludes* and the magnificent booming voice of Brace Beemer, most memorable of the radio actors, the scripts by Fran Striker were virtual textbooks on how to construct radio drama or pulp fiction in general. The combination was unbeatable. The Lone Ranger rode beyond the limits of popular entertainment, and became an imperishable part of Americana.

While the movie serial departed from the original version,

the Lone Ranger still retained more than average appeal on the
screen. In effect, the photoplay stretched the brief opening
events of the radio origin over fifteen film episodes. Within the
context of the serial's own requirements this was not a bad idea.
Even so, the owners of the radio property vigorously objected
to Republic's plans, until Republic pulled their inevitable top
card—the contract gave them the right to do virtually whatever
they pleased with the character. (Apparently, no owner of a
million-dollar property ever bothered to take a look at a Republic serial to see how cavalierly they handled famous creations.)

The film story began with the familiar ambush of a band of
Texas Rangers by the gang headed by Jeffries in Chapter One,
"Heigh-yo, Silver" (as the movies spelled it). The sole survivor, whose face we never were allowed to see, was joined by
four other men in his battle against the outlaw chieftain. The
group numbered five now, plus the survivor's staunch Indian
friend, Tonto. They set up headquarters in an old stockade near
a deserted cave where the Lone Ranger's guns and mask were
concealed. When danger threatened, a mysterious shadow
would fall across that gunbelt and the Lone Ranger would soon
be riding again. (The hearty "Hi-Yo Silver" was dubbed by
the radio series star of that period, Earle Graser. Reportedly
other dialogue was dubbed for the Lone Ranger by Hollywood
stuntman and actor, Billy Bletcher.)

As the pressbook reported: When Jeffries learns Blanchard,
a Federal officer, is coming to Texas for an investigation, he has
a spy plant dynamite at the stockade entrance so that the outlaw troops can get inside. The blast is set off just as the Lone
Ranger rides through the gates.

The Lone Ranger escaped the explosion by luck, or his nim-
ble leap aside. Chapter Two, "Thundering Earth," carried on
with the tight plotting that became certainly *atypical* of Republic serials. The Masked Man captured a Jeffries henchman,
Kester (John Merton) and sent him back to town with a note to

the Federal man, Blanchard, telling him that outlaw troopers were holding the band of Rangers prisoner. The Federal man confronted the leader of the troopers, Jeffries, with the note. Jeffries smirked. Abraham Lincoln had been assassinated. Blanchard's authority would probably be forfeit. The Ranger band was allowed to drive away in a wagon train through a gorge, or at least part way through. In defiance of Blanchard, Jeffries had planted dynamite to wipe out the wagons. Once again, the Lone Ranger, bent on rescue, rode up in time to be caught in an explosion. The resulting landslide threatened to wipe out both him and the wagon train.

In Chapter Three, "The Pitfall," Tonto managed to get the wagon train through the fall of cascading rocks, and the Masked Man got away barely in time. Meanwhile, Jeffries stripped Blanchard of all authority, and sent his own men out to trap the Lone Ranger in a pitfall. Blanchard's pretty daughter, Joan (Lynn Roberts), rode out to warn the masked rider, but with the skill of all serial heroines, only managed to send both herself and the Lone Ranger plunging into the pitfall.

Once again, the good guys lived through what appeared to be certain death, and climbed out of the pit in Chapter Four, "Agent of Treachery." A notorious outlaw, Taggart (Raphael Bennett), seemed ready to turn against Jeffries, and lured the Lone Ranger to a cabin to discuss an alliance. Jeffries' men thought they had captured the Lone Ranger shortly afterward, but quickly discovered that the Masked Man had forced the outlaw to switch clothes with him, and had them covered. Thereafter followed one of the weaker cliffhangers of modern serials—the Lone Ranger was hit in the head by a thrown rock.

After Silver and Tonto rode up in time to save the Lone Ranger in Chapter Five, "The Steaming Cauldron," further treachery by Taggart sent the Rangers off to rescue the priest, Father McKim (silent Western star William Farnum), at an old mill loaded with blasting powder. The explosion killed the first

Ranger "suspect," Jim Clark. (Exit youthful George Montgomery.) The real Lone Ranger was engaged in a fist fight with
Taggart in a cave filled with steaming geysers. The accident-
prone Ranger fell into one of the geyser holes, and was about to
be boiled with his mask and jacket on.

The unknown lawman escaped the fissure in Chapter Six,
"Red Man's Courage," only to find himself framed for the murder of some innocent Indians by Jeffries' men planting incriminating silver bullets by the bodies of the slain braves. The
angry tribe captured Tonto and was prepared to burn him at
the stake when the Lone Ranger arrived on the scene, only to
have Silver trip on a fallen tree, and send the Lone Ranger
sprawling helplessly in the midst of the angry Indians.

The next episode, Chapter Seven, "Wheels of Disaster," had
the Lone Ranger relying on his chief radio attribute—the power
of speech—and talking his way out of the situation, convincing
the Indians that he had been framed. Later, Jeffries tried to get
through a supply of gunpowder for his outlaw troopers, and
put Joan into the wagon to prevent any attack on it. Despite this,
a chase ensued and the Lone Ranger got into the back of the
wagon in an attempt to rescue Joan, just as the careening wagon
turned over, producing another great special effects explosion
for serial buffs.

Besides showing that, of course, the Masked Man and Joan
leaped to safety in time, Chapter Eight, "Fatal Treasure," revealed that even by this point this well-made and expensive
serial was capable of introducing new plot elements. (Most
serials never introduced anything significant after the *first*
episode.) The outlaw leader, Jeffries, substituted Confederate
money for the silver he had collected as government taxes. This
silver became one of the focal points of the serial, rather than
just Jeffries' struggle for power. First, the silver was taken from
him by government men. Next, his outlaws tried to regain it
from the rangers. The men abandoned the silver in a well, and

returned disguised as Mexican peons to rescue the treasure. Two of the Rangers went down into the well itself. The watching outlaws blasted the well apart with their cannon fire. The men appeared trapped in the collapsing stone walls.

Fortunately for the two rangers in the well, there was a secret passage of some sort leading off to the side. Chapter Nine, "The Missing Spur," continued with a free-for-all battle between the outlaw troopers and the band of Rangers. A Federal Cavalry troop took the group into custody for questioning. Later, the Lone Ranger managed to deliver the precious silver to the Federal outpost, Fort Bently, losing only one of his spurs in the effort. That spur was used to try to prove his identity as Jeffries' henchman, Kester, went to the guardhouse where the Rangers were being held to find out which one had slipped away to act as the Lone Ranger and return. Sure enough, one of the Rangers was missing one vital spur!

As a matter of fact, *all* of the four Rangers were missing a spur as revealed by Chapter Ten, "Flaming Fury." (Apparently one must conclude all the spurs were absolutely identical, four matched sets.) This chapter introduced still another element, one more typical of the *silent* serials. Jeffries tried to force lovely Joan into marrying him. Her message via carrier pigeon brought rescue by the Lone Ranger. Soon, the Masked Man and his faithful Indian companion seemed in need of rescue themselves. They were trapped by Jeffries' men in a burning house, with the walls collapsing in on them.

The two heroes managed to escape by the trapdoor that seemed located in every burning cliffhanger building in Chapter Eleven, "The Silver Bullet." They found that Jeffries had once again seized that elusive silver and was holding it at a saloon. The Masked Man dispatched himself to the place, was discovered, and engaged in a terrific fight. In the midst of the fight, a gun muzzle was poked through the window behind his back.

As it happened in Chapter Twelve, "Escape," the gun was

being held by Faithful Tonto who helped the Lone Ranger subdue the crooks. Meanwhile, Joan had found an old picture of
Jeffries establishing that he was a wanted outlaw. The leader
of the outlaw army found out she knew, and she found out that
he knew she knew! The Lone Ranger tried to spirit the girl away
to safety in a stagecoach, and in the desperate chase that followed, that stagecoach went plunging from a towering cliff.

Chapter Thirteen, "The Fatal Plunge," did not prove *that*
unlucky for the Masked Man and Joan who escaped before the
coach went down the cliff. It did prove more unlucky for another Lone Ranger "suspect," Dick Forrest (Lane Chandler, a
rival to Gary Cooper in popularity polls in the days of the
silents). Forrest found himself struggling with another Jeffries'
henchman, Felton (reliable Tom London), and plunging from
still another cliff as the episode ended.

Since he was *not* the real Lone Ranger, Forrest did not escape
unhurt, but was seriously injured in Chapter Fourteen, "Mes-
senger of Doom." He was removed to the hiding place in the
cave, and was cared for by the other Rangers, Joan, and all of
the good guys of the serial. Naturally, they were discovered by
Jeffries' men and a gun battle ensued, causing the entire cavern
roof to fall in on the heroic band.

The fifteenth and final episode, "Last of the Rangers," revealed that the crash did prove fatal to the injured Dick Forrest,
although the others escaped miraculously. They were not yet
out of danger for Jeffries' gang still had them surrounded.
Two of the Rangers, Rogers and King, managed to break
through and ride for help. Later, the outlaws forced Tonto,
Joan, her father, and a boy who had helped them, Sammy Cannon (Sammy McKin) outside into their line of fire. Just then,
the masked Lone Ranger arrived with the help of Federal
troops. The outlaw band was routed, and the Lone Ranger engaged the master villain, Jeffries, in hand-to-hand combat. The
two men fell from a precipice locked in each other's grip, even

as Dr. Watson interpreted the struggle between Sherlock Holmes and Professor Moriarity. Apparently, both men perished. Sometime later, the state of Texas paid homage to the valiant band of Rangers who gave their lives bringing law and order. Then the Lone Ranger's cry of "Hi-Yo Silver" rang out, and he came into view—alive—on the great white stallion. Finally, he was revealed to the audience as the last Ranger—Allen King (played by Lee Powell). The Lone Ranger rode off to new adventure.

This serial has been described at some length because it is at once *typical* of the average Western serial with its usual hazards of explosions, runaway stagecoaches, and plunges from high ledges, and *superior* in plot and execution to the average.

The chapterplay was directed with youthful vigor by the epic team of William Witney and John English. English was the senior member of the duo at twenty-nine years of age at the time, while Witney had just turned twenty-one! It was far from his first directorial assignment either. He had been directing since he was eighteen, after working up through the ranks as a studio janitor, prop boy, guide, electrician, script clerk, assistant cameraman, and assistant director. Only the "old Hollywood" could produce such a totally professional director. If this volume were divided as some books on films are by directors, the significant serials would be more-or-less evenly divided between Spencer G. Bennet and the Witney-English team.

The star of *The Lone Ranger* was Lee Powell, but he had not been officially billed as such. (The Lone Ranger was only "A Man of Mystery" you will recall.) He got into some legal difficulty with The Lone Ranger, Inc. by traveling with a circus and billing himself as "the Lone Ranger." He starred in one other serial for Republic (*The Fighting Devil Dogs*) and made a number of B Western program features for Grand National and P.R.C. before entering the Marine Corps in 1942. Sergeant Lee

Powell, thirty-six, was killed in action on the Pacific island of Tinian on July 29, 1944.

In 1939, Lee Powell was passed over for the lead in the sequel, *The Lone Ranger Rides Again.* This time an established Western star was used—Bob Livingston, leader of Republic's "Three Mesquiteers" in that long-running series of features. This time the element of mystery was completely lacking as the Lone Ranger was clearly revealed to be Bill Andrews (*not* Allen King, the name of the character played by Lee Powell in the first serial). Andrews merely donned the mask of the Lone Ranger when the time was ripe.

The serial returned Chief Thunder Cloud to his role of Tonto and added Duncan Renaldo to the cast in the role of Juan Vasquez, and romantic interest from Jinx Falken (later Falkenburg) and villainy from J. Farrell MacDonald as Craig Dolan.

Dolan was trying to drive the innocent settlers out of the San Ramon Valley by use of masked henchmen known as the Black Raiders. This serial repeated a number of the same cliffhanger situations from the first serial: landslides, explosions, crashing wagons, and plunges from cliffs. Livingston was perhaps too exuberant for the righteous Masked Rider of the plains, but the image stuck with him. He made several later appearances as the Masked Rider (or sometimes a nameless masked rider) in The Three Mesquiteers series of features.

The first serial was released as a feature in 1940 under the title, *Hi-Yo Silver.* The radio series kept alive the fame of the Masked Man until the first television films of the character were made in 1949. The radio Lone Ranger, Brace Beemer, wanted very much to play the role on TV. He was an excellent horseman and marksman, and he had made a terrific battle to get his weight down from its bulky tendencies. Yet he was passed over for an experienced film actor, Clayton Moore, star of several serials. Moore was handsome, slender, perhaps a trifle short, and perhaps more than incidentally, his voice somewhat resembled that of Beemer. The casting of Jay Silverheels as Tonto was nigh perfect. (The radio Tonto was a thin old gentleman past *eighty* years of age named John Todd.) During a contract dispute, Moore was temporarily replaced in the role of the Masked Man by the very youthful John Hart, but soon reclaimed the role through 166 television episodes and two full-length theatrical features. There was a somewhat unsuitable series of TV animated cartoons with the voice of Michael Rye (once radio's Jack Armstrong) as the Lone Ranger. Most recently, Moore re-established his claim on the role by a television commercial (with Silverheels) and by riding Silver in the 1969 Hollywood Santa Claus Lane Parade, and at openings of many of the Lone Ranger franchise restaurants.

The TV films were faithfully made, but reveal their sadly lacking budgets by today's standards. Unfortunately, the well-made serials of 1938 and 1939 are no longer shown anywhere due to their divergence from the "official" Lone Ranger image, and apparently are not even in the hands of private collectors or the studio itself. These fine action films may exist only in memory.

HE'S TRYING TO TELL US SOMETHING

Rin-Tin-Tin was the most popular animal star in the history of motion pictures. More than that, he was a genuine *star*. The first German police dog bearing that name was something of a mutant, *uncannily* intelligent and photogenic. It was more than press agentry and the training of owner Lee Duncan who allegedly found Rinty abandoned by the German troops on a World War I battlefield. The movies of the dog star reveal his skill and his ability to express emotions by facial expressions alone, such as grief, hope, and patience when accused of killing sheep in his feature film of the twenties, *The Night Cry.*

After the retirement and death at an old, old age of the original Rinty, Rin-Tin-Tin, Jr., Rin-Tin-Tin, III and IV continued his fame to the point where the numbering was dropped for the TV series and commercials made right into the 1970s. These dogs bearing Rinty's name, and his competitors such as Strongheart of the silents and Lassie today do depend largely on training and photographic tricks, lacking that one-in-a-million star quality of the original.

Following his sire's serials, *The Lone Defender,* 1930, and *Lightning Warrior,* 1931, Rin-Tin-Tin, Jr., made serials in the sound era. While not the equal to his father as an actor, Rinty, Jr. was certainly more professional than his co-star, Bob Custer.

The Law of the Wild, a 1934 Mascot serial, brought together Custer, Rinty, Jr. and Rex, King of the Wild Horses. The stallion was another prototypical animal star (although only a "liberated" version of Tom Mix's Tony), but like many stars, Rex was a thoroughgoing bastard off the screen, a real killer responsible for injuring many wranglers on the set.

A typical situation had a horse thief named Salters (stocky Richard Alexander, perhaps the last living classic villain of the B Westerns) trying to rustle Rex for profit, even though he hated the animal. "Now there, you black demon—I've got you right where I want you!" Salters shouted, drawing his lariat tight around the rearing stallion's neck.

Nearby was Rex's faithful chum, Rinty. Snarling, the dog leaped and dragged Salters from his saddle. The thief and the dog struggled briefly on the ground, until Salters hurled Rinty from him, and drew his gun. Before he could pull the trigger, the revolver was sent spinning from his grasp by the impact of another man's bullet. The horse thief turned to see the owner of the horse, John Sheldon (Bob Custer), standing on the other side of a boulder.

The hero turned away from Salters (Custer never seemed very bright) toward the stunned dog and the horse still entangled in the thief's lariat. Promptly, Salters beaned Sheldon with a handy rock.

While Rex plunged and reared, Salters mounted Sheldon's tame saddle horse and made the sorrel trample the unconscious form of his master, in an attempt to frame the supposedly wild Rex.

In the following scenes, Salters led Rex away against the animal's will, and Rinty crawled to Sheldon and licked his face gently, laying down beside him. (It took minutes of film and six weeks of story time before Sheldon returned miraculously from the dead.)

With both man and dog up and on the job once again they soon were pursuing a villain named Luger who was horse-napping Rex. Actually the man had a Bill of Sale for Rex but as Luger drove off down the highway in a car and trailer Sheldon realized the legal paper was false.

EXT. INGRAM RANCH—DAY
> SHELDON *crushes the paper in his fist.*
> SHELDON: Come on, Rinty! We've got to get Rex!
> *They start running after* LUGER *in the car and trailer, just then pulling onto the highway and driving off.*

EXT. HIGHWAY—DAY
> RINTY *races ahead of* SHELDON. *The dog catches up with the car and leaps upon* LUGER *in the driver's seat. To protect himself from angry* RINTY, LUGER *slows down the car to battle the dog.*

ANOTHER ANGLE OF THE HIGHWAY.
> SHELDON *runs up to the car now. He leaps on the running board—as* LUGER *knocks* RINTY *away, off the car and back*

onto the highway. SHELDON *and* LUGER *fight. After trading punches—*LUGER *misses a blow.* SHELDON *grabs him and throws him out of the car. (NOTE: The car and trailer are by this time swerving along dangerously.)*

CLOSER ON THE CAR

SHELDON *fights to gain control of the car. But suddenly he looks up and sees a heavy truck rounding a curve up ahead, coming straight towards him on collision course.*

FULL SHOT—HIGHWAY

SHELDON *slams on the brakes and tries to swing out of the impending crash—but it's too late. There's a crash. The car turns over.* SHELDON's *legs are pinned beneath the car. The truck also crashes. But* REX's *trailer hitch breaks during the crash and the trailer rolls to a stop safely a little distance away.*

The death disaster has been averted and the dust clears on this scene. SHELDON *awakens from a momentary unconsciousness to see* RINTY *standing at his fallen side (once again). Of course* SHELDON *is relieved. He pats the dog affectionately.*

SHELDON: I can always rely on you, Rinty! But I can't make it free of here without some more of your help!

He sees a coil of heavy rope laying nearby. This rope fell from the truck when it crashed.

SHELDON: Bring that rope here, Rinty.

The dog gets the rope and brings it to SHELDON *who ties one end to the torque rod of the car. He gives the other end to* RINTY.

SHELDON: Take it, old boy. Now up, Rinty. Up on the hood of the truck, then onto the top.

RINTY *leaps to the hood of the truck, then onto the top.*

SHELDON: Jump now, Rinty! Over the limb of that tree!

RINTY *leaps over a heavy branch of a tree that overhangs the truck. Then with the end of the rope still between his teeth he returns to* SHELDON.

SHELDON: Good boy, Rinty!

SHELDON *makes a loop of the end of the rope.*

SHELDON: Rex! (*whistles signal*)

SHOT ON THE TRAILER AND FOLLOW

> REX *crashes back with his hind legs against the gate. He kicks it down and gets free.* RINTY *runs to him.* RINTY *gets the halter rope and leads* REX *back to* SHELDON, *who tosses the loop of rope around* REX's *neck.*

SHELDON: That's fine, Rinty! Rex, you've got to get me out of here! Lead him away, Rinty!

> *The dog leads the horse away. The rope tightens and slowly the horse begins pulling up on the car.*

SHELDON: Go on, Rex! You can do it! You've got to.

> SHELDON's *faith in* REX *proves true and the horse, led by* RINTY, *successfully pulls up the car thus freeing* SHELDON.
> *The rancher congratulates both horse and dog on a job well done. But there is still more work ahead. The truck-driver is in sad condition and needs help.*
> *And so . . .*

SHELDON: Rinty, old boy, you'll have to go back to Ingram's ranch and get help!

> SHELDON *gets an old envelope out of his pocket, finds a pencil and quickly writes a message. He puts the note into* RINTY's *collar.*

SHELDON: Take this note to Henry! And hurry!

Rinty woofs that he understands the dilemma and then off he goes, back to the ranch to summon help, in Chapter Three of this Mascot serial. The episode was entitled "The Cross Eyed Goony." (Henry is the cross-eyed one.) A colorful chapter title all right but the actual storyline unfolded along rather predictable, standardized Western plotlines.

The Wolf Dog (which introduced Rin-Tin-Tin, Jr.) another Mascot serial in 1933, had Rinty, Jr., the sole animal star of a more fantastic chapterplay. The human star was Frankie Darro, a considerably better actor than Bob Custer, youthful Gene Autry, and other adult heroes he appeared with at Mascot. Darro was the heir to a steamship line, and aboard one of those ships was Bob Whitlock (George Lewis), a radio operator who had invented a deathray in his spare time. The events of the picaresque photoplay took Darro and Lewis to the Canadian wilds where roamed Rin-Tin-Tin, who had reverted to a wolf-like state after being marooned in a plane crash. Even with reawakened primitive instincts, Rinty still helped the man and the boy against criminals who sought the fantastic invention for their own nefarious ends.

Rinty, Jr.'s last movie serial was Mascot's *Adventures of Rex and Rinty* (1935), made in twelve episodes. Rex was enjoying more than his status as "King of the Wild Horses" on Sujan, a primitive island. Natives on the island worshipped the "God Horse, Rex" but three Americans saw only a dollar sign in the magnificent stallion. Capturing Rex, they removed him to America where an unscrupulous buyer named Crawford (Harry Woods) tried to break him as a polo horse. In the United States, Rex teamed up with Rin-Tin-Tin, Jr. and the two almost-human animals evaded every attempt by Crawford to recapture the horse.

Luckily the serial's hero Frank Bradley (Kane Richmond) managed to get Rex back to Sujan. But even on his own island, Rex was not out of danger's way. The natives were tricked into an attempted sacrifice by fire of their equine deity. Frank and Rinty intervened in time to free the stallion from a torturous demise. With Rex saved from death, Frank settled down with him and Rinty on the Island of Sujan.

Animal "stars" played prominent roles in other serials such as Ace, "the Wonder Dog" as Devil in *The Phantom;* Silver in *The Lone Ranger;* Nyoka's dog, Fang, and Vultura's ape, Satan (really a human actor) in *Perils of Nyoka.* Most of these serials as well as the features of the '30s and '40s, tended to be Westerns, the perfect vehicles for stories of a boy, a dog, and a horse.

The "camp" element in these old thrillers is strong. Contemporary audiences are often convulsed by the anthropomorphic qualities given animals in their emotions and their intelligence. Heroes were constantly sending *the* dog or *the* horse for help, mainly it seemed because the really *important* member of the team should be removed from the scene of danger. Then when the animal got to the ranch where help lay, he often seemed hard-pressed to convince the clods that their help was urgently needed. Although it never came to this point, there is no doubt that if necessary Rinty or Tony or Silver could have spelled the message out in the dust with a foreleg.

THE REST OF THE POSSE

The first purely Western serial ever made is generally conceded to be the 1916 Universal chapterplay, *Liberty,* with twenty episodes starring iron-jawed Jack Holt (who would survive into the talking film era to do the 1941 Columbia detective serial, *Holt of the Secret Service*) and short, burly Eddie Polo who rode his white horse through many silent serials, performing amazing demonstrations of strength in a manner similar to Joe Bonomo. Although there had been Western elements in *Perils of Pauline* and other earlier cliffhangers, it was *Liberty* that began the cycle of silent serials about the West that gave work to such directors as Henry MacRae (who co-directed *Liberty* with Jacques Jaccard), W. S. Van Dyke, George B. Seitz, and Spencer Gordon Bennet, and to such stars as Art Acord (*The Moon Riders,* Universal, 1921), and Yakima Canutt (*The Vanishing West,* Mascot, 1928).

As its sound counterpart, the silent Western serial differed little from the Western movie in feature film form. There were the usual fights, chases, stunt leaps. Perhaps the plots tended to become more complex and the stunts more fantastic and less creditable to an adult audience. Above all, like all serials, the silent Western chapterplays were *cheaper* with less important stars and poorer production values. Only *action* gave them their saving entertainment values. Western film historian William K. Everson attributes the most exciting action of the silent period to the Pathé serials of the 1920s.

". . . The serial could really bring nothing new to the Western: the patterns of action had been firmly established . . . The Western serial had to be accepted as a Western rather than as another serial . . ." Everson has gone on to point out. The proper study, conversely, of the Western movie serial is in a study of Westerns, not one of serials. The chief difference between a Western serial and a Western feature film in the sound era was merely the arbitrary insertion of the cliffhanger at the specified point.

The cliffhangers used were far from inventive. In many talking Western serials, the peril was that the hero appeared to have been shot down in a hail of bullets. It often provided the cliffhangers on two or three different chapters per serial (as in *The Miracle Rider, The Scarlet Horseman,* etc.).

The stars of the talking Western serials were drawling Johnny Mack Brown (*The Oregon Trail* and *Fighting with Kit Carson* with villain Noah Beery, Sr., as covered elsewhere); Bob Livingston (*The Vigilantes are Coming,* a Zorro derivative based on the silent Rudolph Valentino vehicle, *The Eagle,* as well as *The Lone Ranger Rides Again*); Bill Elliott (the only Western star to be *created* by a serial when *The Great Adventures of Wild Bill Hickok,* Columbia, 1938, turned actor Gordon Elliott into star Wild Bill Elliott); and old reliable Buck Jones. The rugged Western star made four serials for Universal in the thirties: *Gordon of Ghost City,* 1933; *The Red Rider,* 1934; *Roaring West,* 1935; and *The Phantom Rider,* 1936. After an involuntary retirement, Jones returned in a supporting role to Dick Foran in Universal's 1941 *Riders of Death Valley,* and the same year was again top-lined in his only Columbia serial, *White Eagle,* in which he played an ostensive Indian brave until the familiar last reel cop-out to racial prejudice that he was a white man merely raised as an Indian.

Riders of Death Valley, the first Buck Jones serial of 1941, contributed some of the most enduring stock footage to later Western serials (even though it itself borrowed from ancient silent stock shots). Inevitably, the hero and his sidekick would climb into the fringed buckskins Buck Jones wore or the black shirt and pants affected by Dick Foran and enact events that lead to the two men being trapped on a suspension bridge with huge boulders being rolled down on them by Indians; or even being trapped in that so familiar cattle stampede; or in the stage-coach careening off the edge of the cliff. (*Overland Mail* and *The Scarlet Horsemen* were only two from Universal in the '40s with these shots.)

Otherwise, *Riders of Death Valley* contributed one of the most impressive casts in serial history (Foran, Jones, Lon Chaney, Jr.; Noah Beery, Jr.; Charles Bickford, Monte Blue, Leo Carrillo) and some nice bits of humor. Buck Jones would idly leave Dick Foran hanging from the edge of the cliff while chitchatting amiably with him. Leo Carrillo offered some classic lines of his own contrivance, such as: "Listen, I th*ee*nk I hear foot*prints* . . ."

Following the two serials of 1941, Buck Jones was only to make nine more features (eight of them teamed with Colonel Tim McCoy and Raymond Hatton as The Rough Riders). He had begun as a real-life cow hand on the famous Miller "101" Ranch, had been a Cavalry soldier and military flier, before starting in films in 1920 with *The Last Straw* as an in-studio rival to Tom Mix at Fox. Despite reverses, Jones was the only major Western star of silents to remain a major Western star in the sound era (although Tom Mix, Hoot Gibson, Ken Maynard, Harry Carey, and others had minor or declining careers in sound) and the only significant Western star to make so many sound serials.

Riders of Death Valley revealed the growing shoddiness of serial-making in many areas. Rod Cameron is unmistakably recognizable in many scenes doubling Buck Jones, even in scenes requiring no stunt work. Jones's earlier Universal serial, *Gordon of Ghost City* was as well made as any Western *feature* film of the day.

The Republic serials were always technically well-made, since serials and Westerns were the studio's *main* product to bring in revenue, while episodic thrillers were very secondary pursuits to both Universal and Columbia.

Universal dropped serial-making in 1948 and Republic went over its last cliff in 1955 with Western featured player Harry Lauter in a non-Western role as *King of the Carnival*. It was Columbia that held on to the last even with its poorer product. Although television was discouraging theatre audiences for serials, the same medium was inspiring a vast interest in Western films of all kinds with rescreenings of serials and features of the '30s and '40s, and with its own generally inferior series product. Because of this, the last American movie serial ever made was a Western—*Blazing the Overland Trail* from Columbia in 1956.

This final cliffhanger went back to the rather expensively produced *Overland with Kit Carson* (Columbia, 1939), for the vast amounts of stock footage deemed economically necessary for these last few chapterplays produced. Lee Roberts played Tom Bridger, but wore the same type of fringed buckskins Bill Elliott had worn as Kit Carson, and faced the same menace of the Black Raiders, and the same cliffhangers: the stampede, the runaway wagon, the blazing inferno. Fittingly, Spencer Gordon Bennet directed the new footage on the last serial, even as he had worked on some of the very first silent serials ever made. Bennet's really wondrous career provided the *Yin* and *Yang*, the closed circle, the last cliffhanger.

13

The Classics:
You Say "What Dost Thou Mean By That?"
and Push Him Off the Cliff

THE CASTAWAYS

Movie serials based on classic works of literature served to give answers to the PTA and other organizations concerned with the films watched so fervently on Saturday afternoons by children. Most parents (and organizations created to make decisions for parents) thought serials were all the standard shoot-em-up fare, where the hero wore a white hat and the villain and his gang of thugs wore black hats. The plots, they argued, were all the same, with a dastardly archcrook out to conquer the town or the world, and a lone crime-fighter out to stop him. Between the threads of story, parents said, were the usual violent fights, chases, and devious methods of killing the hero and his friends.

They were right, of course.

Although the serials were in no real danger of extinction from such groups, producers of chapterplays at times tried appeasing the minds of authoritative adults by at least attempting to make their output appear to have some literary quality. They turned to the classics—those same novels read in schools by parents and teachers when *they* were young—and wrote chapter by chapter scripts around them. Surely, the producers believed, parents would find no offense in sending their children to see a serial "written by" Jules Verne, Alexandre Dumas, or Daniel Defoe. These were men to be revered. And what better balance could parents and teachers hope for in juvenile-oriented film than the action required to keep the viewer entertained, plus an added educational boost!

Daniel Defoe's novel *Robinson Crusoe* was first adapted to the serial screen as a silent chapterplay, *Robinson Crusoe*. It was filmed by Universal in 1922 with Robert F. Hill directing the eighteen episodes. The serial, which starred Harry Myers as Robinson Crusoe and Noble Johnson as his "man" Friday, followed the novel rather closely for the first two chapters, "The Sea Raiders" and "Shipwrecked," with Crusoe stranded on a desert island. But the following installments were more the ideas of the script writers. The last six chapters bore even less resemblance to Defoe's classic, with most of the action centered around the escapades of a cave girl running around the island, evading savage natives and hungry alligators. The serial elicited many complaints from dissatisfied exhibitors who argued that the final half dozen chapters did not add to the story and were mere filler.

The first serial to be based on the writings of Jules Verne was the twelve-episode *Around the World,* made in 1923 by Universal, with Reeves Eason and, again, Robert F. Hill directing. Verne's novel, *Around the World in 80 Days* was adapted to a contemporary setting, with William Desmond, star of numerous serials, portraying Phileas Fogg III, a descendant of Verne's character. In the first chapter, "The Wager," Fogg bet that he could circumvent the earth in eighteen days in order to visit the stockholders of a large fuel company in order to get their proxy votes for a company election. An attempt had been made by the company's president to make synthetic fuel. If he succeeded, he would use his discovery to help the needy of the world. His vice-president, opposing him, became the serial's villain. Looking toward a great adventure accompanied by the president's lovely daughter, played by Laura La Plante, Fogg defied the traps set by the villain by traversing the globe by land, sea, and air, and completing his mission by the concluding episode, "The Last Race."

James Fenimore Cooper was introduced to the chapterplay screen with the adaptation of his *Leatherstocking*. The serial was made in 1924 by Pathé with ten episodes, directed by George B. Seitz. It starred Edna Murphy and Walter Miller in the leads, with Frank Lackteen, one of the cliffhanger's most durable villains (who continued acting mean in sound serials), as the villainous redskin Briarthorn. *Leatherstocking* was a story of the American frontier, with Indians on the warpath, attacking panthers, and various forms of sadistic torture devised by the savages.

Joe Bonomo, the he-man body builder and stuntman of primarily silent films, just out of his performance in the Universal serial *The Great Circus Mystery* (1925), starred that same year in the studio's *Perils of the Wild,* directed by Francis Ford. This chapterplay was based on the classic adventure novel *Swiss Family Robinson* by Johann Rudolf Wyss. For this story in which an Australia-bound family with a cargo of gunpowder was shipwrecked in the first chapter, "The Hurricane," on an island of pirates and learned to survive only on the provisions of nature, husky Bonomo was given long sideburns that swooped forward to a point, making him somewhat resemble a stocky Rudolph Valentino. Bonomo portrayed superstrong Frederic Robinson in *Perils of the Wild,* whose feats of sheer power were sometimes hard to accept. He and his family fought the pirates and looked for the island's secret treasure. In those silent days, heroes like rugged Joe Bonomo often did their own superhuman antics on screen, but in his case was at the cost of a fractured leg and an injured sacroiliac.[1]

[1] Joe Bonomo was featured in many serials, silent and sound, including Fred Thompson's starring vehicle *The Eagle's Talons,* William Desmond's *Beasts of Paradise,* Luciano Albertini's *The Iron Man,* William Duncan's *Wolves of the North,* as well as *The Chinatown Mystery, The Vanishing*

James Fenimore Cooper's "Leather Stocking Tale," *Last of the Mohicans,* was made by Mascot Pictures in 1932 as a sound serial in twelve installments. The serial starred a relative new-comer to the chapterplay screen, though a veteran of countless silent features, craggy-faced Harry Carey. He had starred with Joe Bonomo in Mascot's *The Vanishing Legion* and with Ed-wina Booth in the studio's *The Devil Horse,* both 1931.

Last of the Mohicans told the story of Chingachgook, the fated final member of that tribe of Indians, his son Uncas, and his white scout friend Hawkeye (named for his ability to aim a rifle with accuracy akin to the eye of the hawk), and their war with the French army and the marauding, scalp-hungry Huron Indians. In the serial, Harry Carey played Hawkeye, again star-ring with blond, wavy haired Edwina Booth. Ancient-looking Hobart Bosworth played Chingachgook, while young Frank Coghlan, Jr. (who would one day be Shazammed into Captain Marvel) was Uncas.

Directors Ford Beebe and "Breezy" Eason got the most from their actors in *Last of the Mohicans.* At one point, Miss Booth was trapped against a tree as Indians shot arrows tellingly close to her. In a different chapter, Hawkeye and his courageous Indian ally, Uncas, were tied securely to a post, their feet cov-ered with dry branches, and prepared for burning alive. In still another episode, Miss Booth's female companion was forced to the edge of a cliff by the approach of a particularly menacing Huron brave.

Last of the Mohicans may not have been great art, but it was a great action picture of the 1930s, providing many thrills set during the American frontier days, and helping to establish the sound career of Harry Carey, who would continue into numer-

---

Legion, Phantom of the North, Battling with Buffalo Bill, The Last Fron-tier, Phantom of the West, The Golden Stallion, Heroes of the Wild, and another serial based on Sir Arthur Conan Doyle's famous literary piece, *The Lost Special.*

ous feature length movies. He was one of the few stars in Hollywood history to continue successfully playing the leading man into obvious old age.

THE MUSKETEERS STRIKE BACK

Mascot turned from James Fenimore Cooper to Alexandre Dumas in 1933 when the studio filmed the author's most famous novel, *The Three Musketeers*. This twelve-episode "adaptation" was to be different, primarily in that the serial would be set in modern times and given the background of the French Foreign Legion. The Three Musketeers of the title were no longer Athos, Porthos, and Aramis of the original novel, but three Legionnaires, played by Jack Mulhall, Raymond Hatton, and Francis X. Bushman, Jr. Respectively, the trio played Irisher Clancy, the French Renard, and Schmidt, whose comedy gimmick was keeping his German sausages under his regulation cap in case he became hungry.

The role of D'Artagnan was changed to that of American aviator Tom Wayne. For the part of Tom Wayne, producer Nat Levine selected a young actor who had already starred in two serials for Mascot, *Shadow of the Eagle* and *The Hurricane Express,* both in 1932, and had been paid up to $150 for each week he worked on these productions. The actor was a tall, slow-talking ex-gridiron hero who could knock out a villain with but a threat. Later he would become the world's top box office draw and would spend part of the millions he would earn on backing political candidates who stood somewhat to the right of Genghis Khan. He had only recently changed his name from Marion Michael Morrison to the name now often disregarded in favor of "Duke." The star of *The Three Musketeers* was John Wayne.

The serial's first episode showed the youthful actor as flyer

Tom Wayne (a fortunate coincidence of last names) cruising over the African desert (actually, the desert region to the east of the Sierra Mountains), where he found a trio of Foreign Legionnaires at the mercy of an attacking horde of nomadic Arab bandits. Wayne put his flying skill into practice and rescued the soldiers, who identified themselves as Clancy, Renard, and Schmidt. The American smiled as they told him that they called themselves the Three Musketeers, after the characters in the famous Dumas novel. And they even had their own theme song, that told how they fought a murderous sect called the Devil's Circle, and ended with "One for all and all for one!—The Three Musketeers!"

Tom Wayne inquired about the mysterious Devil's Circle. He was told that its main objective was destroying the Foreign Legion, and that it was led by an unknown villain hiding beneath the cloaked identity of El Shaitan—which translated as "Satan." Anxious to help his newfound friends, Tom Wayne agreed to help them smash El Shaitan and his merciless desert cult.

After many instances of escaping death, Tom Wayne finally learned the location of El Shaitan's secret meeting place. Disguised with the robes of the infamous cult, the American cautiously approached the door, knocked, waited for the peephole to open, then spoke the password he'd learned from a captured member of the cult. "The sun rises in the East!" Wayne said boldly as John Wayne said any line, in his own style as American as Coca-Cola. But he managed to fool the cult member and was allowed to enter the Devil's Circle, the secret lair of El Shaitan. The ruse worked—for a while—but then Tom Wayne's true identity was discovered. After a furious battle, he escaped the flailing swords and smashing fists of the villains.

In the last installment, after many "red herrings" who appeared to be the master villain were revealed as men planted by Mascot to take suspicion away from the real El Shaitan, Tom Wayne caught up with, defeated, and unmasked the leader of the Devil's Circle. As usual, the man beneath the robes was the almost insignificant storekeeper, hardly a worthy suspect.

The Three Musketeers was John Wayne's last serial. He would move on to greater things, to become more than a movie star, to be a part of the American legend. For the serials, there were more classics to adapt—and tamper with.

WHO'S MAN FRIDAY?

Republic Pictures turned toward a classic previously filmed as a silent cliffhanger with the fourth serial to come from that studio, *Robinson Crusoe of Clipper Island* in 1936. The fourteen-chapter serial had little, if anything, to do with Daniel Defoe's novel, *Robinson Crusoe*. First of all, there was no Robinson Crusoe in the chapterplay. The closest anyone came to resembling that character was the Polynesian actor Mala, who portrayed himself in the cliffhanger adventure. It was a rare serial casting—a non-Caucasian as the hero. In effect, Defoe's "faithful native," Friday, became the leading character. With Mala were two animal "stars," Buck the Dog and the famed Mascot stallion, Rex the Wonder Horse (also playing themselves).

In Chapter One, "The Mysterious Island," the United States Intelligence Service summoned one of their agents, Mala, to investigate certain acts of sabotage. A giant dirigible the *San Francisco* had been wrecked. Mala then took his canine friend Buck, and his own "Man Friday," Hank (played by William Newell), to Clipper Island, where he discovered that the sabotage had been caused by a ring of enemy spies. To make matters worse, the spies had been ordered to kill Mala.

Discovering the remains of a radio station on the island, the sarong-clad detective began sending out his own messages. But they were intercepted by the saboteurs who were suddenly made to realize that Mala still lived. Infuriated, the fiends used electrical equipment to shoot off the flaming fury of Pelée, the sacred volcano of the island natives.

Naturally, when Princess Melani (Mamo Clark) and her warriors saw the volcano erupt, they appeared and, finding Mala present, blamed the detective for the sacrilege. For provoking their sacred gods, the innocent Mala was sentenced to a horrible death. He was to die in a fiery pit. Only the timely arrival of Hank and Buck rescued him before his consumption by flames.

Mala managed to convince Princess Melani that he was on her side. Together, they thwarted the serial's subconflict, an uprising led by the high priest of Pelée, the scheming Porotu (John Piccori), who wanted to steal her power over the natives.

Later, it was believed by the suppressed high priest that the princess had been killed by a second eruption of the volcano. Taking her sacred headdress of ornate feathers, Porotu proclaimed himself the king of Clipper Island. But Mala acquired the headdress. Then he returned to San Francisco to secure aid in his fight against the spies.

Mala had enough evidence to hang the saboteurs, and to learn who was at their origin. After the police captured the spies reported by Mala, the Polynesian sleuth returned to Clipper Island, where he rescued Princess Melani and restored peace to that savage world, ending Chapter Fourteen, "Thunder Mountain."

Robinson Crusoe of Clipper Island, directed by Mack V. Wright and Ray Taylor, placed Mala in the usual hazards of a primitive island setting. Besides the dangers imposed more than once by the erupting Pelée, the detective was nearly speared to death by an attacking swarm of angry natives, was almost killed by a pouncing jungle cat, and nearly obliterated when the saboteurs tried destroying the dirigible.

Columbia Pictures topped the list of serials based on classics of literature with a total of four. As was typical with studios making chapterplays, a number of changes were in order.

The third serial made by Columbia was, the publicity and title stated, based on Robert Louis Stevenson's novel, *Treasure Island*. The chapterplay, made with fifteen episodes in 1938, was called *The Secret of Treasure Island*. The "secret" was probably that the serial had little relationship with the Stevenson classic.

While the novel had the infamous one-legged pirate Long John Silver and "young Jim Hawkins" searching for buried treasure, the serial, as Republic's *Robinson Crusoe,* updated the story, placing it in modern times. *The Secret of Treasure Island* had hero Larry Kent (played by Don Terry, also known to serial followers for his role of Don Winslow) and his enemies all searching for a hidden trove of gold. The archenemy of Larry Kent was not the rather sympathetic Long John Silver, but a skull-masked swashbuckler in pirate garb, Dr. X. Due to the workings of Dr. X, the hero was nearly buried alive, dynamited to death, sliced up in a slashing sword battle, and caught on a collapsing bridge, before defeating the sinister character in the last installment, suitably entitled "Justice."

In 1946, Columbia turned to the old English stories of Robin Hood and produced their own serial based on the Merrymen of Sherwood Forest. It was *Son of the Guardsman,* with a list of fifteen chapters. Robert Shaw (not the present British star) appeared as David Trent, the darkly handsome hero of the title, and cavorted through Sherwood Forest braving thrown daggers, whizzing arrows, and a wall of fire, in order to save the throne of England and locate another secret treasure. But other than the use of Sherwood Forest as the locale, the serial neglected to include Friar Tuck, Little John, or even Robin Hood himself. At least Robert Shaw was given a wardrobe that made him look like Robin Hood. If the audience could imagine that the characters in the serial were not saying the name David Trent, it was possible to at least pretend that the hero was the original bandit of Sherwood Forest.

Columbia retained the name of the titled hero of their 1949 chapterplay, *The Adventures of Sir Galahad,* in fifteen chapters, based on the tales of King Arthur and his Knights of the Round Table. This was a Sam Katzman-produced serial, which meant that anything could happen, despite the directing of Spencer G. Bennet.

It did, at least in the casting. Ancient-looking William Fawcett, usually seen as an old-timer in Westerns, became the mysterious Merlin the Magician. Galahad was given a sidekick named Bors, portrayed by overweight, mustached Charles King, the late actor who appeared in virtually all of the "poverty row" Western features of the 1940s. Seeing King beat up so many times by cowboy stars made it sometimes difficult to see him now, not only as a good guy, but as the companion of the noble Galahad. The casting of Galahad himself was a bit prophetic. The armor-suited knight was played in the serial by George Reeves, before he became the Man of Steel on television's *Superman* series.

The serial was unique in that it offered something different from the usual arrangement of chases and fist fights. The fact that it was set during the days of King Arthur opened the possibilities. Thus *The Adventures of Sir Galahad* offered possible death by tournament combat, with lances clanging against shields; enormous catapulted arrows; magic, caused by Merlin and by the enchanted sword of Arthur, "Excalibur"; and attacks by an unknown villain who used that most durable of names, the Black Knight.

In Chapter One, "The Stolen Sword," Galahad entered King Arthur's Court with hopes of being knighted. In a tournament, the young Galahad challenged the two victors, Bors and Modred, and defeated them, a triumph which placed him under the favorable eyes of King Arthur. The monarch agreed to reward

Galahad with knighthood, if he could, for one night, guard Excalibur, the sword which made its wearer invincible. During the night, Galahad was drugged and the magic sword stolen. Before he could be made a Knight of the Round Table, Galahad would have to regain the enchanted weapon. His quest for Excalibur took him through the Enchanted Forest, the lair of Arthur's magician and advisor, Merlin. In the woods, Galahad encountered Merlin who tried dooming the courageous fighter in a ring of flames.

The mysterious Lady of the Lake (Lois Hall) used magic to appear at the opening of the second chapter, "Galahad's Daring," and save the young man.

Galahad continued searching for King Arthur's sword week after week. During his quest, he was menaced by such threats as a falling chandelier, a wagon that flew off the side of a cliff, a fall from his mount which placed him in the path of onrushing horsemen, and a giant arrow that whizzed toward his bound body.

In the last installment, suitably titled "Galahad's Triumph," Galahad finally secured the sword Excalibur from the Lady of the Lake. Then he hastened back to Camelot where King Arthur, Bors, and the other knights were at the mercy of the evil Black Knight and his men. Arthur took back his magic weapon from Galahad and defeated the Black Knight, unmasking him as Modred. For a reward, the young fighter was dubbed Sir Galahad, Knight of the Round Table.

ALL'S WELL THAT ENDS WELL

Perhaps the strangest, and outright boldest, alteration of a classic novel for a cliffhanger was in the Sam Katzman-Spencer Bennet Columbia serial of 1951, based on Jules Verne's

Mysterious Island. In the novel, Captain Nemo from Verne's earlier work, *20,000 Leagues Under the Sea,* returned to the Mysterious Island to help a group of men stranded there by secretly offering supplies. The serial *Mysterious Island* followed the plot of the book rather closely. There was a Captain Nemo, played with long white hair by actor Leonard Penn. But there were changes made in the story, drastic changes, made obvious by the title of the first episode, "Lost in Space."

Yes, "Lost in Space!"

The serial, set in the Civil War year 1865, had been transformed into a fifteen-chapter space opera.

The trailer was a harbinger of thrills to come.

EXT. ISLAND CLEARING—DAY
Optical Title Card.
         MERCURY SPACESHIPS
         ZOOMING INTO THIS WORLD!
GIDEON SPILETT *and* NEB *are watching the clearing from concealment amidst nearby mountain boulders as suddenly they see a Mercurian spaceship zoom across the sky and descend to Earth. A moment later out steps* RULU, *a queenly young woman of Mercury, and a pair of Mercurian guards.* GIDEON *and* NEB *react.*
NEB: It looks like some strange craft from some other planet!
GIDEON: I'd like to seek its landing place!

EXT. SKY ABOVE THE OCEAN—DAY
Optical Title Card:
         CAPT. HARDING'S
         FABULOUS ADVENTURES . . .
The balloon sweeps across, propelled by high winds, CAPTAIN HARDING, GIDEON SPILETT, NEB, BERT BROWN *and* JACK PENCROFT *are throwing out the last of their belongings to lighten the load.*
HARDING: We've thrown out all the ballast! There's nothing left . . . except . . .
He starts to leap overboard. The others rush to stop him.
BERT: No, Captain, no!

EXT. OCEAN BEACH—DAY
Optical Title Card:

JULES VERNE'S
MYSTERIOUS ISLAND!

CAPTAIN NEMO *comes out of the ocean carrying* HARDING *unconscious in his arms.*

EXT. CLOSE SHOT AT A BEACH BOULDER—DAY

HARDING *is on the ground, propped up against the boulder. He's reviving.* CAPTAIN NEMO *stands over him masterfully.*

NEMO: Who are you? Why have you come to my island?

EXT. VOLCANO COUNTRY—DAY

BERT, SPILETT *and* PENCROFT *see the Volcano People moving through. They react.*

BERT: Those are the Volcano People. They're carrying Shard with them!

INT. MERCURY SPACESHIP—DAY

RULU *moves away from the Spacial Selector Band Transmitter and turns to her two Mercurian guards.*

RULU: That was a message from our leader on Mercury. He orders us to locate the mineral we came for immediately. Until we find and perfect it our leader will not be able to attack Earth!

EXT. ISLAND COUNTRY—DAY

PENCROFT, SPILETT *and* NEB *are fighting the Mercurians.*
Optical Title Card:

GRAPPLE WITH
THE MEN OF TOMORROW!

EXT. VILLAGE OF THE VOLCANO PEOPLE—DAY

The Volcano People dance around CAPTAIN HARDING, *tied up by his feet and hanging upside down from a wooden crane suspended over the river.* SPILETT, PENCROFT, NEB *and* BERT *enter suddenly. They see the goings-on.*

PENCROFT: Looks like the Volcano People are getting ready for some kind of ceremony.

BERT: Which could be fatal for Captain Harding!

They open fire on the natives. Pandemonium ensues. The

Volcano People scatter. The native clutching the rope of the crane runs off. Immediately HARDING *plunges headfirst into the river and sinks helpless to the bottom.*

EXT. SAILING SHIP—DAY
CAPTAIN HARDING, PENCROFT, BERT, NEB *and* SPILETT *are on deck and watching the volcano erupt, causing the explosion and final destruction of the entire island.*
Optical Title Card:
JULES VERNE'S
MYSTERIOUS ISLAND!
A SPECTACULAR
COLUMBIA SUPERSERIAL!

During the war between the States, Yankee soldier Captain Harding (played by Richard Crane, later seen on television as the star of *Rocky Jones, Space Ranger*) escaped with war correspondent Gideon Spilett (Hugh Prosser), sailor Jack Pencroft (Marshall Reed), his adopted son Bert Brown (Ralph Hodges), and Harding's servant Neb (Bernard Hamilton) from a Confederate prison in the obligatory Verne balloon. For five days, the balloon drifted through the sky. During the flight Harding leaped overboard, hoping the loss of weight in the balloon would save his friends. But as the noble soldier plunged into the water, he was grasped by a weird helmeted giant who suddenly vanished back into the sea. Then the balloon crashed on the nearby Mysterious Island.

It was at that point that the story began to get far out. A rocketship, which had been blasting away from its home planet Mercury, landed on the desert island. Out of the craft stepped a beautiful alien girl and a pair of Mercurian soldiers (wearing shirts somehow snatched away from Flash Gordon, and masks stolen from another serial hero, the Spider, all clothes belonging to Western Costume Company.)

Meanwhile, the survivors of the balloon wreck were being pursued by hostile natives. The castaways fled inside a cave, the roof of which promptly fell down upon them, ending the chapter, telling us that the story would be continued next week.

In the next installment, "Sinister Savages," the party was rescued by Jack Pencroft, whose actions were not spectacular. He merely dug them out of the debris.

Captain Harding was reviving in a secret grotto, where his strange helmeted savior had taken him. Now unmasked, the man from the sea introduced himself as Captain Nemo, a great scientist.

The Mysterious Island had Captain Nemo, primitive natives out for the kill, plus visitors from another world. But there was more. Now a wild man, once a normal castaway named Ayrton (played by movie heavy Terry Frost in a role taken from the novel) attacked Bert in the manner of a savage beast. Bert was saved by his friends, but then the natives resumed their restless chase. Fleeing, the castaways ran to a crevice leading through the mountainside. But they were trapped. A native witch doctor poured powder into the crevice which was filled with fire.

Luckily, Bert discovered an exit at the opening of Chapter Three, "Savage Justice," avoiding the flames.

The plot gradually became more confusing, since there were so many unrelated elements running rampant through *Mysterious Island*. Rulu (Karen Randle) the Mercurian maiden began searching for a certain unnamed metal, the prime reason for her journey to Earth. The witch doctor ranted that the castaways were evil, have angered the gods, and must be killed. Ayrton the wild man continued attacking people without warning. And Captain Nemo proceeded to baffle everyone with his fabulous electrical inventions.

Still, there were *more* plot twists, as if these weren't already too much. In the sixth episode, a new menace entered the story in "The Pirates Attack!" The pirates, led by the evil Shard (played by the massive Gene Roth), were soon attempting to defeat the lovely Rulu.

One element of the complicated plot was eradicated in Chapter Twelve, "Mystery of the Mine," when Ayrton was killed in the exploding pirate ship. In Chapter Fourteen, "Men from Tomorrow," Captain Nemo the mystery man who had saved them more than once, revealed himself to the castaways as the creator and skipper of the supersubmarine *Nautilus*. The captain then told that Rulu was on Earth for a metal necessary for an explosive capable of world-wrecking damage. Unexpectedly, another space ship from Mercury zoomed overhead, and blasted Captain Harding and the pirate Shard in an enormous explosion.

In the last chapter, "The Last of Mysterious Island," only Shard was killed, Harding being saved by his own nobility, his agility, and his studio contract. After a conflict of castaways vs. Mercurians, Rulu planted a superbomb on the island. All would be doomed unless fast action were taken. Working against time, the castaways managed to find and flag down a conveniently passing ship. Safely on board the vessel they watched as the Mysterious Island was blown off the map with its many evils.

Although fantastic beyond credibility, *Mysterious Island* actually contained more elements from the original source than most such adaptations of the sound era.

In the early days of serials, stories taken from classics remained relatively faithful, as with *Perils of the Wild* and *Last of the Mohicans*. During the middle and late 1930s, there were enough changes of the drastic category perpetrated to at least make the long deceased authors rest uneasily in their graves. But by 1951, some of these authors must have been rotating in their crypts as fast as the propellers of Captain Nemo's *Nautilus*.

The ultimate disaster to literature would have been Mascot Pictures' *Hamlet*. Although the account is definitely apocryphal, a recent magazine of limited circulation[2] for cinemaphiles told its version of this hypothetical production as an April Fool's joke.

If this picture were never made, the story is interesting in that it is almost certainly exactly the way Mascot *would* have done it.

Mascot would have played up the action, mystery, and horror in William Shakespeare's play. Heavy drama would have been ignored—and rightfully so, when considering the "all star" and most ideal of serial casts. The role of Hamlet would have been assigned to the youthful star of many Mascot chapterplays, Frankie Darro. The rest of the characters in the play-turned-serial were equally typical, using virtually all of the studio's contract players:

Robert Frazer a villain in many serials, would appear as Claudius, King of Denmark; Eileen Sedgwick as Gertrude, his Queen; Betsy King Ross, Darro's rival at Mascot, as Ophelia; Jack Mulhall, who sounded like a radio sportscaster, as Horatio; slow-talking Henry B. Walthall as Polonius; rugged cowboy star Lane Chandler as Laertes; silent chapterplay hero Walter Miller as Rosencrantz; silent serial daredevil William Desmond as Guildenstern; guttural-voiced Noah Beery, Sr., as the Ghost; Joe Bonomo, the powerful real-life athlete, as Fortinbras; and stuntman supreme Yakima Canutt, Western villain Glenn Strange, and Robert Kortman as pirates.

The serial would have been scripted by William Presley Burt, Harry Fraser, and Ben Cohen, and directed by Richard Thorpe, who directed numerous serials, and would years later become a major director at Metro-Goldwyn-Mayer studios.

We wonder if the famous "To be, or not to be" soliloquy would have been the basis for a cliffhanger, with young Hamlet escaping death the subsequent week by ducking aside as he wielded the dagger toward his own body. As for Shakespeare's

[2] Stringham, James A., " 'Hamlet' Serial Discovery," *Film Fan Monthly*, Number 82, April 1968.

ending, wherein all the principal characters die—including Hamlet, who could have been the only serial hero to meet death after avoiding so many weeks of perils—it is reasonable to speculate that Mascot would have followed the patterns established by studios when adapting the classics to the chapterplay screen. The ending would be changed. Hamlet probably survived the massacre at the end of the play. He had to, with a twelfth and final chapter title "All's Well That Ends Well."

14

The Villains   "All Bad, All Mad"

During a hectic Saturday afternoon in a mint-cool movie theatre, we cheered the cliffhanger heroes—Buster Crabbe as Flash Gordon, Kirk Alyn as Superman, Ralph Byrd as Dick Tracy, and all the others. But, at times, it often seemed that the star of the serial was the villain, so much was he center stage, and at times the actor playing the menace literally got top billing.

The studios realized that audiences admired, or were at least entertained by the deliciously evil actions of the villain, who displayed more wit than the naïve blundering of the hero. True, the hero did manage to fight off with his bare knuckles any number of heavies, to rescue the heroine from any imaginable menace her total imbecility might place her in, to save any scientific miracle or priceless treasure from persistent thievery. But it was the hero who everlastingly plunged into the most transparent of death traps. It was the hero whose fast gun was always knocked out of his hand by a crook's faster foot. It was the courageous and resourceful hero who usually managed to fly off the edge of a cliff in an exploding car, or to find himself strapped to a platform beneath a descending, crushing hydraulic press. And yet it was the criminal mastermind that was able to devise such elaborate instruments of death, such world-wide plots of conquest, such apparent traps that even we, the fans, could not be fooled. The heroes were the ones with the fists. The villains were the ones with the brains.

All through the child's world of the thirties and forties, it seemed much the same—heroes jumping like puppets on strings pulled by the villains. In the movies, on the radio, and in the comics magazines we devoured between Saturdays. In his 1965 book, *The Great Comic Book Heroes,* satirist Jules Feiffer wrote:

> How they toyed with those drab ofay heroes: trap set, trap sprung, into the pit, up comes the water, down comes the pendulum, out from the side come the walls. Through an unconvincing mixture of dumb-luck and general science 1, the hero escaped, just barely; caught and beat up the villain: that wizened ancient who, in toe to toe combat was, of course, no match for the younger man. . . . Villains, whatever fate befell them in the obligatory last panel, were infinitely better equipped than those silly hapless heroes. Not only comics, but life taught us that. Those of us raised in ghetto neighborhoods were being asked to believe crime didn't pay? Tell that to the butcher! Nice guys finished last; landlords, first. Villains by their simple appointment to the role were miles ahead.

"THE BATTIEST OF THEM ALL"

All of his life, Bela Lugosi was pursued by the shadow of his most famous stage and screen portrayal, the Transylvanian vampire, Count Dracula. After his appearance in the 1931 Universal feature, *Dracula,* Lugosi rarely again played a role that was not at least influenced by the vampire image, and in many cases, with an outright imitation of Dracula.

Lugosi appeared as the star of six serials, all in the mold of the sinister figure he projected as the Transylvanian nobleman. Sometimes, a mysterious figure who only *appeared* to be the bad guy; and still other times, as surely the eeriest "hero" ever on the screen. Slight variations in casting really did not matter. As kids, we left the theatre muttering "Wonder what's going to happen to Dracula next week?"

Type-casting has haunted many an actor, but with Lugosi, it was almost inevitable. His portrayals were done in exaggerations of gestures and speech by an actor who never seemed to become familiar with either the art of motion pictures or with the English language, after a long career of playing to the last rows of the balcony in legitimate theatres in Europe. There was no room for subtlety in a Lugosi characterization. Maybe that was why we liked him. As in a Western, there was never the least doubt in a Lugosi vehicle as to who wore the black hat. And the black cloak to go with it.

Such stereotyping actually helped provide Bela Lugosi with steady work he might otherwise have looked for in vain. His film career proceeded through an unimpressive, but *lengthy,* list of productions of the ultra-quickie-cheapie type from Monogram and the absolute cellar of Hollywood, P.R.C. Lugosi was, therefore, a natural for the lowest budgeted theatre fodder of all—serials.

Serial producers blatantly used the Hungarian actor to cash in on the popularity of Universal's well-made, and possibly, classic feature, *Dracula*. Movie posters advertising *Shadow of Chinatown* in 1936 boasted a profile of Lugosi, his eyes staring hypnotically, his hand waving with seeming mesmeric force in the best vampire manner. Producer Nat Levine took advantage of the actor's image in *The Whispering Shadow,* a 1933 Mascot Master-Serial, mimicking Karl Kreund's photography in *Dracula,* filling the entire screen with giant close-ups of the actor's eyes, bordered on top by down-jutting eyebrows and a forehead of forced wrinkles. And although there was no vampire in the serial at all, the audiences could easily identify the bloodthirsty visage of Count Dracula and could expect the worst.

The Whispering Shadow himself was one of those villains who kept both the law and the underworld guessing as to his true identity. In the first chapter, the police try to cajole the real name of the fiend from a ham-handed thug, Kruger:

INT. SHADOW'S HIDEOUT

CROOK: The Shadow!

WHISPERING SHADOW: You've cause to fear my anger. You cowards! Because of your failure, Kruger is in the hands of the police.

CUT TO:

INT. POLICE STATION

DETECTIVE: Are you going to tell us who the Whispering Shadow is? Tell us! Who is he?

KRUGER: Like I've told you before, none of us know! None of us has ever seen him!

DETECTIVE: You're headed for the chair, Kruger! Lying won't save you!

KRUGER: All we know is where to get our orders!

DETECTIVE: Tell us!

CUT TO:

SHADOW'S HIDEOUT

WHISPERING SHADOW: Kruger is weakening. Watch his light—and be *waaaarrrrnnndddd!!!*

Who is . . . the Whispering Shadow? In fact, *what* was the Whispering Shadow? All that was known of this dreaded underworld lord was that he was a diabolically clever mastermind, whose facile genius had produced a device that could render a human being invisible (a favorite technique of serial villains). He would then reappear as a shadow which moved along walls and which, it should come as no surprise, whispered. There was no one who knew to whom the voice of *this* invisible Shadow belonged. If Street and Smith, owners of the original Shadow of magazine and radio fame, had found out the owner of the whisper, they might have sued. As it was, not even the Whispering Shadow's sinister collection of hired toughs gaping around the secret conference room knew the identity of the hushed and unseen menace. However, Kruger being the type of wishy-washy criminal nonentity that thinks for the moment without considering the future wrath of his master, began to crack under the third degree.

Kruger's shivering body almost toppled from the chair to the floor. His eyes were no more than wet glass, streaming from the beams of the overhead light bulb. Around him, pointing, shouting, threatening, was a mob of policemen big enough to deal with a peace demonstration. They fired questions at him and exhaled cigarette smoke, keeping his head turning from one man to another.

In the conference chamber, a hushed voice somehow resembling Bela Lugosi's broadcasts over the heads of the gangsters.

"Kruger . . . is weakening. Watch his light. And *be warned.*"

Like some flock of vultures, the thieves and killers turn to stare at the vacant chair at their table. A weird halo of light, accompanied by the distant sound of throbbing power, encompasses the chair, swelling on and off.

Meanwhile, back at headquarters, Kruger cries out, a relieved smile contorting his face—"I'll tell! He's . . . *arrrrrggghhh!*

Kruger's light has been put out by the Whispering Shadow.

From every conceivable angle, Bela Lugosi appeared menacing in *The Whispering Shadow*. From his sinister, almost carved profile, to his apparently diabolical laboratory with its array of superscience apparatus and his private museum of wax figures that occasionally moved just a bit to assure that actors hired to stand around motionless all day were cheaper than making up statues. That, plus the fact that the unseen menace did sound like Lugosi, made it even more difficult to grasp that in the final episode it was revealed that Bela Lugosi was *not* the Whispering Shadow!

Incredibly enough, Bela Lugosi, who rarely played anything *but* a villain, turned out to be only a "red herring"—an overtly sinister looking character to throw suspicion away from the real master criminal—in this case, a janitor who throughout the chapterplay seemed no more than a harmless, bumbling idiot. Attempts to mislead viewers transpired as Lugosi, a mad look in his power-filled eyes, operated his humming, glowing laboratory devices, followed by a cut to the sibilant Shadow appearing on the side of a truck with the eerie, whispered warning promising destruction.[1]

One could well imagine that if Lugosi were innocent of being the Whispering Shadow, he was probably guilty of a lot of other things.

He was up to more familiar tricks as the evil magician Roxor, matching wits with the good hero of *Chandu the Magician,* a Fox feature, 1932. Lugosi played opposite Edmund Lowe, popular screen star who took the role of the famous radio character played on the air by Jason Robards, Senior, among others. The motion picture followed closely the radio scripts by Harry A. Earnshaw. Chandu—the name adopted by American Frank Chandler—tried to prevent Roxor from gaining the secret of a deathray, invented by Chandu's brother-in-law. As Roxor, Lugosi was once again bent on either conquering the world or destroying it. With the aid of his tutor in mystic arts, a Yogi (played by Nigel de Brulier, who years later played a similar role as the wizard Shazam in the serial *Adventures of Captain Marvel*), Chandu managed to put nefarious Roxor out of commission and retrieve the ghastly weapon. The film, though incorporating many of the plot devices of the serial, was a class feature, partially due to photography by a later Academy Award winning cinematographer, James Wong Howe, who managed to catch much of the Oriental flavor of the story of magic and mystery.

Sol Lesser realized the serial potential in the Chandu story. In 1934, under the Principal banner, Lesser made *Return of Chandu* which was not a direct sequel to the Fox feature.

---

[1] The "shadow" was not cast by any actor, Lugosi or otherwise. The dark outline was drawn in by cartoon animators over the photographed scene.

Lugosi did not play the villain in the serial but graduated to the role of Chandu himself. If it was hard to believe that Lugosi was *not* the villain in *The Whispering Shadow,* it was difficult to grasp that he was now actually supposed to be the *hero.* Yet the casting was not totally unsuccessful. Even a good magician is somehow a sinister figure, filled with forbidden knowledge of black magic. One wondered when Chandu might change his allegiance from white magic to black. Of course with Lugosi in the role, the Orient-trained American spoke with a thick Hungarian accent.

The second serial based on the popular radio series followed the storyline of the broadcasts even more closely than the first. The chapterplay was then adopted into an illustrated book issued by Saalfield in 1935, and departing from the exact title of the second serial it fictionalized was called simply *Chandu the Magician.* The stills, like the actual movie scenes they came from, amply demonstrated Lugosi's rather sinister hypnotic gaze as the supposed hero. Chandu struck terror in the hearts of evil-doers, much as if he were only Count Dracula in a turban. The text of the Saalfield book described one such scene from the film with Lugosi as Frank Chandler, also known as Chandu:

Vindhyan's laugh died in his throat, as he stared back at Chandler. Everyone on deck seemed frozen in his tracks. Breathless, they watched the battle of wills. Before their astonished eyes, Chandler appeared to become enveloped in a whirlpool of smoke, until only his piercing steel-gray eyes were visible, holding Vindhyan in their gaze.

"Release her!" commanded Chandler.

Vindhyan struggled to break the spell, but Chandler's set glare became more intense.

"Release her!" he repeated.

Slowly, Vindhyan's arms relaxed and Nadji slipped to the seat below the rail.

The serial *Return of Chandu* provided a conglomeration of

mad high priests, human sacrifices, poison darts, pagan idols, and an Egyptian princess, through which Bela Lugosi moved in the title role. The trappings were ideally suited for him, but not his role of hero. With Lugosi in the role, Chandu seemed far too mysterious and sinister, producing more shivers than cheers from the audience. Somehow the traps he found himself in seemed to be of his own design. The actor would never again get this close to being a good guy on the screen.

Princess Nadji, Chandu's girl friend, happened to be (with the great coincidences in movie serials) the reincarnated queen of the cat cult of the Magic Isle. By sacrificing Nadji the spirit of the queen would return to her preserved body and thus restore her to life. Chandu and his friends were shipwrecked, providing a cliffhanger, on the Magic Isle which somehow robbed him of his supernatural powers. To make matters worse, Princess Nadji was captured by the cat worshippers and taken through the monstrous gates of the city (actually sets left over from RKO's *King Kong*).

Chandu had to rely on his physical prowess in hoping to rescue Nadji. Perhaps his self-confidence was overly lessened. When he found himself in a hazardous predicament Chandu the Magician would stop, concentrate, and call for help from the man who had given him his powers originally.

"Yogi," Chandu would say as the monotonous drum beat came over the soundtrack and nearly drowned out his dialogue, "My teacher across the sea . . . hear me." Following each plea for help was the voice of the Yogi with his set of instructions as to how to escape the traps of the cat cult.

Chandu nearly died as he approached the sacred temple of the cat worshippers and fell victim to a trap door. His rope broke as he swung Tarzan style over a tiger pit. He was tied to the floor as a gigantic slab of rock creaked . . . moved . . . fell toward his helpless form. Surely this latter peril was devised by Lugosi in his Roxor identity between camera "takes."

The magician escaped death finally, learning to his horror that Princess Nadji had agreed to sacrifice herself to the temple's sacred flames so that her friends could go free. The Princess's lovely body was given to the fire. All seemed lost when the high priest learned that the identical bodies of Nadji and the queen had been switched. The high priest went berserk over the failure and encountered the wrath of Chandu, who, with restored powers blasted the temple apart with magical force from his fingers, and escaped with the Princess.

Chandu's powers included invisibility, which lasted as long as the sands of magical hourglass did not run out. The invisible Chandu rescued a friend who was bound beneath a descending, pendulum-like sword, similar to the torture performed by Lugosi himself in Universal's *The Raven,* 1935, based on works by Edgar Allan Poe. Chandu also fought off a group of cultists who seemed to be punched by empty air. In the final episode the eyes and flashbulbs of newspaper reporters and photographers popped as Chandu and his fiancée Princess Nadji vanished for some privacy.

To audiences of the '30s no one quite so well represented the menace of the *foreigner.* Lugosi's thick Hungarian accent, his mannerisms, forever branded Lugosi as European. His chief rival, the far more successful Boris Karloff, could occasionally get away with playing an eccentric old *American* scientist, for his own accent was not so much English as pure and distinctive Karloff. Not so with Lugosi. He *had* to be a European nobleman, reduced to grave-robbing or possibly even to butlering.

Moviegoers began identifying Lugosi with Europeans causing all the trouble "over there." To some he represented the Nazis; to others the Bolsheviks. He was one of the screen's legion of foreign devils, along with George Zucco, Lionel Atwill, Richard Loo. All of them were cruel, thirsty for power to conquer a brave but defenseless America, to kill, burn, and rule. Lugosi always seemed to head this invading army, if not as their general, then as the high priest of their damnable religion of Foreignism.

In Sam Katzman's Victory Pictures serial, *Shadow of China-town*, 1936, Lugosi played a mad Eurasian scientist who hated both the Caucasian and Oriental races that had sired him. As Victor Poten, Lugosi cheerfully utilized such devices as a death-ray that magnified the sun's rays to fatal potency; a colorless, odorless death gas; and his own small army of mysterious Oriental henchmen including a giant mechanized idol. Poten is finally pursued by the ever-dodging hero, Herman Brix (later known as Bruce Bennett) to seeming certain death as the villain's car plunges off a dock, sinking into a dark ocean.

Brix and his fellow good folk celebrate their good fortune in triumphing over Poten at a banquet, but as usual, the hero relaxed too soon. Poten had survived, and disguised as a waiter, is about to serve poisoned food to the happy group. Brix, granted that good fortune which serves a hero better than wit, somehow sees through the disguise, tackles Poten and turns him over to the police. *"The End"* credit comes up, but one can hardly believe those bumblers will succeed in holding Poten long.

In fact, Poten apparently turns up again under another name in *SOS Coastguard*, 1937. The new name for Bela Lugosi's seemingly constant screen role is significant. Lugosi is now known as "Boroff"—which seems to be a contraction of the name of the rival screen villain, Boris Karloff. As Boroff, Lugosi is a mad munitions inventor, who with the aid of a giant mute henchman, Thorg (Richard Alexander), is a traitor attempting to supply a disintegrating gas of his own manufacture to a foreign country. In this Republic serial, Lugosi has somewhat stiffer competition than usual. As the Coast Guard officer hero, perennial screen Dick Tracy, Ralph Byrd offers more qualities of presence and resourcefulness than the somewhat wooden figures Lugosi was usually pitted against.

But despite the cheerful heroics of Byrd on, over, and beneath the sea, it is not the hero of the serial who finishes off Boroff. It is the lumbering Thorg, wounded by his master's own bullet, who turns on his supposed benefactor and kills him with his iron-thewed hands. As in the countless horror films with which Lugosi became identified, it is the creature who turns on his misguided master and destroys him.

In 1939, Lugosi made his final serial appearance, and appropriately, it seemed a combination, and a culmination, of all his other villain roles. In Universal's *The Phantom Creeps,* it is, of course, villain Bela Lugosi who has the title role of the evil Phantom, and top billing.

Lugosi is now a mad scientist called Zorka (not to be confused with Boroff or Poten). Film director Ford Beebe puts the heroes through cliffhanger after cliffhanger as they are nearly blown-up, gassed, or electrocuted by still another invention of the insidious Zorka . . . yet somehow leap, fall, or are pushed to safety in the nick of time. Zorka can make himself invisible, not unlike the Whispering Shadow. (Can one be absolutely *certain* Lugosi was innocent of being that sibilant shade?) Zorka has a gigantic robot, not unlike Poten's mechanized idol and Boroff's robot-like henchman, Thorg. This mechanical monster of the creepy Phantom's has a scowling face suggesting a bad case of acid indigestion—battery acid, perhaps. Chapter after chapter, Lugosi chortles over his pet robot, rumbling in his thick accent of the destruction the robot will inflict on the whole human race once it is unleashed. Finally, in the last chapter, as the madman is cornered in his own secret laboratory, he pushes the button and the electronic gargoyle lumbers into action. The robot strides out onto the lawn, arms waving, hands grasping the air, stomping toward the waiting forces of the United States Army. They fire one shot. Fifteen seconds after going into motion, the robot is put out of commission.

Zorka shrugs. You can't win 'em all. The only logical course left to him is to destroy the world singlehanded, except for the aid of his one human assistant.

On a maniacal spree of destruction, Zorka unleashes his fury, contributing to world history by blowing up the German Zeppelin *Hindenburg*. (The scenes of the airship's flaming destruction looked remarkably realistic. They should have, since they were newsreel shots of the event.)

Once again, one of Bela Lugosi's henchmen turns on him. The mad scientist's assistant decides there are few career opportunities for an assistant to the man who destroyed the planet Earth. Before that event can take place, the assistant causes Zorka's plane to crash to flaming destruction. It is only a minor holocaust, from which a hero could walk away, whistling. But though he has a villain's cunning, Zorka lacks a hero's luck and it is the end for him. And the hero has contributed little to his destruction.

By the 1940s, even cliffhanger audiences developed some degree of sophistication. They began to prefer at least a Lionel Atwill who could lie to a snooping hero with some degree of credence. Lugosi returned exclusively to the horror feature lengths, where a man could be a monster without ever pretending to be human.

Lugosi disappeared from the serial screen, but he left behind him his shadow. He had been the biggest feature film star ever to be top-billed as a villain in so many chapterplays.

"THAT MOST ELUSIVE MASTERMIND"

Boris Karloff was the foremost movie menace of the sound era, and he did do some of his mischief in serials. However, after his classic portrayal of the Monster in Universal's 1931 feature length, *Frankenstein,* he became too sought-after and expensive a star to do low-budget productions such as chapterplays. Serial producers would very much have *liked* to have used Karloff in the '30s and '40s, could they have got him. Lugosi was given roles well-suited to Karloff, and even that one role with something very much like Karloff's name. But since Karloff was unreachable in later years, all his serial work took place late in the silent era, and in the early years of the talkies.

The English actor had major roles in at least five serials— *The Hope Diamond Mystery,* 1921, and all from Mascot Studios: *Vultures of the Sea,* 1928; *The Fatal Warning,* 1929; *King of the Kongo,* 1929; *King of the Wild,* 1931. (The last two titles represent two separate and distinct productions, and not retitlings of the same film as is sometimes reported.)

Since all of his serial work took place before his major fame as the star of *Frankenstein,* Karloff never commercialized on his reputation as a monster. Lugosi was baldly exploited as "Dracula" in still another menacing guise. Karloff had merely to rely on talent in the early days, and he did quite well with it. If he did not receive top billing (on the initial release at least), Karloff usually got third or fourth billing, just after the hero and heroine, and possibly chief sidekick.

In *The Hope Diamond Mystery,* Karloff played a bald-domed high priest of a cult. The silent production made use of tinted scenes and title cards, so that when Karloff rubbed his hands in glee over the Diamond, it gave off rings of multicolored light.

Karloff looked equally menacing in *King of the Kongo,* which like both *Vultures of the Sea* and *The Fatal Warning,* was a ten-episode thriller directed by Richard Thorpe. However, in *Kongo,* there was a surprise. Although there were shadowy shots of Karloff's sinister features just before some near-fatal catastrophe struck the hero, the final chapter revealed another as the villain and that Karloff was in reality the father of heroine Jacqueline Logan.

In the similarly titled but different film, *King of the Wild,*

Boris Karloff was cast as an Arab sheik, Mustapha, who does not even try to resist the lure of sudden wealth. A boy named Tom is found wandering the desert sands in delirium from a fever. Mustapha's bearers bring him to camp where he blurts out to the sheik the existence of a fabulous diamond field of incalculable wealth.

Mustapha's eyes light, and he strokes his lean, calculating face.

But for all his fevered ravings, Tom does not divulge the secret location of the diamonds.

"When the fever is gone from him—we'll make him talk!" murmurs the sheik confidently.

Later, a man enters Mustapha's tent with a wild tale. "May it please, master. A strange jungle beast leaped out upon our people at the water hole, killing a camel."

The sheik gives an impatient wave of his robed arm. "What kind of beast? A lion?"

"Like no lion that we ever saw, Excellency. We dug a pit and baited it with the slain camel and the beast fell into the trap."

"Let me see this strange beast," Mustapha commands.

The sheik hurries to the iron grating that covers the pit. From below comes the growl of a wild beast. Amid the jabbering of the Arabs (more of Hollywood's ever-present "superstitious natives"), Mustapha exclaims, "An Indian tiger in Africa! The steamer that was wrecked had such animals on board. Doubtless this one managed to reach shore."

"Wilt thou slay him, master?" asks the man who had brought the news, aiming at the great striped cat with a long-barrelled musket.

Boris Karloff as Mustapha contorts his face into the countenance of pure evil that he could effect. He pushes aside the Arab's gun. "I have other plans."

The sheik has the partially recovered Tom brought from his tent, and places before the boy a simple proposition. Either he will tell where the diamonds are, or he will be thrown into the pit with the tiger. The confused boy can give no answer. Then, Mustapha shows a certain lack of caution where his only lead to the treasure is concerned. He has Tom flung into the pit with the snarling, raging beast.

Once again, as the episode comes to a close, it does not look well for one of the good guys.

However, as the next chapter opens, with superhuman strength and skill born of desperation, Tom manages to scramble from the pit and to ever-so-temporary safety.

Meanwhile, the hero, Grant (played by Walter Miller), has been falsely accused of the murder of Rajah, a crime not to be taken lightly. There exists a letter which can clear Grant, ascribing the crime to a convict named Dakka. However the letter has been written in *invisible ink,* and the only man in the world who knows how to bring out this secret writing is the evil sheik Mustapha.

Harris, a scoundrel who has mastery over a shaggy half-man half-ape named Bimi, wants the letter for his own evil ends. The sly sheik gives Harris what appears to be the letter, but what actually is a forgery, keeping the *real* document he has obtained from Grant for himself.

When Mustapha is later attacked by a leopard, he is saved from a bloody death by Grant. The hero immediately draws a gun on him and demands his letter.

"My friend," says the Arab sheik in the British lisp of Karloff, "I do not understand. One minute you save my life and with the will of Allah I thank you. The next minute you threaten to shoot me for something which I do not possess."

Grant steps closer to the Arab. "I know you gave Harris a fake copy of the Rajah's letter. Hand over the real one."

Reluctantly, Mustapha gives up the letter to Grant, his shifty eyes catching a welcome sight coming through the jungle. A group of Mustapha's bloodthirsty tribesmen are on their way to help the sheik. He hurls himself at Grant, knocking the gun aside, and a hand-to-hand fight is on.

It is the classic serial confrontation—the quick-witted villain against the fast-punching (if somewhat punchy) hero. The result was inevitable. Grant could not outwit Mustapha but he could outslug him. Grant drops the sheik with a solid haymaker, and flees into the jungle from the howling Arabs.

Unlike the spectacular demises of most serial archfiends, Mustapha in the twelfth and final chapter of *King of the Wild* meets no spectacular death but is only captured. Mustapha and his murderous band are stopped from killing Grant, young Tom, and the good guys by a jungle version of the U. S. Cavalry— an army of troopers—just in the very nick of time. The secret location of the diamonds is revealed to be in the crater of a volcano.

To clear up the final loose end, the shady Harris snatches the coveted letter and tries to escape on horseback. But so desperate is his ride that the horse becomes frightened, bolts sharply, spilling Harris into a death plunge from the edge of a cliff. The brutish, half-human Bimi who has doggedly followed Harris throughout the serial, eager to carry out his every command, paws at the broken body, whimpering, trying to understand what death means for his master.[1]

While it is almost certainly coincidence pure and simple, it is interesting to note that Boris Karloff's last serial contained as a minor element the same theme that would make Karloff an immortal of the screen in the feature film that would follow the same year—*Frankenstein*. Karloff's Monster was another

[1] Serials were a genre almost exclusively concerned with action, but the final scene of the *King of the Wild* script contains a rare shot meant to suggest pathos. It reads:

127. LONG SHOT TOWARD THE SETTING SUN as beautiful as we can make it. Bimi with Harris' body in his arms, goes from camera up the rocky hillside moaning his sorrows to the open sky on and on and on as the scene slowly fades into darkness.

half-human creature like Bimi, asking for sympathy and love. Of course, it took a feature film to develop such a theme, because in a serial, the action could not stop long enough for characterization. Not even when the serials were employing one of the greatest of all character actors, Boris Karloff.

"THE DEVIL YOU SAY"

The gangster film of the thirties was as classic a source for movie villains as the horror films that created the screen image of Lugosi and gave Karloff his best medium. Since in a gangster film, the villain was the top-billed star in most cases, few celebrated movie gangsters ever agreed to work in economy productions like multi-episode thrillers. One can hardly imagine a James Cagney or an Edward G. Robinson in a serial. However, one fine actor in many class gangster epics, Eduardo Ciannelli, did star in a well-made Republic serial in the title role of *The Mysterious Dr. Satan.*

Certainly, Ciannelli held more of the audience's interest than handsome but colorless Robert Wilcox, the film's hero. He disguised himself with a Copperhead mask, but even without it, it would have been difficult to pick Wilcox out of a crowd.

Originally, popular villain Henry Brandon, who had played the insidious Oriental mastermind in *Drums of Fu Manchu* earlier in the year, was considered in 1939 for the role of Dr. Satan. Brandon would wear a regular Devil's costume, horns and all. However, the '30s were running out, and with them, something of the suspension of disbelief of serial fans. Brandon was replaced with Ciannelli who played the villain as he did all his other villains—a sleek gangster. The audience of the '30s could readily believe in such a menace.

It was the hero who wore a mask in the manner of comic book heroes like Batman who were just then becoming popular. The metallic-scaled hood of the Copperhead suggested the appearance of the dangerous snake of the Southwest—a sure killer when he struck! Beneath the mask, the Copperhead is Bob Wayne, the son of a fabled character from the days of the old West (then only some forty years past) who rode for justice in this mask, but who was called by many an outlaw. Young Wayne wants to prove to the world that the Copperhead has always fought for law and order, and to do it, he dedicates himself to thwarting the plans of the mysterious Dr. Satan.

Those plans of the doctor included the usual goal of conquering the world, and by the not-usual means of an army of robots. The only thing stopping him from putting his ambitious plan into effect is his lack of a remote control device by which he can work his electronic monsters from a distance. One man possesses such a device, Professor Thomas Scott (played by C. Montague Shaw, himself an actor often cast as a serial villain, though not here). Dr. Satan promptly abducts the professor, and employs the charming methods of Satan to force the professor to employ his knowledge and talents for the master plan.

As episode after episode unfolds, the Copperhead risks death time after time to keep Satan from completing the construction of his robot army. The hero is trapped underwater, lured beneath a spray of naked electricity, driven into a dancing wall of flame, and apparently trapped in a coffin-like box and shoved into a raging furnace. Yet somehow the Copperhead manages to escape each one of these traps as Dr. Satan smirks and frowns and plots new devilment. (Certainly, it was easier for Ciannelli to bump off guys in his more familiar role as head of the Mafia in countless films, the latest being the 1969 production, *The Brotherhood*.)

At last, Dr. Satan prepares to destroy the Copperhead with the most dangerous invention of them all—his own man of steel automaton.

In the fifteenth and final episode, titled "Dr. Satan Strikes," the robot, a walking water heater (a man of Steele—famed stunt-man Tom Steele inside the contraption) is guided by his sinister creator to destroy all the good guys, tied to chairs in Satan's lair. But the Copperhead does manage to break into the sanctu-ary. He confronts the evil doctor and in a furious battle of flying fists and smashing furniture (with stuntman Dave Sharpe now wearing the Copperhead mask) Satan is laid cold. Wayne takes off the Copperhead mask and slips it on Satan. With the typical lack of brains of serial henchmen, Satan's men mistake their boss for the real Copperhead, and order the robot to attack him. The robot strides toward the mastermind, metal arms wav-ing, clamp-like hands closing and unclosing. The villain edges back, ever backward, until both the man and his monster plummet out the window, many stories above the street. Once again the villain has perished at the hands of his own villainy.

Despite its bland hero and inevitable clichés, *The Mysterious Dr. Satan* was one of Republic's best serials, and one that set the pace for others that followed. The film had slick direction by the best talents in the serial field, William Witney and John English; music both moody and exciting, scored by Cy Feuer; superior and atmospheric lighting; and some of the greatest stunt work in the fights to ever appear on the screen in any kind of film. Despite their budget limitations, what serials did best— *action*—they did better than even major feature productions.

Villainy was another product in which the serials excelled. Ciannelli received top billing for *Satan,* enjoyed the best scenes, the meatiest dialogue, and was lit and photographed better than the rest of the cast (to make him look genuinely satanic). He had the ability to make all of these factors work for him.

Ciannelli went over to Universal to make two more serials, both air adventures, *Sky Raiders* (1941) and *Adventures of the Flying Cadets* (1943). Apparently the studio saw value in his own first name, for he was called respectively "Edward" and "Eduardo" in these two chapterplays.

It was, however, as Dr. Satan that Ciannelli is most fondly remembered by serial fans. In one of the five or six greatest serials ever made by Republic, it was the villain who stole not only the money and secret plans, but also the show.

"NOW HERE'S MY PLAN"

Villains were as plentiful in Western serials and features as they were in horror and crime films, but somehow they tended to be less memorable. The town gambler Kenneth MacDonald and his chief henchman Roy Barcroft became rather ingratiatingly familiar, but few indeed were actors who have achieved star status by playing the heavy in cowboy sagas.

Noah Beery, Sr., was the only personality of star caliber to play the villain in the countless Western chapterplays of the sound era. During the silent period, he had been even more prominent in features, only a notch below his brother, Wallace Beery, who was often the good-bad man, not the outright crook with few redeeming features that Noah portrayed. (His son, Noah Beery, Jr., reverted more to his uncle's type, and in fact, was usually on the side of the just.)

Frontier villains tended to be somewhat less devious and infallible than their big city colleagues in crime. In the 1937 Republic serial, *Zorro Rides Again,* the bulky mustached Noah Beery, Sr., makes a small mistake. In the thriller set in a modern-day era that must have surprised the author of the original novels of Zorro, Johnston McCulley, Beery sits comfortably in his office in an urban skyscraper and radios orders to his chief bad man, El Lobo (actor Richard Alexander) in the California-Yucatán area. Beery's error is in paying El Lobo's band of horse thieves and train wreckers by *check*.

("Do not fold, spindle or mutilate.") When the check is found by the modern Zorro (John Carroll) after a lot of songs, fist fights, and seemingly innumerable times in which Zorro gets his foot caught in the railroad tracks with a train bearing down on him, the jig is up for Beery.

In the 1935 Mascot Master-serial, *Fighting with Kit Carson,* Beery plays the crafty Kraft who is out to seize a huge supply of gold, despite the best efforts of Johnny Mack Brown as the famous scout. Beery figures in a very well-done cliffhanger in the serial. Still not known to be the crook behind all the trouble, Beery talks with Kit Carson about getting the scout to put an old man named Fargo into his custody for "safe-keeping." Fargo is the only one who knows the location of the gold. One of Beery's band hides behind a boulder, waiting for a prearranged signal to kill Carson if the talk does not go well. Beery will drop his knife as a signal to the outlaw to hurl his own knife into Carson's back.

Near the boulder, Beery smiles ingratiatingly at Fargo and his daughter, "Johnny," who is dressed as a boy, and speaks to Kit Carson, as he idly tosses his hunting knife up in the air, and catches it by the handle, time after time. "Carson, those Mystery Riders will still be trying to get the gold. And suppose something happens to Fargo before he tells us where the gold is?"

"I'm going to see that nothing happens to him," Kit Carson says confidently.

The knife is tossed into the air, but this time Noah Beery lets it land point-first in the dirt. Instantly, his henchman throws his own blade straight at Kit Carson's back.

This is where we expect to see the action cut and the famous CONTINUED NEXT WEEK title card go up, but instead we see the girl, "Johnny," cry out a warning to Carson and to throw herself in front of him heroically. She screams, clutches at her breast, and topples to the ground. And *that* is the real climax to the episode.

In the following chapter, Kit Carson shoots down the sneaking outlaw before he can finish the job with a gun. The scout turns to young "Johnny," but with the infallible luck of all decent folk menaced in serials, she has only been lightly grazed by the blade. Beery grumbles his feigned sympathy and retrieves his own knife for later use.

The final chapter offers a spectacular end to Beery's conniving Kraft. He has rigged a gun to fire a shot into a barrel of gunpowder in an old cabin as a death trap for Carson. But after being exposed, the villain makes a frantic dash for freedom and triggers the earth-shaking explosion himself. It may not have been as fantastic as Dr. Satan's robot, but once again a serial villain was destroyed by his own mechanism.

"THE REST OF THE GANG"

For the countless other villains required for the sound serials, producers went back to that rich ground for the heavies—the horror features. One actor whose character always fluctuated between villain and hero in countless monster features was Lon Chaney, Jr. He showed this indecision in serials, playing the hero in RKO's only serial *The Last Frontier* in 1932 and in Universal's *Overland Mail* ten years later. In the former serial, the actor, still using the name "Creighton" Chaney, became a Zorro-type hero in order to thwart the villain, played by Francis X. Bushman. Putting on fake mustache and sideburns, plus a dark and flamboyant costume, he was transformed into the Black Ghost. Perhaps the "transformation" was prophetic of his later roles in horror films. In *Overland Mail* Chaney uttered a classic bit of good-natured (if simple-minded) charity as the villain (played by Noah Beery, Sr.) confessed to his countless murders and other crimes just before he died. "He wasn't such a bad sport after all."

But just as he could not resist the periodic ominous change of his most famous role, *The Wolf Man* from Universal's 1941 feature, so Chaney could not escape being one of the bad guys in a number of serials. He was a henchman in Mascot's 1933 John Wayne starrer *The Three Musketeers* which concerned the modern French Foreign Legion; and another in Universal's all-star, high budget Western cliffhanger *Riders of Death Valley*, which also featured Dick Foran, Buck Jones, Leo Carrillo, and Charles Bickford among others.

Probably Chaney's most colorful henchman was Captain Hakur, the commander of the Black Robes, the army of the sunken continent Atlantis in *Undersea Kingdom,* Republic's second serial in 1936. In this Flash Gordon-type epic of a mad dictator and his arsenal of zap guns and the same robots which proved experimental models for those later used by Dr. Satan, an expedition of surface dwellers led by Ray "Crash" Corrigan (name sounding suspiciously like "Flash") arrived in Atlantis via supersubmarine.

Atlantis, like so many supercivilizations as Superman's Krypton and Flash Gordon's adopted Mongo, relied heavily upon superscience. Miracle inventions, such as space vehicles, deathrays, and mechanical men, were often used *when* the characters were not otherwise engaged in sword battles on horseback or modeling the latest fashions of ancient Rome or Greece. We can only wonder what these advanced "people" wore when their technology was on a par with ours.

Corrigan fought Hakur's army, the robots, the Roman-style gladiators, and finally in Chapter Six, "The Juggernaut Strikes," found himself in real trouble.

Chaney as Captain Hakur was only tenth in the acting credits, but he was responsible for a lot of Corrigan's trouble. The fairly trim and rather handsome Hakur tied the beefy Corrigan to the front of a Juggernaut, a swift, armed ultra-tank. Hakur, at the controls, peers out the window at his captive who has information as to the location of a strange priming powder that can help raise Atlantis back to the surface of the sea, where it can attack the surface world at will.

"This is your last chance, Corrigan," growls Hakur. "Tell me where you've hidden that priming powder, or I'm going to ram you into those gates!"

Corrigan's gaze turns toward the locked gates of the city. His friends are watching in terror from atop the walls. Without looking at Hakur, staring straight ahead, he orders: *"Go ahead and ram."*

Grinning, Hakur guns the Juggernaut, speeding toward the gates with cheerful velocity, smashing the vehicle into that barrier with a cloud of dust and flying debris. Has our hero been reduced to jelly?

The seventh installment begins with the usual recap scenes of the situation: Hakur delivers his threat, Corrigan sounds his defiance, and the whining Juggernaut careens toward the wall. But this time, there is a departure. Someone inside the city yells, "Open the gates!"

The gates are indeed opened, and the Juggernaut roars through the gap, with Corrigan still tied to the front of it, but unharmed. (The "solution" was obviously filmed before the cliffhanger ending wrecked those gates.)[2]

---

[2] Serial fans always regarded a situation where the events shown in the cliffhanger are simply changed, so that the menace never really occurred, to be a "cheat." Cliffhanger chapter endings were resolved in the next episode in various approved ways. To simply follow up the cliffhanger action in the solution with the escape was the most honest and desirable. (The hero did fall off the cliff but he caught a tree limb on the way down.) Showing in the solution the escape, during the same time but from different camera angles, was tolerated. (The car did go off the bridge, but we see the hero jumping to safety a moment before.) The "cheat," however, was always booed, since the cliffhanger itself was altered so as to be inconsistent with the last chapter ending. (The hero jumps his horse across a terrific gap, but the horse falters, and plunges into the canyon below. Next episode, the hero jumps his horse across and simply makes the jump successfully and rides on.) Mascot, Columbia, and the independent studios were more guilty of cheating than Republic.

Another performer familiar to horror movie fans, just below Lugosi, Karloff, and Chaney in popularity, was the celebrated English stage actor, Lionel Atwill. While he never achieved top-billing as the villain in a serial (unlike Lugosi), studio records reveal he sometimes received a higher salary than the leading man.

Atwill was his usual mad, but *sly,* scientist in *Captain America,* Republic, 1943. Atwill played Dr. Maldor, alias the Scarab. He was an elderly museum curator out to retrieve archaeological treasures he felt rightfully belonged to him, since he had headed the expeditions. In his secret identity of the Scarab he employed disintegrating rays, remote control devices, and a gang of armed thugs to obtain his desires. His nemesis District Attorney Grant Gardner assumed his own secret identity, that of the patriotically garbed Captain America. In beautifully choreographed fights he could beat up two or three of the Scarab's hoodlums, but when he tackled the aging Scarab in the final climactic fist fight he seemed to have a match on his hands, thanks to Atwill's stuntman Fred Graham. Finally with a punch that would kill an ox, Captain America knocked out the old man.

Villains die hard but they do die, and so do the actors that portray them. Following the serial *Junior G-Men of the Air,* Universal, 1943, in which the distinguished English actor played a Japanese spy out to wreck America's defenses in spite of the opposition of the famed (and reformed) Dead End Kids, and *Raiders of Ghost City,* Universal, 1944, with another villainous performance, Atwill became the lead heavy in his last serial *Lost City of the Jungle,* Universal, 1946.

Before Atwill could complete his screen plan for seizing a new and deadly atomic ore, the actor died of pneumonia. Many of his scenes as the foreign spy chief were shot, and since serials were always made for notoriously low production costs, the studio felt it could not junk Atwill's scenes and start over with another actor in his role.

A new actor did come into the film as supposedly an even more important spy than Atwill, who gave Atwill his orders. A double resembling Atwill from the back was used in many scenes. With the double with his back to the camera, one of the thugs would say to him something like: "Now I understand you want us to shoot the plane right out of the sky, and leave no survivors. Right, Boss?" Then there was a cut to an enlarged and grainy shot of Lionel Atwill nodding, rather disinterestedly. The same blown-up shot turned up so many times that one could memorize the grain pattern.

The most evil mastermind of them all was an actor who was not famous from horror films, crime pictures, or Westerns. In fact, he never really seemed to get a good role *outside* of serials. Because he was largely ignored for major parts in features, his most famous portrayal will always be that of Ming the Merciless in Universal's three Flash Gordon serials. Ming's real name was Charles Middleton.

Middleton came from a wealthy family and did not really have to act for a living, but he enjoyed it. His face seemed carved into an image of evil, as if some starving sculptor had chiseled out his idea of what his landlord looked like. No one but Middleton could *enjoy* it so much as with a chuckling sneer, he ordered "Throw Flash Gordon into the Arena of Death! The sacred Orangapoid will finish him!"

As Ming, he was Emperor of the planet Mongo and self-proclaimed Ruler of the Universe. His plans to destroy the planet Earth and reign over the rest of the Solar System were constantly being thwarted by the Earthman, Flash Gordon, his girl friend, Dale Arden, and the old scientist, Zarkov. Yet Ming never gave up. With a mere handful of soldiers, dressed like ancient Romans, armed with swords and an occasional raygun, and with a fleet of rickety, *putt-putting* rocketships, Ming threatened our whole world in *Flash Gordon,* 1936. Though he seemingly met death in the final chapter, he next showed up on Mars in *Flash Gordon's Trip to Mars,* 1938. Even after being *disintegrated* in that one, he came back in *Flash Gordon Conquers the Universe,* 1940.

Charles Middleton hugely enjoyed the role of Ming, overacting with just enough gusto to make his menace believable within the context of that very special serial world. You could almost read his inner feelings when, beholding the golden beauty of Dale Arden for the first time, he advances with clutching, rigid fingers that must have been both clammy and slimy, and slowly speaks in a commanding voice, "Ah, you are beautiful!" At times, the Emperor of Mongo thought of conquering more than just the Earth.

Although he was chiefly known as Ming, Charles Middleton played other roles in serials, even an occasional good guy, such as an old prospector in Columbia's 1943 *The Batman.* Even aside from Ming, his best known roles continued to be villains.

It was a classic confrontation of Evil vs. Good when Middleton, *the* screen villain in the opinion of many, faced Tom Mix, *the* screen hero in the opinion of many others, over the fate of a tribe of Indians threatened by the rockets and rayguns of Middleton's superscience in *The Miracle Rider,* Mascot, 1935.

At other times, Middleton was sinister Pa Stark fighting Ralph Byrd as the hawk-nosed hawkshaw in *Dick Tracy Returns,* Republic, 1938; he was Cassib, a nefarious Arab killer who brooded no good for Kay Aldridge as the jungle girl in *Perils of Nyoka,* Republic, 1942; and the perfectly named Jason Grood making things tough for John Hart as *Jack Armstrong,* Columbia, 1947.

Probably his best villain role outside the Gordon serials was in *Daredevils of the Red Circle,* Republic, 1939. In his cliffhanger, Middleton fought not one but *three* heroes—Charles Quigley, Herman Brix, and Dave Sharpe, three circus athletes who were known as the Daredevils of the Red Circle. As for

Middleton, he was known simply by a prison number, 39013. He has escaped prison to take revenge on his former cohort, Granville, by wrecking the latter's factory through sabotage.

To carry out his deviltry, 39013 dons a mask of Granville so lifelike that we could be justified in assuming Middleton is replaced by the real Granville (played by Miles Mandor) whenever he allegedly puts on the face mask.

Even *three* athletic young heroes have trouble in defeating the elderly and cadaverous 39013. Like Dr. Satan and so many serial villains before and after, 39013 was destroyed by one of his own creations—a bomb rigged to explode in an automobile when the speedometer hit seventy. Unconscious in the rumble seat of his careening escape vehicle, driven by a partner in crime who knows nothing of the bomb, 39013 comes to just in time to see the needle strike the fatal number before they are blasted into eternity.

From Charles Middleton to Bela Lugosi, serial *villains* tended to be impressive. They could have—and in several cases, *did*—stand up well as the menace in many major feature films. Their bland opposition, leading men like Robert Wilcox and Charles Quigley, had trouble carrying a chapterplay, much less a high-budgeted production. Only occasionally did a serial villain face competition from a strong personality like Tom Mix, Dick Foran, or Buster Crabbe.

In the end, it did not matter. No matter how much the villain had going for him, he lost. The production code demanded it. Moreover, we expected it. On those Saturday afternoons in ice-box cold theatres all that time back, our faith was still unshaken that good guys *always* won.

15

Last Chapter   The Final Cliffhanger

We might like to think that serials were a victim of a society that decries fictional violence, apparently because it prefers to practice the real thing. However, the serial disappeared due to the successful competition of a new medium, television, whose very *instant* quality worked against continued stories in all media.

The last American motion picture serial was released in 1956: Columbia's *Blazing the Overland Trail*. We can subtract nearly another ten years from that date when considering the last *great* chapterplays. Movie audiences, then, have been without new serials of any quality for more than two decades.

Movie serials would seem a dead form of entertainment in this light. In the strictest sense, that is true. In another sense, the format of continued stories with cliffhanger endings running episodically to capture sustained viewer interest has managed to survive even into these times of allegedly adult films and television programs.

Admittedly, the United States has not produced any new serials for theatrical distribution. However, numerous serials for both theatrical and television release are currently being made overseas, some of which, both live-action and animated, occasionally turn up on American TV.

The serial approach is still popular in the daytime television soap operas, that alternate mystery and adventure cliffhanger endings (as in the supernatural serial, *Dark Shadows*) with those of tear-splattered domestic drama borrowed from drama-tized radio (*The Guiding Light,* an old radio title). Prime-time

American television, with entries like Disney's *Zorro* series of a few seasons back, *Peyton Place, Lost in Space,* and the craze-setting *Batman* have capitalized on cliffhanging their audiences to lure them back tomorrow, the day after tomorrow, or the next week.

Certainly, the James Bond films and all the imitations of them were only movie serials made acceptable to adults. The mad scientists were better characterized to make them more believable; their inventions made to look more convincing; sexy girls were added; the week-to-week continuation was subracted for a jaded, impatient audience.

As for the real thing—the subject matter of this book—those old serials live today in more than merely the nostalgic memories of fans, and new, pop culture enthusiasts. Flash Gordon, Commando Cody, and their contemporaries still manage to battle their way across television screens and in theatre revivals. Even before the *Batman* television show, the original fifteen episodes of the 1943 Columbia serial was offered to theatres for one big marathon showing as *An Evening with Batman and Robin.* Exploited for its camp value, that serial was followed to theatres by Republic's rerelease of the vastly superior *Adventures of Captain Marvel.* Many other serials which are not available to theatres and television may be rented from 16-mm libraries, or purchased in condensed 8-mm editions from places as near as the neighborhood camera shop.

The year 1966 was a big year for the revival of the old chapterplays. Not only did Columbia make available a number of cliffhanger titles to television—including *Monster and the Ape, Blackhawk,* and *The Vigilante*—but Republic released to TV twenty-six of their serials, each one edited into a one-hundred minute feature. These were retitled to sound more in tune with the 1960s spy adventure and muscleman costume epic. Thus, a nostalgic property like *Undersea Kingdom* became *Sharad of Atlantis; The Purple Monster Strikes* became *D-Day on Mars;*

Jungle Drums of Africa became *U28 and the Witch Doctor;* and *Darkest Africa,* once rereleased as *King of the Jungleland,* capitalized on the Batman craze as *Batmen of Africa.*

There are other serials still in the vaults that may be eventually rereleased, usually in feature form. However, it is unlikely *new* serials as we knew them will ever be produced for theatres, or even for television, considering the economic factors and today's audience.

The *continued story* will probably be ever with us as long as people continue to tell each other stories, and to enjoy the bittersweetness of waiting to hear how it all comes out.

Yet, in the strictest sense, the movie serial is gone forever. It was a part of childhood, designed for the child of the '30s and '40s. (Silent serials were intended to appeal to adults as well.) Such children no longer exist. Going to the movies once a week was an anticipated event. With the easy access to television such anticipation can never again be sustained.

The same television set has, of course, opened up new worlds of knowledge to children. They are no longer amused by the rickety sham that enthralled the children of earlier decades. Actually, it is their loss that these children can see only that Batman was overweight (in the first Columbia serial) and that the Blackhawk team had only one old-fashioned airplane between them. Only fools fail to grow up, but we may be producing a generation which were never children.

Ours is a world where both the young and not-so-young could do well to escape to a world of harmless violence where Nyoka could always be about to be sliced in two by the giant pendulum of the Sacred Idol, where Billy Batson could cry "Shazam!" and be transformed into Captain Marvel to face *any* peril successfully, and where a forever young Flash Gordon and Dale Arden could rocket toward the mysterious and magical world called Mongo.

The heroes always escaped the final cliffhanger in the last

chapter. Perhaps that can be some consolation for us. As we live through a time of the greatest environmental hazard to human life, and the greatest authoritarian hazard to human liberty, we have grown up to be *living* the greatest cliffhanger of all time.

Index